Nala H. Lee
A Grammar of Modern Baba Malay

Mouton Grammar Library

Edited by
Georg Bossong
Bernard Comrie
Patience L. Epps
Irina Nikolaeva

Volume 90

Nala H. Lee
A Grammar of Modern Baba Malay

DE GRUYTER
MOUTON

ISBN 978-3-11-135860-4
e-ISBN (PDF) 978-3-11-074506-1
e-ISBN (EPUB) 978-3-11-074515-3
ISSN 0933-7636

Library of Congress Control Number: 2021948492

Bibliographic information published by the Deutsche Nationalbibliothek
The Deutsche Nationalbibliothek lists this publication in the Deutsche Nationalbibliografie; detailed bibliographic data are available on the Internet at http://dnb.dnb.de.

© 2023 Walter de Gruyter GmbH, Berlin/Boston
This volume is text- and page-identical with the hardback published in 2022.
Typesetting: Integra Software Services Pvt. Ltd
Printing and binding: CPI books GmbH, Leck

www.degruyter.com

Acknowledgements

This work is due in no small part, to the encouragement and support of many people. I owe a debt of gratitude to my key language consultants, who have been nothing but generous with their time and expertise. A huge *kamsiah* 'thank you' to the late Baba Peter Wee, Baba Victor Goh, Nyonya Jane Quek, Baba Albert Ku, and my own Uncle Chan. I am also thankful to the Gunong Sayang Association, the Peranakan Association Singapore, and other members of the Peranakan community who have extended their generosity to me in some way or other.

This work is a much revised version of the doctoral dissertation that I submitted to the University of Hawai'i in 2014, *A Grammar of Baba Malay with Sociophonetic Considerations*. I am indebted to my dissertation committee, including my chairperson, Lyle Campbell, and committee members: Andrea Berez, Robert Blust, Katie Drager, and Barbara Watson Andaya. Their genuine interest, encouragement, and critical comments have much improved this grammar. I am grateful to Felicity Meakins for having read through a working draft, and for offering her suggestions. This volume, as it stands in its published form, has benefited from the careful eye and well-thought out suggestions of my editor, Georg Bossong. Much thanks also to the other series editors behind Mouton Grammar Library for their support of this grammar: Bernard Comrie, Patience L. Epps, and Irina Nikolaeva. I wish to extend my sincere thanks to Katie Gao for providing me her cartographic expertise as well.

Finally, I am thankful for the support of my family, in particular, my Hockchia mother, for evoking my initial interest in my paternal lineage, and my life partner, Iswen, for his unwavering support.

This work was made possible by the start up grant conferred at the National University of Singapore by the Ministry of Education Singapore in 2017 (MOE AcRF Tier 1: R-103-000-150-133), and a subsequent Humanities and Social Sciences Research Fellowship awarded in 2020.

Contents

Acknowledgements — V

1		**Introduction — 1**
1.1		An overview of Baba Malay typology — 3
1.1.1		Overview of sound system — 3
1.1.2		Overview of morphology — 4
1.1.3		Overview of syntax — 6
1.2		The speakers behind this grammar — 10
1.3		A guide to this grammar — 11
1.3.1		Example sentence features — 12
1.3.2		List of abbreviations used — 13
1.3.3		Transcription conventions — 14
1.3.4		Structure of this grammar — 14
2		**Baba Malay and its speakers — 16**
2.1		What is in a name? — 20
2.2		Geographical location — 24
2.3		Dialects and ecologies — 25
2.4		Speaker numbers — 28
2.5		The endangerment of Baba Malay — 29
2.6		Community responses to language endangerment — 31
3		**Phonetics and phonology — 33**
3.1		Phoneme inventory — 33
3.1.1		Consonants — 33
3.1.1.1		Minimal and near-minimal pairs of consonants — 33
3.1.1.2		The use of waveforms and spectrograms — 36
3.1.1.3		Bilabials — 37
3.1.1.4		Alveolars — 39
3.1.1.5		Post-alveolars — 43
3.1.1.6		Velars — 45
3.1.1.7		Glottals — 47
3.1.1.8		Glides — 49
3.1.2		Vowels — 50
3.1.2.1		Minimal pairs of vowels — 50
3.1.2.2		Monophthongs — 52
3.1.2.3		Diphthongs — 57
3.1.2.4		Vowel sequences across syllables — 57
3.2		Phonotactics — 58
3.2.1		Resyllabification and reduplication — 60

3.3	Phonological rules —— 62	
3.3.1	Syllable-final velar plosive to glottal stop rule —— 65	
3.3.2	Deletion of word-initial *h* rule —— 65	
3.3.3	Metathesis of ə and *r* rule —— 66	
3.3.4	Assimilation of V to *u* before *lw* rule —— 67	
3.3.5	Vowel raising to ɛ and final *l*, *r*, *s* deletion in refined style rules —— 67	
3.4	Rule ordering —— 69	
3.4.1	Vowel raising to ɛ, then deletion of final *l*, *r*, *s* —— 69	
3.4.2	*u* assimilation, then vowel raising to ɛ, followed by deletion of final *l*, *r*, *s* —— 69	
3.5	Fast speech —— 70	
3.6	Writing system of this grammar —— 71	
3.7	Stress and intonation —— 73	
3.7.1	Word stress and pitch —— 74	
3.7.2	Tones on Hokkien-derived words —— 78	
3.7.3	Sentence intonation —— 82	
3.8	Phonological change —— 85	
4	**Parts of speech —— 91**	
4.1	Nouns —— 92	
4.1.1	Nominal morphology —— 93	
4.1.1.1	Derivational noun morphology —— 94	
4.1.1.2	Nominal compounds —— 95	
4.1.2	Noun classifiers and partitives —— 96	
4.1.3	Pronouns —— 99	
4.1.3.1	Personal pronouns —— 99	
4.1.3.2	Reflexives —— 101	
4.1.3.3	Reciprocals —— 103	
4.1.3.4	Interrogative pronouns —— 104	
4.2	Verbs —— 105	
4.2.1	Verbal morphology —— 106	
4.2.1.1	Derivational verb morphology —— 107	
4.2.1.2	Non-productive verb morphology —— 110	
4.2.1.3	Verbal compounds —— 114	
4.3	Adjectives —— 115	
4.3.1	Adjectival morphology —— 116	
4.4	Adverbs —— 117	
4.4.1	Adverbial morphology —— 117	
4.4.2	Interrogative adverbs —— 119	
4.5	Determiners —— 120	
4.5.1	Person marker —— 120	
4.5.2	Demonstratives —— 121	

4.5.3	Numerals —— 123	
4.5.3.1	Other numerical expressions —— 125	
4.5.4	Quantifiers —— 126	
4.6	Prepositions —— 127	
4.7	Conjunctions —— 135	
4.8	Discourse elements —— 137	
4.8.1	Interjections —— 137	
4.8.2	Particles —— 139	
5	**Syntax** —— 142	
5.1	Noun phrases —— 142	
5.1.1	Genitive —— 144	
5.1.2	Noun phrases with determiners —— 147	
5.1.2.1	Noun phrases with demonstratives —— 147	
5.1.2.2	Noun phrases with person marker —— 150	
5.1.2.3	Noun phrases with numerals, noun classifiers and partitives —— 150	
5.1.2.4	Noun phrases with quantifiers —— 153	
5.1.3	Noun phrases with adjectival modifiers —— 154	
5.1.4	Negation of noun phrases —— 156	
5.1.5	Order of elements in noun phrases —— 157	
5.2	Verb phrases —— 157	
5.2.1	Copula constructions —— 159	
5.2.2	Modality —— 160	
5.2.3	Passivization —— 164	
5.2.4	Ditransitive, causative and benefactive constructions —— 166	
5.2.4.1	Ditransitive constructions —— 166	
5.2.4.2	Causative and benefactive constructions —— 169	
5.2.5	Aspect and tense —— 170	
5.2.5.1	Perfective aspect —— 171	
5.2.5.2	Recent perfect aspect —— 172	
5.2.5.3	Experiential perfect aspect —— 173	
5.2.5.4	Progressive aspect —— 173	
5.2.5.5	Habitual aspect —— 174	
5.2.5.6	Tentative aspect —— 175	
5.2.5.7	Future tense —— 175	
5.2.6	Serial verb constructions —— 177	
5.2.7	Verb phrases with adverbial modifiers —— 178	
5.2.8	Negation of verb phrases —— 180	
5.2.9	Order of elements in verb phrases —— 183	
5.3	Adjectival phrases —— 183	
5.3.1	Comparatives —— 185	
5.3.2	Comparison of equality —— 186	

5.3.3	Comparison of similarity —— 187
5.3.4	Superlatives —— 188
5.3.5	Excessive degree —— 188
5.3.6	Adjectival phrases with adverbial modifiers —— 190
5.3.7	Order of elements in adjectival phrases —— 191
5.4	Adverbial phrases —— 191
5.4.1	Temporal adverbial phrases —— 192
5.4.2	Location adverbial phrases —— 192
5.4.3	Manner adverbial phrases —— 193
5.4.4	Order of elements in adverbial phrases —— 194
5.5	Summary of word order at the phrase level —— 194
5.6	Clauses —— 195
5.6.1	Word order at the clause level —— 195
5.6.2	Grammatical relations and alignment —— 197
5.6.3	Relative clauses —— 198
5.6.4	Complement clauses —— 201
5.6.5	Direct and indirect speech —— 203
5.6.6	Adverbial clauses —— 204
5.6.6.1	Temporal adverbial clauses —— 205
5.6.6.2	Location adverbial clauses —— 206
5.6.6.3	Manner adverbial clauses —— 207
5.6.7	Conditional —— 208
5.6.8	Conjunctions —— 209
5.6.8.1	Coordinating conjunctions —— 209
5.6.8.2	Subordinating conjunctions —— 211
5.6.9	Topicalization —— 214
5.6.10	Questions —— 216
5.6.10.1	Content questions —— 216
5.6.10.2	Tag questions —— 222
5.6.11	Imperatives —— 228
6	**Differences between Baba Malay Spoken in Singapore and Malacca —— 230**
6.1	Phonetic and phonological differences —— 230
6.1.1	Vowel [ɔ] —— 230
6.1.2	[e], [o] versus [aj], [aw] —— 232
6.2	Morphological differences —— 234
6.2.1	*Ke- -an* nominalizing circumfix —— 234
6.2.2	Other affixes —— 236
6.3	Syntactic differences —— 238
6.3.1	Noun phrase —— 238
6.3.1.1	Demonstrative determiners —— 238
6.3.2	Verb phrase —— 240

6.3.2.1	Progressive aspect —— **240**	
6.3.2.2	Perfective aspect —— **241**	
6.3.3	Adjectival and adverbial phrases —— **242**	
6.3.3.1	*Daripada* comparatives —— **243**	
6.3.3.2	*Dengan* 'with' adverbial phrase —— **243**	
6.3.4	Conjunctions —— **244**	
6.3.4.1	*Dan/sama* 'and' coordinating conjunction —— **245**	
6.3.4.2	*Atau/ka* 'or' coordinating conjunction —— **245**	
6.4	Diverging ecologies —— **246**	
7	**Appendices —— 248**	
7.1	Word lists —— **248**	
7.1.1	Swadesh 100-word list —— **248**	
7.1.2	Kinship terms —— **250**	
7.1.3	Expressions for day, month and time —— **254**	
7.2	Texts —— **257**	
7.2.1	Cherita Pear sama Baba Peter Wee —— **258**	
7.2.2	Anjing Sama Tulang sama Baba Peter Wee —— **282**	
7.2.3	Bangkuang Besair sama Baba Victor Goh —— **292**	
7.2.4	Chakapan sama Aunty Jane Quek —— **304**	
7.2.5	Ten Pantuns by Baba Albert Ku —— **338**	
7.3	Lexicon and reversal index —— **342**	
7.3.1	Baba Malay- English lexicon —— **342**	
7.3.2	English- Baba Malay reversal index —— **358**	

List of Tables —— 375

List of Figures —— 377

References —— 379

Index —— 385

1 Introduction

Baba Malay (ISO 639-3: mbf), also known as *Peranakan* to its speakers, is an Austronesian-based contact language with a Sinitic substrate that is spoken by the Chinese Peranakans in Southeast Asia. The language was formed via early intermarriages of Hokkien traders from China and indigenous women in the region. While the term *Peranakan* is an endonym used by the community, researchers have commonly used the term *Baba Malay*. The language is highly endangered, with less than 1,000 speakers in Malacca (a state within Malaysia) and less than 1,000 speakers in Singapore. There are also Baba Malay speakers who live outside of these regions, such as in the Malaysian capital state of Kuala Lumpur and in Australia, but their number is far fewer than those who reside in Malacca and Singapore.

In the past, it has been suggested that Baba Malay is a dialect of Malay with heavy borrowing from Hokkien, a variety of Southern Min, in terms of both lexical and grammatical structures (Pakir 1986; Thurgood 1998). Others viewed Baba Malay as a "somewhat simplified" dialect, postulating it to be a nativized version of Bazaar Malay (Reinecke et al. 1975: 746), Bazaar Malay here referring to the lingua franca used for early trade in the region. Notably, Baba Malay lacks the more complex features of Malay, such as most of its system of affixes, which exists only partially or in fossilized remnants (see Sections 4.1.1.1, 4.2.1.1 and 4.2.1.2 for examples). Nevertheless, the perspective that Baba Malay is a simplified dialect of Malay can be discarded, considering that the language is not exceptionally simplified in many other ways, for example, in its speakers' use of extensive grammatical features, such as classifiers (Section 4.1.2) and relative clauses (Section 5.6.3) or in their usage of elaborate sociolinguistic features, such as its system of *kasar* 'coarse' and *halus* 'refined' registers (Section 3.3.5; also Lee 2020). The view that Baba Malay might be a nativized version of Bazaar Malay can also be discarded if one bears in mind that the historical development of Bazaar Malay has never been linked to any specific community of speakers (Ansaldo 2009: 60).

In more recent literature, Baba Malay has been characterized as a creole, given its emergence and expansion as part of a hybrid culture (Lim 1981; Lim 1988; Ansaldo & Matthews 1999; Shih 2009; Lee 2014). However, it is acknowledged that Baba Malay would be a sociologically atypical creole if it were to be classified as such – unlike other creoles, Baba Malay did not undergo a traumatic displacement of its creators. Neither does it represent unequal social relations between the speakers of the target language and its learners, nor has it ever been related to a break in the transmission of the lexifier (given that contact language exists in the same environment as its lexifier) (Ansaldo, Lim & Mufwene 2007; also see Chapter 2 for more sociolinguistic information). Structurally, whether Baba Malay should be regarded as a creole depends on the definition utilised. If one were to use the notion that creoles are intrinsically simple (see for example, McWhorter 2001), then Baba Malay might not qualify in light of its complexities such as those highlighted in the paragraph above. But if a more encompassing definition were used, and a creole is to be viewed as system comprising a lexicon derived mainly from one language and a grammatical subsystem that bridges its component languages (see Thomason 2003), then Baba Malay would duly qualify as one. While significant Hokkien influence is felt in particular areas of the lexicon, it is relegated largely to the domains of customs, culture and affect (Pakir 1986; also see appendix for kinship terms and terms for marking significant religious and customary dates based on the lunar calendar). To a lesser extent, Baba Malay has also adopted words from English, Portuguese, Dutch, and Tamil, among other languages (Pakir 1986; Shellabear 1913). For example, the word for window, *menjéla* is derived from Portuguese *janela*, and the word for money, *duit* originated as the coin of the Dutch East Indies. The main bulk of the lexicon is conspicuously Malay in nature. Grammatically, while some structures are distinctly derived from the substrate language Hokkien, including the adversative passive construction (Section 5.2.3), and the benefactive and causative constructions (Section 5.2.4.2), Baba Malay has a complex system that incorporates grammatical characteristics of both its component languages. This is exemplified in its aspectual system, which integrates structures that are directly derived from Malay (including the *sudah* perfective structure, the *baru* recent perfect structure, and the *pernah* experiential perfect structure) and Hokkien (including reduplication for the tentative aspect and relexified structures for the perfective, progressive, experiential perfect, and habitual functions originating from Hokkien possessive verb *u*) (Section 5.2.5). As a separate case in point, the language's relativization strategies have also been derived from the grammatical subsystems of both component languages, with prenominal relativization originating from Hokkien and postnominal relativization originating from Malay (Section 5.6.3). All that being said, this grammar necessarily treats the contact language as a coherent complex language system in its own right, rather than viewing it as a sum of its component languages, which might inadvertently promote the view that contact languages are simple or simply some variety of its component languages.

The varieties of Baba Malay in Malacca and Singapore bear a large similarity with each other, except for differences that are mostly lexical resulting from a more dominant Malay influence in Malacca. The variety of Baba Malay in Singapore shows greater Hokkien influence. For example, while Hokkien-derived *huahi* can be used to express the notion of 'happy' in Singapore Baba Malay, Baba Malay speakers in Malacca use Malay-derived *gembira* or *suka hati* 'literally: like heart' to express a similar concept (Lee 2018). This grammar is based mostly on the variety of Baba Malay that is spoken in Singapore, but also lists major differences between Malacca Baba Malay and Singapore Baba Malay, particularly where these differences impinge upon phonology, morphology and syntax. These two varieties that constitute Modern Baba Malay should be distinguished from Old Baba Malay, which survives in written records from the nineteenth century. These written records include newspapers published in Baba Malay and collections of old conversations. It has been postulated that there are clear differences between Old Baba Malay and Modern Baba Malay – the modern variety is said to show considerably more Hokkien influence due to a large influx of Hokkien speakers at the end of the nineteenth century and the beginning of the twentieth century (Thurgood 1998). It is also highly plausible that Modern Baba Malay is less variable in form than Old Baba Malay. Older records of the language also include translations of Chinese classics written in the late 1800s and 1900s.[1] Aside from different systems of codification, the authors were said to differ in terms of how much Malay or Hokkien they used (Tan 1979: 124). These early records that were published predominantly in Singapore[2] showed that the writers had some command of the substrate language, Hokkien, and the superstrate language, Malay, choosing to use lexical and functional features from these languages optionally when writing in Baba Malay (Lee in prep). It is rarer for Baba Malay speakers today, particularly in Singapore, to speak these component languages, with English being a much more dominant home language amongst them (see Sections 2.5 and 6.4). Therefore, whereas early language records are distinguished by a more typical language contact continuum, the variety of Baba Malay that is captured by this grammar is notably a more stable variety.

1.1 An overview of Baba Malay typology

A brief overview of Baba Malay's typology is provided in this section. The overview includes notes on the language's vowel and consonant inventories, morphology, word order, argument alignment and case.

1.1.1 Overview of sound system

Baba Malay has eight phonemic vowels, and its vowel inventory is as follows in Table 1.

---

[1] For a comprehensive overview of literature written in and about Baba Malay, please refer to Tan (2007). For a bibliometric survey of Chinese classics translated Baba Malay between 1889 and 1939, please see Yoong and Zainab (2002).
[2] *Cherita dulu kala* 'stories from long ago', which are mainly translations of Chinese classics, were also published in Batavia, but these were written in Peranakan Indonesian. None appears to have been published in Malacca.

Table 1: The vowel inventory of Baba Malay.

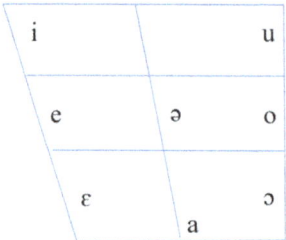

Its 19 phonemic consonants are as follows in Table 2.

Table 2: The consonant inventory of Baba Malay.

		Labial	Alveolar	Post-alveolar	Palatal	Velar	Glottal
Plosives	Voiceless	p	t			k	ʔ
	Voiced	b	d			g	
Affricates	Voiceless			tʃ			
	Voiced			dʒ			
Fricatives	Voiceless		s				h
Nasals		m	n		ɲ	ŋ	
Lateral			l				
Flap			r				
Glides		w (labiodental)			j		

1.1.2 Overview of morphology

There is some affixation in Baba Malay. All of its affixes are derived from Malay, in which the corresponding affixes are obligatory (Marsden 1812).[3] Most of these affixes are optional and may not be meaningful to the speakers of Baba Malay. For example, in Malay the prefix *meN-* is used as an active or progressive marker. But in Baba Malay, the use of this marker is not mandatory, and it makes no difference to the meaning of the verb onto which it is attached. This is demonstrated below by the examples in (1) and (2), where *meN-* is non-existent in (1), but is attached to *nangis* 'cry' in (2).

---

[3] Earlier versions of Malay plausibly contributed more to the formation of Baba Malay, but the language continues to be influenced by Standard Malay which is spoken in its environment.

Alternatively, *menangis* can be used in the context of (1) and *nangis* can be used in the context of (2) to express the same notions.

(1) Téngok, bapak dia mati, dia tak nangis.
    look   father 3SG die 3SG NEG cry
    'Look, his father died, (and) he did not cry.'
    (Victor, oai:scholarspace.manoa.hawaii.edu: NL1-021, 00:32:44.0-00:32:46.3)[4]

(2) Dia kulair dari rumah menangis.
    3SG go.out from house cry
    'She left the house crying.'
    (Victor, oai:scholarspace.manoa.hawaii.edu: NL1-043, 00:04:18.3-00:04:20.9)

Very few affixes are obligatory. The only two affixes that are more commonly used are the prefix, *ter-* 'accidental, movement', and the transitivizing suffix *-kan*. The different usages of *ter-* are shown in (4) and (5), and these examples can be compared to (3), where *ter-* is not affixed on the verb. In (6), the verb *jatoh* 'to fall' is intransitive, whereas it is made transitive with the affixation of *-kan* in (7).

(3) Masok ini kebun.
    enter this garden
    'Enter this garden.'
    (Peter Wee, oai:scholarspace.manoa.hawaii.edu: NL1-022, 00:00:31.2-00:00:32.8)

(4) Ter-masok kat dalam ayé.
    ACD-enter PREP inside water
    'Fell into the water.'
    (Jane Quek, oai:scholarspace.manoa.hawaii.edu: NL1-044, 00:14:33.2-00:16:34.8)

(5) Ter-balék-kan   itu ikan pun boléh lah.
    MVT-turn.over-TR   that fish also can   EMP
    'It is also okay to turn over that fish.'
    (Jane Quek, oai:scholarspace.manoa.hawaii.edu: NL1-044, 00:10:32.3-00:10:33.8)

(6) Budak jatoh,
    child fall
    'The child falls,'
    (Peter Wee, oai:scholarspace.manoa.hawaii.edu: NL1-022, 00:03:46.6-00:03:50.7)

---

[4] Section 1.3.1 provides explanatory notes on how these handles can be used to locate the relevant audio files.

(7) Jatoh-kan dia,
    fall-TR   3SG
    'drop it,'
    (Peter Wee, oai:scholarspace.manoa.hawaii.edu: NL1-022, 00:00:59.2-00:01:02.5)

1.1.3 Overview of syntax

The basic clausal level word order for transitive clauses in Baba Malay is SVO (Subject Verb Object). This word order is demonstrated in (8), (9) and (10). Intransitive clauses have the word order SV, as demonstrated by (11) and (12).

(8) Itu   kuching makan ikan.
    that cat   eat   fish
    'That cat eats fish.'
    (Victor, oai:scholarspace.manoa.hawaii.edu: NL1-009, 00:00:35.9-00:00:37.7)

(9) Tukang   kebun   tarék itu   bangkuang.
    laborer garden pull   that turnip
    The gardener pulled that turnip.'
    (Peter Wee, oai:scholarspace.manoa.hawaii.edu: NL1-034, 00:00:52.7-00:01:00.5)

(10) Budak pakay baju.
     boy   wear   clothes
     'The boy is wearing clothes.'
     (Jane Quek, oai:scholarspace.manoa.hawaii.edu: NL1-088, 00:00:59.2-00:01:01.8)

(11) Kupukupu   trebang.
     butterfly fly
     'The butterfly is flying.'
     (Peter Wee, oai:scholarspace.manoa.hawaii.edu: NL1-030, 00:01:36.8-00:01:39.7)

(12) Kupukupu   datang.
     butterfly come
     'The butterfly is coming.'
     (Peter Wee, oai:scholarspace.manoa.hawaii.edu: NL1-030, 00:03:18.9-00:03:20.9)

The subject is not always obligatory, particularly when the unexpressed subject is known to the participants in the conversation. In (13), the speaker was asked about the activity she was carrying out, to which she responds *kopék bawang* 'peeling onions'. In (14), the speaker was talking about what elderly people do to stay healthy. She states that those who *makan ikan manyak* 'eat a lot of fish' stay healthy, the unexpressed subject here being elderly people. In (15), the unexpressed subject is a boy who is brushing his teeth.

(13) *Kopék bawang lah.*
     Peel   onion EMP
     '(I am) peeling onions.'
     (Kim Choo, oai:scholarspace.manoa.hawaii.edu: NL1-079, 00:12:49.8-00:12:51.2)

(14) *Makan ikan manyak.*
     Eat   fish many
     '(Elderly people who stay healthy) eat a lot of fish.'
     (Lilian, oai:scholarspace.manoa.hawaii.edu: NL1-079, 00:03:44.4-00:03:46.2)

(15) *Berus   gigi.*
     brush   teeth
     '(The boy is) brushing (his) teeth.'
     (Jane Quek, oai:scholarspace.manoa.hawaii.edu: NL1-088, 00:01:04.5-00:01:05.9)

At the phrasal level, Baba Malay has word orders of ADJ N (Adjective Noun) *and* N ADJ, GEN N (Genitive Noun) and N GEN, as well as PREP N (Preposition Noun), Relative clauses occur both prenominally and postnominally. Example (16) illustrates the ADJ N word order, while (17) shows the N ADJ word order. Although the ADJ N word order is mitigated by a relative clause marker, which makes it more structurally-marked, the ADJ N structure is commonly used, as with the N ADJ word order.

(16) *Betol mia[5] cherita.*
     real REL   story
     'Story that is real'
     (Jane Quek, oai:scholarspace.manoa.hawaii.edu: NL1-028, 00:03:24.8-00:03:26.0)

(17) *Idong panjang.*
     nose long
     'Long nose.'
     (Lillian, oai:scholarspace.manoa.hawaii.edu: NL1-079, 00:00:13.7-00:00:15.0)

The GEN N word order is demonstrated in example (18), while the N GEN order is demonstrated in (19). The possessor in the N GEN construction has to be a pronoun, making this word order less basic than GEN N.

---

[5] *Punya*, which can be shortened to *nia* and *mia*, is a possessive marker that can also be analyzed as a relative clause marker.

(18) *Peter punya bapak,*
    Peter REL   father
    'Peter's father,'
    (Victor, oai:scholarspace.manoa.hawaii.edu: NL1-009, 00:45:01.7-00:45:06.9)

(19) *Badan lu.*
    body   2SG
    'Your body.'
    (Lilian, oai:scholarspace.manoa.hawaii.edu: NL1-079, 00:11:33.1-00:11:36:1)

The PREP N word order is demonstrated in (20) and (21).

(20) *Kebun   dekat Europe ini.*
    garden PREP   this
    'This garden is in Europe.'
    (Peter Wee, oai:scholarspace.manoa.hawaii.edu: NL1-022, 00:00:32.8-00:00:34.6)

(21) *Tulang di   mulot, buang di   sunggay.*
    bone   PREP mouth   throw PREP river
    'Bone in the mouth, thrown into the river.'
    (Peter Wee, oai:scholarspace.manoa.hawaii.edu: NL1-030, 00:02:14.1-00:02:17.3)

Prenominal relativization is shown in (22) while (23) shows postnominal relativization. Both are equally common in Baba Malay.

(22) *[Anak perompuan nia] satu.*
    child female   REL   one
    'The one that is a girl.'
    (Jane Quek, oai:scholarspace.manoa.hawaii.edu: NL1-142, 00:00:44.8-00:00:47.0)

(23) *Ini   sumua dia mia kawan [nang[6] jaga   kambing].*
    This all   3SG REL friend REL   guard sheep
    'These (are) all his friends that guard the sheep.'
    (Peter Wee, oai:scholarspace.manoa.hawaii.edu: NL1-030, 00:05:58.2-00:06:00.8)

In terms of argument alignment and case, Baba Malay is a nominative-accusative language, as can be established by word order. The subject and object in Baba Malay are not differentiated morphologically (also in the case of pronouns). The subject of

---

6 Also *yang*.

intransitive verbs is treated equivalently to the agent of the transitive verb. Both of these precede the verb phrase, as shown in (24) and (25). Example (8) is replicated here as (25).

(24) Budak tu senyum.
 child that smile
 'That child smiles.'
 (Jane Quek, oai:scholarspace.manoa.hawaii.edu: NL1-088, 00:00:35.9-00:00:37.7)

(25) Itu kuching makan ikan.
 That cat eat fish
 'That cat eats fish.'
 (Victor, oai:scholarspace.manoa.hawaii.edu: NL1-009, 00:37:23.3-00:37:25.5)

In addition, the object of an active sentence is able to undergo passivization with the use of the adversative passive markers *kasi* (lexical meanings: 'give', 'cause', 'let') and *kena* (lexical meaning: 'subjected to'). In these instances, the object is promoted to the subject function. Note that the logical subject is not expressed overtly when *kena* is used. Example (27) is the passive counterpart of (26), while (29) is the passive sentence that corresponds to (28). Example (28) replicates (25) and (8).

(26) Mary bunoh dia.
  kill 3SG
 'Mary killed him.'
 (Victor, oai:scholarspace.manoa.hawaii.edu: NL1-037, 00:39:17.1-00:39:18.8)

(27) Dia kasi Mary bunoh.
 3SG PASS kill
 'He was killed by Mary.'
 (Victor, oai:scholarspace.manoa.hawaii.edu: NL1-037, 00:40:01.8-00:40:14.9)

(28) Itu kuching makan ikan.
 that cat eat fish
 'That cat eats fish.'
 (Victor, oai:scholarspace.manoa.hawaii.edu: NL1-009, 00:37:23.3-00:37:25.5)

(29) Itu ikan sudah kena makan.
 That fish already PASS eat
 'That fish has already been eaten.'
 (Victor, oai:scholarspace.manoa.hawaii.edu: NL1-009, 00:38:17.8-00:38:19.9)

In topicalization, logical objects can also be fronted without passivization. Topicalization is highly productive in Baba Malay, generating sentences such as (30) and (31).

(30) *Itu   ikan   sudah   kuching   makan.*
 that   fish   already   cat   eat
 'That fish, the cat already ate.'
 (Victor, oai:scholarspace.manoa.hawaii.edu: NL1-009, 00:37.37.1-00:39:39.8)

(31) *[Teloh],   goréng.*
 Egg   fry
 'The egg, fry (it).'
 (Jane Quek, oai:scholarspace.manoa.hawaii.edu: NL1-142, 00:07:44.8-00:07:47.5)

1.2 The speakers behind this grammar

This grammar owes much to the time and expertise of four key consultants and their acquaintances. Among these key consultants, three speakers are from Singapore and one from Malacca. These consultants serve as contact points to other speakers from within the Peranakan cultural scene or their families. The ages of these four speakers ranged from 70 to 84 at the time of their participation in this language documentation project. All of these speakers are bilingual in English, but identify Baba Malay as their dominant native language and use it on a daily basis. None of the key consultants were monolingual, given the frailty of monolingual speakers, who would be in their late nineties.

The three key consultants from Singapore who were involved in this project are Baba Peter Wee, Baba Victor Goh, and Bibik Jane Quek.[7] Until 2018, the late Baba Peter Wee was the president of the Peranakan Association Singapore, a clan association established in 1900 with links to sister associations in Malacca and Penang in Malaysia, and Melbourne, Sydney, and Perth in Australia, where a number of Peranakans have migrated to in recent years. Baba Peter Wee also operated the Katong Antique House, which is part shop and part private museum. The Antique House, located along East Coast Road (a traditional Peranakan enclave), served as a communal space, visited by tourists and crucially also by visitors who spoke Baba Malay. Recording sessions with Baba Peter Wee took place at this location. Some of the conversations that took place between Baba Peter Wee and his visitors were recorded and archived.

---

7 *Baba* and *Bibik* are polite terms of addresses for Peranakan men and older Peranakan women, see Section 2.1 for more information.

Another location that was important to this project was the Gunong Sayang[8] Association clubhouse. It was located in Geylang until 2017, and is now located in Joo Chiat. Both locations are also situated within the traditional Peranakan enclave on the eastern side of Singapore. The Gunong Sayang Association, a social club established in 1910, aims to create an awareness of Peranakan culture and Baba Malay by promoting Peranakan performance arts, such as *dondang sayang* 'art of singing Malay poetry' (see footnote 10), *wayang Peranakan* 'Peranakan plays', music and dance. In addition to eliciting data from Baba Victor Goh, the club's cultural advisor, recordings were also made of conversations that took place at the club's dinner table and at rehearsal sessions.

The third key Singaporean speaker for the language documentation is Bibik Jane Quek. Besides being an active member of the Gunong Sayang Association, Bibik Jane Quek is known for her Peranakan home-cooking in Singapore. Recording sessions with her usually took place at her home or in the shops selling Peranakan food and fashion along East Coast Road, where she would further engage others who can speak the language.

The Malaccan contact for this project was Baba Albert Ku. Most recordings took place at his home in Malacca. A retiree, he speaks the language with his family and is proficient at writing Baba Malay *pantun* 'poetry'. He also provided further points of contact within the Malacca community.

All key consultants and others involved in the recordings provided informed consent for their data to be recorded and archived.

In relation to the community, it may also be useful information that the author identifies as being Peranakan through her paternal lineage, and is recognised as a member of the community. She is a heritage speaker of Baba Malay.

1.3 A guide to this grammar

This is a descriptive grammar that has been written to be of use to a wide audience. Where possible, the use of any theoretical framework that would require specific training to understand is kept to a minimum. Some basic background in linguistics is however necessary, as basic grammatical terms have to be used so that Baba Malay can be adequately described, and so that researchers can make comparisons to other languages where relevant. This grammar has also adopted the following features, structure, use of linguistic abbreviations, and transcription conventions.

---

8 The words *Gunong Sayang* translate directly into 'mountain love' to mean 'mountain of love'.

1.3.1 Example sentence features

The following feature of this grammar caters to readers who may wish to listen to the examples in more detail. Example sentences are provided with timecodes and handles,[9] providing a reference to where each example can be found within the relevant archive. Example (32) illustrates this.

(32) Dia   chakap   sama   dia.
      3SG   speak   with   3SG
      'He speaks with him.'
      (Peter Wee, oai:scholarspace.manoa.hawaii.edu: NL1-042, 00:02:44.4-00:02:46.0)

Data collected from the fieldwork that supports this grammar is hosted in the Kaipuleohone Language Archive, belonging to the University of Hawai'i (scholarspace.manoa.hawaii.edu). If a reader wanted to search for a specific example, such as (32) within the archived file, she or he would have the information that this example uttered by the speaker Peter Wee, can be found on the site in the file labeled NL1-042, and more specifically, that this utterance can be heard between 00:02:44.4–02:46.0 (between the 2 minute and 44 seconds mark and the 2 minutes and 46 seconds mark). Unless otherwise cited, most examples in this grammar are derived from primary fieldwork.

Fieldwork for this grammar was mostly carried out between 2012 and 2014. Sound files and selected transcripts associated with the grammar are hosted at the above-mentioned Kaipuleohone Language Archive. Example sentences are taken from both naturally-occurring and elicited texts. Where elicited data is used, other consultants are also consulted to ensure that the elicited utterances are acceptable in Baba Malay. In addition, these examples also come from different genres, such as conversations and narratives. While texts collected include *pantun* 'traditional poetry',[10] these are not generally used to illustrate the grammar of spoken Baba Malay, since the *pantun*

---

9 This method of referencing examples to their locations within specific archives follows that of Berez (2011).
10 A *pantun* is a traditional Malay verse form with an *abab* rhyme system. The significant lines in a *pantun* are the third and fourth lines, in which the main message of the *pantun* is embedded. *Pantun* can be sung to a tune called *dondang sayang* 'melody (of) love', and singers used to exchange verses they would compose on the spot (Chia 1994: 70). As compared to the Malay *pantun*, the subject of the Peranakan *pantun* is often a matter that the Peranakan community can relate to. It is interesting that even in Peranakan *pantun*, the grammar of standard Malay language is followed as much as possible, and standard Malay lexical items are also used (Chia 1994: 70). While some Peranakan *pantun* adhere to the strophic structure of classical Malay *pantun*, not all do. Singing *pantun* to *dondang sayang* is now an endangered art form, but still performed by groups such as the Gunong Sayang Association in Singapore.

is highly stylized, and does not reflect everyday language use. Some *pantun* have been included in the selection of texts that accompany this grammar.

1.3.2 List of abbreviations used

The following are a list of abbreviations used within the glosses of examples. Leipzig glossing conventions are used where possible.

ACD	Accidental marker
ADJ	Adjective
ADV	Adverb
AdvP	Adverbial phrase
AUX	Auxiliary verb
AP	Adjectival phrase
CLF	Noun classifier
COP	Copula
COMP	Complement
CONF	Confirmative particle
DEM	Demonstrative
EMP	Emphatic particle
EXCLAM	Exclamation
EXIST	Existential marker
GEN	Genitive
HAB	Habitual marker
MVT	Uncontrolled movement marker
N	Noun
NEG	Negation marker
NMZ	Nominalizer
NP	Noun phrase
NUM	Numeral
PFV	Perfective marker
PL	Plural
POSS	Possessive marker
PREP	Preposition
PROG	Progressive marker
Q	Question particle
REL	Relative clause marker
SG	Singular
TR	Transitive marker
V	Verb
VP	Verb phrase
1	First person
2	Second person
3	Third person

1.3.3 Transcription conventions

The transcription in this grammar (including the transcripts that appear at the end) is based mostly on Du Bois et al. (1992)'s conventions for discourse transcriptions. Speech streams are segmented by the intonation unit, which can be identified as a spurt of speech (Du Bois et al. 1992: 16) or a stretch of speech that is accompanied by a single coherent intonation contour (Du Bois et al. 1992: 21). However, when presented in the grammar to demonstrate a particular grammatical pattern or a well-formed phrase or sentence, the intonation units are conflated for ease of interpretation. An example such as (33), which has two intonation units, would be produced in a section on transitivity as (34).

(33) *Anjing   tutop-kan.*
    dog   close-TR
    'The dog turned off.'

   Itu   aloji.
   that   alarm.clock
   'That alarm clock.'
   (Jane Quek, oai:scholarspace.manoa.hawaii.edu: NL1-088, 00:00:25.6-00:00:29.9)

(34) *Anjing   tutop-kan   itu   aloji.*
    Dog   close-TR   that   alarm.clock
    'The dog turned off that alarm clock.'
    (Jane Quek, oai:scholarspace.manoa.hawaii.edu: NL1-088, 00:00:25.6-00:00:29.9)

For the purpose of this grammar, a medium to broad transcription is utilized. A period at the end of the utterance indicates finality, a comma signals continuity (that the speaker has more to say), whereas a question mark signals that the speaker is seeking a response from her or his interlocutor. These are dependent on intonation (see Section 3.7). A list of more detailed transcription conventions for understanding the appended full transcripts at the end of this grammar are included with the transcripts for ease of reference. Transcription is orthographic (see Section 3.6 for orthographic conventions).

1.3.4 Structure of this grammar

This grammar is organized as follows. Chapter 2 provides historical and sociological perspectives on the Baba Malay speech community, highlighting in part the threat of endangerment the language is facing, and the actions taken by the community to reclaim their language. Chapter 3 describes the phonetics and phonology of Baba

Malay. Chapter 4 describes the different parts of speech, and Chapter 5 provides information concerning the syntax of the language. Chapter 6 then provides a general discussion on the differences between Baba Malay spoken in Singapore and Malacca, particularly where differences pervade areas of phonology, morphology and syntax. Appended to the grammar are vocabulary lists (including a 100 word list, kinship terms, expressions for day, month and time, as well as a general Baba Malay-English lexicon, and an English-Baba Malay lexicon) and a collection of texts (including three narratives, a conversation and several *pantun*).

2 Baba Malay and its speakers

Records show that the Chinese were aware of the Malay Archipelago as early as the second century AD, and Indonesian products such as the clove had begun appearing in Funan, China, during this time, although it was only in the fifth century AD that it became popular for Chinese traders to engage in trade in the Malay Archipelago region by sea (Andaya & Andaya 2001). The ports in the Malacca[11] Strait region were geographically advantaged, being at the receiving ends of both northeast and southwest monsoons. The northeast monsoon aided vessels in their southwest journey from China to the Malacca Strait, where they awaited changes in the wind direction to continue their journeys, or to return home, and the Malacca Strait provided a sheltered maritime route, as compared to the open seas beyond (Andaya & Andaya 2001). The development of Chinese settlements in these regions then began as early as the fifteenth century AD, or at least, these dates have been recorded for the travels of the Chinese admiral Zheng He, who led trading exchanges in the South China Sea, Java Sea, and Malacca Strait between 1405 and 1433 (Wade 1994; Wang 1964; Widodo 2002). Out of a total seven voyages made by Zheng He during the Ming dynasty, five visits were made to Malacca, which was notably the first kingdom at that time to receive an official inscription on a tablet by the Chinese emperor, Yong Le (Wang 1964; Widodo 2002).[12] After Zheng He's death in 1433, a scholar on his ship by the name of Fei Xin wrote in *Xing Cha Sheng Lan*[13] 'The Overall Survey of the Star Raft' that besides dark-skinned people, he had also observed fairer-looking people of Chinese descent in Malacca (Fei 1436). In 1537, about a century later, a Chinese traveler by the name of Huang Zhong[14] wrote in his travel journal, *Hai Yu* 'News from the Ocean', that the Chinese in Malacca ate pork, lived in hotels, and had female slaves who served them food and drinks (Groeneveldt 1880). These narratives complement the account that many of the Chinese men who had come to trade at the new port in Malacca did not return to China. Most of these Chinese immigrants were men, as it was rare for women to make these voyages out of China. Women were expected to stay behind to take care of the households, observe filial piety and ancestor worship, and it was only

---

11 In Malaysia and in the Malay language used in the region, Malacca is *Melaka* orthographically.
12 Malacca was then a kingdom in its own right (Windstedt 1948). Malacca became part of the Crown Colony together with Singapore and Penang in 1867, before becoming part of the Malayan Union in 1946. The union was then reformed as the federation of Malaysia, which gained independence from the British in 1957. Singapore later gained its independence from Malaysia in 1965. For more details, see Ryan (1976).
13 Hanyu Pinyin is used for Mandarin elements in the main text. Fei Xin appears as Fei Hsin and *Xing Cha Sheng Lang* as *Hsing-ch'a sheng-lan* in the original source; Chinese names are represented here in the Sinitic tradition of family names preceding personal ones.
14 Huang Zhong appears as Hwang Chung in the original source.

https://doi.org/10.1515/9783110745061-002

after 1853, that Chinese female migration to Malaya began, especially with the Taiping Rebellion[15] of 1850–1864 (Lim 1967).

Eventually, the Hokkien-speaking male settlers who mostly originated from the Zhangzhou and Quanzhou regions in the Fujian province on the south-east coast of China, married indigenous spouses. It remains disputed if these women were of Malay origin (Tan 1979), or if they also comprised the Batak, Balinese, and Javanese (Purcell 1980). On the related subject matter of which variety of Malay constitutes Baba Malay, it has been postulated that Baba Malay's precursor is possibly found in a diffused notion of varieties that share a cluster of mostly grammatical features, considering the range of Malay varieties, contact languages, trade jargons and pidgins that were known to have existed in the region (Ansaldo 2009). Notably, knowledge of some trading variety of Malay was also clearly important to the migrant traders from China, as evidenced by an early Sinitic-Malay dictionary *Hua yi tong yu* 'Chinese migrants' vernacular' (Lin 1883), that was published with the specific aim of helping migrants conduct their business more effectively (Lee 2016). Pages from *Hua yi tong yu* are shown in Figure 1 below.

Figure 1: Pages in *Hua yi tong yu* provide Sinicized pronunciations for various numerals and silver currencies in Malay (Collection of National Library, Singapore).

---

15 The Taiping Rebellion was a period of peasant revolt against the Qing dynasty, which resulted in an estimated 20 million casualties (Michael 1971).

By 1750, it was reported by then Governor of Malacca, Balthasar Bort, that the Chinese population in Malacca had grown to 2161, a fifth of the total population (Purcell 1980), and that the number of China-born Chinese only contributed minimally to this figure (Skinner 1996). Descendants of the locally-formed community are referred to as 'Straits-born Chinese', or *Peranakan*, and it is their language, *Baba Malay*, that this grammar describes.

Notably, while Chinese-Malay intermarriages still occur in Malaysia, Singapore, and beyond, these intermarriages result in neither Peranakan ethnicity nor culture. *Peranakan* refers to more than the descendants of mixed marriages, but also to a home language that some term a *patois*, and to a unique culture that is an amalgamation of Chinese, local, and Western customs and traditions. The largest of these influences is that of the Chinese (Wee 2013). Traditionally, the Peranakans adopted Chinese religious practices.[16] In addition to ancestral worship, they traditionally prayed to *ti gong* 'sky god' and the *datok dapor* 'deity of the stove'. Peranakan celebrations for major life events and festivals also customarily follow Chinese traditions, such as celebrating one's *tua séhjit* 'big birthday' when one turns sixty and celebrating the Lunar New Year. Malay influence, on the other hand, is apparent in Baba Malay with its lexicon having been derived for the most part from Malay, and in the female dress. While Peranakan men traditionally wore the baju *lokchuan*, a Chinese attire made of silk, the females wore the *baju panjang*, a long blouse over a *sarong*, reminiscent of what other local women such as the Malay would wear. Eventually, the men began to favor English suits due to British colonial influence, and the women favored the *sarong kebaya*, the *kebaya* being a short jacket made of European material such as voile, and often elaborately embroidered by hand around the edges with Chinese motifs, such as the dragon to symbolize luck and success, and mandarin ducks to symbolize love. The *kebaya* is fastened in the front by three brooches, linked together by a common chain. This set of brooches is called the *kerosang*. Women also wore beaded shoes called the *kasot manek*, with similar Chinese motifs. Most Peranakans no longer wear traditional outfits on a daily basis, except for some older women. The *sarong kebaya* is only worn for special occasions, such as weddings, and the men have begun wearing batik shirts at these events, as with other men in Southeast Asia. The photograph in Figure 2 was taken in the 1920s, and it shows a Peranakan woman dressed in a *baju panjang* fastened together with *kerosang*, worn over a *sarong*, and a Peranakan man dressed in an English suit.

---

[16] While some of these early intermarriages that constituted the Peranakan community were Chinese-Malay intermarriages, these families did not adopt Islam in general, whereas modern Chinese-Malay intermarriages would usually require that the Chinese partner adopts Islam as a religion (see Tan 1979).

2 Baba Malay and its speakers — 19

Figure 2: A 1920s photograph of a Peranakan couple in Singapore.¹⁷

As far as cuisine is concerned, Peranakan cooking is a fusion of Chinese, local, and Western ingredients. *Iték tim* 'duck soup' for example, comprises Chinese preserved

---

17 It was common for Peranakans to patronize commercial photography studios in the late 1800s and early 1900s (Peranakan Museum 2018). The subjects in this picture are the author's great-grand mother and step-great-grandfather. The picture was taken at a now-defunct photography studio, Wong Fong, which used to be at 809 North Bridge Road, Singapore.

vegetables, the Southeast Asian tamarind, and Western brandy, among other ingredients (Wee 2013).

Western influence brought about by British colonialism cannot be taken too lightly. With the British settlement of Penang, Malacca and Singapore in the early nineteenth century, English medium schools were set up, and the Peranakans were among the first to send their children to these schools. The English-educated Peranakans often served as middlemen who mediated between the new migrants who had arrived from places such as China, and the English colonial administrators (Lim 2016a). Whether or not it was indeed the case,[18] the Peranakans were perceived to be among the best educated and wealthiest of the Chinese population (Nathan 1922; Ansaldo, Lim & Mufwene 2007).

In a conscious effort to differentiate themselves from other Chinese migrants, the Peranakans went as far as identifying themselves as the King's Chinese (Song 1967; Hardwick 2008). Eventually, a group of Peranakans set up the Straits Chinese British Association in 1900, the name of the association reflecting the Peranakans' ties with the British administrators. After World War II, the British completely removed themselves from Malaya in 1963, and only then was the association renamed the Singapore Chinese Peranakan Association. It was later renamed the Peranakan Association Singapore in 1966, and the association's name has since remained the same (Wee 2013).

2.1 What is in a name?

The term *Peranakan* was conceivably formed via one of these processes – *Peranakan* comprises middle voice prefix *ber-*, which combines with *anak* 'child', giving rise to *beranak*, which means 'to give birth'. The verb is then combined with the nominalizer *-an* to indicate 'womb'. The word initial *b* may dissimilate in voicing with the following sequence. This construal is in fact reminiscent of *Crioulo in* Portuguese, which is derived from *criar* 'to raise or to bring up children', in view of the conceptual overlap between raising children (Portuguese *criar*) and having children (Malay *beranak*). That there might be some Portuguese influence in this regard is not implausible, given that the Portuguese colonized Malacca between 1511 and 1641, coinciding with the early period of the Peranakans.[19] In a second interpretation, *Peranakan* constitutes the person prefix *pe-*, the word for child, *anak*, and a nominalizer suffix, *-an* to denote 'descendants'. The more plausible explanation might be the first, which provides a morphologically well-formed word at each stage of word formation and requires that the nominalizer *-an* be suffixed onto a verb. In this case, the verb would be *beranak* 'to give birth'. The second interpretation is less plausible because it would require the

---

18 While it is commonly assumed in the literature that Peranakans were at one point among the most well-educated and wealthy, the author also encountered older Peranakans in rural parts of Malaysia who came from farming families, some of whom are illiterate.

19 Credit is owed to the editor, Georg Bossong, for pointing out these conceptual similarities.

person prefix that is usually attached to a verb to be attached to a noun, and the nominalizer -*an* would have to be suffixed onto a noun, either *anak* 'child' or **peranak*, which has no meaning on its own. All affixes here are of Malay origin. While the nominalizer -*an* is a productive suffix in Baba Malay, person prefix *pe-* and middle voice *ber-* are not. In the Malay Peninsula, *Peranakan* can be used to indicate a person born of an indigenous or Malay mother and a foreign father, and it is also frequently taken to mean 'locally-born', as with *Peranakan Yahudi* (locally-born Jews), *Peranakan Chitty* (locally-born Hindus of indigenous and Tamil origins), and *Peranakan Jawi* (locally-born Muslims of indigenous and Arab or South Asian ancestry).[20] While the term *Peranakan Cina* (locally-born Chinese) was more popularly used in the past, the Peranakan Chinese are now commonly referred to simply as *Peranakan* by the speakers themselves and by those outside the community. The generic term *Peranakan* is used to refer to the Peranakan Chinese, presumably due to the larger numbers of this particular community (Pakir 1986: 23).

Within the Peranakan community, the males are referred to as *baba*, while the females are referred to as *nyonya*. The term *baba*, which also constitutes a part of the language name, *Baba Malay*, is of unclear etymology. According to one account, the term was said to be derived from Turkish, and used by Bengal natives for European children, and was introduced by Indian convicts in Penang to describe Chinese children (Vaughan 1879). In a separate account, it was postulated that *baba* is a loanword borrowed from Persian by Malay speakers. Used as an honorific for grandparents, the term was said to have been imported to the Malay Peninsula by Hindustani speakers such as vendors and traders (Khoo 1996). A third, simpler and more direct explanation can also be proposed. The term could have come from Hokkien, which the Chinese traders would have spoken originally. The Hokkien address for one's father is [papa] with an unaspirated [p], with a low falling tone on the first syllable, and a rising tone on the second syllable. The children of these Chinese-indigenous intermarriages may have used the Hokkien term to address their fathers, considering that most of the kinship terms in Baba Malay are derived from Hokkien (see Pakir 1986 and section 7.1.2). It is plausible that the term [papa] evolved into [baba], as unaspirated [p] is aurally close to [b]. Today, Peranakans either address their fathers [bapaʔ] or [baba], the latter term being more commonly used in Malacca.

Nyonya, which refers to the female Peranakan, has a clearer etymology. It is most likely derived from the Portuguese form *dona* – the dates of the first Chinese settlement in Malacca and the Portuguese colonization of this place seem to support this account.

---

[20] *Peranakan Jawi* and *Peranakan Yahudi* are most likely exonyms. *Peranakan* is an endonym to the Peranakan Chinese, who use it to refer to their community and the language that they speak, and the Chitty use the terms *Peranakan Chitty* or *Peranakan Indian* to refer to their community. The Peranakan Chitty are said to use a version of Malay with Tamil loanwords. On a separate note, it is common perception that there are not many Peranakan Jawi and Peranakan Yahudi left in Malaysia and Singapore. There is a small community of Chitty left in Malacca in Gajah Berang (Dhoraisingam 2006) and in Singapore.

Malacca was colonized by Portugal between 1511 and 1641, the Portuguese having arrived a century after Chinese traders had begun settling in Malacca. Within a century, the Chinese-indigenous marriages that led to the development of the Peranakan culture and identity would have taken place, and it would have been possible for the Peranakans to borrow the term for 'female' from the then-dominant Portuguese. The remarkable salience of the word *dona* or *nona* is attested to by the fact that this word from that era is still preserved in the region through a popular Malacca Creole Portuguese song, *Jingli Nona* 'Dancing Girl'.

Other essential terms associated with the *Peranakan* identity are *peranakan jati*, *peranakan chelop*, *embok-embok*, *embok jantan*, *wawak* and *bibik*. Both *peranakan jati* and *peranakan chelop* relate to lineage. *Jati* is a term for 'teak' in Malay, and a *peranakan jati* is one whose parents are both Peranakan. *Peranakan jati* are often described as being "true-blue" Peranakans, in comparison to the *peranakan chelop*. *Chelop* means to 'dip in dye' in Malay, and a *peranakan chelop* is no longer "pure", since one of her or his parents would be non-Peranakan. These concepts are paradoxical, considering that the Peranakan community itself arose out of intermarriages across ethnic lines. Notably, in the years after the formation of the Peranakan identity, marriages within the community were common and even preferred (Clammer 1980; Tan 1979). The Peranakans differentiated themselves from the new Chinese migrants or *sinkék* (Hokkien-derived term meaning 'newcomers'), although in the nineteenth century, when the British first colonized Malaya and Singapore, Chinese males were encouraged to migrate to Singapore to fulfil a demand for labor, during which time, Peranakans looked to Chinese migrants for sons-in-law, as they preferred their daughters to not marry Malay men (Tan 1979). Marriages within the community became rare after the Japanese invasion of the Malay Archipelago (1942–1945). Consequently, there are not many *Peranakan jati* left.

The term *embok-embok* is close in nature to that of *peranakan jati*. *Embok-embok* refers to elderly Peranakan women who are highly traditional in their beliefs and customs. It has been suggested that *embok-embok* could have originated from Javanese in which [əm.boʔ] would mean 'mother', or be a 'term of address for an older woman, especially of the servant class' (Pakir 1986: 23). The term also is said to exist in Betawi Malay, spoken in Jakarta – Betawi Malay speakers use the term [mboʔ- mboʔ] to mean 'older woman' (Pakir 1986: 23). The word can possibly be traced further back to an earlier existence in Hokkien, since the Hokkien were among the most dominant Chinese in the region. There exists in Hokkien [po] with a rising tone, a word that refers to 'grandaunt'. This word would appear as [ŋ.po] in the Zhangzhou variety of Hokkien, Zhangzhou and Quanzhou being where most Peranakans trace their ancestral roots to. [ŋ] is a vocative particle in the Zhangzhou variety of Hokkien, used commonly in kinship terms (Freedman 1979). The meaning of [ŋ.po], which denotes grand-aunt and connotes a much older woman, is semantically congruous with the Peranakan, Javanese and Betawi Malay terms. In Peranakan, *embok-embok* can also mean 'highly traditional Peranakan elders' collectively. However, the term is never used to refer to elderly Peranakan men. This is perhaps due to the fact that the original term from which *embok-embok* was coined refers to 'grandmother' or 'elderly woman'

Figure 3: Map of key locales in the development of Baba Malay.

in Hokkien. The male counterpart of the female *embok-embok* is the *embok-jantan*, wherein *jantan* means 'male' in Malay.[21] Interestingly, traditional forms of Peranakan cuisine are called *lauk embok-embok*. Finally, another term that is utilized to mean a much older Peranakan woman of a grandmother's or even great-grandmother's age is *wawak*. The term has no male equivalent.

---

[21] While *jantan* 'male' is used when referring to animals in Malay, it can also be used for human beings in Baba Malay. Interestingly, the term for female animals in Malay, *betina*, is not used to refer to human beings in Baba Malay. Instead, Baba Malay speakers use *perompuan* 'female, woman'.

The last term that is highly indicative of the Peranakan identity is *bibik*. *Bibik* refers to a 'mature Peranakan woman'. It is said that *bibik* may have been derived from Hindustani, and has a similar meaning, 'aunt' in Indonesian (Pakir 1986: 25). There is no direct male equivalent to *bibik*. The *bibik* is usually perceived to be younger than the *embok-embok* or *wawak*. At the time of writing, *bibik* and its contracted form *bik* remain highly used within the community, while the other terms, *embok-embok*, *embok-jantan*, and *wawak* are falling out of use.

2.2 Geographical location

Although the Peranakans first developed their identity, language, and culture in Malacca (2.2000° N, 102.2510° E), some of them may have moved later to Penang (5.4000° N, 100.2333° E) and most definitely, to Singapore (1.3667° N, 103.7500° E). While Penang is 475km (or 295 miles) north of Malacca, Singapore is 232km (or 144 miles) south of Malacca (see Figure 3 for a map of key locales in the development of Baba Malay).

Penang is about 1,048km², Malacca is about 1,664 km², and Singapore is about 710 km². Both Penang and Malacca are states in current-day Malaysia, while Singapore is a nation state on its own. The local names for Penang and Malacca in Malay are *Pulau Pinang* 'Island Penang' and *Melaka*. Penang and Malacca are positioned on the west coast of the Malay Peninsula, while Singapore occupies the southern-most tip of this peninsula. All three locations are littoral, strung along the Malacca Strait, which was made prosperous by trading ships. The Malacca Strait is still a vital shipping channel, being the main artery that links the Indian Ocean and the Pacific Ocean.

Malacca flourished as a trading port under the Portuguese rule between 1511 and 1641. In contrast, it was considerably less successful under the Dutch rule between 1641 and 1825. The Dutch had only occupied Malacca to prevent other European powers from occupying it, during which time they still preferred to use Batavia, present-day Jakarta, as their main center of trade and other economic activities (De Witt 2008). The Peranakans were greatly affected by these events, being involved in trade and commerce. In 1786, a number of Peranakans moved to Penang, after the British annexed it, because, unlike Malacca, Penang was thriving as a trading port at the expense of Malacca. In a letter dated 1 February 1787, the colonial administrator of Penang, Captain Francis Light, wrote that "[d]id not the Dutch keep a strict watch over the Chinese, most of them would leave Malacca" (Purcell 1967: 244). Following that, a significant number of Peranakans also moved to Singapore at the beginning of the 19th century, shortly after the founding of Singapore by Thomas Stamford Raffles in 1819 (Skinner 1996).

A separate account has also been put forth for the presence of Peranakan Chinese in Penang. It is said that this community emerged from the intermarriages between Chinese traders from Southern Thailand and Northern Sumatra, and women of Malay, Siamese and Burmese descent (Khoo 1998: 6). It has also been observed that the Peranakans in Penang still have extensive ties with families in Southern Thailand and Northern Sumatra (Teoh, Lim & Lee 2017: 172).

In addition to the Peranakans of Malacca, Penang, and Singapore, it should be noted that there is also a Peranakan population in Java, Indonesia (7.5028° S, 111.2631° E). This population is not directly related to the communities in Malacca, Penang, and Singapore. It is said that even though Chinese immigrants arrived in Java prior to the eighteenth century, they had mostly assimilated to the indigenous society. It was only during the eighteenth century that the Peranakan community began to develop, with its own practices and language (Skinner 1996). The language spoken by this community is called Peranakan Indonesian (ISO 639-3: pea), and it is said to be based on Indonesian (ISO 639-3: ind) and Javanese (ISO 639-3: jav), with Mandarin elements as compared to Baba Malay, which instead has Hokkien elements (Lewis, Simons & Fennig 2015). Notably, these intertwined and separate histories have had effects on what language or language variety each community speaks.

2.3 Dialects and ecologies

There are two varieties of Baba Malay spoken today. The Peranakans from Singapore speak a different variety of Baba Malay from the Peranakans in Malacca. Conversely, the Peranakans in Penang do not speak Baba Malay. Instead they speak Penang Peranakan Hokkien (Teoh, Lim & Lee 2017). There are a few reasons for this. First, the community in Penang might have evolved separately, with a Penang-southern Thailand/northern Sumatra pattern of intermarriage (Skinner 1996; Khoo 1998). Second, the trading patterns of Penang and Singapore were likewise different. Penang was an entrepot for Phuket in southern Thailand, and Medan in northeastern Sumatra, where Hokkien speakers predominated among the traders, and Singapore was an entrepot for ports that lined the north coast of Java, where Indonesian Peranakans predominated among the traders (Skinner 1996). These trading patterns possibly explain why Hokkien continued to be a more dominant language among the Peranakans in Penang, and why a variety of Baba Malay never did take off there (although such an account would be less successful at explaining why Baba Malay in Singapore is not more influenced by Peranakan Indonesian). Third, while there possibly had been a population of Peranakans in Penang who did originate from Malacca, they might have assimilated into the stable settlement of married Hokkien speakers in Penang, since such a settlement preceded the arrival of the Peranakans from Malacca (Skinner 1996). The Peranakans who migrated to Penang from Malacca would have had strong ties with Hokkien speakers who were traders like themselves, and the stable Hokkien settlement would have provided a model the Peranakans could emulate. No such settlement of married Hokkien speakers existed in Singapore prior to the arrival of the Peranakans. Interestingly, while the Peranakans in Penang speak Hokkien, their variety is said to contain numerous loanwords from Malay (Teoh, Lim & Lee 2017). Their culture is similarly a mixture of Chinese, indigenous and Western, although it is predominantly Chinese. They share, for example, Chinese kinship terms that are also used by the Peranakans in Malacca and in Singapore (see section 7.1.2 for kinship terms in Baba Malay).

The two varieties of Baba Malay in Malacca and in Singapore have since diverged due to their different ecologies (Lee 2018). Census data on Singapore only begins from the 1820s, but population trends become quickly apparent. Table 3 compares the populations of Malacca and Singapore in 1836. These numbers are derived from Newbold (1839). The Chinese categories here include the Teochew, Hakka, Cantonese and Hailam populations, in addition to the Hokkiens.

Table 3: Population of Malacca and Singapore in 1836 (Newbold 1839: 136, 283).

Malacca		Singapore	
Malays	21,220	Malays	9,632
Chinese	4,102	Chinese	13,749
Chulias	2,273	Natives of Coromandel (Chulias) and Malabar Coasts	2,348
Bataks	317	Bugis, Balinese, etc.	1,952
Javanese	252	Javanese	903
Siamese	230	Siamese	3
Arabs	72	Arabs	41
Africans	2	Africans	41
Christians (including all Europeans)	2,389	Europeans	141
Hindus	880	Natives of Hindustan and Bengal	582
Bengalis	88	Armenians	34
Total	31,825	Indo-Britons	117
		Native Christians	425
		Parsis	2
		Jews	4
		Total	29974[22]

---

[22] Newbold (1939) calculates 29984, when the total should be 29974.

Table 3 shows that the ecologies of Malacca and Singapore were clearly different in 1836. The largest group in Malacca were the Malays, followed by the Chinese, whereas the largest group in Singapore were the Chinese, followed by the Malays. At both locations, the Hokkiens predominated among the Chinese, and still do today. From the outset, the Hokkiens have always been the most dominant Chinese group in Malacca, since the arrival of Chinese settlers in the 1400s (Pan 2006: 173). In Singapore, while there were once more Teochews than Hokkiens, soil deterioration in Singapore is said to have driven many Teochews who were engaged in gambier and pepper planting to Johor in the 1850s (Pan 2006: 204). By 1901, there were almost twice as many Hokkiens as there were Teochews (Hayes 1921: 362). These population trends continue to perdure. Table 4 illustrates recent population trends derived from official government census reports in Malacca and Singapore.

Table 4: Ethnic composition of Malacca and Singapore (Malaysia 2016; Singapore 2015).

Malacca		Singapore	
Malays	58.7%	Malays	13.3%
Chinese	28.5%	Chinese	74.3%
Indians	5.1%	Indians	9.1%
Others	7.7%	Others	3.2%
Total resident population	931,210	Total resident population	3,900,000

A comparison of Tables 3 and 4 shows that the Chinese population has more than doubled in Singapore since the 1800s, and a recent census among the Chinese resident population in Singapore shows that the Hokkien population far outnumbers the rest of the Chinese groups at 1,151,285, the next largest Chinese population being the Teochews, at 574,793 (Singapore 2015). In Malaysia, the largest group were and still are the Malays.

Yet another factor to consider when looking at the different ways in which Malacca Baba Malay and Singapore Baba Malay have diverged is that the Peranakans in Malacca are multilingual in a different way than the Peranakans in Singapore. Most Peranakans in Malacca who speak Baba Malay can also speak Malay, which is the language of administration and education in Malaysia (Rappa & Wee 2006), and some speak English. Conversely, Peranakans in Singapore who speak Baba Malay tend to be proficient in English, but not in Malay, due to the fact that English is the language of administration and mainstream education in Singapore. In addition, younger Peranakans, who are administratively categorized and regarded as "Chinese" would also be required to learn Mandarin in addition to English in schools, under a bilingual language policy that begun in Singapore in 1966 (see Pakir 1994). At both locations, the only monolingual speakers are in their 90s, and it is difficult to find Peranakans who speak Baba Malay under the age of 50.

In terms of interaction patterns, there are Peranakans in Singapore who have relatives living in Malacca that they may visit on the occasion. Active members of both communities also meet annually at the Baba Nyonya Convention, but interaction rarely takes place on an everyday extensive basis.

Against these differing and perduring linguistic backdrops, the two varieties of Baba Malay were formed, with observable stable differences. Singapore Baba Malay has more Hokkien lexical items than Malacca Baba Malay, which seems more Malay to Peranakans in Singapore. For example, words such as *riyang*, meaning 'lively', are used in Malacca Baba Malay, but are deemed by Singapore Baba Malay speakers as being "too Malay". Singapore Baba Malay speakers use the term *laujiet* to express 'lively', *laujiet* having been derived from Hokkien. Syntactically, the two varieties are slightly different from one another. It is possible to construct phrases with both sequences of 'Noun Determiner', and 'Determiner Noun' in Singapore Baba Malay, whereas the sequence 'Determiner Noun' is not usually found in current-day Malacca Baba Malay. In Malay, only the sequence 'Noun Determiner' is permitted, while in Hokkien, the opposite is true. While this grammar is mostly based on Baba Malay as it is spoken in Singapore, Chapter 6 outlines the major differences between both varieties.

2.4 Speaker numbers

It is difficult to pinpoint how many Peranakans and Baba Malay speakers there are in Malaysia and Singapore. Both countries consider the Peranakans to be ethnically Chinese and census reports usually do not list Peranakans in a separate category. Similarly, Baba Malay is not an official language, and would be subsumed under a more general "Others" category if the census takers were at all interested in non-official languages. In 1986, based on a 1957 census report of Singapore that stated that 2.1% of 442,707 people had "Malaysian dialects" as their mother tongue, Pakir (1986) postulated that there was possibly an ethnic population of 10,000 Peranakans in Singapore. Among the Peranakans in Singapore then, it was estimated that there were at least 5,000 speakers of Baba Malay. This number comprises both fluent and non-fluent speakers. Monolingual speakers were also reported to be at least 70 years old. Thirty-three years on, Baba Malay is a moribund language, more so than ever. It is no longer being learnt by younger generations. Speakers themselves claim that there are less than 1,000 speakers in Singapore who can speak the language fluently. Based on Pakir's (1986) numbers, all surviving monolingual speakers would be in their late 90s at the very least, and this is indeed the observed trend within both the Singapore and Malaccan community. The situation in Malacca is similar. In 2006, it was reported that there were an estimated 2,000 Peranakans in Malaysia (Salleh 2006). There are no official numbers on how many of them speak Baba Malay. Given that the language is also moribund in Malacca and that speakers under the age of 50 are rare, and assuming that there are equal numbers of Peranakans below and above the age of 50, it can be estimated that there are less than 1,000 speakers in Malacca.

Outside of Singapore and Malacca, Peranakans have also moved to locales such as Kuala Lumpur in Malaysia, and also Australia, especially to Melbourne, Sydney, and Perth where there now exist chapters of the Peranakan Association Australia. It is less clear how many Peranakans and speakers of Baba Malay there are in those communities, although it is highly likely that there are fewer Peranakans and speakers of Baba Malay outside of Singapore and Malacca than within these areas.

2.5 The endangerment of Baba Malay

It is evident that the number of Baba Malay speakers is decreasing, when the numbers of speakers then and now are compared. This section focuses centrally on the circumstances of endangerment in Singapore, which is the locus of the variety that this grammar documents. As early as the 1980s, the fact that Baba Malay was endangered was recognized (Lee 2019). The threat of language loss was then addressed by Felix Chia, a writer in the Peranakan community who wrote several *wayang Peranakan* 'plays in Baba Malay', as well as commentaries on the social lives and histories of the Peranakans (Chia 1980; Chia 1983a; Chia 1983b; Chia 1994). The circumstances of endangerment have not been ameliorated, and in fact have become exacerbated since.

The endangerment of Baba Malay can be attributed to three main causes – the dominance of English over the lives of the Peranakans, the language education policy that required Peranakans to learn Mandarin in schools in addition to English, and the fact that community numbers are inherently declining (Lee 2019). The dominance of British culture and the English language in the lives of the Peranakans is well recognized by those who have commented on Baba Malay's state of endangerment (Lim 2016a; Lim 2016b). With the British settlement of Singapore and Malacca in the early nineteenth century (Singapore in 1819, and Malacca in 1824) came the establishment of English medium schools. Previously, a handful of wealthy Peranakans were sending their sons to China for education. Now, most are sending their children to English medium schools (Tan 1979). With their knowledge of English, Peranakan men were often employed as intermediaries who mediated between the migrants and the British colonial administrators. They were also themselves well-placed to be highly involved in trade and commerce. As such, many Peranakans were socially influential and economically advantaged (Ansaldo, Lim & Mufwene 2007). Ironically, the circumstances that led to the socio-economic heyday of the Peranakans, also led to the current state of language endangerment (Lim 2016b). The influence of the British over the Peranakans extended beyond language – the Peranakans aligned themselves with the British rather than with the Chinese, particularly the newer migrants whom they called *sinkék* 'new arrivals'. They incorporated Western elements into their culture, such as the use of brandy in their cuisine and the suit in their dressing. At an entrenched level, the Peranakans identified themselves as the King's Chinese (Song 1967), and in 1900, they set up the Singapore Chinese British Association (Lee 1960), the name of the clan association reflecting the early ties between the Peranakans and the administrators. During World War I, leaders of the association further demonstrated their allegiance to the British, with the donation of funds and the purchase of warplanes to aid Britain's war efforts (Yeo 2017). After World War II, with the exit of the British administration from Singapore, the Singapore Chinese British Association was renamed the Singapore Chinese Peranakan Association in 1964, and then the Peranakan Association in 1966 (Lim 2003: 20). The dominance of the English language in the lives of the Peranakans continues. In 1966, a bilingual language education policy was implemented in Singapore (Pakir 1994) – students were broadly categorized into officially recognized ethnic groups, and assigned a "mother tongue"[23] that they learnt as an academic subject, while English was chosen as the medium of instruction for all other subjects. This policy still stands, and English remains the main medium of education and administration in Singapore.

The aforementioned bilingual language policy is also significant. Peranakans, who were and still are officially classified as being ethnically "Chinese", are required to learn Mandarin in school. Incontrovertibly, the policy has had an impact on Baba Malay, with fluent speakers of Baba Malay being above the age of 50 (Lee 2014; Lee 2019). At home, instead of encouraging their children to speak Baba Malay, some Peranakans were encouraging their children to speak Mandarin. The dominance of Mandarin then, and its contribution to Baba Malay's decline at home is actually more saliently recognized by community members than the influence of English (Hong 2017). Today, within the home domain, the language is highly threatened. Recent census data in Singapore reinforces this impression (Lee 2019): English is the most frequently spoken language at home for 36.9% of the residents in Singapore. The same census also reports that the Chinese (a more general label under which the Peranakan community is subsumed) literate population aged 15 years and over are mostly literate in two languages, these being two of the official languages in Singapore, English and Mandarin, at 58.0% and 62.6% respectively (Department of Statistics Singapore 2015).

The last identifiable reason, for which Baba Malay has become critically endangered, is just as noteworthy – this is the fact that the Peranakan community itself is not expanding in the most traditional way (Lee 2019). While Chinese-Malay intermarriages still do occur, and intermarriages are becoming increasingly common, with one in five marriages in Singapore being intermarriages (Department of Statistics Singapore 2015), these intermarriages do not result in Peranakan ethnicity, since "Peranakan-ness" denotes more than an intermarriage and is a unique composite of various cultures. At one point, Peranakans were indeed marrying among themselves

---

[23] The concept of a "mother tongue" here is more akin to that of a second language that is taught in schools than a language that one's parent or parents speak.

(Pakir 1986), hoping to keep the bloodline "pure", ironically since these the Peranakan ethnicity and culture arose from early intermarriages. These intra-community marriages however, are no longer the norm (Tan 1979). Instead, it is has become increasingly common for Peranakans to marry spouses from other Chinese groups, such as the Hokkiens, Teochews, Cantonese, and Hakkas, among others. This was documented as a trend in Malacca in the 1970s (Tan 1979), and the trend continues today, even in Singapore, given an increasingly limited pool of potential Peranakan spouses. Newer figures are not available, as Peranakans have for a long time been subsumed under a wider Chinese label for official purposes. But a census of the population taken much earlier in 1911 shows that of the 194,016 Chinese in Singapore, 155,132 were China-born, as compared to the 38,884 who were Straits-born (or Peranakan in other words) (Song 1967: 24). More than a century has since passed, and with the progression of time and the inevitable reduction in the number of Peranakan considering that intermarriages have long ceased to result in Peranakan ethnicity, it has become more common for Peranakans to marry outside their own community, whether it be to a person from another Chinese group, or to a person outside the ethnic Chinese framework. Hence, in addition to English and Mandarin, which are recognized official languages that have been adopted as home languages, Peranakans of child-bearing age also have the options of passing on Baba Malay and or the language of their spouse's family to their children. More often than not, parents tend to choose a more dominant home language for socio-economic reasons (Wee 2003), or one that they are more fluent in for practical reasons. The option of passing on Baba Malay to children is now becoming less viable, considering that the language is no longer spoken by most people of child-bearing age. The language is moribund, with mostly those of the grandparent generation speaking the language (Lee 2014). The odds of Baba Malay being transmitted to the younger generation then, as a language spoken by 1,000 people out of 5.61 million people in Singapore (Department of Statistics Singapore 2017), are extremely low.

All factors considered, Baba Malay is assessed as a "critically endangered" language according to the Language Endangerment Index (Lee & Van Way 2016) that is utilized by the Catalogue of Endangered Languages (www.endangeredlanguages.com) and a "shifting" language according to the Expanded Graded Intergenerational Disruption Scale (Lewis & Simons 2010) that is utilized on Ethnologue (Simons & Fennig 2017).

2.6 Community responses to language endangerment

In general, the Peranakan community is extremely concerned about language endangerment. A survey on language attitudes was carried out during the course of the language documentation project that informs this grammar. Most respondents felt that Baba Malay was endangered and were concerned about its future. While they felt that a person could still be Peranakan without speaking the language, they also stated that it was a language that they would want the younger generation to speak (Lee 2014).

Various ongoing efforts to revitalize the language are underway, all of which are community-driven. Publications that aim to promote the learning of Baba Malay include works of Baba William Gwee, Baba Philip Chan, and Baba Kenneth Chan. In 1993, Baba William Gwee published *Mas Sepuloh: Baba Conversational Gems*,[24] a glossary of Peranakan terms and idioms, and in 2006, he published a Baba Malay-English dictionary (Gwee 1993; Gwee 2006). In 2007, *Speak Baba Malay: The Easy Way* was published by Baba Philip Chan (Chan 2007).[25] More recently, *Mari Chakap Baba* 'Let's Speak Baba' was published, with the support of Gunong Sayang Association (Chan 2018). *Mari Chakap Baba* was created by Baba Kenneth Chan with Nyonya Amelyn Thompson, both of whom are trained in language pedagogy as ESL teachers, and based in part on the unpublished version of this current grammar.[26] The book was launched in conjunction with a series of language classes modeled on the Common European Framework of Reference for Languages. The language classes are opened to all, but have been attracting mostly Peranakans, or those affiliated in some way to the culture or community, such as docents at the Peranakan museum. It is hoped that these classes will be sustainable into the future.

Other possible projects that have been discussed or broached for the future include the creation of Baba Malay podcasts and the translation of children books into Baba Malay. Where the podcasts are concerned, an individual has scripted fifty dialogues in Baba Malay under the guidance of an experienced Peranakan stage actor who performs in *wayang Peranakan* 'Peranakan plays'. These dialogues are meant to be recorded and released with an accompanying book of transcripts and translations in the future. All in all, the projects mentioned are all community-driven and represent an entirely bottom-up approach to revitalization. There is a clear sense of ownership with regard to what has to be done, and who is responsible for revitalizing the language (Lee 2019).

In response to the circumstances of endangerment and community efforts aimed at language revitalization or reclamation, this descriptive grammar aims to function not only as a reference point for specialists interested in Baba Malay or in the typology of contact languages, but also as base for those who are interested in developing pedagogical material.

---

24 *Mas Sepuloh* literally translates to ten pieces of gold, with *mas* indicating 'gold' and *sepuloh* indicating 'ten'.
25 Baba Philip Chan had planned on conducting language classes based on *Speak Baba Malay: The Easy Way*, but passed away before he could do so.
26 This grammar is a much revised, updated, and focused version of the author's PhD dissertation that was submitted to the University of Hawai'i in 2014. The more exploratory scope of the PhD dissertation included a sociophonetic study and an extended discussion of the type of contact language Baba Malay is. For the sociophonetic study, see Lee (2020).

3 Phonetics and phonology

At the very core, a comprehensive description of the sound system of Baba Malay must take into account that Baba Malay is a contact language. While the main lexifier of Baba Malay is Malay, Baba Malay has also derived a significant portion of its lexicon from Hokkien, including terms of emotion and terms that have to do with traditional customs and practices (Pakir 1986). To a lesser extent, the contact language has also incorporated words from Portuguese, Dutch, English, and Tamil, among other languages (Shellabear 1913; Pakir 1986). This chapter describes Baba Malay's phonological system. It also explains how it differs from that of the Standard Malay that is spoken in Singapore and Malaysia, and how words from Hokkien and other languages have been incorporated into the language based on its own unique phonological template.

3.1 Phoneme inventory

The phoneme inventory of Baba Malay accounts for words of Malay origin, words of Hokkien origin, and words of origins other than Malay and Hokkien that have long existed in the Baba Malay speakers' repertoire. This inventory comprises 19 consonants and 8 vowels that can also be combined to form diphthongs and long vowels. Where relevant, acoustic representations of the different phones are also utilized. Differences between the Baba Malay phoneme inventory and that of Malay, as well as that of Hokkien, are also discussed where relevant.

3.1.1 Consonants

Baba Malay has the following 19 phonemic consonants. Table 2 is replicated here as Table 5, for the readers' convenience.

3.1.1.1 Minimal and near-minimal pairs of consonants

Minimal pairs[27] are used to establish the phonemic status of the consonants that have been introduced in section 3.1.1. Where necessary, near-minimal pairs are utilized as well.

(35) /b/ : /p/
[**b**agi] 'similar to' : [**p**agi] 'morning'

---

[27] For the non-linguist reader, minimal pairs refer to two words with different meanings that differ in only one sound. These attest to the meaning potential of those sounds in the language.

https://doi.org/10.1515/9783110745061-003

Table 5: Consonant chart of Baba Malay.

		Labial	Alveolar	Post-alveolar	Velar	Glottal
Plosives	Voiceless	p	t		k	ʔ
	Voiced	b	d		g	
Affricates	Voiceless			tʃ		
	Voiced			dʒ		
Fricatives	Voiceless		s			h
Nasals		m	n	ɲ	ŋ	
Lateral			l			
Flap			ɾ			

Glides: w (voiced labiovelar); j (voiced palatal)

(36) /b/ : /w/
[bajaŋ] 'shadow' : [wajaŋ] 'play'

(37) /p/ : /w/
[paʔ] 'male fellow' : [waʔ] 'elderly Malay person'

(38) /m/ : /w/
[majaŋ] 'palm blossom' : [wajaŋ] 'play'

(39) /m/ : /n/
[mja] 'life' : [nja] 'contracted form of possessor and relative clause marker *punya*'

(40) /m/ : /p/
[mati] 'die' : [pati] 'first cream of coconut'

(41) /d/ : /t/
[da.own] 'leaf' – [ta.own] 'year'

(42) /d/ : /ɾ/
[dʒaɾi] 'finger' – [dʒadi] 'happen, become'

(43) /t/ : /tʃ/
[taɾeʔ] 'pull' – [tʃaɾeʔ] 'search'

(44) /d/ : /dʒ/
[daɾi] 'from' – [dʒaɾi] 'finger'

(45) /tʃ/ : /dʒ/
[tʃam] 'observe' –   [dʒam] 'time, hour'

(46) /n/ : /l/
[nama] 'name' – [lama] 'long (describing time)'

(47) /ɾ/ : /l/
[ɾupa] 'appearance' – [lupa] 'forget'

(48) /ɾ/ : /n/
[kuɾaŋ] 'less' – [kunaŋ] 'under the influence of black magic'

(49) /n/ : /ŋ/
[piŋgan] 'plate' – [piŋgaŋ] 'waist'

(50) /n/ : /ɲ/
/na/ 'here you go' – [ɲa] 'mother'

(51) /dʒ/ : /g/
[dʒantoŋ] 'heart' – [gantoŋ] 'hang'

(52) /k/ : /g/
[kaja] 'rich'– [gaja] 'splurge'

(53) /k/ : /tʃ/
[kjam] 'stingy'– '[tʃjam] – 'divination stick'

(54) /g/ : /ŋ/
[gaga] 'daring' – [ŋaŋa] 'mouth agape

(55) /ŋ/ : /k/
[pəŋat] 'sweet dessert of thick coconut milk with banana chunks' – [pəkat] 'thick (describing liquid)'

(56) /ʔ/ : /ŋ/
[pulaʔ] 'instead' – [pulaŋ] 'return'

(57) /s/ : /h/
[so] 'burn' – [ho] 'good'

(58) /h/ : /ŋ/
[hantoʔ] 'bang' – [ŋantoʔ] 'sleepy'

(59) /ʔ/ : /k/
    [baʔu] 'smell' – [baku] 'standard'

A near minimal pair that establishes the phoneme statuses of /ʔ/ and /g/ is:

(60) /ʔ/ : /g/
    [baʔu] 'smell' – [bagus] 'good'

3.1.1.2 The use of waveforms and spectrograms

In the following subsections, acoustic representations of consonants are provided in the form of waveforms and spectrograms. The purpose of acoustic analysis is two-fold here. In addition to being more precise than a purely auditory analysis, an acoustic analysis can form the basis of comparison in the future, for example if one would like to investigate changes to particular phones. All waveforms and spectrograms were generated using Praat version 5.3.59 (Boersma & Weenink 2013). All recordings utilized in these subsections are made using a Zoom H4 recorder paired with either a Shure WH30XLR cardioid headset microphone or a Countryman E6 XLR ominidirectional earpiece microphone (Lee 2013). For the purpose of making the characteristics of these phones comparable, speech from the same speaker is utilized. The words used in these instances are derived from naturally-occurring data. While phoneticians have been, and still are, debating over whether it is preferable to use word-list data or naturally occurring data, this grammar as a product of language documentation maintains that it is important to understand language as a natural occurrence. Hence, word-list data has not been used. Although naturally occurring forms are used, it is still possible to choose tokens whose acoustic characteristics of the phones in question can appear distinctly. For example, it may be more useful to look at plosives in the word initial position, so that the waveform is able to capture information such as whether there is aspiration, whereas the aspiration of a plosive occurring between other phones would be less distinct. In comparison, a nasal's own formants show up better on the spectrogram when the nasal is flanked by vowels. Tokens in stressed positions are also preferred, so that acoustic information in the waveforms and on the spectrograms appear clearer. In general, Baba Malay is a syllable-timed language rather than a stressed-time language, and in most instances, this means that syllables may receive equal stress in a multi-syllabic word. It should be noted that being extracted from language documentation data recorded in natural environments, these featured clips might have some extent of background noise, although the use of noisier clips is avoided. The formant settings used for this section are – Maximum formant: 5000Hz, number of formants: 5, window length: 5 milliseconds, dynamic range: 40dB, dot size of 2.0mm. To facilitate comparison, all waveforms and spectrograms presented are normalized to 0.5 seconds in length. Formant dots are only used on spectrograms to illustrate nasal formants.

3.1.1.3 Bilabials

There are three bilabials in Baba Malay, these being the voiceless plosive [p], voiced plosive [b], and the nasal [m]. The items in the greyed-out boxes are words of Hokkien origin. Note that Hokkien is an isolating language (Wright 1983), meaning that while it lacks inflectional morphology, it has many compound words comprising more than one syllable (see Bodman 1955 and 1958 for examples of these). Hokkien compound words are however transferred directly into Baba Malay – Baba Malay speakers who do not speak Hokkien, are unable to identify the individual original components of these compound words. These words are often incorporated into Baba Malay as whole, monomorphemic items that cannot be broken down further, and these also abide by the phonotactics of Baba Malay words in general (see section 3.2 for discussion on phonotactics). Table 6 demonstrates the various positions in which these bilabials can be found.

Table 6: Bilabial consonants by position.

	Initial position	Medial position	Final position
p	[pokoʔ] 'tree'	[kəpeʔ] 'pinch'	[tʃukop] 'enough'
	[peʔpeʔ] 'father's elder brother'	[peʔ.peʔ][28] 'father's elder brother'	[tʃap] 'ten'
b	[bawaŋ] 'onion'	[tʃobeʔ] 'long-jawed'	[dʒawab] 'answer'
	[bapaʔ] 'father'	[awban] 'selfish'	[tʃanab] 'decorative altar stand'
m	[masaʔ] 'cook'	[gəmoʔ] 'fat'	[malam] 'night'
	[mja] 'life'	[chut.mja] 'famous'	[geʔsim] 'unhappy'

[p]
Figure 4 in the following is an example of how [p] appears on a waveform and spectrogram.

Notice from the waveform that the plosive [p] in Baba Malay has very little aspiration and the vowel begins very quickly after a complete closure by the articulators have been made. The plosive is also voiceless, as indicated by the lack of a voice bar in the corresponding area on the spectrogram. The locus of F2 and F3 (second and third formants) in the following vowel are also relatively low, as characteristic of preceding labials (see Ladefoged and Johnson 2011).

---

[28] Examples such as [ʔ.p] in [peʔ.peʔ] and [t.m] in [chut.mja] are not regarded as true consonant clusters, as the consonants that appear adjacent to each other belong to separate syllables.

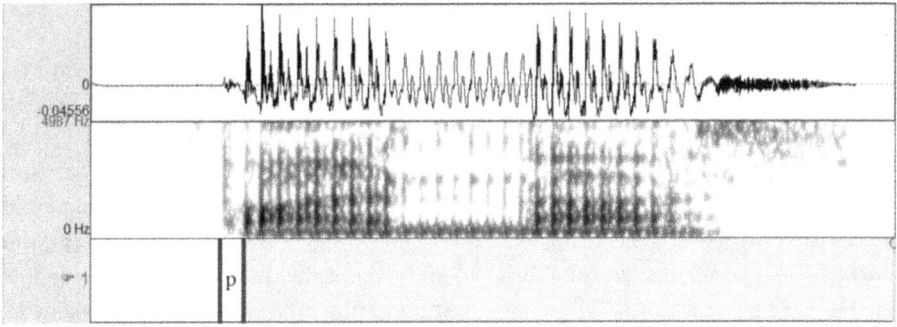

Figure 4: Waveform and spectrogram of [p] in [panas] 'hot'.

[b]

Figure 5 shows an example of how [b] appears on a waveform and spectrogram.

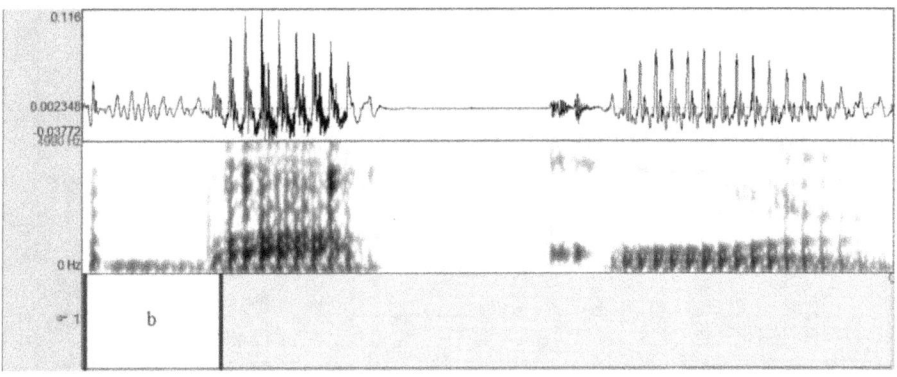

Figure 5: Waveform and spectrogram of [b] in [bakol] 'basket'.

The corresponding voiced bilabial counterpart of [p] is [b], the main difference being that there is no aspiration at all in this instance. Voicing is present during the closure period for the articulators and there is a negative voice onset time. As expected of a bilabial, the locus of F2 and F3 in the following vowel are relatively low as well.

[m]

Figure 6 is an example of the waveform and spectrogram that demonstrates the realization of the bilabial nasal [m]

As characteristic of the bilabial nasal [m], there is considerable energy at the base at about 240Hz (hertz), at about 1000Hz, and at about 2300Hz. Again, the relatively low locus of F1 and F2 are expected due to the bilabial nature of [m].

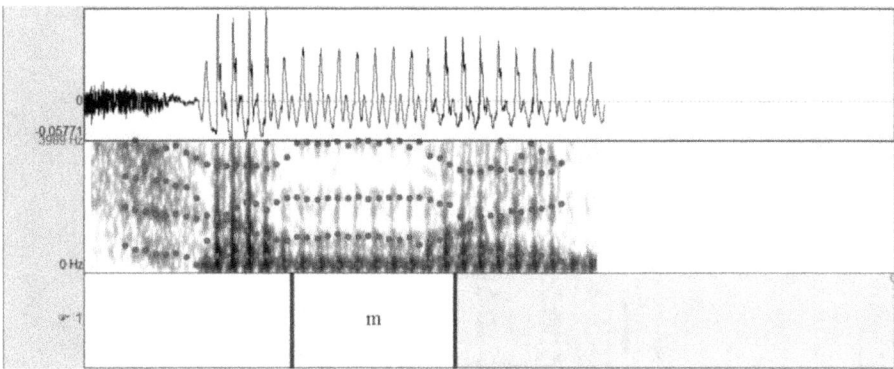

Figure 6: Wave form and spectrogram of [m] in [sama] 'same, and, with'.

3.1.1.4 Alveolars

The alveolars found in Baba Malay are the voiceless plosive [t], the voiced plosive [d], the voiceless fricative [s], nasal [n], lateral [l], and flap [ɾ]. Table 7 demonstrates the various positions in which they can be found.

Table 7: Alveolar consonants by position.

	Initial position	Medial position	Final position
t	[taw] 'know'	[rəti] 'understand'	[lipat] 'fold'
	[tu] 'cupboard'	[kam.tio?] 'develop an illness'	[tʃwe.it] 'first day of the lunar month'
d	[da.own] 'leaves'	[bodoh] 'stupid'	
	[djam] 'quiet'	[djam.djam] 'quietly'	
s	[sədap] 'delicious'	[kasi] 'give, let, cause, Pass'	[ləkas] 'quick'
	[sehjit] 'birthday'	[tʃut.si] 'birth'	
n	[naɲis] 'cry'	[mənaŋ] 'win'	[ta.own] 'year'
	[njo] 'mother-in-law'	[anchəŋ] 'blessing of the marital bed'	[tʃin] 'close to one another'
l	[lipat] 'fold'	[kalu] 'if'	[dəgil] 'stubborn'
	[lotʃeŋ] 'bell'	[haw.lam] 'male mourner'	
r	[rəti] 'understand'	[buro?] 'ugly'	[kasar] 'coarse'

[t]
Figure 7 is an example waveform and spectrogram of [t].

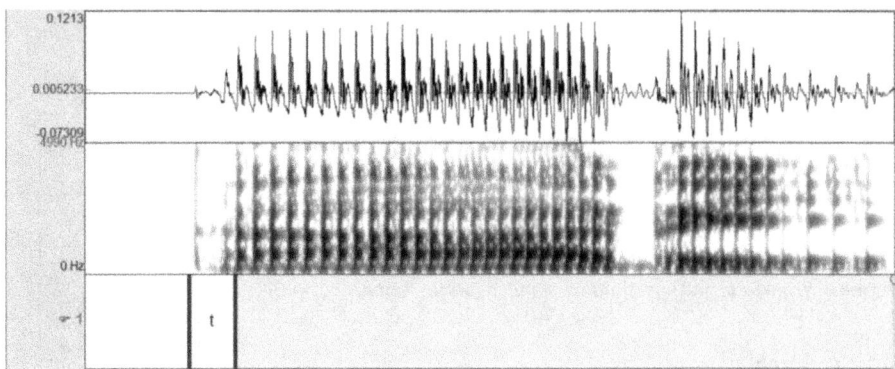

Figure 7: Waveform and spectrogram of [t] in [tareʔ] 'pull'.

There is slight aspiration after the closure at the alveolar ridge made for [t] in Figure 7, and [t] is accompanied by almost no voicing, being a voiceless plosive. The locus of F2 is about 1700Hz, which is characteristic of alveolars (see Ladefoged and Johnson 2011).

[d]
Figure 8 demonstrates an example waveform and spectrogram of the voiced plosive [d].

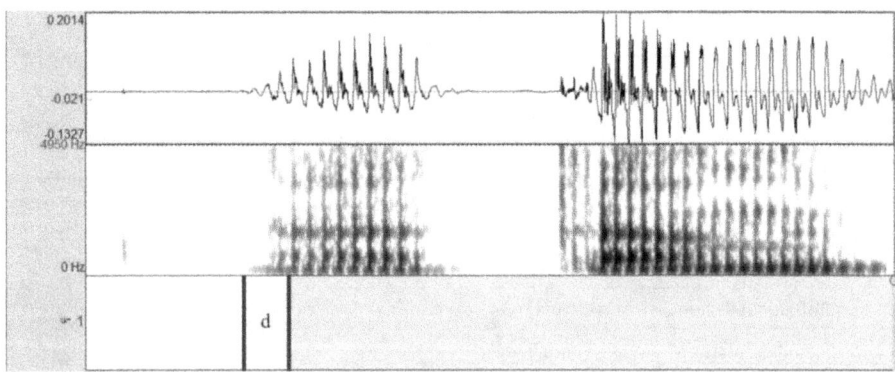

Figure 8: Waveform and spectrogram of [d] in [dataŋ] 'come'.

At the word initial position, [t] and [d] do not look very different, but compared to [t], no aspiration is involved at all when producing [d], and a voice bar appears in the spectrogram accompanying the voiced alveolar plosive [d].

[s]

Figure 9 is representative of the waveform and spectrogram for [s].

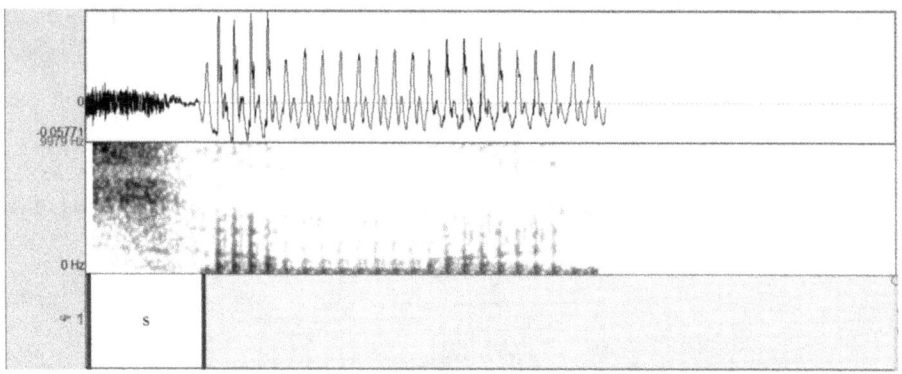

Figure 9: Waveform and spectrogram of [s] in [sama] 'same, and, with'.

As a sibilant, the [s] fricative has a lot of energy in the spectrogram above 5200Hz until 10,000Hz or so. The fact that there is energy concentrated in the higher range (just under 10,000Hz) indicates that [s] is more fronted than what is typical for alveolar sibilants. Frication noise can also be seen in the waveform. This range indicates that [s] is a clear alveolar sibilant, bearing in mind that the palatoalveolar sibilant does not show energy above 7,000Hz (see Evers et al. 1998: 348).

[n]

Figure 10 shows an example waveform and spectrogram for alveolar nasal [n].

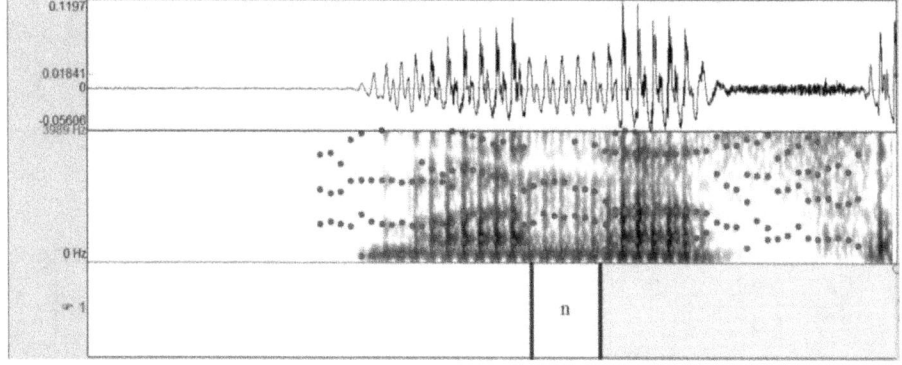

Figure 10: Waveform and spectrogram of [n] in [mana] 'where, which'.

As with nasals at the initial position, faint formants can be seen, and there is energy at about 250Hz, 1,300Hz and 2,400Hz in the case of Figure 10. Formants are weak at the nasal murmur portion, nasal formants comprising extra resonances that arise due to the nasal passage being used in addition to the oral tract. The nasal formants occur weakly at about 300Hz for the alveolar nasal.

[l]
Figures 11 and 12 demonstrate example waveforms and spectrograms of the alveolar lateral [l]. Both figures are necessary due to the very different manifestations of [l] typically expected in non-coda and coda positions.

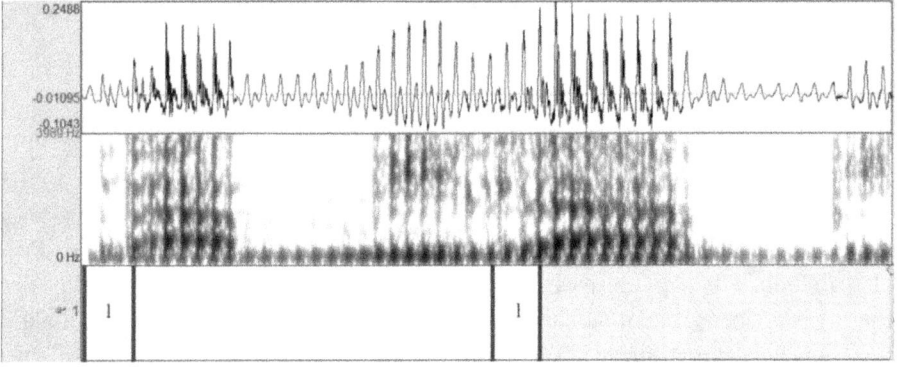

Figure 11: Waveform and spectrogram of [l] in [labilabi] 'tortoise'.

When in initial position, the clear [l] has a second formant of about 1,400Hz.

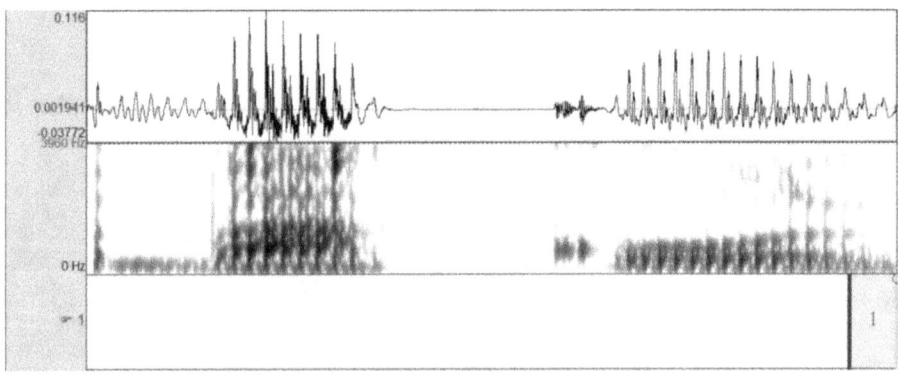

Figure 12: Waveform and spectrogram of [l] in [bakol].

There is no dark [l] in the word final position, with very little to no vocalization in the position.

[r]

Figure 13 demonstrates an example waveform and spectrogram of the alveolar flap [ɾ].

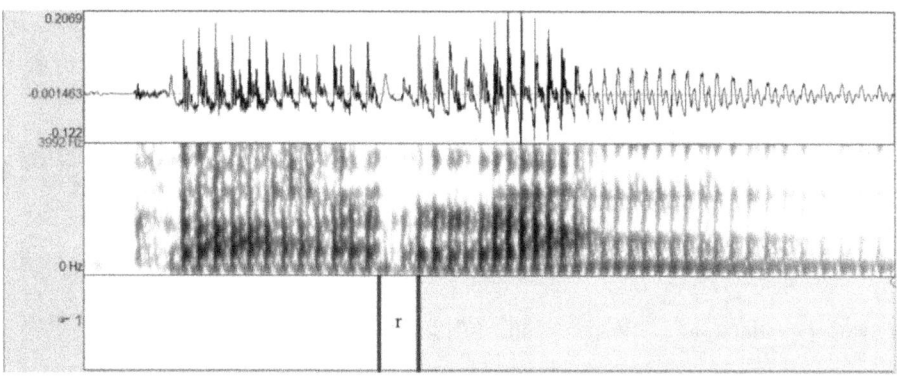

Figure 13: Waveform and spectrogram of [ɾ] in [garaŋ] 'fierce'.

There is very little rhoticity or r-coloring that accompanies the alveolar flap [ɾ], with the relatively high formant value at about 1,600Hz (see Ladefoged 2003 for what is typical of the alveolar flap).

3.1.1.5 Post-alveolars

The three post-alveolar consonants in Baba Malay are two affricates – the voiceless affricate /tʃ/ and the voiced affricate /dʒ/, as well as a nasal /ɲ/. Table 8 demonstrates the various positions that these post-alveolar consonants can be found in.

Table 8: Post-alveolar consonants by position.

	Initial position	Medial position	Final position
tʃ	[tʃam.por] 'mix'	[bun.tʃit] 'distended stomach'	
	[tʃaj.ki] 'banner'	[lap.tʃaj] 'wedding gift exchange ceremony'	
dʒ	[dʒum.pa] 'meet'	[badʒu] 'clothes'	
	[dʒi] 'two'	[peʔ.dʒi] 'eight characters for Chinese horoscope'	
ɲ	[ɲoɲa] 'Peranakan lady'	[ɲoɲa] 'Peranakan lady'	

[tʃ]

Figure 14 is an example waveform and spectrogram of a realization of voiceless affricate [tʃ].

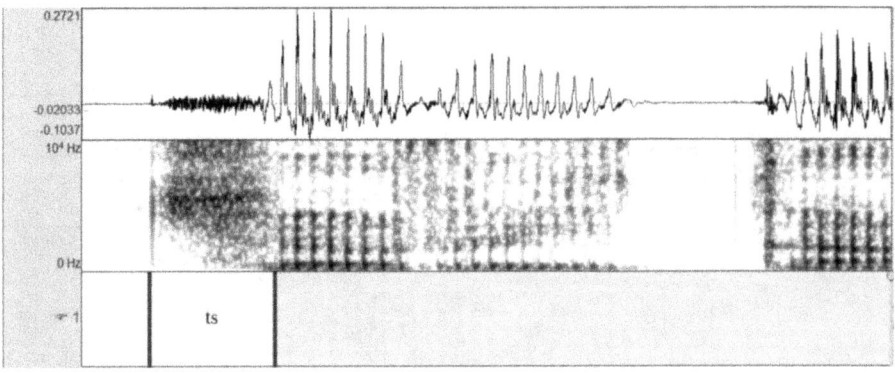

Figure 14: Waveform and spectrogram of [tʃ] in [tʃərita] 'story'.

In the spectrogram and especially the waveform of Figure 14, there is clear frication that immediately follows the post-alveolar closure for production of the affricate [tʃ].

[dʒ]

Figure 15 demonstrates a realization of the voiced affricate [dʒ] in a waveform and its accompanying spectrogram.

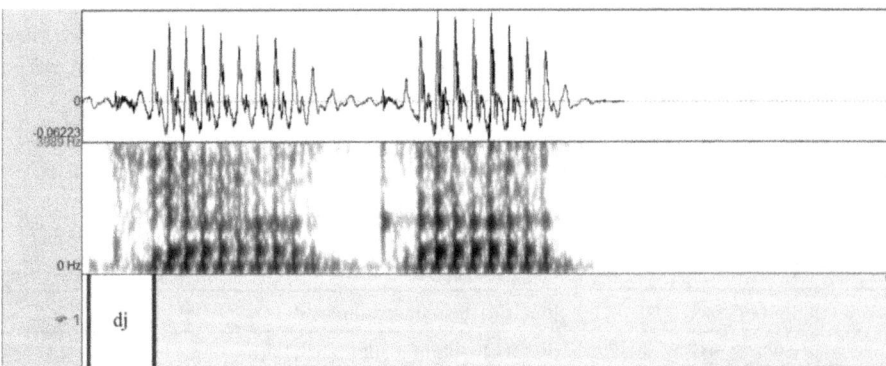

Figure 15: Waveform and spectrogram of [dʒ] in [dʒaga] 'take care of someone or something, guard'.

There is some prevoicing in the realization of voiced affricate [dʒ], as seen from the voice bar on the spectrogram. There is also frication in the waveform, albeit to a lesser extent when compared to the waveform that accompanies the production of [tʃ].

[ɲ]
Figure 16 demonstrates the acoustic properties of post-alveolar nasal [ɲ].

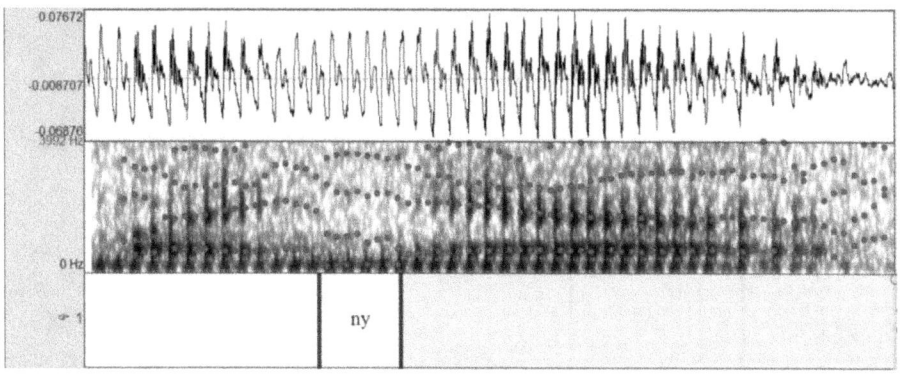

Figure 16: Waveform and spectrogram of [ɲ] in [maɲaʔ] 'many'.

As is common with nasals universally, some nasal formants can be seen between the flanking vowels for post-alveolar nasal [ɲ] in Baba Malay. Energy in this instance can be seen at around 200Hz, 900Hz, and about 2,400Hz.

3.1.1.6 Velars
The velar consonants in Baba Malay are voiceless plosive [k], voiced plosive [g], and nasal [ŋ]. Table 9 demonstrates the positions in which velar consonants can occur within the word.

Table 9: Velar consonants by position.

	Initial position	Medial position	Final position
k	[kalo] 'if'	[ləkas] 'quick'	
	[ko] 'paternal aunt'	[laŋ.kéʔ] 'guest'	
g	[gəmoʔ] 'fat'	[pagi] 'morning'	
	[gwa] '1SG'	[lun.gweʔ] 'Chinese intercalary month'	
ŋ	[ŋantoʔ] 'sleepy'	[naŋis] 'cry'	[bisiŋ] 'noisy'
	[ŋe.ŋe] 'obstinate'	[laŋ.kéʔ] 'guest'	[lotʃeŋ] 'bell'

[k]
Figure 17 shows an example waveform and spectrogram of voiceless velar plosive [k].

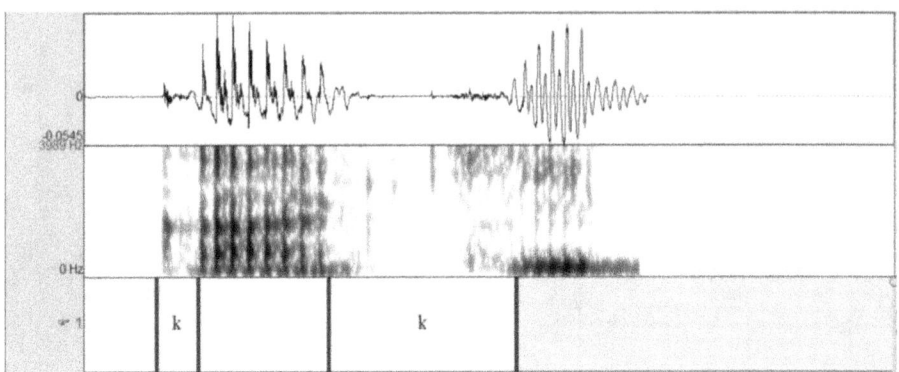

Figure 17: Waveform and spectrogram of [k] in [ka**k**i] 'leg'.

There is minimal aspiration following closure as observed from both word initial [k] and medial [k] on the waveform. The velar pinch is much clearer for intervocalic [k] than for word initial [k]. The velar pinch is where F2 and F3 appear to converge on the spectrogram.

[g]
Figure 18 demonstrates a realization of voiced velar plosive [g] on a waveform and spectrogram.

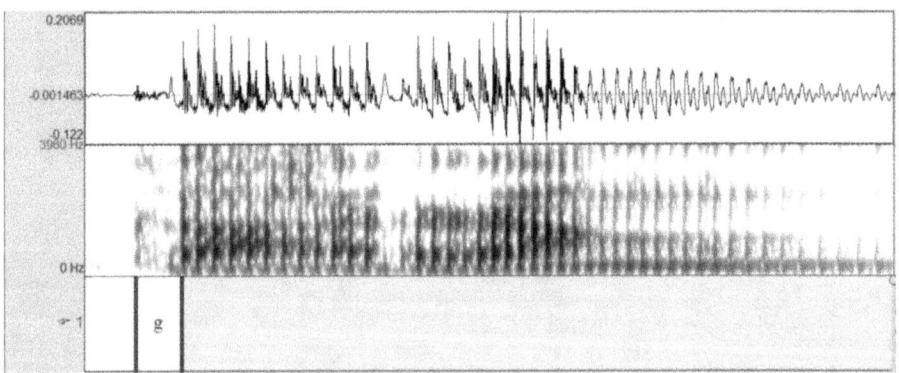

Figure 18: Waveform and spectrogram of [g] in [**g**araŋ] 'fierce'.

Acoustically, [k] and [g] do not appear to be very different, apart from slightly more voicing associated with the voiced plosive [g]. Similar to [k], there also appears to be some aspiration where [g] is concerned.

[ŋ]

The waveform and spectrogram in Figure 18 are replicated in Figure 19 to demonstrate the acoustic characteristics of velar nasal [ŋ].

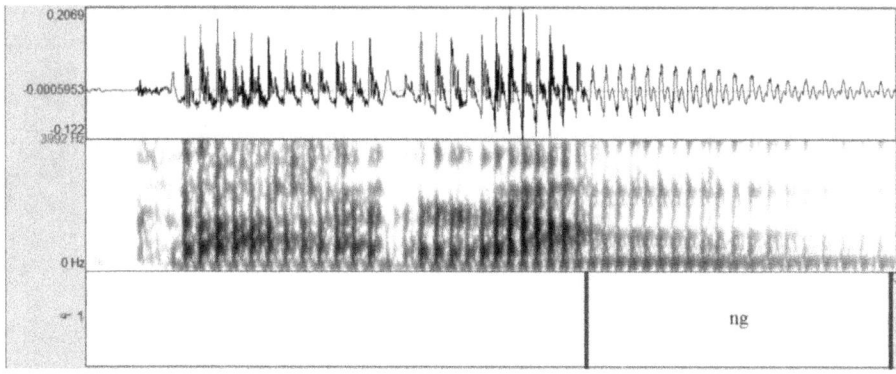

Figure 19: Waveform and spectrogram of [ŋ] in [garaŋ] 'fierce'.

Weak formants, characteristic of nasals, are seen in the region of [ŋ]. The velar pinch at 1,200Hz demonstrates the velar nature of this nasal. The same type of pinch is not present in the spectrograms of other types of nasals such as the alveolar nasal.

3.1.1.7 Glottals

There are two glottal consonants in Baba Malay, these being the voiceless plosive [ʔ],[29] and the voiceless fricative [h]. Table 10 shows the positions in which these glottal consonants can be found.

Table 10: Glottal consonants by position.

	Initial position	Medial position	Final position
ʔ		[a.ʔus] 'thirsty'	[kəpeʔ] 'pinch'
		[geʔ.sim] 'unhappy'	[sin.keʔ] 'newcomer'
h	[habis] 'finish'	[dahi] 'forehead'	[mən.tah] 'raw'
	[hwan.tjoʔ] 'meet ill spiritual forces'	[lihaj] 'cunning'	

---

[29] It is worth noting that words with final consonants such as glottal stops, have been derived from both Malay and Hokkien. For example, [gəmoʔ] 'fat' is derived from Malay, while [peʔpeʔ] is derived from Hokkien.

[h]

Figure 20 shows a spectrogram and waveform that demonstrate that acoustic properties of voiceless glottal fricative [h].

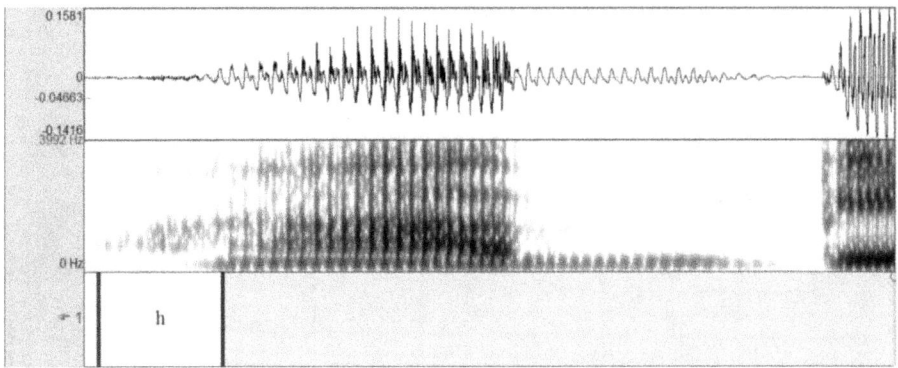

Figure 20: Waveform and spectrogram of [h] in [habis] 'finish'.

Even though there is very little striation in the spectrogram due to the voiceless quality of [h], some glottal frication can still be observed on the spectrogram.

[ʔ]

Figure 21 is an example of an acoustic representation of glottal plosive [ʔ].

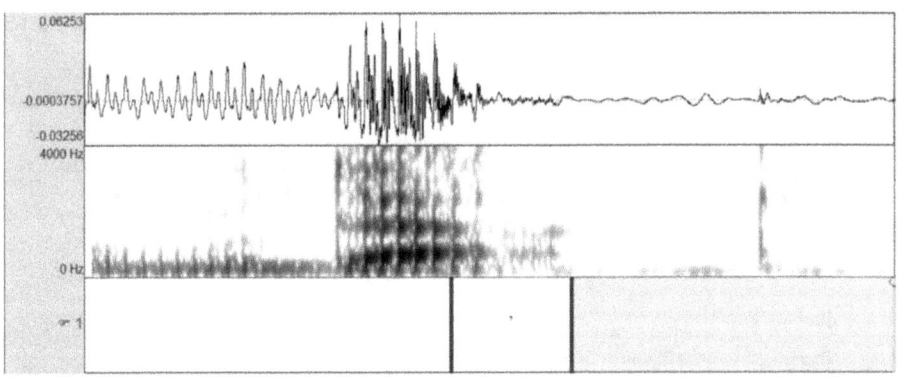

Figure 21: Waveform and spectrogram of [ʔ] in [budaʔ] 'child'.

Some glottal frication shows up at the position of plosive [ʔ].

3.1.1.8 Glides

There are two glides in Baba Malay, these being the labiovelar approximant [w] and the palatal approximant [j]. Table 11 lists the various positions that these glides can be found in.

Table 11: Glides by position.

	Initial position	Medial position	Final position
w	[waɲi] 'fragrant'	[bawaŋ] 'onion'	[taw] 'know'
	[wilɔ] 'Lunar New year reunion dinner'	[kawin] 'marry'	[hor.paw] 'purse'
j	[jang] 'REL'	[səmajaŋ] 'pray'	[pandaj] 'clever'
	[jen.tʃi] 'rouge'	[tʃaj.jen] 'jelly'	[jau.gwaj] 'demon'

[w]

Figure 22 is an example of a waveform and spectrogram of labiovelar approximant [w].

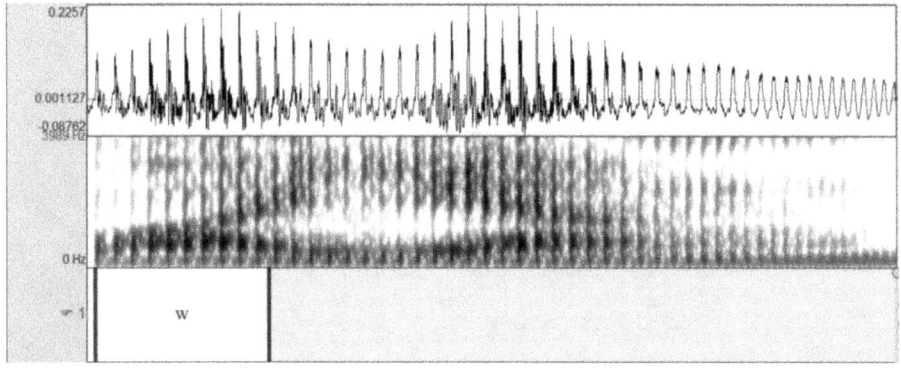

Figure 22: Waveform and spectrogram of [w] in [wajaŋ] 'play (performance)'.

The labiovelar approximant [w] appears to have formants, but no steady state. There is a gradual dip in its F2, but the F2 does not descend below 700Hz, showing that the lips were not very rounded in the production of [w] (see Ladefoged 2003 for acoustic characteristics of lip rounding).

[j]

The waveform and spectrogram in Figure 22 are replicated here in Figure 23, to demonstrate the acoustic characteristics of palatal approximant [j].

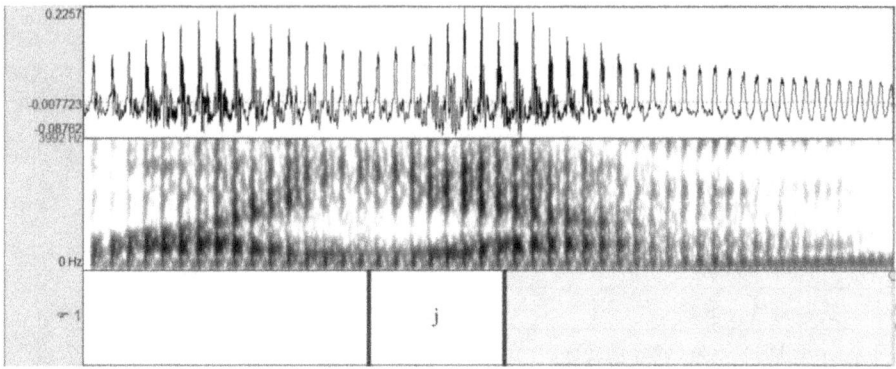

Figure 23: Waveform and spectrogram of [j] in [wajaŋ] 'play (performance)'.

Similar to the labiovelar approximant [w], the palatal approximant [j] also shows vowel-like qualities, but has no steady state. The tongue is at the highest front position at about 2,100Hz, and is retracted and lowered as F2 falls.

3.1.2 Vowels

The eight phonemic vowels are represented in the vowel chart below:

Table 12: Vowel chart of Baba Malay.

	Front	Central	Back
	Non-rounded	Non-rounded	Rounded
Close	i		u
Close-mid	e	ə	o
Open-mid	ɛ		ɔ
Open		a	

Among these vowels, /ɛ/ and /a/ are contrasting phonemes, and /a/ becomes [ɛ] before /l/, /r/ and /s/ (see section 3.3.5). Both do also form minimal pairs.

3.1.2.1 Minimal pairs of vowels

The minimal pairs in the language and hence the vowel phonemes are as follows:

(61) /i/ : /e/
     [tapi] 'but' : '[tape] 'fermented rice dessert'

(62) /i/ : /ə/
[siɾam] 'flush' : [səɾam] 'frightening'

(63) /i/ : /u/
[abi] 'then, but' : [abu] 'ash'

(64) /u/ : /ə/
[kunaŋ] 'under the influence of black magic' : [kənaŋ] 'reminisce'

(65) /u/ : /o/
[ku] 'maternal uncle' : [ko] 'paternal aunt'

(66) /o/ : /ə/
[kopeʔ] 'peel' : [kəpeʔ] 'pinch'

(67) /o/ : /a/
[ikot] 'follow' : [ikat] 'tie'

(68) /o/ : /ɔ/
[toʔ] 'table' : [tɔʔ] 'poisonous, evil'

(69) /ɔ/ : /ə/
[ɔŋ] 'prosperous' : [əŋ] 'honorific prefix for familial relations'

(70) /ɔ/ : /a/
[gantɔŋ] 'hang' : [gantaŋ] 'a cylindrical measure of one gallon of rice'

(71) /a/ : /ɛ/
[kena] 'PASS' : [kenɛ] 'know' (refined)[30]

(72) /a/ : /ə/
[basi] 'stale' : [bəsi] 'iron'

(73) /a/ : /e/
[tʃobaʔ] 'taste' : [tʃobeʔ] 'long-jawed'

(74) /e/ : /ə/
[bedeʔ] 'tell a lie' : [bədeʔ] 'pummel'

---

[30] The *kasar* 'coarse'-*halus* 'refined' style distinctions in Baba Malay are described in section 3.3.5.

3.1.2.2 Monophthongs

The vowels in Baba Malay are represented here acoustically. The vowels of the same proficient speaker whose consonants were represented from subsections 3.1.1.3 to 3.1.1.8 are used. Again, the data comes from naturally occurring forms in narratives including story-telling and conversational data, and tokens are chosen if their relevant acoustic characteristics appear distinctly. Ten tokens are measured for each vowel and the resultant vowel plot in F1-F2 space is presented at the end of this section. It has been proposed that vowel formants are acoustic correlates of vowel features and are more representative of vowels than their articulatory properties.[31]

Formant values are read manually at the midpoint steady state of the vowel, as shown in Figure 24. The settings used for the analysis of this speaker are: Maximum formant: 5000Hz, number of formants: 5, window length: 5 milliseconds, dynamic range: 40dB, dot size of 2.0mm. F1 and F2 values are derived for all vowels. F1 corresponds approximately to vowel height while F2 corresponds roughly to vowel frontness. The higher F1 is, the lower the vowel, the higher F2 is, the more front the vowel. F3 is less essential for the vowels in Baba Malay, as it is primarily used for differentiating between vowels that are only distinguishable by lip-rounding (Ladefoged 2003), and there are none of these in Baba Malay. Analysis is carried out in Praat (Boersma & Weenink 2013). Again, vowel tokens are selected with the following characteristics: Vowels in stressed positions are preferred, as their formants are easier to read on a spectrogram than the formants of unstressed vowels. For the same reason, creaky voice data is discarded, as are clips in which any noise obscures the token vowels given that these clips are taken from naturally occurring language documentation data. In addition, it is preferable to use vowels that are not flanked by consonants in their immediate environment – this ensures that the measurement derived is purely that of the vowel, and not that of a consonant's effect on the vowel. As this is not always possible, in the instances where preceding or following consonants are used, [h] initial and glottal stop finals are preferred since these do not affect formant values are much as other consonants.[32] Also, due to the fact that many tokens are preceded by labials in the available data, these can also be used consistently for different vowel measurements. Tokens outside of these environments are only used when there are not enough tokens to constitute the ten required for each vowel. Figure 24 is used to demonstrate how the formants are measured for individual tokens.

---

[31] This is due to idiosyncratic differences in vowel articulation as well as inconsistencies between patterns of linguistic vowel height and frontness and measured tongue height and frontness during vowel production (Johnson 2012, Johnson et al. 1993, Ladefoged et al. 1972).
[32] For example, laterals lower formant values of vowels that follow.

3.1 Phoneme inventory — 53

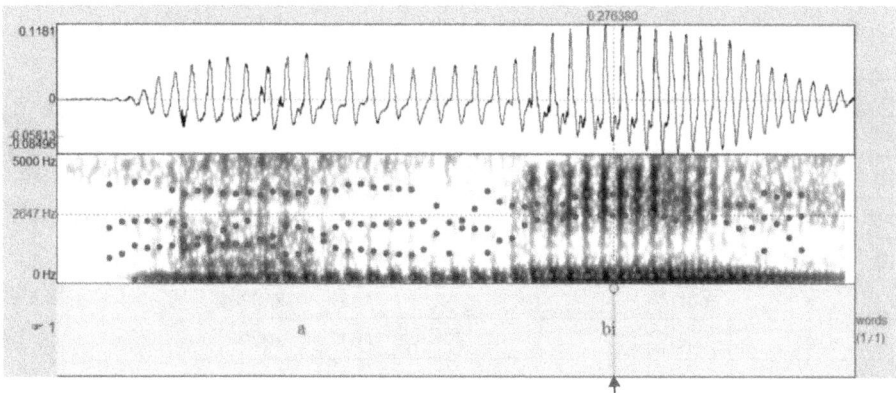

Figure 24: Waveform and spectrogram of [i] in [abi] 'then'.

In the spectrogram generated by Praat, the dots correspond to where the darkest horizontal stripes are. These dark horizontal stripes represent concentrations of energy, and also the formants to be measured. F1 is indicated by the lowest stripe, and F2, by the one above it. The arrow indicates where the formants of the vowel [i] are measured, at the midpoint of the vowel's steady state. The measurements along the left axis of the spectrogram shows that the value of [i]'s F2 is 2647Hz (F1 whose value not seen here is 282Hz). The relatively low F1 value and the relatively high F2 value indicate that [i] is a high front vowel.

Table 13 shows the different F1 and F2 values generated for the different vowels and their tokens. Where relevant, the preceding and or following context across word boundary is provided, since this potentially influences formant values.

Table 13: Vowels and formant values for a proficient speaker of Baba Malay in Singapore.[33]

No.	Vowel	Word(s)	Environment	F1	F2
1	i	labilabi	b_	286	2145
2	i	labilabi	b_	267	2165
3	i	habi	b_	286	2242
4	i	tapi	p_	286	2203
5	i	labilabi	b_	267	2300
6	i	labilabi	b_	267	2397
7	i	habi	b_	305	2591
8	i	təpi	p_	267	2203

---

[33] It is necessary to indicate that this is the vowel space of a Baba Malay speaker in Singapore, noting that [ɔ] is not found in the data gathered for Malacca Baba Malay speakers.

Table 13 (continued)

No.	Vowel	Word(s)	Environment	F1	F2
9	i	babi	b_	286	2242
10	i	abi ilaŋ	i#_	267	2397
11	e	beloʔ	b_	402	2010
12	e	pile	l_	441	2203
13	e	pəteʔ	t_ʔ	402	2107
14	e	tareʔ	r_ʔ	402	2029
15	e	tʃareʔ	r_ʔ	421	2107
16	e	teŋoʔ	t_ŋ	383	2010
17	e	habes	b_s	383	2145
18	e	sampe	p_	421	2436
19	e	habes	b_s	344	2262
20	e	beloʔ	b_	402	2010
21	ɛ	laŋɛ	ŋ_	538	2107
22	ɛ	laŋɛ	ŋ_	538	2087
23	ɛ	kərɛ	r_	615	2242
24	ɛ	sɛ	s_	538	2149
25	ɛ	bərgətɛ	t_	538	2203
26	ɛ	kərdʒɛ	dʒ_	557	2184
27	ɛ	dəŋɛ	ŋ_	576	2107
28	ɛ	hospitɛ	t_	596	1971
29	ɛ	hospitɛ	t_	615	2087
30	ɛ	gambɛ	b_	596	1855
31	ə	pəteʔ	p_	383	1448
32	ə	pəteʔ	p_	441	1526
33	ə	tərlaŋɛ	t_r	480	1545
34	ə	tərlaŋɛ	t_r	460	1545
35	ə	məntah	m_n	499	1506
36	ə	tərkəleʔkəleʔ	t_r	441	1603
37	ə	tərkəleʔkəleʔ	k_	480	1546
38	ə	tərkəleʔkəleʔ	k_	383	1564
39	ə	təpi	t_	421	1564
40	ə	kəna	k_	480	1661
41	a	mata	m_	789	1255

Table 13 (continued)

No.	Vowel	Word(s)	Environment	F1	F2
42	a	mari	m_	770	1545
43	a	masoʔ	m_	789	1448
44	a	mja apa	a#_	770	1506
45	a	apa	p_	634	1255
46	a	babi	b_	809	1390
47	a	taw apa	w#_	731	1216
48	a	apa	p_	751	1235
49	a	sudah apa	h#_	673	1351
50	a	apa	p_	770	1371
51	u	kəbun	b_n	267	809
52	u	kəbun	b_n	247	906
53	u	budaʔ	b_	286	903
54	u	mulot	m_	247	925
55	u	mulot	m_	286	906
56	u	bukit	b_	247	925
57	u	budaʔ	b_	286	925
58	u	budaʔ	b_	286	867
59	u	budaʔ	b_	247	867
60	u	bulan	b_	305	886
61	o	pokoʔ	p_	408	698
62	o	mo	m_	383	777
63	o	mo	m_	363	777
64	o	mo	m_	344	750
65	o	lotʃeŋ	l_	354	830
66	o	dʒatoh	t_h	407	803
67	o	toloŋ	t_	407	1015
68	o	mo	m_	354	750
69	o	mo	m_	354	803
70	o	katʃo	tʃ_	381	1094
71	ɔ	ala ɔraŋ	a_	468	964
72	ɔ	lambɔŋ	b_ŋ	538	698
73	ɔ	teŋɔʔ	ŋ_ʔ	539	936
74	ɔ	lambɔŋ	b_ŋ	518	645

Table 13 (continued)

No.	Vowel	Word(s)	Environment	F1	F2
75	ɔ	tarɔʔ	r_ʔ	513	1041
76	ɔ	lɔmpat	l_m	518	1068
77	ɔ	tɔŋkat	t_ŋ	538	990
78	ɔ	teŋɔʔ	ŋ_ʔ	576	1068
79	ɔ	tɔŋ	t_ŋ	513	989
80	ɔ	bəgi ɔraŋ	i#_	500	1068

It is worth mentioning that [ɔ] exists in words derived from Malay (such as in [teŋɔʔ] indicating 'look, see', [lambɔŋ] 'toss', [lɔmpat] 'jump'). It was earlier observed that [ɔ] only existed in loanwords (Pakir 1986: 56). It is also important to note that there is variability in production, wherein a word such as [ɔraŋ] 'person' may be pronounced as [oraŋ] by others. Note however that a vowel merger appears to be taking place, whereby [ɔ] is falling out of use (see section 3.8 for more information regarding change in the vowel space).

The F1 and F2 values tabulated in Table 13 are presented in Figure 25, which is a vowel plot with F1 values on the Y-axis and F2 values on the X-axis.

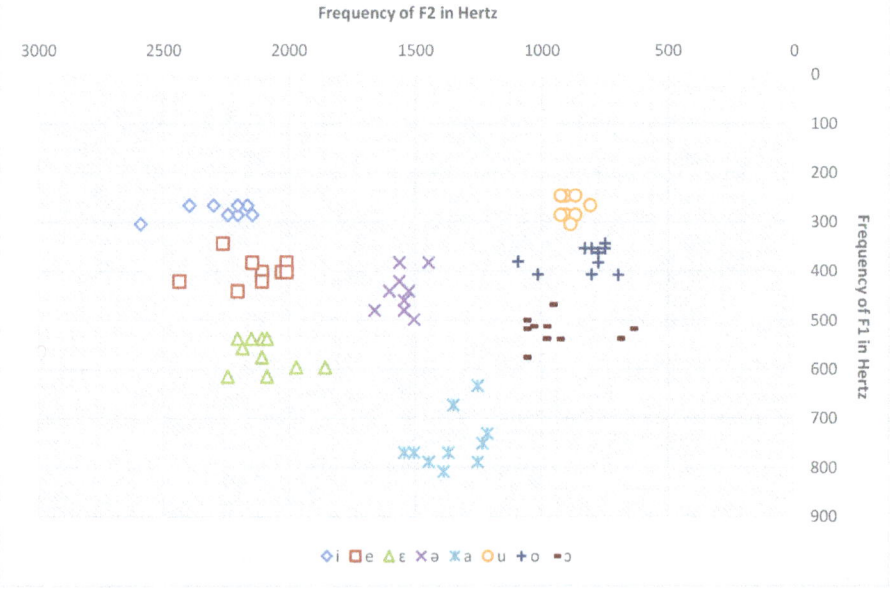

Figure 25: Vowel space of a Baba Malay speaker in Singapore.

The speaker whose vowels are represented in Figure 25 is the same proficient speaker whose consonants were examined in the earlier sections – the chart is an accurate depiction of the general vowel space in Baba Malay. In section 3.8, the vowel spaces of six speakers are contrasted to give a fuller picture of ongoing change and variation.

3.1.2.3 Diphthongs

Diphthongs here refer to sequences of vowels and glides that occur within the same syllable,[34] as compared to sequences of vocoids that occur disjointed across two separate syllables (see section 3.1.2.4 for these). All diphthongs in Baba Malay are found in words of Malay origin as well as words of Hokkien origin. Words that are derived from Hokkien are marked with (H) in the following list. Note that these words are often phonologically adapted into Baba Malay and sound different from their original Hokkien lexical bases (see section 3.7.2 for example).

(75) [aj]
Examples: [bə.kə.**laj**] 'quarrel', [tʃ**aj**.tən] 'nunnery that serves vegetarian food (H)'

(76) [aw]
Examples: [t**aw**] 'know', [ɔːp**aw**] 'purse (H)'

(77) [oj]
Examples: [amb**oj**] 'exclamation of surprise', [b**oj**ʔ] 'socks (H)'

(78) [ow]
Examples: [da.**ow**n] 'leaves', [b**ow**] 'NEG (H)'

3.1.2.4 Vowel sequences across syllables

The [a.o] vowel sequence can occur disjointed across two different syllables. These cannot be analyzed as diphthongs comprising vowel and glide, since each syllable requires its own nucleus, and each vowel in the [a.o] sequence forms the nucleus of its own syllable.

(79) [ao]
Examples: [d**a.o**wn] 'leaves', [t**a.o**wn] 'years', [ɡ**a.o**] 'mix'

---

[34] This is similar to the treatment of diphthongs in Austronesian where diphthongs are viewed to be combinations of vowel and semivowel (Dempwolff 1934–1938, Blust 1998), and such a treatment extends to many other languages.

3.2 Phonotactics

The Baba Malay syllable structure is (C)(C)V(C)(C) with some restrictions (C: consonants, V: vowels). Onsets and codas are optional, and syllables are of the type V, CV, CCV, VC, CVC, CCVC, and CVCC. However, no examples are found with VCC and CCVCC. The consonant clusters that occur within the same syllable must have a glide occur as one of the consonants in the cluster. This is demonstrated by examples such as the CCV syllable [mwi] in [mwi.laŋ] 'matchmaker', the CCVC syllable [bwaŋ] 'throw', and the CVCC syllable [bajʔ] 'good'. Other consonant clusters that are found in Baba Malay occur as a product of local metathesis (switching of position of phones) or fast speech. For example, [kr] in [krə.dʒar] 'work', [gr] in [grə.taʔ] 'threat', and [tr] in [trə.baŋ] 'fly' are derived from [kər.dʒar],[35] [gər.taʔ], and [tər.baŋ] respectively. An example of a consonant cluster in fast speech occurs when [ə] is reduced, as in [bla.tʃu] for [bə.la.tʃu] 'unbleached cotton outfit used for mourning'. In all these instances, where fast speech results in a consonant cluster, at least one of the consonants is a glide [j, w] or a liquid [l, r]. In general, the glottal stop [ʔ] cannot occur in the onset of the first syllable, while affricates [tʃ] and [dʒ] cannot occur in the coda. The following examples in (80) to (86) illustrate permutations of various syllable types that can occur in Baba Malay. Restrictions on each permutation are also listed. Syllable boundaries are marked with '.' All of these syllable types are found in words of Malay and Hokkien origins. In the examples, words of Hokkien origin are marked by (H).

(80) V
Examples: [**a**.deʔ] 'sibling', [**o**.pan] 'freckles (H)'

All vowels can occur as the obligatory, individually-occurring nucleus that comprises the entire syllable.

(81) CV
Examples: [**da**.pat] 'receive', [kweh.**ji**] 'glutinous rice balls (H)'

There are no restrictions on V in this sort of syllable, and the only restriction on C is that it cannot be a glottal stop. Glottal stops are only allowed in the onset of the second syllable, such as in [ba.ʔu] 'smell' and in the word [pe.ʔe] 'good character', which is borrowed from the Arabic word, [fi.ʔil].

(82) CCV
Examples: [**trə**.baŋ] 'fly' (after metathesis), [**mwi**.lang] 'matchmaker (H)'

---

[35] Note that whereas the Baba Malay versions of work are [kər. ʒar], [krə.ʒar] (coarse), and [krə.ʒɛ], the Malay version is [ker.ja].

There are no restrictions on V, whereas the restriction for all consonant clusters is that one of the consonants must be a glide, or a liquid in the case of metathesis or fast speech. In the case of CCV, the second consonant has to be a glide or a liquid. The glottal stop should also not occur in the onset of the first syllable.

(83) VC

Examples: [aŋ.kat] 'lift, hold, pick up, carry', [aw.ban] 'selfish (H)'

Both glides and full consonants, except for affricates, can occur in the C position in VC. Note that it is more common for [ŋ] to follow a vowel as a coda than to precede it as an onset.

(84) CVC

Example: [ti.**mun**] 'cucumber', [**joʔ**.hun] 'Chinese medicinal powder (H)'

The glottal stop is not permitted in the onset of the first syllable, while affricates are not permitted in the coda. An example of a glottal stop occurring in the second syllable is in the word [a.ʔus] 'thirsty'.

(85) CCVC

Example: [pə.**rjoʔ**] 'cooking pot', [**hwat**] 'expand (H)'

Again, the glottal stop is not permitted in the onset of the first syllable, while affricates are not permitted in the coda. The second consonant in the CCVC consonant cluster has to be a glide.

(86) CVCC

Examples: [**bajʔ**] 'good',[36] [**bojʔ**] 'socks (H)'

In CVCC syllables, the penultimate consonant must be a glide. Similarly, the glottal stop is not permitted in the onset of the first syllable, while affricates are not permitted in the coda.

Words are usually between one to three syllables in length, with two syllable words being the most commonly found ones in the data gathered from fieldwork. All possible syllabic permutations are found in words of Malay origin, as well as words of Hokkien origin. Words borrowed from other languages into Baba Malay also follow the above phonotactic constraints. For example, Dutch [lamp] for 'lamp' is incorporated into Baba Malay as [lampu], given that there are no consonant cluster codas in Baba Malay that do not comprise a glide or a liquid, and the Portuguese word [padri]

---

36 Originally from Dutch, borrowed into Malay.

is borrowed into the language as [padəri] 'priest', as consonant clusters with liquids are not common, unless as a product of metathesis or fast speech.

3.2.1 Resyllabification and reduplication

Other processes that affect the syllable shape in Baba Malay are resyllabification and reduplication. Resyllabification can occur with the use of suffixes. For example, when nominalizer [-an] is attached to [ma.ɲak] 'many' to derive a noun out of an adjective (see section 4.1.1.1), the new word is [ma.ɲa.kan], and [k] is no longer the coda of the ultimate syllable but its onset. Similarly, when the same nominalizer [-an] is attached to the adjective [ka.saɾ] 'coarse', the word [ka.sa.ɾan] 'coarse manner' results, and [ɾ] is not part of the penultimate syllable like the rest of that original syllable, but is now the onset of the ultimate syllable. However, resyllabification is not a common process in Baba Malay, because the use of most affixes, including nominalizer [-an] is optional. The most common suffix is the transitive suffix [-kan] (see section 4.2.1.1), which has no effects on resyllabification since the suffix comprises one syllable that has its own onset. Reduplication is also not always a productive process in Baba Malay. Words that appear reduplicated, such as in examples (87) to (93), are often not recognized by speakers as being composed of a shorter component that has meaning by itself, that is repeated in the reduplicated form to express a more complex meaning.

(87) labi-labi 'turtle, tortoise'

(88) kupu-kupu 'butterfly'

(89) kuɾa-kuɾa 'tortoise'

(90) antiŋ-antiŋ 'earrings'

(91) gədəbaʔ-gədəbuʔ 'onomatopoeia: thudding of the heart'

(92) gədəbaŋ-gədəboŋ 'onomatopoeia: loud noises'

(93) embɛ-embɛ 'half-cooked'

Labi in (87) *labi-labi* 'turtle' does not mean a singular turtle, given that reduplication functions as a plural marker as with many other varieties of Malay, such as with Manado Malay, Ambon Malay, Kupang Malay (Paauw 2009), Bahasa Melayu, and Bahasa Indonesia, to name a few. In fact, on its own, *labi* does not constitute a word in any of these languages and in Baba Malay. In varieties such as Bahasa Melayu and Bahasa Indonesia, *kupu* indicates 'equal in social or familial statuses', but is in no way related to (88) *kupukupu* 'butterfly'. Similarly, *kura* means 'spleen' in Bahasa Melayu and Bahasa Indonesia, and this meaning is unrelated to that of (89) *kurakura* 'tortoise'. The word *antiŋ* means 'weight on a scale' in the same language, and the word for earrings (90) *antiŋ-antiŋ* may have come from the fact that the long earrings worn might have looked like the weights on traditional balancing scales, but the word *antiŋ* by itself does not exist in Baba Malay and any such historical connection there may be is unknown to speakers. Where (91) is concerned, the components *gədəbaʔ* and *gədəbuʔ* have no meaning on their own in Baba Malay. In related varieties such as Bahasa Melayu and Bahasa Indonesia, *gədəbuʔ* is the onomatopoeic sound for stamping and pounding. These seemingly reduplicated words in examples (87) to (91) appear to have been directly derived from other Malay varieties, in which these words exist.

There are also instances of "reduplications" in Baba Malay that are unique to the language, not having been derived directly from any source. In (92), *gədəbaŋ* and *gədəboŋ* have no individual meanings in Baba Malay, but *gədəbam* is the onomatopoeic sound made by falling things in Bahasa Indonesia. Baba Malay speakers might have analogized and innovated *gədəbaŋ-gədəboŋ* as an onomatopoeia for loud noise themselves, following the template for *gədəbaʔ-gədəbuʔ*, in which the first component ends with an open low vowel followed by a velar, and the second component ends with a rounded back vowel also followed by a velar. In other cases such as (93), neither component nor "reduplicated" word is known to exist in any other associated variety of Malay, and *embɛ-embɛ* 'half-cooked' appears to be unique to Baba Malay (*embɛ* on its own does not exist as a word).

In other instances, words are reduplicated meaningfully, some more productively than others:

(94) peʔ-peʔ 'father's elder brother' / dʒi peʔ 'father's second eldest brother'

(95) kim-kim 'mother's brother' wife' / tua kim 'mother's eldest brother's wife'

(96) adeʔ-bəradeʔ 'siblings' / adeʔ 'sibling'

(97) rumah-rumah 'houses'/ rumah 'house'

(98) pəlan-pəlan 'slowly' / pəlan 'slow'

(99) ləkas-ləkas 'quickly' / ləkas 'quick'

(100) tauwɛ-tauwɛ 'somewhat tasteless' / tauwɛ 'tasteless'

(101) asien-asin 'somewhat salty' / asin 'salty'

(102) dʒalan-dʒalan 'to take a walk' / jalan 'walk'

(103) matʃam-matʃam 'like this and that'/ matʃam 'seems, like, like this'

There are five patterns of reduplication observed here. (95) and (96) are examples of kinship terms in Baba Malay that have been derived from Hokkien. The individual components on their own have the same meanings as the reduplicated components, for example, both *peʔ* and *peʔ-peʔ* mean 'father's elder brother', but these stems are seldom used on their own in Baba Malay. Rather, they are combined with Hokkien numerals to indicate the position of this relative in relation to oneself, thus *dʒi peʔ* would mean 'father's second eldest brother', *dʒi* meaning 'two' (see section 7.1.2).

Whereas reduplication for plurals is common in other varieties of Malay such as Bahasa Melayu and Bahasa Indonesia, reduplication for plurals is not common in Baba Malay. Plurals in Baba Malay are usually indicated by adding the word *maɲak* 'many' before the noun. Reduplicated plurals found in the corpus include (96) *adeʔ-bəradeʔ* 'siblings', reduplicated from *adeʔ* 'sibling' and, and *rumah-rumah* 'houses', reduplicated from (97) *rumah* 'house'.

Examples (98) to (103) are more productive and typical in Baba Malay. Adjectives can be reduplicated to become adverbs, as with example (98), where *pəlan* means 'slow' and *pəlan-pəlan* indicates 'slowly', and example (99), where *ləkas* is 'quick' and *ləkas-ləkas* means 'quickly'. Adjectives can also be reduplicated to express tentativeness or moderateness, as with (100) and (101), where *tauwɛ* means 'tasteless' and *tauwɛ-tauwɛ* indicates 'somewhat tasteless', and *asin* means 'salty' whereas *asien-asin* indicates 'somewhat salty'. Similarly, tentativeness can be expressed by reduplicating other word classes. On its own, *dʒalan* would mean 'walk' but (102) *dʒalan-dʒalan* means 'to take a walk' or to stroll with no general goal or purpose, and *matʃam* means 'seems, like, like this' whereas (103) *matʃam-matʃam* indicates 'like this and that' or 'nothing in general'.

It is notable that phonologically, some of these reduplications appear to be interesting, for example, *adeʔ-bəradeʔ* 'siblings' and '*asien-asin*' but none of these patterns are productive in Baba Malay. Monosyllabic, disyllabic and trisyllabic roots can all be reduplicated, with the monosyllabic forms being derived entirely from Hokkien.

3.3 Phonological rules

This section covers the phonological rules in Baba Malay, including both mandatory and optional rules. As Baba Malay is a separate and distinct language in its own right, its phonology must be analyzed as such, and the rules in this section generate surface forms from underlying Baba Malay forms, rather than assume that the underlying forms will coincide with equivalent Malay words. It is therefore neither technically necessary nor appropriate to use the phonologies of either Malay or Hokkien as preliminary points of comparison for the development of phonological rules in Baba Malay However, there are several systematic and non-systematic differences between Baba Malay and Malay that should and can be noted.

Where words end with [aj] and [aw] word-finally in Malay, they end with [e] and [o] respectively in Baba Malay. These close-mid monophthongs have the same degree of frontness and backness as their corresponding semivowels [j] and [w] in the diphthongs [aj] and [aw]. For example, forms such as [kedaj] 'shop', [pandaj] 'clever', [halaw] 'chase away' and [pisaw] 'knife' in Malay correspond to [kede], [pande], [halo], and [piso] in Baba Malay. The only word found to vary among Baba Malay speakers is [kalo] 'if', which sometimes manifests itself as [kalu] in free variation. This described phenomenon does not constitute a phonological monophthongization rule in Baba Malay (where the diphthongs /ai/ and /au/ become close-mid monophthongs [e] and [o] with similar degrees of frontness and backness as the high vowels /i/ and /u/ in the diphthongs /ai/ and /au/) since there is no surface alternation that shows up with [ai] or [au].

In a separate phenomenon, where vowel sequences of [a] and [i], and [a] and [u] are mediated with [h] in Malay, they occur without [h] as [aj] and [aw] in Baba Malay. For example, [dʒahit] 'sew', [pahit] 'bitter' and [tahu] 'know' in Malay correspond to [dʒajt], [pajt] and [taw] in Baba Malay. Again, this does not constitute an intervocalic h-deletion rule and a vowel to glide rule (/ai/ to [aj] and /au/ to [aw]) in Baba Malay, since there are no surface alternations that show up with [ahi] and [ahu] in Baba Malay itself. An exception to this phenomenon is the word [mo] 'want' in Baba Malay (instead of [mau]), which corresponds to [mahu] in Malay.

In addition to understanding systematic differences between Baba Malay and Malay where they exist, it is also interesting to note the non-systematic differences that exist between the two languages. For example, Baba Malay [bawak] corresponds to Malay [bawa] 'bring', Baba Malay [mesti] corresponds to Malay [misti], Baba Malay [amek] to Malay [ambil], Baba Malay [tʃarek] to Malay [tʃari] 'find', and Baba Malay [muŋka] to Malay [muka] 'face'. The forms of these words are uniquely different in Baba Malay and attempts to derive these Baba Malay word forms from the Malay base forms would not be productive or appropriate.

The following tables provide distinctive features of individual segments, as distinctive features are used in the description of the phonological rules that exist in Baba Malay. Inasmuch as possible, non-redundant features are used here. In a strict view, where economy is valued, Baba Malay would not require all of these features. For example, the feature [approximant] is redundant in this table of distinctive features of vowels and glides, as glides can be specified as [-syllabic]. However, since this feature captures a natural class of glides and liquids (which are represented in Table 14), it is included both Tables 14 and 15. Table 14 lists the distinctive features of vowels and glides in Baba Malay.

Table 14: Distinctive features of vowels and glides in Baba Malay spoken in Singapore.[37]

	i	e	ɛ	a	ə	o	ɔ	u	j	w
syllabic	+	+	+	+	+	+	+	+	-	-
high	+	-	-	-	-	-	-	+	+	+
low	-	-	-	+	-	-	+	-	-	-
back	-	-	-	+	+	+	+	+	-	+
round	-	-	-	-	-	+	+	+	-	+
tense	+	+	-	+	-	+	-	+	-	-
approximant	-	-	-	-	-	-	-	-	+	+

Table 15 lists the distinctive features of consonants in Baba Malay (not including glides).

Table 15: Distinctive features of consonants in Baba Malay.

	p	b	m	t	d	s	n	l	r
syllabic	-	-	-	-	-	-	-	-	-
voice	-	+	+	-	+	-	+	+	+
back	-	-	-	-	-	-	-	-	-
coronal	-	-	-	+	+	+	+	+	+
anterior	+	+	+	+	+	+	+	+	+
lateral	-	-	-	-	-	-	-	+	-
nasal	-	-	+	-	-	-	+	-	-
continuant	-	-	-	-	-	+	-	+	+
approximant	-	-	-	-	-	-	-	+	+

	tʃ	dʒ	ɲ	k	g	ŋ	ʔ	h
syllabic	-	-	-	-	-	-	-	-
voice	-	+	+	-	+	+	-	-
back	-	-	-	+	+	+	-	-
coronal	+	+	+	-	-	-	-	-
anterior	-	-	-	-	-	-	-	-
lateral	-	-	-	-	-	-	-	-
nasal	-	-	+	-	-	+	-	-
continuant	-	-	-	-	-	-	-	+
approximant	-	-	-	-	-	-	-	-

---

37 Note that [ɔ] is not found in the data gathered for speakers of Baba Malay in Malacca.

3.3.1 Syllable-final velar plosive to glottal stop rule

(104) $\begin{bmatrix} \text{- syllabic} \\ \text{+ back} \\ \text{- nasal} \end{bmatrix} \rightarrow \begin{bmatrix} \text{- back} \\ \text{- coronal} \\ \text{- anterior} \\ \text{- continuant} \end{bmatrix} / \_\$$

g → ʔ / _$
k → ʔ / _$

At the end of a syllable, velar plosives (including /k/ and /g/) become a glottal stop [ʔ] obligatorily. In other positions, velar plosives remain on the surface as /k/ or /g/. To illustrate this, the word *manyak* [maɲaʔ] is produced with a glottal stop in the syllable-final position, but when nominalizer *-an* is suffixed to it, the glottal stop remains as a /k/, as in [maɲak-an] 'many-NMZ'. In another example, /g/ remains /g/ in [gasaʔ] 'guess', while the syllable-final velar plosive becomes [ʔ]. Table 16 provides more of these examples, illustrating the different realizations of /k/ and /g/ in different positions.

Table 16: Examples illustrating syllable-final velar plosive to glottal stop rule.

Underlying forms	beg 'bag'	pekpek 'father's elder brother'	masok 'enter, put in'	gasak 'guess'	maɲak-an 'many-NMZ'	bikin 'make, do'
syllable final plosive to glottal stop rule	beʔ	peʔpeʔ	masoʔ	gasaʔ	maɲakan	bikin

3.3.2 Deletion of word-initial *h* rule

(105) $\begin{bmatrix} \text{- coronal} \\ \text{+ continuant} \end{bmatrix} \rightarrow (\emptyset) / \#\_$

h → (∅) / #_

Word initially, /h/ is deleted optionally. Table 17 demonstrates the operation of this rule in the appropriate position, and the manifestation of /h/ in non-word initial positions.

Table 17: Examples illustrating optional word-initial *h* deletion rule.

Underlying forms	haʔus 'thirsty, worn-out'	hudʒan 'rain'	hitam 'black'	mahal 'expensive'	dʒahat 'evil'	bohoŋ 'lie'
word initial *h* deletion rule	aʔus	udʒan	itam	mahal	dʒahat	bohoŋ

This rule does not apply to all Hokkien-derived words with initial [h], for example, [hawlam] for 'female mourners', [hauli] 'male mourners', and [huahi] 'happy'. For words derived from Malay, the rule is optional. Speakers produce both forms with and without [h] (speakers can produce both [udʒan] and [hudʒan] for 'rain'), although the general consensus is that the forms that lack [h] are more Baba Malay in nature, since the forms with [h] exist in the standard Bahasa Melayu as well.

3.3.3 Metathesis of *ə* and *r* rule

(106) $\begin{bmatrix} +\text{syllabic} \\ -\text{high} \\ -\text{low} \\ +\text{back} \\ -\text{round} \end{bmatrix} \begin{bmatrix} -\text{syllabic} \\ -\text{lateral} \\ +\text{approximant} \end{bmatrix} \Rightarrow (\begin{bmatrix} -\text{syllabic} \\ -\text{lateral} \\ +\text{approximant} \end{bmatrix} \begin{bmatrix} +\text{syllabic} \\ -\text{high} \\ -\text{low} \\ +\text{back} \\ -\text{round} \end{bmatrix}) / \_ \begin{bmatrix} -\text{syllabic} \end{bmatrix}$

ər ⇒ (rə) / __ C

Metathesis occurs as the sounds /ər/ become transposed within the word and result in [rə] instead. This occurrence of such metathesis is limited to pre-consonantal positions. While it is reasonable to assume that laterals following /ə/ might cause such metathesis too, since both /r/ and /l/ are liquids, there are no instances of /l/ followed immediately by a consonant in Baba Malay, and it is not necessary to further define the liquid by including [-lateral]. The metathesis rule applies optionally, although the word for work, [krədʒa] appears consistently as such in the corpus. /ər/ is postulated as the underlying segment and not [rə], because the segment /ər/ occurs in more general conditions elsewhere, such as in [bərat] 'heavy'. Table 18 illustrates manifestations and non-manifestations of the optional *ə* and *r* metathesis rule.

Table 18: Examples illustrating optional *ə* and *r* metathesis rule.

Underlying forms	gərdʒa 'church'	kərdʒa 'work'	bərsi 'clean'	tərban 'fly'	bərat 'heavy'	pəletʃok 'twist foot'
ər to *rə* metathesis rule	grədʒa	krədʒa	brəsi	trəban	bərat	pəletʃok

3.3.4 Assimilation of V to *u* before *lw* rule

(107) $\begin{bmatrix} +\text{syllabic} \end{bmatrix} \rightarrow (\begin{bmatrix} +\text{high} \\ +\text{round} \end{bmatrix})/\_\begin{bmatrix} +\text{lateral} \end{bmatrix}\begin{bmatrix} -\text{syllabic} \\ +\text{round} \end{bmatrix}$

$V \rightarrow (u)/\_lw$

Optionally, vowels before /lw/ can assimilate towards the rounded, back and high /w/, so they appear as round, back and high vowel [u]. This anticipatory assimilation is triggered specifically by a subsequent /lw/ and not by an intervening lateral, /lj/ or any lV environment. Words such as [səlwaɾ] 'pants' are phonologically manifested as [sulwaɾ]. The positions that involve such assimilation and other positions that do not (including a position with subsequent /lj/ and another with a subsequent /lu/) are presented in Table 19.

Table 19: Examples illustrating optional V to *u* before *lw* assimilation rule.

Underlying forms	səlwar 'pants'	kəlwar 'go out, take out'	dilwar 'outside'	kalu 'if'	halja 'ginger'	katʃua 'cockroach'
u assimilation rule	sulwar	kulwar	dulwar	kalu	halia	katʃua

3.3.5 Vowel raising to *ɛ* and final *l, r, s* deletion in refined style rules

Word-finally, /al/, /aɾ/, and /as/ optionally become [ɛ] (noted by Pakir 1986). However, such a phonological alternation is dependent on the social meaning that is intended by the speaker. Words that end with /al/, /aɾ/, and /as/ are recognized by speakers to be *kasar* 'coarse'. These words are used interchangeably with their *halus* or *alus* 'refined' counterparts that end with [ɛ], depending on what the intention of the speaker is – While speakers of other languages differentiate between formal and informal registers, Baba Malay speakers differentiate between two registers depending on whether the speaker is attempting to come across as being particularly refined, or coarse (Lee 2014). Notably, *kasar* and *halus* are used to describe not only the way people speak, but also their behavior and dressing. While speakers can reflect these values in whether they are speaking loudly (*kasar*) or softly (*halus*), whether or not they use *gua* (*kasar*) or *saya* (*halus*) as first person singular pronoun,[38] and whether they use the correct terms of address when speaking to others rather than the second person singular pronoun *lu*, most of the *kasar-halus* contrast is dependent on whether words that end with /al/, /aɾ/, and /as/ are produced with an [ɛ] at the end instead.

---

[38] *Gua* as first person pronoun is derived from Hokkien while *saya* is derived from Malay. See 4.1.3.1.

Two rules have to be posited for the manifestation of [ɛ] refined forms, since it is phonologically more plausible and theoretically preferable for phonological rules to change only a single segment at any one time. These rules are identified in (108) and (109).

(108) $\begin{bmatrix} +\text{syllabic} \\ +\text{low} \\ -\text{round} \end{bmatrix} \rightarrow (\begin{bmatrix} +\text{syllabic} \\ -\text{back} \\ -\text{tense} \end{bmatrix}) / \_ \begin{bmatrix} +\text{anterior} \\ +\text{continuant} \end{bmatrix} \#$

a → (ɛ) / _l #
a → (ɛ) / _ɾ #
a → (ɛ) / _s #

In the vowel raising rule, /a/ becomes [ɛ] when followed by /l/, /ɾ/, or /s/, although this only occurs for refined forms. Table 20 demonstrates the application of the vowel raising rule.

Table 20: Examples illustrating vowel raising to ɛ rule.

Underlying forms	kənal 'know (a person)'	tampal 'mend'	bənaɾ 'logical'	kasaɾ 'coarse'	panas 'hot'	nanas 'pineapple'
vowel raising rule	kənɛl	tampɛl	bənɛl	kasɛl	panɛl	nanɛl

(109) $\begin{bmatrix} +\text{anterior} \\ +\text{continuant} \end{bmatrix} \rightarrow \emptyset / \begin{bmatrix} +\text{syllabic} \\ -\text{back} \\ -\text{tense} \end{bmatrix} \_$

l → Ø / ɛ __
ɾ → Ø / ɛ __
s → Ø / ɛ __

The vowel raising rule then feeds the rule that deletes the final /l/, /ɾ/ or /s/ segment that follows [ɛ]. Table 21 shows how final /l/, /ɾ/ or /s/ is deleted in the position after [ɛ]. With the application of both rules, words such as /tampal/ 'mend', / bənaɾ/ 'logical' and /panas/ 'hot' manifest as [tampɛ], [bənɛ] and [panɛ]. These examples are shown along with others in Table 21 and have to be understood in the context of the rule applied in Table 20.

Table 21: Examples illustrating final l, r, s deletion post- ɛ vowel raising.

Underlying forms	kənɛl 'know (a person)'	tampɛl 'mend'	bənɛɾ 'logical'	kasɛɾ 'coarse'	panɛs 'hot'	nanɛs 'pineapple'
final l, r, s deletion rule	kənɛ	tampɛ	bənɛ	kasɛ	panɛ	nanɛ

3.4 Rule ordering

Note that there are appropriate orders in which two sets of phonological rules apply.

3.4.1 Vowel raising to ɛ, then deletion of final l, r, s

The vowel raising rule feeds the final *l*, *ɾ*, *s* deletion rule (see section 3.3.5). The final *l*, *ɾ*, or *s* segments are only deleted following the rule in section 3.3.5 when they occur after the vowel [ɛ], which is created from the vowel raising rule. Examples that demonstrate this feeding process are shown in Table 22.

Table 22: Ordering of vowel raising to ɛ, then final *l*, *ɾ*, *s* deletion.

Underlying forms	nanas 'pineapple'	pasar 'market'	kenal 'know'
vowel raising rule	nanɛs	pasɛr	kenɛl
final *l*, *ɾ*, *s* -deletion rule	nanɛ	pasɛ	kenɛ
Surface forms	nanɛ	pasɛ	kenɛ

The rule feeding order would be disrupted if the rules were applied in the wrong sequence – there would be no change to the surface forms of words such as /nanas/ 'pineapple', /pasar/ 'market', and /kenal/ 'know'.

3.4.2 *u* assimilation, then vowel raising to ɛ, followed by deletion of final *l*, *ɾ*, *s*

Vowel raising and the deletion of final *l*, *ɾ* or *s* (see sections 3.3.5 and 3.4.1) can only take place after the application of the rule that assimilates a vowel before lw to u (see section 3.3.4). Examples that illustrate this particular order of application are listed in Table 23.

Table 23: Ordering of vowel raising to ɛ and final *l*, *ɾ*, *s* deletion, then *u* assimilation.

Underlying forms	kəlwar 'go out, take out'	səlwar 'pants'
u assimilation rule (Surface forms)	kulwar	sulwar
vowel raising rule	kulwɛr	sulwɛr
final *l*, *ɾ*, *s* deletion rule	kulwɛ	sulwɛ
Surface forms	kulwɛ	sulwɛ

The rule ordering in Table 23 is supported by the observation that non-refined forms (ending in l, ɾ or s) also undergo optional u assimilation before lw, so that forms such as [sulwaɾ] and [kulwaɾ] exist in addition to [səlwaɾ] and [kəlwaɾ] for non-refined forms. Vowel raising to ɛ, followed by the loss of final l, ɾ are optionally applied after u assimilation, producing [kulwɛ] and [sulwɛ] for the refined versions of 'go out, take out' and 'pants'. Otherwise, the surface forms [kəlwɛɾ] and [səlwɛɾ] would be expected.

3.5 Fast speech

Fast speech in Baba Malay is characterized by the use of contracted forms of lexical items, the omission of certain vowels, and the linking up of words, so that the original word boundaries are lost. The fast speech phenomena in Baba Malay has been presented extensively by Pakir (1986).

The contracted forms that can be found of certain lexical items in fast speech are not phonologically governed. Examples of these include: [swa] for [sudah] 'already', [kat] for [dəkat] 'near, at', [sapa] for [sjapa] 'who', [pi] for [pərgi] 'go', [ni] for [ini] 'this', and [tu] for [itu] 'that'. These contracted forms are usually function words or words that are very commonly used, so that very little context is required to understand what these words refer to. Among these contracted forms, [dʒoraŋ] is an interesting contraction for [dia-oraŋ] meaning 'they'. The word initial [d] appears to be undergoing palatalization, brought about by anticipatory articulation before [i] with the sequence [ia-o] reducing to just [o]. This is not a commonly used contracted form though, and in fact, whether it should be represented in writing for the stage has been a source of dispute among playwrights.[39]

The vowel [ə] is also often reduced in fast speech in Baba Malay (Pakir 1986). The reduction usually occurs within the first syllable, so that [səkali] 'very' becomes [skali], [sərono] becomes [srono] 'proper', [kəriŋ] 'dry' becomes [kriŋ], [bərapa] 'how many' becomes [brapa], and [tʃəlop] 'dip in dye' becomes [tʃlop]. While one might observe a preference for [ə] to be omitted if it is followed by a liquid, this is not always the case, as with [səkali] and [skali]. Such a phenomenon appears to be connected to the optional /ər/ to [rə] metathesis rule, although the metathesis rule has no effect on the number of syllables. For example, [bərsi] ends up optionally as [brəsi] 'clean', both forms having the same number of syllables. In the instances of [ə] reduction in fast speech, the number of syllables is reduced. For example, whereas there are two syllables in [kəriŋ] 'dry', there is only one syllable in [kriŋ].

The other phenomenon that is common in fast speech is that word-finally, liquids and the glottal fricative can be omitted. For example, in their coarse forms, [kapal] 'ship' becomes [kapa] in fast speech, and [bəladʒar] 'study' becomes [bəladʒa]. Non-

---

[39] Relevant information is recorded in an interview with Victor (oai:scholarspace.manoa.hawaii.edu: NL1-015, 00:00:00–00:03:43.0).

coarse forms are affected too. For example, [dapor] 'kitchen' becomes [dapo], [pe'el] 'good character' becomes [pe'e], and [buah] becomes [bua] 'fruit'. This final segment omission is similar to the rule that deletes final /l/, /r/, or /s/ after vowel raising to [ɛ] in refined speech. The difference between these two phenomena is that final /l/, /r/, /s/ is mandatorily deleted after raising to [ɛ] in refined speech, whereas word-final liquids and the glottal fricative are not mandatorily deleted in fast speech.

Fast speech can also compound words together, common ones being [taʔ-a] and [taʔ-da] for [taʔ ada] 'there isn't', [taʔ-pa] for [taʔ apa] 'it is nothing', [toʔ-sa] for [toʔ usa] 'there is no need', and [niaɾi] for [ini aɾi] 'this day'. These are also recorded in Pakir (1986). She has more examples of these that show up in her data than in the archived data used. At the time of her work, she observed that disyllabic structures were "the favoured output" (Pakir 1986:80).

3.6 Writing system of this grammar

As a non-official language that is not taught in the schools, Baba Malay has no official writing system of its own. There are however, individual systems used by authors who write about Peranakan subject matters (see for example, Chia 1980 and Chia 1983) and playwrights who create Peranakan plays, also known as *wayang Peranakan* (Gunong Sayang Association 2018). These systems are usually closely modelled on the Standard Malay writing system that is used in Singapore, Malaysia, and Brunei. Until the early 1900s, Malay was written using the Jawi script, modified for use from the original Arabic system (Omar 1989; Omar 1993). Only in 1904 was the writing system reformulated and Romanized by Richard James Wilkinson, a Malay scholar and member of the colonial administration. This was the system adopted in Malaysia, Singapore, and Brunei. In fact, Wilkinson systematized the writing system predominantly based on the English writing system, whereas the Romanized writing system in Indonesia introduced by Charles Adriaan Van Ophuijsen was influenced by the Dutch writing system (Omar 1989, Omar 1993). The Standard Malay orthography was then revamped several times, with key changes taking place in 1972, during which administrators attempted to unify the spelling systems of Malay in Malaysia and Singapore with the one in Indonesia.

The system that this grammar uses is closest to the one that was developed by Baba William Gwee, a prominent Peranakan community member in Singapore who has published a Baba Malay-English dictionary (Gwee 2006) and a compendium of Baba Malay sayings (Gwee 1998), the reasons being that his works may be familiar to the Peranakan community, and that the system he uses is logical and mostly easy to follow for general readers. Table 24 shows the corresponding phonetic values, writing system used for this grammar adapted from Gwee (2006), and the corresponding equivalents used in modern Malay orthography. The sense of the word 'orthography' as it is used here refers to standard usage.

Table 24: Writing system of Baba Malay used by this grammar.

IPA	Writing system of this grammar (adapted in part from Gwee 2006)	Modern Malay orthography
a	*a*	*a*
i	*i*	*i*
e	*é*[40] except syllable-finally where it is represented by *ay*	*e* except before a coda where it is represented by *i*.[41]
ɛ	*air*	
ə	*e*	*e*
u	*u*	*u*
o	*o*	*o* except before a coda where it is represented by *u*.
ɔ	*or*	
p	*p*	*p*
b	*b*	*b*
m	*m*	*m*
t	*t*	*t*
d	*d*	*d*
s	*s*	*s*
n	*n*	*n*
l	*l*	*l*
r	*r*	*r*
tʃ	*ch*	*c*
dʒ	*j*	*j*
ɲ	*ny*	*ny*
k	*k*	*k*, except for words borrowed from Arabic that originally contained velar fricative, these are spelled *kh*.
g	*g*	*g*
ŋ	*ng*	*ng*
ʔ	*'* except in word-final position, *k* or *g*	
h	*h*	*h*
w	*w* except in non-onset position, *u*	*w*
j	*y* except in non-onset position, *i*	*y*

---

40 Differs from Gwee (2006), where both [e] and [ə] are represented by *e*.
41 Vowel lowering takes place in Malay before a consonant coda, so that /i/ becomes [e], and /u/ becomes [o]. See Onn (1980); Teoh (1994). There is no evidence that this takes place in Baba Malay.

There are several points to note:

The sound [ɛ] is represented by *air* as the vowel sounds similar to the vowel in the English word 'air'. Singaporeans' pronunciation of this English word is similar to that of the Received Pronunciation vowel. This would be familiar to most literate Peranakans who would also be exposed to English, be it in Singapore or in Malaysia. In fact, it should be recalled that the Romanized Malay script itself was formulated based on English in these areas (Omar 1989, Omar 1993).

The two sounds [e] and [ə] are represented by the same symbol, *e* in Malay orthography and in Gwee's publications (Gwee 1998, Gwee 2006). Whereas [ə] is still represented as *e* in this grammar, [e] is represented by *é*, given that it is not predictable where [ə] occurs, or where [e] occurs. For example, [bedeʔ] 'tell a lie' and [bədeʔ] 'pummel' form a minimal pair in Baba Malay. It is also more economical to mark [e] with an extra diacritic as opposed to [ə] since [ə] occurs much more frequently than [e] does. Note however, that at the end of a word, the vowel sound [e] is written *ay*, such as with *sampay* for [sampe], meaning 'until, reach'. This marks a salient difference between Baba Malay and Malay. For example, [sampe] in Baba Malay would correspond to [sampaj] in Malay. In addition, while [ɔ] does not exist in Malay, [o] and [ɔ] are represented by *o* and *or* respectively, so as to be consistent with Gwee (2006).

Diphthong combinations are represented using *i* for [j] and *u* for [w] when [j] or [w] are not found in the onset. For example, [ja] is written as *ia* and [wa] can be written as *ua*. For example, [sjut] 'singe' is written as *siut* and [kwat] 'strong' is represented as *kuat*. In onset positions, the glide [j] is represented as *y* and [w] is represented as *w*. For example, the word [wa.jaŋ] 'play' is written as *wayang*. This follows Gwee (2006).

Although word-final glottal plosives manifest as [ʔ], these are still represented as *k* or *g* (see section 3.3.1) since it should be relatively easy for readers to apply the word-final plosive to glottal stop rule. Word-final *k* and *g* are also used by Gwee (2006).

For readers familiar with Malay, it is interesting to note that the sounds [f] and [z] do not exist in Baba Malay, even though they exist in Malay.

Whereas Hokkien is a tone language, Baba Malay words of Hokkien origin do not have consistent tones on them and are thus not marked for tonal contrasts. Note that they do however receive regular lexical stress (see section 3.7.2).

3.7 Stress and intonation

In general, Baba Malay is a syllable-timed system, where the duration of each syllable is approximately equal. This should come across as being unsurprising, considering that both its lexifier language, Malay as well as its substrate language, Hokkien, are syllable-timed instead of stress-timed (see Wan 2012 and Hung 1996).

3.7.1 Word stress and pitch

While the lexical stress system is not based on duration, pitch (and to some extent, intensity) is used for the purpose of emphasizing lexical stress. In Baba Malay, the ultimate syllable tends to receive the most stress. Wee (2000) characterizes this as a 'step-up' progression', However, when there are three syllables, the final syllable receives the most stress, followed by the first syllable. Lexical stress allocation begins from the final syllable, and stress then alternates backwards between syllables. Words with four syllables are rare, but when they do occur, they follow the general lexical stress template, where the ultimate syllable receives the most stress, the penultimate syllable is not stressed, and the second syllable is stressed. This differs from Wee's (2000) findings, where the step-up progression is also observed for words that are more than two syllables long.

The following waveform and spectrogram capture natural speech comprising words of two syllables. There are two sets of non-striated contour lines on the spectrogram. The lower line represents pitch while the upper line represents intensity. The dynamic range on each spectrogram in this section is set at 40dB so that both pitch and intensity contours can be seen more clearly. For the same purpose, both pitch range and intensity range are adjusted for individual spectrograms, so that none of the relevant contours are cut off. Otherwise, the settings in Praat (Boersma & Weenink 2013) for this section are: Maximum formant: 5000Hz,[42] number of formants: 5, window length: 5 milliseconds. Words are orthographically transcribed in this section.

(110) *Orang   panjat   pokok.*
     person   climbs   tree
    A person climbs a tree.
    (Victor, oai:scholarspace.manoa.hawaii.edu: NL1-028, 00:00:15.6-00:00:17.6)

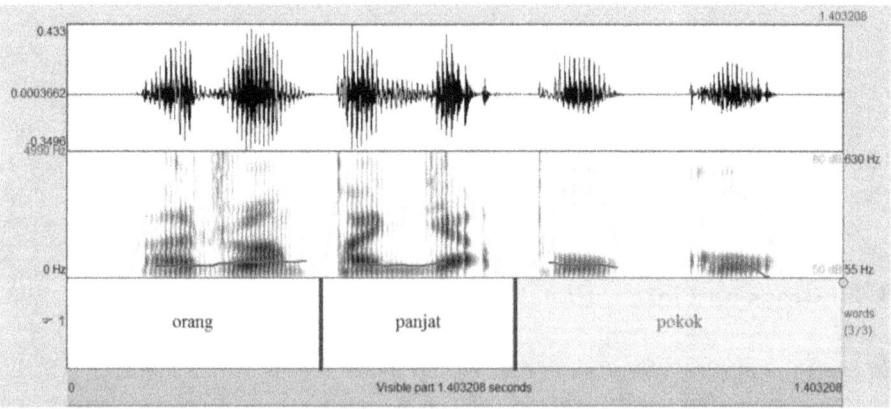

---

42 This setting is also suitable for the female speaker whose voice is featured in this section, as she has a low voice.

Featuring a series of three two-syllable words, example (110) shows that each syllable within each word is equivalently the length of the other word (as with syllable-timed systems), and each syllable within each word also has almost similar intensity patterns as the other. Besides a slight drop in pitch towards the end of *pokok* 'tree' which appears to indicate sentence finality, the other disyllabic items show a slight step-up in pitch within the word. These can be represented as *o.'rang* 'person' and *pan.'jat* 'climb' respectively, where ' represents primary stress. In this sequence of two-syllable words, stress can be said to fall on the final syllable since the accompanying higher pitch indicates more prominence. Note that while (110) shows examples of closed syllables, (111) demonstrates that the same word stress pattern occurs in open syllables.

(111) Gua rasa kita luka   sikit.
      1SG think 1PL   wound little
      'I think we are a little wounded.'
      (Victor, oai:scholarspace.manoa.hawaii.edu: NL1-028, 00:03:42.5-00:03:44.9)

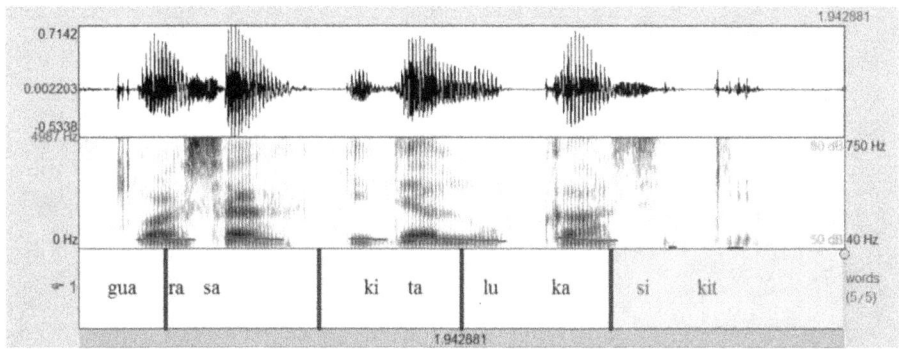

The disyllabic words in (111) can be represented as *ra.'sa* 'think', *ki.'ta* '1PL' and *lu.'ka* 'wound'. In addition to the step-up progression in pitch, the second syllable in each word is also accompanied by higher intensity. Thus, in disyllabic words featuring both open and closed syllables, lexical stress always occurs on the ultimate syllable.

The following two examples in (112) and (113) demonstrate lexical stress in trisyllabic words.

(112) Satu kerosi boléh sandah.
      one   chair   can   lean
      'one chair (that) can lean.'
      (Jane Quek, oai:scholarspace.manoa.hawaii.edu: NL1-044, 00:05:46.6-00:05:48.1)

76 — 3 Phonetics and phonology

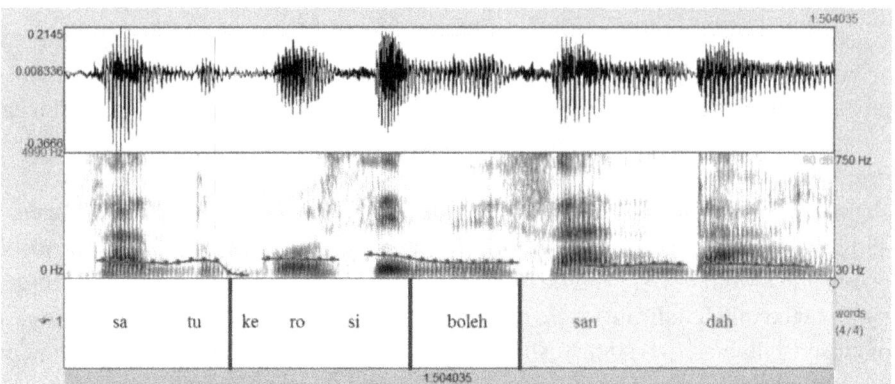

In (112), the trisyllabic word for chair can be represented as ˌke.ro.ˈsi 'chair', where ˌ indicates secondary stress and ˈ indicates primary stress, with pitch being the most accurate indicator of stress. The following is another example of a trisyllabic word.

(113) Balék-kan   itu   ikan,
       turn.over-TR that   fish
       'Turn over that fish,'
       (Jane Quek, oai:scholarspace.manoa.hawaii.edu: NL1-044, 00:10:30.7-
       00:10:32.3)

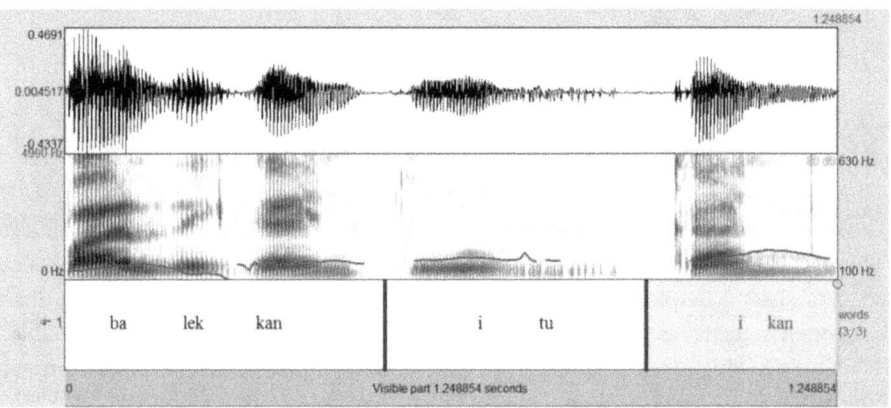

In example (113), 'turn over-TR' can be represented as ˌba.lék.ˈkan, with pitch being the most prominent on the ultimate syllable followed by the first syllable. Hence in trisyllabic Baba Malay words, primary stress falls on the ultimate syllable, followed by the first syllable.

Words of four syllables are rare in Baba Malay, but they follow the template where the ultimate syllable receives primary stress, and the second syllable receives secondary stress. Example (113) can be compared to (114), where the prefix *ter-* 'MVT' is attached to ˌba.lék.ˈkan 'turn over-TR'. The word now comprises four syllables instead of three.

(114) *Ter-balék-kan   itu   ikan pun boléh lah*
      MVT-turn.over-TR that fish also can   EMP
      'Turn over that fish is also okay.'
      (Jane Quek, oai:scholarspace.manoa.hawaii.edu:
      NL1-044, 00:10:32.3-00:10:33.8)

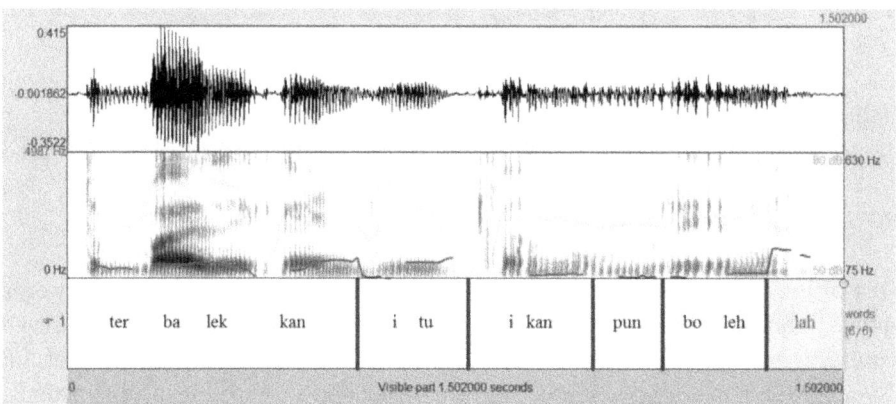

With an additional prefix, the four syllable word can be expressed as *terˌ.ba.lék.ˈkan* 'MVT-turn.over-TR'. The same syllables receive the same stress as ˌba.lék.ˈkan 'turn over-TR'. This adheres to the pattern of stress allocation that begins from the ultimate syllable; the ultimate syllable receives the primary stress, while the alternate syllable receives the secondary stress. Lexical stress is mainly indicated by pitch. (115) is another example of lexical stress allocation on a word comprising four syllables.

(115) *Ini   kupukupu   trebang,*
      this butterfly fly
      'This butterfly flies,'
      (Peter Wee, oai:scholarspace.manoa.hawaii.edu: NL1-030, 00:01:37.5-
      00:01:39.2)

78 — 3 Phonetics and phonology

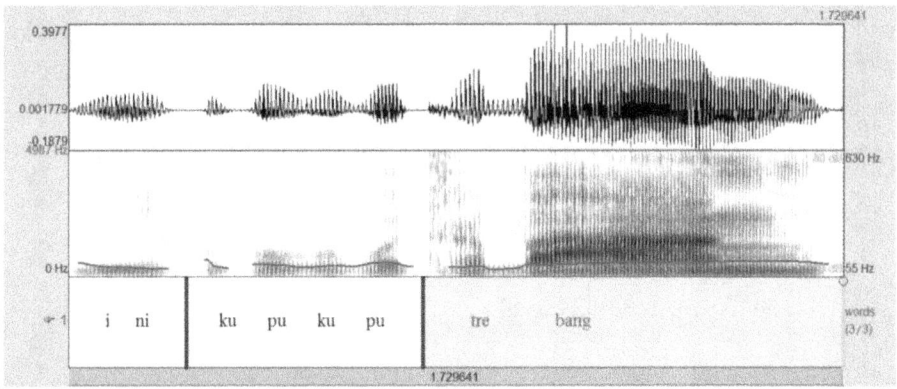

The word for butterfly can be represented as ku.ˌpu.ku.ˈpu, based on the pitch patterns, with stress alternating between syllables.

3.7.2 Tones on Hokkien-derived words

One of the more interesting questions regarding pitch is whether tones in words derived from Hokkien have been preserved. Hokkien is a tone language with seven contrastive tones, where changes in pitch can change the lexical meaning of a word. Pakir (1986) states that words derived from Hokkien show no tonal distinctions, and this is mostly accurate where the current corpus is concerned. On monosyllabic items, Baba Malay speakers appear to produce no contrastive tone in comparison with Hokkien speakers, and on disyllabic items, Baba Malay speakers produce pitch on these Hokkien-derived lexical items that are unlike Hokkien tones, but consistent with general Baba Malay patterns for other words. These are essentially step-up progressions like the ones recorded in the previous section. Trisyllabic words from Hokkien are rare.

The following is an example of a monosyllabic word as it would have been produced in Hokkien. The speaker speaks Baba Malay, but is aware that Hokkien words sound different in Baba Malay than the corresponding forms in Hokkien.

(116) *Hu*
 amulet
 'amulet'
 (Victor, oai:scholarspace.manoa.hawaii.edu: NL1-169, 00:06:25.0-00:06:25.5)

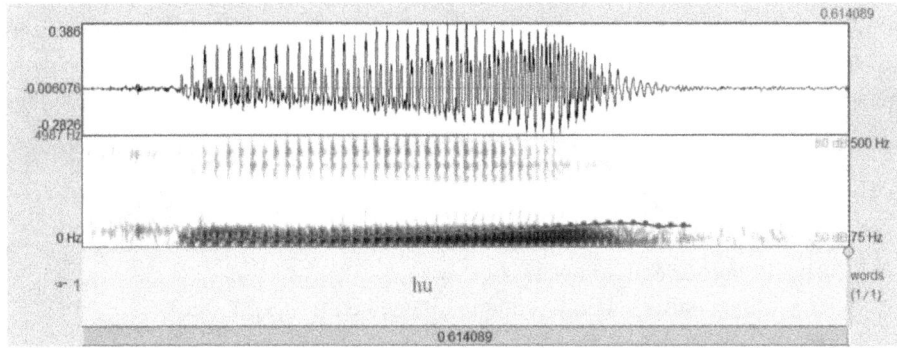

In example (116), the speaker states that *hu13*⁴³ is usually pronounced with a rising tone in Hokkien. In example (117), the Baba Malay speaker uses *hu* in a Baba Malay sentence. There is no rise in pitch accompanying *hu*. In fact, pitch falls slightly owing to *hu*'s sentence-final position.

(117) *Pi   bakair   hu.*
      go   burn   amulet
      'Go burn an amulet.
      (Victor, oai:scholarspace.manoa.hawaii.edu: NL1-169, 00:06:26.7-00:06:27.3)

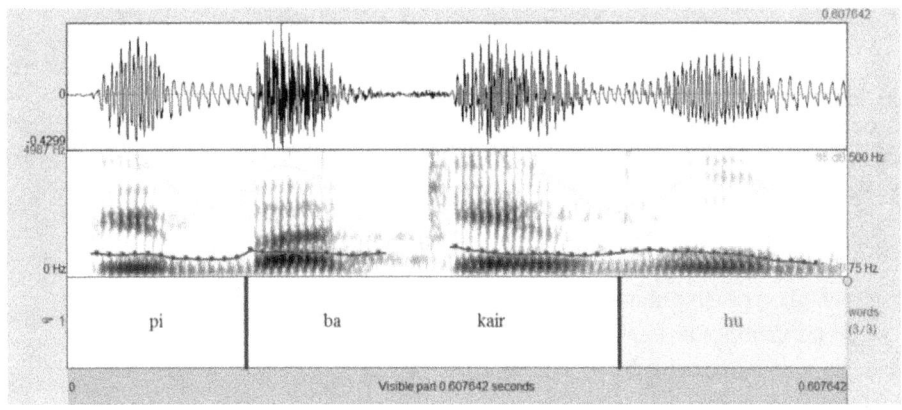

---

43 Chao (1930)'s system is used to annotate tones here. The numerals 1–5 are used, and the first number in the transcription indicates the starting point of the tone, while the second number indicates the ending point of the tone. 1 represents the lowest pitch, and 5 the highest.

While monosyllabic items appear to lack tone, disyllabic items are accompanied in Baba Malay by pitches different from those in Hokkien. The following is taken from a speaker of both Baba Malay and Hokkien who differentiates between the two languages.

(118) *That is called siki.*
                death.anniversary
      'That is called death anniversary.'
      (Jane Quek, oai:scholarspace.manoa.hawaii.edu: NL1-173, 00:08:01.1-00:08:02.6)

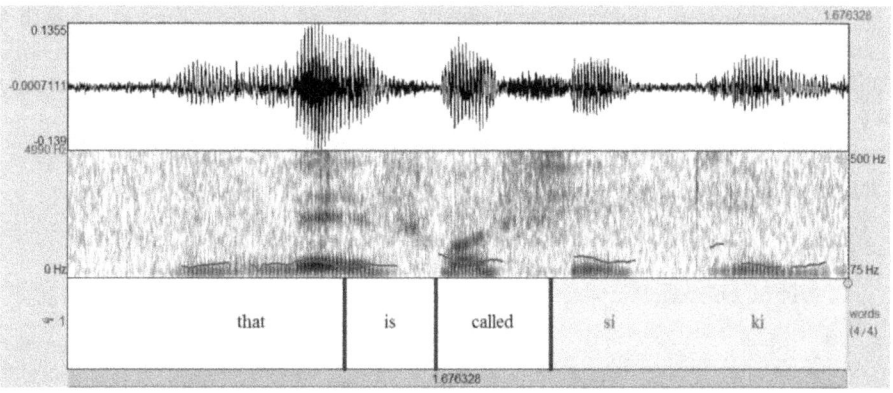

In example (118), the speaker states explicitly that in Hokkien, 'death anniversary' is pronounced *si53 ki32*, whereas in example (119), when the same speaker is speaking Baba Malay, there is a step-up progression in *si'ki*, where the second syllable ends slightly on a higher pitch than the first.

(119) *Bikin   siki   lah*
      make   death.anniversary   EMP
      'Commemorate death anniversary.'
      (Jane Quek, oai:scholarspace.manoa.hawaii.edu: NL1-173, 00:08:04.6-00:08:05.8)

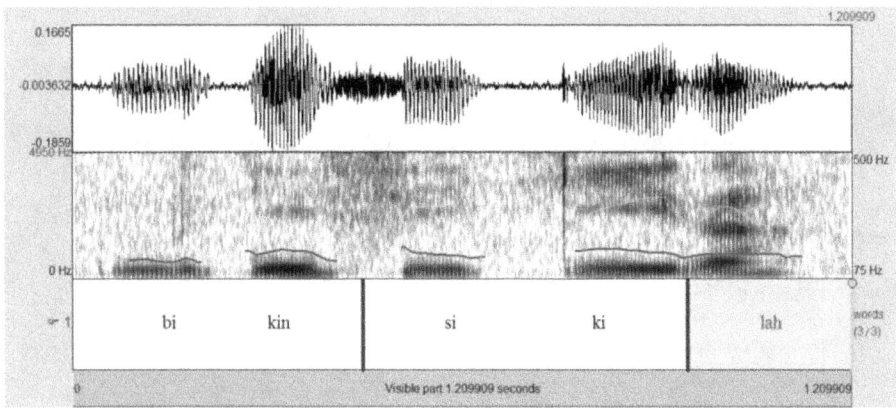

The following is another example taken from a different speaker, who also says that Hokkien as spoken by the Chinese is different from Hokkien as spoken by Baba Malay speakers.

(120) *Actually called binpo.*
                       face.cloth (Hokkien)
     'Actually called facecloth.'
     (Victor, oai:scholarspace.manoa.hawaii.edu: NL1-171, 00:34:35.2-00:34:36.2)

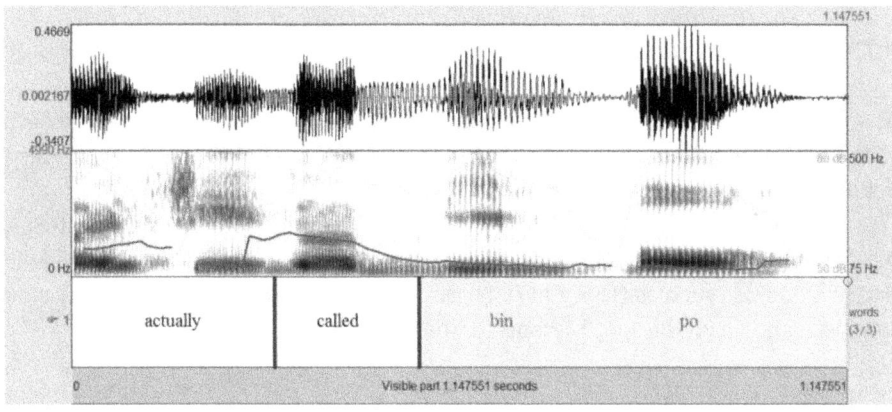

In example (120), the speaker states that in Hokkien, the word for 'facecloth' is *bin21po22*. It is interesting to note that *binpo* means 'handkerchief' and not 'facecloth' in Baba Malay. In comparison to example (120) which shows that a low tone accompanies *po*, example (121) shows how *bin* starts lower, and *po* ends on a higher pitch, so that the word can be represented as *bin'po*.

(121) amék   binpo   gua,
      take   handkerchief 1SG
      'Take my handkerchief,'
      (Victor, oai:scholarspace.manoa.hawaii.edu: NL1-171, 00:34:34.1-00:34:35.2)

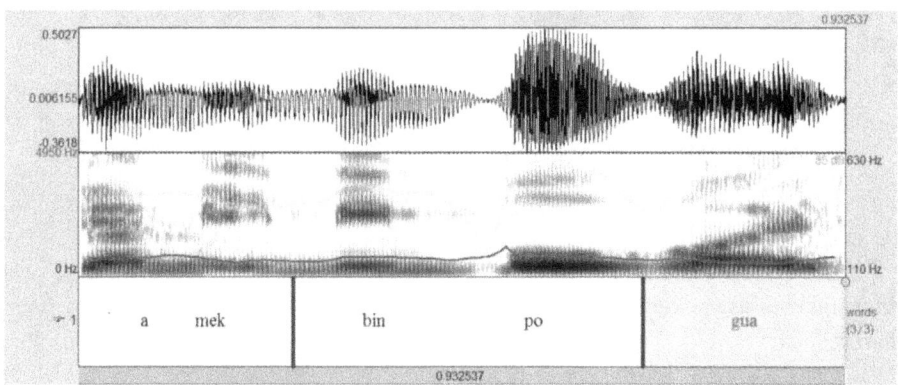

Although there is a slight up-step progression accompanying these words, there is technically no tone on these words, if tones are defined as what differentiates one lexical item from another.

3.7.3 Sentence intonation

There are four main types of sentential intonation that can be observed in the speech of Baba Malay speakers. These are found in declaratives, clauses signaling continuity, content questions, and tag questions.

Declarative sentences end with a fall in the overall pitch contour of the sentence, as also observed by Wee (2000). This is demonstrated in example (122), and also in earlier examples such as (110) and (112). Only pitch contours (and not intensity contours) are shown on the spectrograms for this section.

(122) Tak   tau   apa   mia   tulang   itu.
      NEG   know   what   REL   bone   that
      'Don't know what bone that is.'
      (Peter Wee, oai:scholarspace.manoa.hawaii.edu: NL1-030, 00:02:40.8-00:02:42.5)

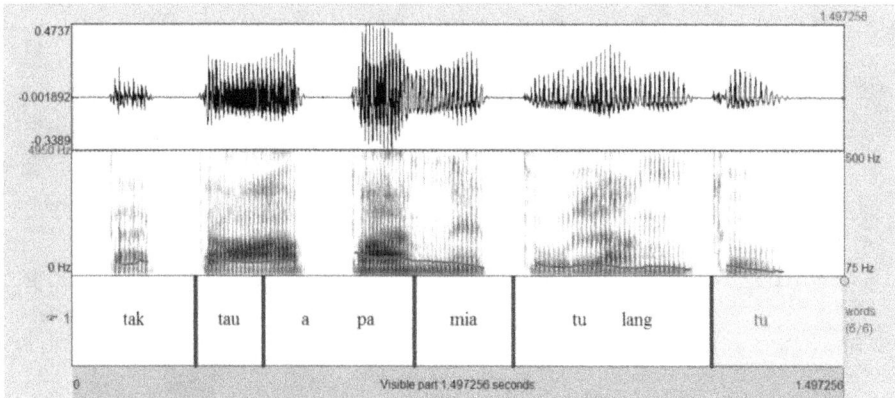

With a different pattern, Baba Malay speakers signal continuity, that they have more to say on the subject matter, even though they may have come to a pause. The pitch of the sentence rises towards the end of the clause, as shown in example (123).

(123) Lu   mo   pakay   ka,
      2SG want use   or
      'You want to use (it) or,'
      (Peter Wee, oai:scholarspace.manoa.hawaii.edu: NL1-170, 00:04:10.5-00:04:12.4)

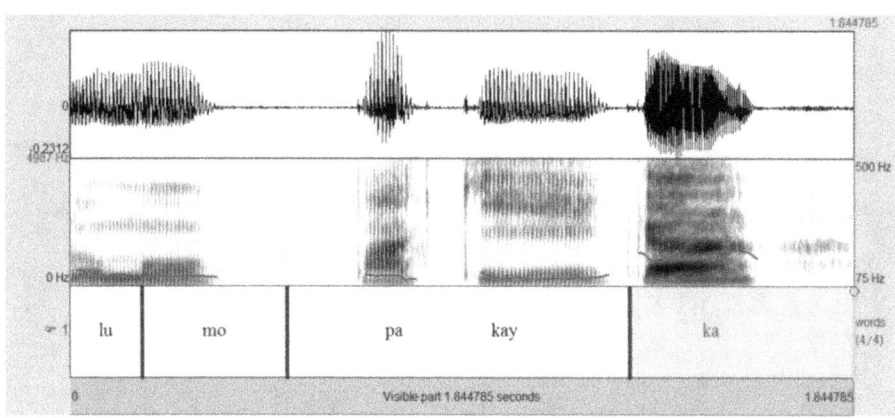

There are two separate intonation patterns that accompany content questions, depending on the position of the question word. When the question word occurs at the beginning of the utterance, pitch rises at the beginning and falls towards the end, as with example (124). This is in line with the observations of Wee (2000) that a rise-fall intonation accompanies interrogatives in Baba Malay.

(124) Apa   macham   dia   mo   bikin?
       what   like.that 3SG   want   do
       'How does she/he want to do this?'
       (Victor, oai:scholarspace.manoa.hawaii.edu: NL1-37, 00:42:37.6-00:42:39.3)

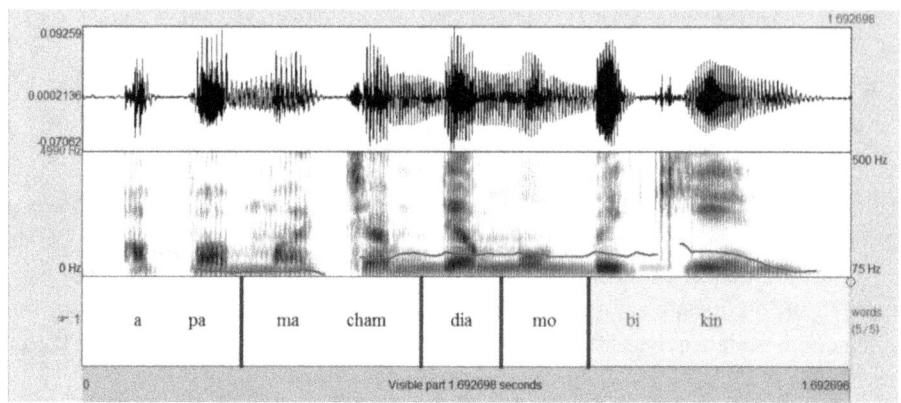

Conversely, when the question word is at the end of the utterance, pitch rises towards the end of it, as with example (125).

(125) Lu   pakay   chanték   mo   pi   mana?
       2SG   wear   beautiful want   go   where
       'Where do you want to go dressed (so) beautifully?'
       (Victor, oai:scholarspace.manoa.hawaii.edu: NL1-37, 00:07:04.0-00:07:05.9)

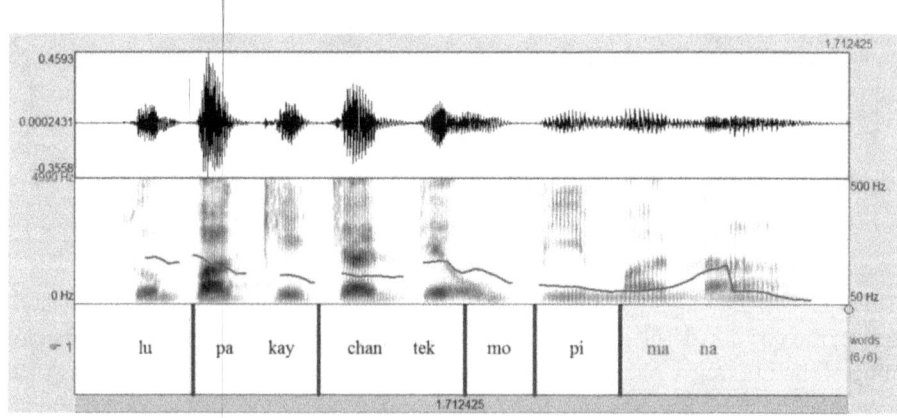

Similarly, tag questions have a rise that come towards the end of question, as also observed by Wee (2000).[44] This is demonstrated by example (126).

(126) Buah   pear bukan?
       CLF.fruit   no
      'Is this pear?'
      (Peter Wee, oai:scholarspace.manoa.hawaii.edu: NL1-022, 00:00:42.3-00:00:43.8)

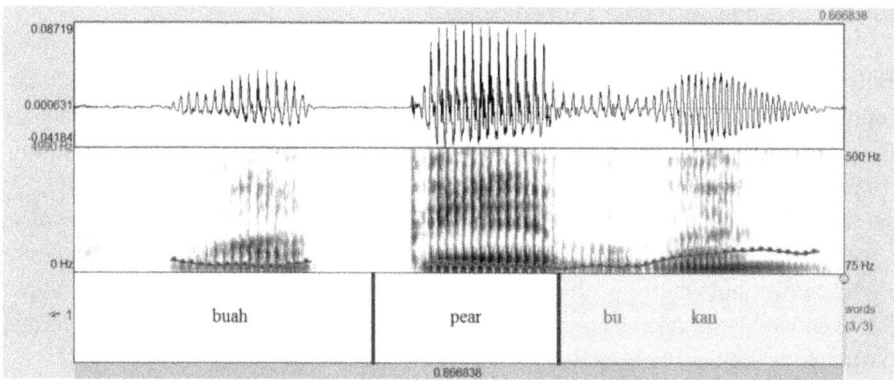

Hence, there are a four distinct intonation contours at the sentential level in Baba Malay. Declaratives fall in pitch towards the end of the utterance, a final rise can signal continuity, and content questions are accompanied by rise-fall when the question word occurs at the beginning of the interrogative. When the question word occurs at the end of the interrogative, or when a tag question is asked, pitch tends to rise at the end of the utterance.

3.8 Phonological change

The loss of phonetic information is common in situations of language decay (Tsunoda 2005). Even though phonological variation takes place in languages that are not threatened, it has been demonstrated that phonetic or phonological variation can become more apparent in minority communities when the viability of the language is threatened (Babel 2009; Brunelle 2009; Campbell & Muntzel 1989). This is true of Baba Malay, where the number of phonemic contrasts is being reduced as speakers become less proficient in the language, and more proficient in other dominant languages, such as English. In fact, the vowel space appears to be contracting, so that it is becoming more similar to that of Standard Malay. The essential difference between the vowel

---

44 Wee (2000)'s term for tag questions is yes-no questions.

spaces of Standard Malay and that of Baba Malay, is that the open-mid front and back vowels [ɛ] and [ɔ], which are found in Baba Malay do not occur in Standard Malay.[45]

The vowels of six Baba Malay speakers are plotted in this section. These speakers are between the ages of 60 to 80, four of them are male and two are female. All of these speakers stated that Baba Malay was their first language. In addition, all of these speakers are bilingual in English, and profess to have different levels of proficiency in Baba Malay. Four speakers identified themselves to be proficient in Baba Malay, while two others stated that they have become less proficient in the language as English is now their dominant language.[46]

Ten tokens of each vowel (identified in section 3.1.2.2) were extracted from naturally occurring speech (not wordlist data) and their formants were measured in Praat, following the methodology in section 3.1.2.2. The settings used for this analysis are the same as the ones used for the earlier analysis of vowels, except that the maximum formant is set to 5500Hz for one female speaker (speaker B in Figure 28), while it is set to 5000Hz for the rest of the speakers (including one female who has a low voice; speaker A in Figure 28). Where possible, ten [ɛ] and ten [ɔ] tokens are measured for each speaker, but where speakers only seem to produce [e] and not [ɛ], or [o] and not [ɔ], twenty [e] or [o] tokens are measured instead. Where vowels appeared to overlap, participants' beliefs were used to identify if a vowel was [e] or [ɛ], and [o] or [ɔ].[47]

For the purpose of a quick general comparison, the following two vowel charts in Figures 26 and 27 illustrate the vowel spaces of a more proficient speaker, and a less proficient speaker, respectively, the difference being that the more proficient speaker produces open-mid front and back vowels, [ɛ] and [ɔ], whereas the less proficient speaker produces neither of these. Both speakers are males in their sixties. While the more proficient speaker still uses Baba Malay daily, the less proficient speaker has stopped using Baba Malay as much as he used to. This speaker stopped using the language daily when his parents who predominantly spoke Baba Malay passed away – more than ten years prior to the time of recording. Figure 26 replicates Figure 25.

While the above figures are provided for the purpose of quickly illustrating the phonological differences between a more proficient speaker and a less proficient one, vowel normalization is required when comparing between different speakers – nor-

---

45 This is based on a comparison with a phonetic account of Standard Malay spoken in Brunei (Clynes and Deterding 2011). Crucially, this variety is similar to those spoken in Singapore and Malaysia, and different from the variety that is spoken in Indonesia. In the absence of information from Singapore, it is reasonable to assume that the vowel system of the standard variety in Singapore is comparable to the one that Clynes and Deterding (2011) describe.
46 Speakers are not named here, so as to protect their identities in this discussion of language attrition.
47 This was done due to the fact that consultants differed in how they felt some words should be pronounced. For example, [ɔraŋ] versus [oraŋ] for 'people'.

3.8 Phonological change

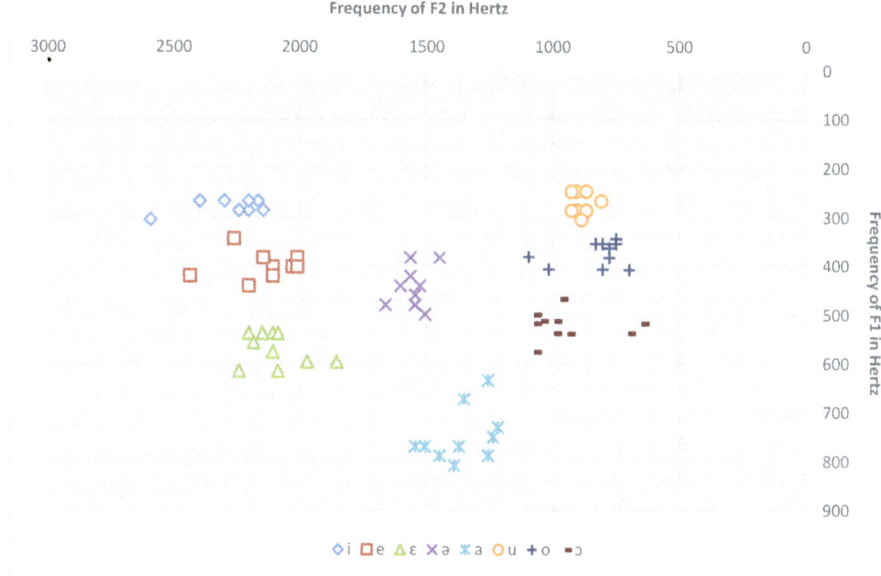

Figure 26: Vowel space of a more proficient Baba Malay speaker in Singapore.

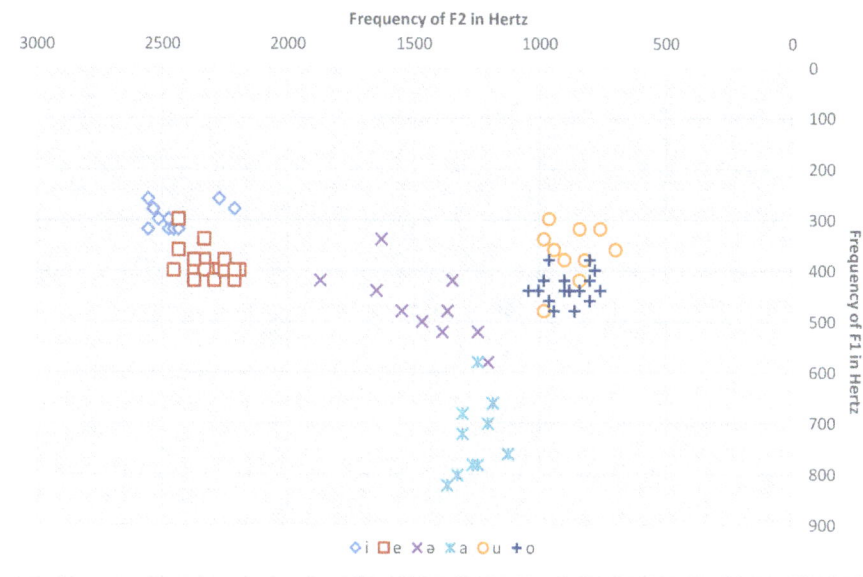

Figure 27: Vowel space of a less proficient Baba Malay speaker in Singapore.

malization controls for the different lengths and shapes of the vocal tracts of different speakers. The Lobanov method is utilized in this instance. (see Lobanov 1971).[48] Figure 28 shows the resultant vowel plots.

Figure 28: Normalized vowel plots of six Baba Malay speakers in Singapore.

---

48 There are vowel intrinsic and vowel extrinsic methods of normalization (Ainsworth 1975, Nearey 1989). Vowel intrinsic methods use only acoustic information contained within a single vowel to normalize that vowel token, while vowel extrinsic methods rely on information distributed across more than one vowel of the speaker. Vowel extrinsic methods such as the Lobanov have been shown to perform better than vowel intrinsic methods. The Lobanov method is represented by the following formula $F_{n[V]}^{N} = (F_{n[V]} - MEAN_n)/S_n$, where $F_{n[V]}^{N}$ is the normalized value for $F_{n[V]}$ (formant n of vowel V), $MEAN_n$ is the mean value for formant n for the speaker, and S_n is the standard deviation for the speaker's formant n.

The vowel plot shown is obtained through vowel normalization and plotting suite, NORM (Thomas and Kendall 2014).

According to the vowel plots, two out of six speakers, B and F, do not produce anything in the region of the open-mid front vowel [ɛ], while only speakers A, B, C and D produce tokens in the region of open-mid back vowel [ɔ]. It is not surprising that speakers B and F identified themselves during the data collection sessions as speakers who are no longer proficient in Baba Malay, now that English is their dominant language. Although speaker E states that he is a proficient Baba Malay speaker, and is observed to use the language regularly with community members and family, he does not produce [ɔ] tokens. All other speakers state that they are proficient in Baba Malay. There is ongoing change, as two vowels are on the verge of being lost. The emerging vowel plot can be compared to the one that Pakir (1986) describes, which was characteristic of the variety when it was more stable, wherein [ɛ] and [ɔ] can both be distinguished from other vowels. It is also noteworthy that vowels [u], [o], and [ɔ] all appear to be in the process of merging.

It is notable that [ɛ] only occurs in refined speech, corresponding to words in coarse speech that end with phonological /aɾ/, /al/ or /as/ (see section 3.4.2). That [ɛ] is not produced as often as /aɾ/, /al/ or /as/ shows that Baba Malay speakers are producing less 'refined' speech, and using more 'coarse' speech instead. Words with the /aɾ/, /al/, and /as/ endings are acknowledged by speakers to be *kasar* [kasaɾ] or even *kasair* [kasɛ], literally meaning 'coarse'. Their [ɛ] counterparts are *halus* or *alus*, the literal meaning being 'refined'. When speakers engage either form, it has little to do with the level of familiarity the speaker has with the interlocutor, their social statuses or the social circumstances surrounding language use, but rather, that the speaker simply wants to be perceived as being more refined (hence the use of the terms *halus* 'refined' and *kasar* 'coarse', indicating that the notion of an elevated versus colloquial style is more appropriate than formal versus informal). Synchronic change is taking place – a recent survey showed that younger and less proficient speakers of Baba Malay did not identify forms ending with [ɛ] as being *halus* and forms ending with /aɾ/, /al/ or /as being *kasar*. Instead, they perceived the [ɛ] variants as being more Peranakan in nature, since the [ɛ] forms do not exist in Standard Malay which is spoken around them, whereas the other forms do (Lee 2020). However, [ɛ] variants are being produced less in naturally-occurring speech by the same group of people.

With regard to [ɔ], two reasons may be postulated for its loss. One plausible reason is that phonological systems tend to not be completely symmetrical, having more front than back vowels, due to the narrowing of the vocal track towards the back of the mouth. What is happening in Baba Malay is consistent with this fact, as speakers appear to produce fewer cases of [ɔ] than [ɛ]. This is especially evident with male speaker, E in Figure 28. Next, Pakir (1986) states that [ɔ] is only found in words of Hokkien origin. The phone [ɔ] may be used less simply if words of Hokkien origin are being used less frequently. This may also be caused by language contact influence from Standard Malay. Still, this explanation is not entirely satisfactory because it has been observed that some speakers of Baba Malay produce [ɔ] in words of Malay origin (for example, a speaker may produce ɔraŋ for oraŋ 'person'). Yet, the notion of language change due to contact with a more dominant language does not have to be abandoned. In fact, speakers are producing [o] where they would traditionally produce [ɔ]. For example, speakers may produce [binpo] 'handkerchief' where originally, the word is pronounced [binpɔ] in Hokkien. Language change in which the contact language becomes more like its lexifier language, due to contact influence may explain for the change in phonetic space, since Malay has the same vowels as Baba Malay, apart from [ɛ] and [ɔ].

4 Parts of speech

Baba Malay is an isolating language, more so than Malay (which utilizes a number of affixes). Word order is therefore crucial in expressing grammatical relations. In view of this, the different parts of speech in Baba Malay can only be identified by appropriately using the individual distribution of the word. This is more accurate than purely looking at word meaning, especially when words can be used in multiple contexts. For example, the word *salah* 'mistake, wrong' can be both a noun and an adjective depending on how it is used. When *salah* is used following a transitive verb, it is the object complement of the verb, as with (127). When it is used immediately after a subject noun phrase, it can be assumed to most likely be an adjective (the copula verb is usually not expressed explicitly in Baba Malay), as with (128).

(127) Gua   bikin   **salah.**
 1SG   make   **mistake**
 'I make mistake.'
 (Jane Quek, oai:scholarspace.manoa.hawaii.edu: NL1-043, 00:19:04.0-00:19:05.8)

(128) Gua   **salah.**
 1SG   **wrong**
 'I (am) wrong.'
 (Jane Quek, oai:scholarspace.manoa.hawaii.edu: NL1-043, 00:40:04.0-00:40:05.2)

Similarly, *marah* 'angry' can be used as an adjective or a transitive verb. After *jangan* 'do not', it is used as a verb (section 5.2.8) and where it precedes a noun phrase object complement as with (130), it is a transitive verb.

(129) Jangan   **marah.**
 do.not   **angry**
 'Do not (be) angry'.
 (Peter Wee, oai:scholarspace.manoa.hawaii.edu: NL1-042, 00:20:18.1-00:20:19.2)

(130) Dia-orang   sumua   **marah**   dia   lah.
 3PL   all   **angry**   3SG   EMP
 'They are all angry at him.'
 (Peter Wee, oai:scholarspace.manoa.hawaii.edu: NL1-030, 00:04:37.9-00:04:40.4)

Hence, the different parts of speech are differentiated based on syntactic distribution rather than semantic content or morphology.

4.1 Nouns

Nouns in Baba Malay can be identified by the following distributional patterns. They can be used after noun classifiers (section 5.1.2.3), before and after demonstratives (section 5.1.2.1), and after numerals (section 5.1.2.3). The following examples (131)-(134) demonstrate these respective patterns.

(131) Satu **batang** *payong*
one **CLF.LONG.THIN** umbrella
'One umbrella'
(Victor, oai:scholarspace.manoa.hawaii.edu: NL1-156, 00:05:43.5-00:05:45.0)

(132) Budak **ini.**
child **this**
'this child.'
(Peter Wee, oai:scholarspace.manoa.hawaii.edu: NL1-022, 00:03:23.5-00:03:24.0)

(133) Gua mo beli **ni kayu.**
1SG want buy **this wood**
'I want to buy this wood.'
(Victor, oai:scholarspace.manoa.hawaii.edu: NL1-035, 00:02:23.3-00:02:24.8)

(134) Ni tiga ékor **babi** kuluair rumah.
this three CLF.ANIMAL **pig** go.out house
'These three pigs went out of the house.'
(Victor, oai:scholarspace.manoa.hawaii.edu: NL1-035, 00:00:43.7-00:00:47.2)

Proper nouns (not personal pronouns) can be used after the person marker *si*, although this is optional (section 4.5.1). This is reflected in (135).

(135) Kat mana **si** Mary mo jumpa John?
PREP where **PERSON** want meet
'Where does Mary want to meet John at?'
(Victor, oai:scholarspace.manoa.hawaii.edu: NL1-037, 00:02:44.4-00:02:47.3)

Also, in general, the noun phrase can precede the verb phrase as subject, or follow the verb as object (section 5.2). In (136) and (137), the relevant noun phrases both precede and follow the verb. The noun phrases *orang* 'person' and *dia* '3SG' precede the verb phrase as subjects, while the noun phrases *pokok* 'tree' and *tu orang* 'that person' follow the verb phrase as objects predicated by the verb.

(136) **Orang** *panjat* **pokok**.
  person climb **tree**
  'A person climbs a tree.'
  (Victor, oai:scholarspace.manoa.hawaii.edu: NL1-028, 00:00:15.6-00:00:17.6)

(137) **Dia** *téngok* **tu** *orang*.
  3SG look **that** person
  'He looked at that person.'
  (Victor, oai:scholarspace.manoa.hawaii.edu: NL1-028, 00:02:29.7-00:02:30.9)

4.1.1 Nominal morphology

Nouns can occur on their own, without any affixation. This is the most common form for nouns in Baba Malay. In examples (138) and (139), *anjing* 'dog and *pokok* 'tree' occur without any affixation.

(138) **Anjing** *tu* *gonggong*.
  dog that bark
  'That dog barked.'
  (Victor, oai:scholarspace.manoa.hawaii.edu: NL1-034, 00:01:48.9-00:01:51.8)

(139) *Empat* **pokok**.
  four **tree**
  'Four trees.'
  (Peter Wee, oai:scholarspace.manoa.hawaii.edu: NL1-022, 00:00:25.7-00:00:26.8)

Nouns may also be reduplicated. In example (140), *adék* is singular for 'sibling' while the reduplicated form *adék-beradék* denotes the plural form 'siblings'. In example (141), *pék* represents father's elder brother, but this stem is never used on its own, and the form *pék-pék* is preferred.

(140) *Pangkat* **adék-beradék**.
  rank **sibling-PL**
  'Cousins.'
  (Jane Quek, oai:scholarspace.manoa.hawaii.edu: NL1-132, 00:03:41.4-00:03:43.8)

(141) **Pék-pék.**[49]
'father's elder brother.'
(Jane Quek, oai:scholarspace.manoa.hawaii.edu: NL1-132, 00:07:10.4-00:07:11.4)

Noun reduplication is not as productive as verb reduplication. Noun reduplication appears largely limited to the reduplication of kinship terms as demonstrated by example (141) (see section 3.2.1 for more details). In addition to reduplicated forms, a noun may be created using the *-an* nominalizer suffix, as presented in section 4.1.1.1.

4.1.1.1 Derivational noun morphology

Derivational morphology that create new nouns is non-productive. In fact, the nominalizer suffix *-an* is only found with adjectives *manyak* 'many' and *kasair* 'coarse' in the Singapore Baba Malay corpus. This suffix creates nouns *manyak-an* 'many', as in examples (142) and (143), and *kasair-an* 'coarse manner' as in example (144).

(142) **Manyak-an** chakap bikin manyak.
many-NMZ speak make/do many
'Many say *bikin* a lot.'
(Jane Quek, oai:scholarspace.manoa.hawaii.edu: NL1-043, 00:00:36.8-00:00:40.0)

(143) **Manyak-an** chakap tua.hia.
Many-NMZ speak big.brother
'Many say *tua.hia*.'
(Jane Quek, oai:scholarspace.manoa.hawaii.edu: NL1-132, 00:01:38.6-00:01:38.5)

(144) **Kasair-an.**
coarse-NMZ
'Coarse manner.'

Aside from nominalizer *-an*, there is no other nominal derivational morphology in Singapore Baba Malay. This is unlike Standard Malay, which has a number of derivational affixes: the *ke- -an* and *peN -an* nominalizing circumfixes for deriving nouns of an abstract nature (*ke- -an* is also found in Malacca Baba Malay; see section 6.2.1) and the *peN-* prefix used to derive a noun indicating a person who carries out the action of the root verb.

---

[49] Earlier, *pék-pék* was represented as [peʔ-peʔ] since the phonological form was being cited. Here, the orthographic form is used.

4.1.1.2 Nominal compounds

Nominal compounds in Baba Malay are noun phrases comprising a noun modified by either noun, adjective, verb, or even classifier. Table 25 in the following lists examples of nominal compounds found in the language, as well as their patterns of modification. For the purpose of illustration, nominal compounds that use *ati* 'heart', *mata* 'eye' and *mulot* 'mouth' are listed. Again, note that none of these patterns are productive ones.

Table 25: Some nominal compounds in Baba Malay using *ati* 'heart', *mata* 'eye' and *mulot* 'mouth'.

Nominal compound	Meaning of individual lexemes	Meaning of compound	Parts of speech
ati baik	heart good	kind	N + A
ati busok	heart smelly	cruel	N + A
ati it gor it chap	heart one five one ten	nervous	N + NUM + NUM + NUM + NUM
jantong ati	Heart	beloved	N + N
mata ari	eye day	sun	N + N
mata ayé	eye water	sweetheart	N + N
mata beliak	eye glare	protruding eyes	N + V
mata gelap	eye dark	detective	N + A
mata ikan	eye fish	wart	N + N
mata juling	eye squinty	cockeye	N + A
mata kuching	eye cat	longan fruit	N + N
mata lembu	eye cow	fried egg with yolk intact	N + N
mata mata	eye eye	policeman	N + N
mata piso	eye knife	blade of knife	N + N
bijik mata	CLF.small.round eye	favorite child, apple of one's eye	CLF + N
tanda mata	sign eye	heirloom	N + N
mulot asin	mouth salty	ability to make accurate predictions	N + A
mulot béngok	mouth twisted	twisted mouth	N + A
mulot berat	mouth heavy	inability to express oneself	N + A
mulot bocho	mouth leaky	inability to keep a secret	N + A
mulot busok	mouth smelly	bad breath	N + A
mulot gatair	mouth itchy	uncontrollable mouth	N + A

Table 25 (continued)

Nominal compound	Meaning of individual lexemes	Meaning of compound	Parts of speech
mulot dunya	mouth world	public opinions	N + N
mulot jahat	mouth evil	caustic mouth	N + A
mulot kering	mouth dry	inability to say more	N + A
mulot manis	mouth sweet	ability to speak sweetly	N + A
mulot pantat ayam	mouth buttocks chicken	deceitful mouth	N + N + N
mulot ringan	mouth slim	polite character	N + A

In the nominal compounds of Table 25, the modifier occurs after the head, except for *bijik mata* 'favorite child, apple of one's eye', where a classifier precedes the noun. The head+modifier form of these nominal compounds is interesting because modifiers do not always occur after nouns in Baba Malay (See sections 4.5.2 and 5.1.5 for examples). With most modifiers following nouns, except for classifiers, the word order of nominal compounds in Baba Malay is similar to the word order of nominal compounds in the lexifier language, Malay. Modifiers occur after noun heads, except for classifiers. For example, two blue cars would be expressed in Malay as *dua buah keréta biru* 'two CLF.big.object cars blue'. Note that modifiers occur before nominal heads in the substrate language Hokkien.

4.1.2 Noun classifiers and partitives

The use of noun classifiers and partitives (classifiers for mass or uncountable nouns) is common in Baba Malay, but non-obligatory. Noun classifiers are presented in Table 26.

Table 26: Noun classifiers in Baba Malay.

Noun classifiers	Use
ékor	animals and young children
buah	fruit
kuntum	bloom
daon	leaves
bijik	small round items
uluair (ular, uluair: snake)	durian flesh
batang	long thin items
pasang	pair

These noun classifiers can be used independently of the nouns that they modify, athough in general, they are used before nouns, together with numerals that precede the classifiers. Some examples of noun classifiers are as follows:

(145) Dua **ékor** ikan.
two **CLF.animal** fish
'two fish.'
(Peter Wee, oai:scholarspace.manoa.hawaii.edu: NL1-148, 00:01:57.9-00:01:59.1)

(146) Ini **buah** pear.
this **CLF.fruit**
'These are pears.'
(Peter Wee, oai:scholarspace.manoa.hawaii.edu: NL1-022, 00:00:27.9-00:00:28.9)

(147) Se-**kuntum** bunga.
one-**CLF.bloom** flower
'One flower.'
(Victor, oai:scholarspace.manoa.hawaii.edu: NL1-160, 00:02:04.7-00:02:05.7)

(148) Dua **bijik** intan.
Two **CLF.small.round** diamond.chip
'Two diamond chips.'
(Peter Wee, oai:scholarspace.manoa.hawaii.edu: NL1-148, 00:07:12.9-00:07:16.2)

(149) Dua **uluair** durian.
two **CLF.durian.flesh/snake**
'Two pieces of durian.'
(Peter Wee, oai:scholarspace.manoa.hawaii.edu: NL1-148, 00:04:39.5-00:04:41.3)

In addition to noun classifiers, measure words or partitives are also used by Baba Malay speakers when they quantify mass nouns (that otherwise cannot be counted) in partitive phrases. Some of these mass classifiers are presented in Table 27.

Table 27: Mass classifiers in Baba Malay.

Mass classifiers	Use
bungkus	bundle
botol	bottle

Table 27 (continued)

Mass classifiers	Use
kepéng	slice
ketol	chunk
changkay	cup
mangkok	bowl
séndok	spoon
hélay, lay, éla	sheet
gantang	gallon
chupak	quarter gallon

Some examples in which these mass classifiers are used are as follows:

(150)   Satu **bungkus** nasik
        One **bundle** cooked.rice
        'One bundle of rice.'
        (Jane Quek, oai:scholarspace.manoa.hawaii.edu: NL1-149, 00:27:14.4-00:27:15.7)

(151)   Potong-kan satu **kepéng** kék.
        cut-TR   one   **piece**   cake
        'One piece of cake.'
        (Jane Quek, oai:scholarspace.manoa.hawaii.edu: NL1-149, 00:01:55.5-00:01:59.3)

(152)   Tuang-kan satu **changkay** kopi.
        pour-TR   one   **cup**   coffee
        'One cup of coffee.'
        (Victor, oai:scholarspace.manoa.hawaii.edu: NL1-156, 00:16:08.0-00:16:10.1)

(153)   Satu **mangkok** nasik.
        One **bowl**   cooked.rice
        'One bowl of rice.'
        (Peter Wee, oai:scholarspace.manoa.hawaii.edu: NL1-148, 00:26:58.0-00:27:01.4)

(154)   Kasi gua dua **séndok** nasik.
        Give 1SG two **spoon**   cooked.rice
        'Give me two spoons of rice.'
        (Peter Wee, oai:scholarspace.manoa.hawaii.edu: NL1-148, 00:24:47.0-00:24:50.0)

(155) *Satu* **lay** *kain.*
One sheet cloth
'One sheet of cloth.'
(Jane Quek, oai:scholarspace.manoa.hawaii.edu: NL1-149, 00:08:02.5-00:08:06.0)

4.1.3 Pronouns

Pronouns here refer to a closed set of grammatical items that may substitute a noun phrase. The set of pronouns in Baba Malay includes personal pronouns, reflexives, reciprocals, and interrogative pronouns.

4.1.3.1 Personal pronouns

The following table in 28 represents the system of personal pronouns used in Baba Malay.

Table 28: Personal pronouns in Baba Malay.[50]

Personal pronouns	Use
saya	1SG (refined)[50]
gua	1SG (coarse)
kita	1PL
lu	2SG
lu-orang/ lu	2-PL
dia	3SG
dia-orang/ dia	3-PL

The personal pronominal system is a mixed system derived from Hokkien and Malay. The words for the first person (coarse) *gua* and second person *lu* are derived from Hokkien, while the rest of the terms originate from Malay.

Baba Malay speakers differentiate between two registers depending on whether they want to sound *alus* 'refined', or *kasair* 'coarse' (see section 3.8). Within the pronominal system, the first person singular is the only concept that is ostensibly marked as being *alus* or *kasair*. The word that Baba Malay derives from Malay, *saya*, is used as an *alus* term, while the word that it derives from Hokkien, *gua*, is used as a *kasair* term. It is notable that that older females appear to use *saya* more often than males

---

[50] See 3.3.5 and 3.8

or younger females.[51] That *gua* is used more often than *saya* among the Singapore Baba Malay-speaking community may be indicative that the language is undergoing change, whereby the younger speakers are no longer familiar with what is *alus* 'refined' and what is *kasair* 'coarse'. In addition to these two forms of first personal singular pronouns, Chia (1983) notes that it was common for pre-war[52] Peranakans to refer to themselves in the third person as a show of humility. This is no longer common nowadays. Other personal pronouns are not outwardly *alus* or *kasair*, although when addressing an interlocutor, it is more *alus* to use the interlocutor's name (and title if appropriate) rather than the second person singular *lu*. For example, when enquiring if one has eaten, it is more *alus* to say "Uncle Peter sudah makan? (Has Uncle Peter eaten?)", rather than "lu sudah makan? (Have you eaten?)".

Other aspects of the Baba Malay pronominal system are noteworthy. While terms are derived from both the lexifier language, Malay, and the substrate language, Hokkien, calquing occurs wherein terms for the second person and third person plurals are directly translated from Hokkien terms. The second person plural in Hokkien is *lin-lâng* '2SG-people', while the third person plural in Hokkien is *i-lâng* '3SG-people'. In the Baba Malay versions of these words, the Hokkien word for people, *lâng* is replaced by the Malay word for people, *orang*. It is curious that the first person plural in this modern Baba Malay dataset is not a direct calque of *goá-lâng* '1SG-people (Hokkien)'. There used to be a distinction between the first person plural inclusive and the first person plural exclusive, but not anymore. In earlier work, Pakir (1986:146) showed that speakers used *kita-orang* to indicate the first person inclusive pronoun and *gua-orang* to indicate the first person exclusive pronoun. This parellels the use of *kita* "1PL inclusive' and *kami* '1PL exclusive' in Malay, and *lán-lâng* '1PL inclusive' and *goá-lâng* '1PL exclusive' in Hokkien. Notably, Baba Malay speakers would have had a unique system wherein the first person plural inclusive pronoun was adapted mainly from Malay *kita* and the first person plural exclusive pronoun from Hokkien *goá-lâng*. This distinction is not found in the current dataset. These are also not reported by Lee (1999). While one might expect such an inclusive-exclusive distinction to be crucial in Baba Malay, given that it occurs in both of its component languages, speakers appear to be shifting away from both Malay and Hokkien. Conceivably, Baba Malay speakers primarily speak English in their home domain these days, and are less likely to know or be fluent in Malay or Hokkien (see section 2.5).

Terms for the second person plural pronoun, *lu-orang* and the third person plural pronoun, *dia-orang* are also undergoing change. Some speakers use *lu* (derived from Hokkien) and *dia* (derived from Malay) instead of the Hokkien-based calques for these

---

51 In fact, while females have also been observed to use *gua* for the first person singular, the researcher was told that it was not appropriate for her to use *gua* by an older male speaker during the course of fieldwork.

52 War here refers to the 1942–1945 period of the Second World War, when the Malay Archipelago was invaded by the Japanese.

concepts. This variation is also observed by Lee (1999:20), but not in the earlier work of Pakir (1986).

4.1.3.2 Reflexives

In Baba Malay, reflexives are formed by using the reflexive pronoun, *sendiri* (noted by Lee 1999). *Sendiri*, which originates from Malay, etymologically comprises *diri*, indicating 'self', and the prefix *sen-*, which is a contracted form of the numeral 'one', *satu*.[53]

As a reflexive marker, *sendiri* denotes the same referent with one of the noun phrases in a sentence. In the more typical instances, the subject and object would have the same referent, such as with examples (156), (157) and (158). The word *sendiri* replaces the pronoun or noun referent in the object noun phrase position.

(156) Gua boléh mandi **sendiri**.
 1SG   can   bathe **self**
 'I can bathe myself.'
 (Jane Quek, oai:scholarspace.manoa.hawaii.edu: NL1-150, 00:12:45.2-00:12:46.4)

(157) Budak-budak sumua pi mandi **sendiri**.
 Child-PL   all   go bathe **self**
 'All the children go bathe themselves.'
 (Peter Wee, oai:scholarspace.manoa.hawaii.edu: NL1-154, 00:12:20.9-00:12:22.6)

(158) Kita mandi **sendiri**.
 1PL   bathe **self**
 'We bathe ourselves.'
 (Peter Wee, oai:scholarspace.manoa.hawaii.edu: NL1-154, 00:09:38.5-00:09:39.5)

In instances where the reflexive replaces the object in a sentence, *sendiri* can also be used immediately after the subject as an emphatic reflexive, to reinforce the notion that the predicate concerns the subject himself, herself or itself. This is demonstrated by examples (159) and (160).

(159) Lu   **sendiri** suap **sendiri**.
 2SG **self**   feed **self**
 'You yourself feed yourself.'
 (Jane Quek, oai:scholarspace.manoa.hawaii.edu: NL1-150, 00:15:29.5-00:15:32.6)

---

53 In Malay, *sen-* is specifically used when it is followed by a voiced alveolar plosive. In other phonological environments it appears as *se-*.

(160) Dia **sendiri** mandi **sendiri.**
 3SG **self** bathe **self**
 'He himself bathes himself.'
 (Jane Quek, oai:scholarspace.manoa.hawaii.edu: NL1-150, 00:17:13.4-00:17:16.0)

Similarly, *sendiri* can be used as an emphatic reflexive in intransitive constructions where there is no object, reinforcing that the subject carried out the action himself or herself, and not someone else. Examples (161), (162) and (163) show how the reflexive is used in such intransitive constructions.

(161) Gua **sendiri** makan, lu jangan suap gua.
 1SG **self** eat, 2SG do.not feed 1SG
 'I eat (by) myself, you do not (have to) feed me.'
 (Peter Wee, oai:scholarspace.manoa.hawaii.edu: NL1-154, 00:13:08.5-00:13:14.7)

(162) Dia **sendiri** jatoh.
 3SG **self** fell
 'He himself fell.'
 (Jane Quek, oai:scholarspace.manoa.hawaii.edu: NL1-150, 00:27:33.2-00:27:34.9)

(163) Kita **sendiri** tau mandi.
 1PL **self** know bathe.
 We ourselves know how to bathe.'
 (Jane Quek, oai:scholarspace.manoa.hawaii.edu: NL1-150, 00:14:35.9-00:14:37.6)

Finally, while Lee (1999:21) suggests that reflexives can also be formed with the expression *mia diri* 'POSS self', this expression is more accurately analysed as being part of the object phrase. For instance, in example (164), *kita mia diri* refers to 'our selves or bodies', where *diri* is not an anaphora of *kita*. In fact, this expression was judged to be strange by some but not by others due to the subject matter.

(164) Kita boléh mandi **kita mia diri.**
 1PL can bathe **1PL POSS self**
 'We can bathe our selves/bodies.'
 (Jane Quek, oai:scholarspace.manoa.hawaii.edu: NL1-150, 00:14:50.4-00:14:53.5)

4.1.3.3 Reciprocals

Reciprocals in Baba Malay are indicated by the expressions *satu sama satu* 'one with one', or *satu sama lain* 'one with all' depending on the number of people involved in the predicated activity. When there are only two people involved in a reciprocal relationship, the expression *satu sama satu* 'one with one' is used as an object noun phrase, as with example (165). When more than two people are involved, the expression *satu sama lain* 'one with other' is used in the same position, as with examples (166), (167) and (168).

(165) Mary sama Lucy sayang **satu sama satu**.
       with   love   one   with   one
'Mary and Lucy love each another.'
(Peter Wee, oai:scholarspace.manoa.hawaii.edu: NL1-154, 00:00:16.0-00:00:20.2)

(166) Ini   budak-budak sumua sayang **satu sama lain**.
      this child-PL   all   love   one   with other
'These children love one another.'
(Peter Wee, oai:scholarspace.manoa.hawaii.edu: NL1-154, 00:03:12.2-00:03:18.0)

(167) Dia   adék-beradék sayang **satu sama lain**.
      3SG   sibling-PL   love   one   with other
'Them siblings love one another.'
(Victor, oai:scholarspace.manoa.hawaii.edu: NL1-161, 00:00:28.0-00:00:32.7)

(168) Itu   empat budak   sayang **satu sama lain**.
      that four   children love   one   with other
'Those four children love one another.'
(Jane Quek, oai:scholarspace.manoa.hawaii.edu: NL1-150, 00:05:03.6-00:05:15.8)

There is also some individual variation in expressing reciprocity. The following are examples of how one consultant prefers to express reciprocity, even though she is aware of the *satu sama satu/ satu sama lain* expressions. In examples (169) and (170), the expression *sama sama* 'same same' is used either before or after the predicate (note that *sama* can mean both 'with' and 'same').

(169) Mark sama Lucy **sama   sama**   sayang.
       with   same   same   love
'Mark and Lucy love each other.'
(Jane Quek, oai:scholarspace.manoa.hawaii.edu: NL1-150, 00:00:14.4-00:00:24.0)

(170) Dia empat budak sayang **sama sama**.
      3SG four child love   **same same**
      'Them four children love one another.'
      (Jane Quek, oai:scholarspace.manoa.hawaii.edu: NL1-150, 00:03:34.8-
      00:03:42.5)

4.1.3.4 Interrogative pronouns

In Baba Malay, there are five interrogative pronouns. These are *apa* 'what', *siapa* 'who', *siapa punya* 'whose', *berapa* 'how many', and *mana* for 'which'. Interrogative pronouns as used in this section refer to interrogatives that can substitute noun phrases. Not all question words are interrogative pronouns as not all can substitute noun phrases. Interrogative adverbs include *bila* 'when', *mana*[54] 'where', *apa pasal/ pasair/ sair* 'what reason (why)', *apa macham/ apacham/ amcham* 'what like (how)' and the rhetorical *mana ada* 'where EXIST' (see section 4.4.2 for more details on interrogative adverbs). A list of interrogative pronouns is provided in Table 29.

Table 29: Interrogative pronouns in Baba Malay.

Interrogative pronouns	Use
apa	what
siapa	who
siapa punya / mia / nia	whose
berapa	how many
mana	which

The following instances in examples (171) to (175) demonstrate how interrogative pronouns are used by Baba Malay speakers. More details can be found in section 5.6.10.1.

(171) Ini   ***apa?***
      This **what**
      'This (is) what?'
      (Victor, oai:scholarspace.manoa.hawaii.edu: NL1-037, 00:23:11.1-00:23:12.5)

(172) ***Siapa*** itu?
      who   that
      'Who (is) that?'
      (Peter Wee, oai:scholarspace.manoa.hawaii.edu: NL1-042, 00:23:11.1-
      00:23:12.5)

---

54 Note that *mana* means both 'where' and 'which' in Baba Malay.

(173) **Siapa punya** bubor itu?
     who POSS porridge that
     'Whose porridge (is) that?'
     (Victor, oai:scholarspace.manoa.hawaii.edu: NL1-032, 00:04:10.1-00:04:12.1)

(174) Umor lu **berapa** taon?
     age 2SG **how.many** year
     'How many years old are you?'
     (Peter Wee, oai:scholarspace.manoa.hawaii.edu: NL1-052, 00:14:51.4-00:14:53.7)

(175) **Mana** baik, **mana** satu tak baik?
     Which good **which** one NEG good
     'Which (is) good, which one (is) not good?'
     (Peter Wee, oai:scholarspace.manoa.hawaii.edu: NL1-022, 00:01:23.2-00:01:26.3)

4.2 Verbs

Verbs in Baba Malay can be identified by the following distribution patterns. They occur after noun subjects. Transitive verbs precede noun complements. Verbs also may occur after aspect markers such as progressive *ada*, and with other verbs in serial verb constructions. The following are respective examples of these distributional patterns. Example (176) illustrates the verb's position in an intransitive sentence, and example (177) does the same for a transitive sentence. Example (178) shows the verb's position after an aspect marker, and example (179) shows how verbs can be combined with other verbs in a serial verb construction.

(176) Budak itu **ketawa.**
     child that **laughs**
     'That child laughs.'
     (Jane Quek, oai:scholarspace.manoa.hawaii.edu: NL1-088, 00:09:16.0-00:09:17.8)

(177) Anjing **ambék** bakol.
     dog **take** basket
     'The dog takes the basket.'
     (Jane Quek, oai:scholarspace.manoa.hawaii.edu: NL1-088, 00:01:19.6-00:01:21.9)

(178) Dia **ada** **bikin** kuéh.
    3SG **PROG** **make** cake
    'She is making cake.'
    (Victor, oai:scholarspace.manoa.hawaii.edu: NL1-037, 00:26:46.5-00:26:47.6)

(179) **Pi tidor.**[55]
    go sleep
    'Go sleep.'
    (Jane Quek, oai:scholarspace.manoa.hawaii.edu: NL1-142, 00:03:24.1-00:03:25.5)

4.2.1 Verbal morphology

Verbs can occur on their own without affixes, such as with both *dapat* 'get' and *makan* 'eat' in example (180) and *senyum* 'smile' in example (181).

(180) **Dapat makan.**
    Get   eat
    'Gets to eat.'
    (Lilian, oai:scholarspace.manoa.hawaii.edu: NL1-079, 00:00:18.2-00:00:19.3)

(181) Budak[56] tu **senyum.**
    child   that **smile**
    'That child smiles.'
    (Jane Quek, oai:scholarspace.manoa.hawaii.edu: NL1-088, 00:00:35.9-00:00:37.7)

Verbs may also occur in reduplicated forms. In the following instances, these verbs express tentativeness, meaning that the agents are not walking anywhere or looking at anything in particular, as in examples (182) and (183) (see section 3.2.1 for more information on reduplication).

(182) **Jalan jalan**
    walk walk
    'Take a walk'
    (Jane Quek, oai:scholarspace.manoa.hawaii.edu: NL1-142, 00:02:13.1-00:02:14.6)

---

55 Subjects are commonly omitted in Baba Malay, and in this sentence, the speaker was referring to what she herself does – the sentence is not meant as an imperative.
56 For both male and female. Gender can be differentiated by adding the words *perompuan* 'female' or *jantan* 'male'. Hence *budak jantan* would indicate 'boy', while *budak perompuan* would indicate 'girl'.

(183) **Téngok téngok**
 look look
 'Take a look'
 (Jane Quek, oai:scholarspace.manoa.hawaii.edu: NL1-142, 00:02:14.6-00:02:16.2)

Other than in reduplicated forms, verbs also can take on affixes. In general, verbs undergo more affixation than nouns. The different types of affixation are discussed in sections 4.2.1.1 and 4.2.1.2.

4.2.1.1 Derivational verb morphology

In Baba Malay, there are no inflectional affixes, but a few derivational ones that change lexical meanings. This is unlike Standard Malay that utilizes *meN-* as an active or progressive marker, *di-* as a passive marker, and *ber-* as a stative marker. These derivational affixes in Baba Malay can change the part of speech. Two derivational suffixes that are productive are the transitive suffix *-kan* and the prefix *ter-* that is attached to verbs to emphasize that something was done accidentally or involved uncontrolled movement.

In Baba Malay, transitivity, or the number of arguments a verbal predicate takes, can be increased by the use of the suffix *-kan*. The addition of the suffix requires that that verb takes at least two arguments instead of one. The productive transitive marker *-kan* is attached to verbs, regardless of whether they are inherently transitive, as with examples (184) and (185), or intransitive as with examples (186) and (187).

(184) **Amék-kan** gua mia aloji.
 Take-TR 1SG POSS small.clock
 'Take my small clock.'
 (Jane Quek, oai:scholarspace.manoa.hawaii.edu: NL1-043, 00:10:09.4-00:10:11.7)

(185) **Bukak-kan** itu kepok.
 open-TR that box
 'Open that box.'
 (Jane Quek, oai:scholarspace.manoa.hawaii.edu: NL1-044, 00:02:07.9-00:02:09.4)

(186) Auntie Jane selalu **ketawa-kan** gua.
 always **laugh-TR** 1SG
 'Auntie Jane always laughs (at) me.'
 (Jane Quek, oai:scholarspace.manoa.hawaii.edu: NL1-043, 00:18:03.5-00:18:06.4)

(187) Tak   tau   apa   sair   dia   **pekék-kan**   si   John.
      NEG   know   what reason 3SG   **shout-TR**   PERSON
      'Don't know why she shouted (at) John.'
      (Jane Quek, oai:scholarspace.manoa.hawaii.edu: NL1-043, 00:11:50.7-
      00:11:53.2)

While -*kan* has an inherent grammatical function, it is best classified as a derivational suffix, rather than an inflectional one, for the reason that it is also class-changing. The suffix -*kan* can be attached to adjectives and adverbs to convert them into transitive verbs. In example (188), *panas* 'hot' is an adjective, while in example (189), *panas-kan* is a transitive verb meaning 'to heat something up'. Similarly, in example (190), *kechik* 'small' is an adjective, while in example (191), it is a transitive verb meaning 'to make something small.' Example (191) also shows how –*kan* can be suffixed to an adverb (*kurang* 'less') to make it a transitive verb.

(188) Ala   **panas** sair,   pakay kopiah   dia.
      EXCLAM   **hot**   CONF   wear   hat   3SG
      '(Goodness it is) hot indeed, wearing a hat he is.
      (Peter Wee, oai:scholarspace.manoa.hawaii.edu: NL1-043, 00:02:26.7-
      00:02:29.2)

(189) **Panas-kan** itu   kuah.
      hot-TR   that   gravy
      'Heat (up) that gravy.'
      (Jane Quek, oai:scholarspace.manoa.hawaii.edu: NL1-043, 00:44:57.0-
      00:44:59.9)

(190) Tidor   ranjang   **kechik.**
      sleep   bed   **small**
      'Sleep (on the) small bed.'
      (Victor, oai:scholarspace.manoa.hawaii.edu: NL1-043, 00:02:01.3-00:02:03.3)

(191) Kalo   mo   **kechik-kan** badan   **kurang-kan**   roti.
      if   want   **small-TR**   body   **less-TR**   bread
      'If (you) want to make your body smaller, lessen (your intake of) bread.'
      (Victor, oai:scholarspace.manoa.hawaii.edu: NL1-053, 00:12:27.5-00:12:32.0)

The other productive derivational affix in Baba Malay is the derivational prefix *ter-*. It has two main uses in Baba Malay, the first of which is to indicate that an action occurred accidentally, as shown in examples (192), (193), and (194), while the second emphasizes that the action taking place involves uncontrolled movement, as shown in examples (195), (196), and (197). It is plausible that the function of *ter-* meaning 'uncontrolled movement' extended from its use as an accidental marker, since the accidental interpretation is also associated with *ter-* in Bahasa Melayu and Bahasa Indonesia. Some of the examples could possibly be interpreted as expressing either 'accidental' or 'uncontrolled movement.' The glosses in the examples given below are hence based on context.

(192) *Itu   tortoise, dia   sendiri **ter**-balék.*
      that   3SG   self   **ACD**-return
      'That tortoise accidentally flipped itself (upside down).'
      (Jane Quek, oai:scholarspace.manoa.hawaii.edu: NL1-044, 00:10:54.4-00:10:56.6)

(193) *Dia   **ter**-gui.*
      3SG   **ACD**-kneel
      'He accidentally fell on his knees.'
      (Jane Quek, oai:scholarspace.manoa.hawaii.edu: NL1-044, 00:07:44.9-00:07:46.1)

(194) *Dia   jalan   **ter**-peléchok.*
      3SG   walk   **ACD**-twist.foot
      'He walked (and) accidentally twisted his foot.'
      (Jane Quek, oai:scholarspace.manoa.hawaii.edu: NL1-044, 00:07:43.1-00:07:44.9)

(195) *Mata   dia   **ter**-kelék.kelék.*
      eye   3SG   **MVT**-blink
      'His eyes blinked.'
      (Peter Wee, oai:scholarspace.manoa.hawaii.edu: NL1-030, 00:00:23.9-00:00:24.9)

(196) ***Ter**-lompat   lompat.*
      MVT-hop   hop
      'Hopping (here and there).'
      (Peter Wee, oai:scholarspace.manoa.hawaii.edu: NL1-030, 00:00:38.6-00:00:39.8)

(197) ***Ter**-kejar   ni   mia   apa?*
      MVT-chase this   REL   what
      '(It) chased what is this?'
      (Peter Wee, oai:scholarspace.manoa.hawaii.edu: NL1-030, 00:02:08.7-00:02:10.0)

While *ter-* is necessary in indicating that something is accidentally taking place, it is optional in indicating movement. This is demonstrated by example (198), which can be compared to example (196).

(198) Dia   lompat sini, dia   lompat sana.
      3SG   hop   here   3SG   hop   there
      'He hops here and there.'
      (Peter Wee, oai:scholarspace.manoa.hawaii.edu: NL1-030, 00:02:08.7-00:02:10.0)

The two suffixes that have been discussed in this section are derived from Malay. The transitive suffix *–kan* occurs in Malay (both spoken in Singapore/ Malaysia and Indonesia), where it is said to license arguments that are not syntactically licensed by the base verb (Cole and Son 2004), in effect, changing the valency of the verb. The prefix *ter-* also occurs in both varieties of Standard Malay, but its meaning differs slightly from Baba Malay. Again, in the Standard Malay of Malaysia and Indonesia, *ter-* has been analysed as an accidental marker (Sneddon 1996, Wee 1995), as well as an active marker, a superlative marker, a passive marker, and an abilitative marker (Chung 2011). The prefix *ter-* in Baba Malay which has the same 'accidental' meaning, has developed its own function, indicating 'uncontrolled movement'. However, it cannot be used as an active marker, a superlative marker, or as an abilitative marker.

4.2.1.2 Non-productive verb morphology

There are two more affix forms in Baba Malay that are unproductive. These are the *ber-* and *meN-* prefixes. The prefix *ber-* in Malay is recognized to correlate with the notion of middle voice (Benjamin 2009, Windstedt 1927, Windstedt 1945), wherein the agent of the verb performs an action that involves the agent herself or himself. In Baba Malay, some verbs retain reflexes of the *ber-* prefix but this prefix has no lexical meaning of its own. Examples (199) to (202) feature words that begin with the prefix form *ber-*. While a Malay speaker would recognize that there are two components in example (199), and *bergerak* would comprise the *ber-* middle voice prefix and *gerak*, meaning 'movement', a Baba Malay speaker would not perceive this word as having separate components, as with the bolded words in examples (200), (201) and (202).

(199) Tu   bangkuang tak   **bergerak.**
      that turnip   NEG   **move**
      'That turnip does not move.'
      (Victor, oai:scholarspace.manoa.hawaii.edu: NL1-034, 00:01:00.5-00:01:03.3)

(200) *Itu orang tak tau* **berenang.**
that person NEG know **swim**
'He doesn't know (how to) swim.'
(Jane Quek, oai:scholarspace.manoa.hawaii.edu: NL1-044, 00:16:31.0-00:16:33.2)

(201) *Dia-orang* **bertengkar.**
3-PL **argue**
'They argued.'
(Jane Quek, oai:scholarspace.manoa.hawaii.edu: NL1-044, 00:11:47.4-00:11:50.7)

(202) **Bergetair** *lah.*
Tremble EMP
'Tremble.'
(Peter Wee, oai:scholarspace.manoa.hawaii.edu: NL1-030, 00:05:00.2-00:05:01.7)

The presence of *ber-* is infrequent, and not used to indicate middle voice. Instead, where speakers of Standard Malay would use *ber-* to form middle voice forms of *berchakap* 'speak', *berfikir* 'think',[57] and *berlari* 'run' respectively in examples (203), (204), and (205), Baba Malay speakers prefer to produce forms without *ber-*.

(203) *Kita* **chakap** *Peranakan.*
1PL **speak**
'We speak Peranakan.'
(Peter Wee, oai:scholarspace.manoa.hawaii.edu: NL1-030, 00:05:00.2-00:05:01.7)

(204) *Goldilocks tak* **pikay** *siapa punya bubor itu.*
NEG **think** who REL porridge that
'Goldilocks did not think whose porridge that (was).'
(Victor, oai:scholarspace.manoa.hawaii.edu: NL1-032, 00:04:08.7-00:04:12.1)

(205) *Terus dia* **lari.**
straight 3SG **run**
'Straight he ran.'
(Victor, oai:scholarspace.manoa.hawaii.edu: NL1-028, 00:03:01.5-00:03:02.8)

---

57 Malay *fikir* 'think' corresponds to Baba Malay *pikay*.

In addition to the prefix form *ber-*, the prefix form *meN-* is also found, frozen as it is now occurring unproductively in Baba Malay. The prefix *meN-* is commonly analyzed as an active voice or progressive marker in the Standard Malays of Singapore and Malaysia, as well as Indonesia (Chung 1976, Nomoto and Shoho 2007, Son and Cole 2008). Again, in examples (206) to (209) below, Baba Malay speakers do not analyze these words as having two separate components, namely a *meN-* active prefix and a stem. The component words *nyalap* 'howl' in example (207) or *ngantok* 'yawn' in example (208) would not be recognized by speakers of Baba Malay who are not familiar with Standard Malay.

(206) Itu kuah sudah **menidi.**
 that gravy already **boil**
 'That gravy (is) already boiled.'
 (Jane Quek, oai:scholarspace.manoa.hawaii.edu: NL1-043, 00:45:15.2-00:45:17.3)

(207) Tu anjing **menyalap.**
 that dog howl
 'That dog howled.'
 (Victor, oai:scholarspace.manoa.hawaii.edu: NL1-034, 00:01:40.2-00:01:44.6)

(208) **Mengantok.**
 yawn
 'Yawn.'
 (Victor, oai:scholarspace.manoa.hawaii.edu: NL1-009, 00:29:44.0-00:29:45.5)

(209) Sini dua ékor **memisék.**[58]
 here two CLF.animal **whisper**
 'Here (these) two are whispering.'
 (Jane Quek, oai:scholarspace.manoa.hawaii.edu: NL1-043,00:13:10.2-00:13:13.5)

In other instances, speakers produce two versions of the verb, one with the *me-* prefix and one without the *me-* prefix. Out of over 1,100 words collected for the lexicon component of this grammar, there are only two words that commonly show up with differing forms. They are *nyanyi* and *menyanyi* 'sing' in examples (210) and (211), as well as *nangis* and *menangis* 'cry' in examples (212) and (213). While the form of *nyanyi* in (210) might be explained by the fact that the sentence is an imperative, as compared

---

[58] Note that the Malay version of *meN-bisek* is *membisek* 'whisper', the coda of the suffix agreeing in place of articulation with the onset of the first syllable on the root form *bisek*. This does not occur in Baba Malay.

to (211), examples (212) and (213) show that *meN-* does not appear to be particularly indicative of the active or progressive form as it would have been in Malay, otherwise both verb forms in (212) would have to take on the *meN-* prefix. Examples (1) and (2) are replicated as (212) and (213) here.

(210) **Nyanyi** lah, lagu terang bulan ka,
sing EMP song bright moon or
'Sing the Bright Moon song or (something else),'
(Jane Quek, oai:scholarspace.manoa.hawaii.edu: NL1-043, 00:08:26.2-00:08:28.9)

(211) Kita sama sama **menyanyi**.
1PL same same **sing**
'We sing together.'
(Jane Quek, oai:scholarspace.manoa.hawaii.edu: NL1-043, 00:08:26.2-00:08:28.9)

(212) Téngok bapak dia mati, dia tak **nangis**.
look father 3SG die 3SG NEG **cry**
'Look, his father passed away, (and) he did not cry.'
(Victor, oai:scholarspace.manoa.hawaii.edu: NL1-021, 00:32:44.0-00:32:46.3)

(213) Dia kuluair dari rumah **menangis**.
3SG go.out from house **cry**
'She left the house crying.'
(Victor, oai:scholarspace.manoa.hawaii.edu: NL1-043, 00:04:18.3-00:04:20.9)

As *meN-* is not lexically meaningful, both versions of each word above can be treated as different variations of the same word, but denoting the same notion. Again, it is much more common for Baba Malay speakers to not use the *meN-* form at all, as demonstrated in the following examples. Malay speakers would otherwise replace *bacha* 'read' with *membacha* in (214), *dengair* 'listen' with *mendengar*[59] in (215), and *jual* 'sell' with *menjual* in (216) to indicate that these verbs are active or progressive.

(214) Mak tu ada **bacha** lagik.
mother that PROG **read** more
'That mother is reading more.'
(Jane Quek, oai:scholarspace.manoa.hawaii.edu: NL1-043, 00:08:53.3-00:08:57.0)

---

59 There is no *-air* form in Malay.

(215) Gua tak **dengair** apa lu chakap.
    1SG NEG **hear** what 2SG speak
    'I do not hear what you speak.'
    (Jane Quek, oai:scholarspace.manoa.hawaii.edu: NL1-043, 00:09:17.6-00:09:20.7)

(216) Orang **jual** batu.
    person **sell** stone
    'The person sells stone.'
    (Victor, oai:scholarspace.manoa.hawaii.edu: NL1-043, 00:03:06.1-00:03:07.7)

Hence, both *ber-* (middle voice marker in Malay) and *meN-* (active or progressive marker in Malay) prefix forms are neither productive nor lexically meaningful in Baba Malay.

4.2.1.3 Verbal compounds

Verbal compounds in Baba Malay are verb phrases comprising a verb and a modifier. Modifiers include noun, adjective, verb, as well as preposition phrase. Table 30 lists examples of verbal compounds found in the language, as well as their patterns of modification. For the purpose of demonstration, the verbs *buang* 'throw', *buat* 'do, make', and *naik* 'ascend' are used (note that there are two words for 'do, make' in Baba Malay, the other word being *bikin*). None of these verbal patterns are productive.

Table 30: List of some verbal compounds in Baba Malay.

Verbal compound	Meaning of individual lexemes	Meaning of compound	Parts of speech
buang ayé	throw water	urinate	V + N
buang ayé besair	throw water big	defecate	V + N + A
buang ayé kechik	throw water small	urinate	V + N + A
buang buang	throw throw	exorcise	V + V
buang mata	throw eye	keep an eye on someone or something	V + N
buang mulot	throw mouth	convey by speaking (as opposed to writing)	V + N
buang se-belah	throw one-side	aside from	V + Num + Prep
buang segan	throw shy	stretch upon waking up	V + A
buang terbiat	throw attitude	throw tantrum	V + N
buat bodoh	do/ make stupid	feign ignorance	V + N
buat mahal	do/ make expensive	play hard to get	V + A

Table 30 (continued)

Verbal compound	Meaning of individual lexemes	Meaning of compound	Parts of speech
buat malu	do/ make embarrassed	cause embarrassment	V + A
buat mungka	do/ make face	be sour-faced	V + N
buat suay	do/ make unlucky	cause misfortune	V + A
buat susah	do/ make difficult	cause difficulty	V + A
buat tak dengair	do/ make not hear	pretend to not hear	V + NEG + V
naik baik	ascend good	change for good	V + A
naik chuan	ascend breathless	be breathless	V + A
naik darah	ascend blood	be angry	V + N
naik geléték	ascend tickle	be up to mischief	V + V
naik geram	ascend furious	be furious	V + A
naik gila	ascend mad	be mad	V + A
naik lemak	ascend cooked.in.coconut.milk	be up to mischief	V + A
naik pangkat	ascend rank	be promoted	V + N
naik sedap	ascend delicious	be satisfied	V + A
naik seram	ascend frightening	be frightened	V + A

In general, the shape of verbal compounds follows that of a verb phrase comprising verb and complement (see section 5.2.9).

4.3 Adjectives

Adjectives in Baba Malay occur before or after the nouns that they modify. This pattern of modification is illustrated by example (217). When used before a noun, adjectives usually occur with relative clause marker *punya* (contracted forms being *mia* and *nia*), as with example (218). Adjectives may also occur after the verb *ada* when it functions as a copula as in example (219) (see section 5.2.5 for other usages of *ada*). It is however much more common for the copula to be omitted, as with example (220).

(217) Beruang **kechik** ada mangkok **kechik**.
       bear   small   have bowl   small
       'Small bear has (a) small bowl.'
       (Victor, oai:scholarspace.manoa.hawaii.edu: NL1-028, 00:01:20.9-00:01:22.4)

(218) *Cherita-kan gua **betol** mia cherita.*
story-TR 1SG **real** REL story
'Tell me a real story.'
(Jane Quek, oai:scholarspace.manoa.hawaii.edu: NL1-028, 00:03:20.8-00:03:26.7)

(219) *Ada **baik** tak a?*
COP **good** NEG COP
'Are (you) good or not?'
(Jane Quek, oai:scholarspace.manoa.hawaii.edu: NL1-142, 00:00:09.9-00:00:11.2)

(220) *Taukay kebun ni **kiam** sair.*
boss garden this **miserly** CONF
'This boss (of the) garden is miserly indeed.'
(Victor, oai:scholarspace.manoa.hawaii.edu: NL1-028, 00:01:03.7-00:01:05.8)

4.3.1 Adjectival morphology

Adjectives can and most often occur independently, without any suffixation, as with *mahal* 'expensive' and *chanték* 'beautiful' in examples (221) and (222).

(221) *Tapi **mahal** lah.*
but **expensive** EMP
'But (it is) expensive.'
(Jane Quek, oai:scholarspace.manoa.hawaii.edu: NL1-142, 00:02:30.8-00:02:32.9)

(222) ***Chanték** sekali.*
beautiful very
'Very beautiful.'
(Jane Quek, oai:scholarspace.manoa.hawaii.edu: NL1-142, 00:02:35.7-00:02:37.2)

Adjectives can also occur in reduplicated forms, to indicate tentativeness (see section 3.2.1 and section 5.2.5.6).

(223) ***Tawair-tawair.***
Tasteless-tasteless
'Kind of tasteless.'
(Jane Quek, oai:scholarspace.manoa.hawaii.edu: NL1-142, 00:11:12.7-00:11:15.0)

In other instances, when reduplicated, adjectives function as adverbs (see sections 3.2.1 and 4.4). Adjectives are also not formed with affixes. When adjectives are affixed with nominalizer *-an*, nouns are formed instead (see section 4.1.1.1).

4.4 Adverbs

Adverbs modify adjectives or verbs. They may precede or follow adjectives, as with examples (224) and (225). They may also precede or follow the verb phrases that they modify, as with examples (226) and (227).

(224) Kambing dia kuat **sekali.**
goat 3SG strong **very**
'The goat, it (is) very strong.'
(Peter Wee, oai:scholarspace.manoa.hawaii.edu: NL1-142, 00:01:52.8-00:01:54.6)

(225) Ada satu bangkuang dia téngok **betol** besair.
EXIST one turnip 3SG see **really** big
'There was one turnip he saw (that was) really big.'
(Victor, oai:scholarspace.manoa.hawaii.edu: NL1-034, 00:00:27.0-00:00:30.5)

(226) Dia [peték tu buah pear] **lagik.**
3SG pluck that CLF.fruit **again**
'He plucked those pears again.'
(Victor, oai:scholarspace.manoa.hawaii.edu: NL1-028, 00:01:50.5-00:01:53.0)

(227) Si tua tu **pelan-pelan** [angkat satu-satu.]
PERSON old that **slow-slow** lift one-one
'That old person slowly lifted one by one.'
(Peter Wee, oai:scholarspace.manoa.hawaii.edu: NL1-028, 00:04:10.4-00:04:11.5)

4.4.1 Adverbial morphology

Adverbs occur independently on their own, as with *selalu* 'always' and *macham* 'like that' in examples (228) and (229). Note that the short form of *pegi* 'go' is *pi*.

(228) Dia **selalu** pi sana.
3SG **always** go there
'She always goes there.'
(Jane Quek, oai:scholarspace.manoa.hawaii.edu: NL1-142, 00:02:39.8-00:02:41.2)

(229) *Dia-orang sudah biasa* **macham.**
 3-PL already used.to.it **like.that**
 'They are already used to it more or less.'
 (Jane Quek, oai:scholarspace.manoa.hawaii.edu: NL1-142, 00:04:58.9-00:05:01.1)

There is no affixation process that creates adverbs. However, reduplication of adjectives does result in the formation of adverbs. Examples (230) to (233) illustrate how adverbs are created from the reduplication of adjectives.

(230) **Pelan-pelan,** *satu-satu, budak masok-kan.*
 slow-slow one-one child enter-TR
 'Slowly, one-by-one, the children put (the pears) in.'
 (Peter Wee, oai:scholarspace.manoa.hawaii.edu: NL1-022, 00:04:58.9-00:05:01.1)

(231) *Apa sair gua chakap lu dudok* **diam-diam?**
 what reason 1SG speak 2SG sit **quiet-quiet**
 'Why are you sitting quietly (while) I speak?'
 (Jane Quek, oai:scholarspace.manoa.hawaii.edu: NL1-045, 00:19:50.6-00:19:52.8)

(232) *Sandah* **baik-baik.**
 lean **good-good**
 'Lean properly.'
 (Jane Quek, oai:scholarspace.manoa.hawaii.edu: NL1-044, 00:06:23.4-00:06:24.7)

(233) *Misti angkat* **baik-baik.**
 Must carry **good-good**
 'Must carry properly.'
 (Peter Wee, oai:scholarspace.manoa.hawaii.edu: NL1-022, 00:01:05.5-00:01:07.2)

It is notable that these adverbs typically formed by reduplication may also occur in a non-reduplicated form in casual speech, as with examples (234) and (235). Essentially, adjectives can function as adverbs. Note that example (234) features both the reduplicated form *lekas-lekas* 'quickly', and the non-reduplicated form *lekas*, which also functions as an adverb that modifies the verb, instead of as an adjective.

(234) **Lekas-lekas** datang **lekas** datang.
 quick-quick come quick come
 'Quickly come quickly come.'
 (Peter Wee, oai:scholarspace.manoa.hawaii.edu: NL1-022, 00:04:58.9-
 00:05:01.1)

(235) Ketawa ketawa **lekair** senyum.
 laugh laugh quick smile
 'Laugh, laugh and quickly smile.'
 (Jane Quek, oai:scholarspace.manoa.hawaii.edu: NL1-044, 00:06:16.5-
 00:06:18.0)

Besides not having affixes that form adverbs, Baba Malay also does not have adverbial compounds.

4.4.2 Interrogative adverbs

Interrogative adverbs include: *bila* 'when', *mana* 'where', *apa pasal*, literally 'what reason', and *apa macham*, 'what like'. *Apa pasal* and *apa macham* function as 'why' and 'how' respectively. *Mana ada*, literally meaning 'where EXIST' is used as a rhetorical question, in cases where the implied answer is in the negative. While interrogative pronouns can substitute for the noun phrase, interrogative adverbs can be used to substitute the adverbial clause. Interrogative adverbs usually concern time, location, or the manner in which something is done, except for *mana ada* 'where EXIST'. Note that there are two other forms for *pasal* 'reason' in *apa pasal* 'why', the first being the refined form *pasair* (see section 3.3.5), the second being *sair*, a shortened version of *pasair*. *Sair* is the most commonly used form in casual speech. The shortened version of *macham* 'like' in *apa macham* 'how' is *cham*. *Amcham* is also used as a contracted form of *apa macham*. The complete list of interrogative adverbs in Baba Malay is provided in Table 31.

Table 31: Interrogative adverbs in Baba Malay.

Interrogative adverbs	Use
bila	when
mana	where
apa pasal/ apa pasair/ apa sair	why 'what reason'
apa macham/ apa cham/ amcham	how 'what like'
mana ada	rhetorical 'where EXIST'

Examples (236) to (240) demonstrate how these interrogative adverbs are used in Baba Malay. More details can be found in section 5.6.10.1.

(236) **Bila**   gua   panggay   John   datang?
      when   1SG   ask   come
      'When did I ask to come?'
      (Jane Quek, oai:scholarspace.manoa.hawaii.edu: NL1-093, 00:07:47.7-00:07:49.6)

(237) **Mana**   pi   si   Mary?
      where   go   PERSON
      'Where goes Mary?'
      (Victor, oai:scholarspace.manoa.hawaii.edu: NL1-037, 00:08:42.2-00:08:43.5)

(238) **Apa**   **sair**   gua   chakap   lu   tak   jawab   gua?
      what   **reason**   1SG   speak   2SG   NEG   answer   1SG
      'Why are you not answering when I speak?'
      (Jane Quek, oai:scholarspace.manoa.hawaii.edu: NL1-045, 00:20:03.9-00:20:06.9)

(239) **Apa**   **macham**   mo   masak   iték   tim?
      what **like**   want   cook   duck   double-boil
      'How (do I) want to cook double-boiled duck (soup)?'
      (Victor, oai:scholarspace.manoa.hawaii.edu: NL1-037, 00:04:30.9-00:04:33.1)

(240) **Mana**   ada   piso?
      where EXIST   knife
      'Where is the knife (implying there is no knife)?'
      (Victor, oai:scholarspace.manoa.hawaii.edu: NL1-037, 00:21:02.8-00:21:05.6)

4.5 Determiners

Determiners in Baba Malay include person markers, demonstratives, numerals, and other quantifiers.

4.5.1 Person marker

Si is used as a person marker in Baba Malay. It can be used directly before a person's name, or with attributes that describe a person (usually with personal pronouns, nouns and adjectives), to indicate that a particular person is being spoken about. Examples (241) to (244) demonstrate how *si* is used in the language. The usage of *si* is not mandatory. For example, *si* does not precede *John* in (241), even though it precedes *Mary* in the same sentence.

(241) Apa   sair   **si**   Mary   bunoh John?
      what   reason **PERSON**   Mary   kill   John?
      'Why did Mary kill John?'
      (Victor, oai:scholarspace.manoa.hawaii.edu: NL1-037, 00:01:06.7-00:01:09.1)

(242) **Si**   sa   ko   bongsu.
      PERSON   third   paternal.aunt   youngest.child
      'Youngest third paternal aunt.'
      (Lilian, oai:scholarspace.manoa.hawaii.edu: NL1-079, 00:09:01.2-00:09:02.9)

(243) Téngok **si**   tua   tu   peték   dia   mia   pear.
      look   **PERSON**   old   that   pluck   3SG   POSS
      'Look at the old man plucking his pear.'
      (Peter Wee, oai:scholarspace.manoa.hawaii.edu: NL1-022, 00:05:36.9-00:05:38.7)

(244) Bila   gua   boléh   jumpa   **si**   ano   ni?
      when   1SG   can   meet   **PERSON**   anonymous   this
      'When can I meet this anonymous person?'
      (Peter Wee, oai:scholarspace.manoa.hawaii.edu: NL1-107, 00:12:11.7-00:12:15.2)

The usage of *si* in Baba Malay can be attributed to Malay, where it is also used as an optional person marker. There is no similar person marker in Hokkien, except for *eng* which is used in specific kinship terms (see section 7.1.2).

4.5.2 Demonstratives

The four demonstratives in Baba Malay are *ini* 'this' and *itu* 'that', as well as *sini* 'here' and *sana* 'there'. The shortened forms of *ini* 'this' and *itu* 'that' are *ni* and *tu* respectively. *Ini* and *itu* can be used as demonstrative pronouns as with (245) and (246), where these words stand in for nouns in a deictic way – these words can only be understood in context.

(245) **Ini**   buah   pear.
      this   CLF.fruit
      'This is a pear.'
      (Peter Wee, oai:scholarspace.manoa.hawaii.edu: NL1-022, 00:00:27.9-00:00:28.9)

(246) Lepas **itu** kita boléh buat soup bangkuang.
after **that** 1PL can make turnip
'After that we can make turnip soup'
(Victor, oai:scholarspace.manoa.hawaii.edu: NL1-034, 00:00:38.8-00:00:46.6)

Besides demonstrative pronouns, *ini* and *itu* can also be used as demonstrative determiners that occur together with nouns. As determiners, *ini* and *itu* can precede or follow nouns, as with examples (247) and (248), and examples (249) and (250) respectively.

(247) **Ni** tiga ékor babi tinggal sama mak babi.
this three CLF.animal pig live with mother pig
'These three pigs live with mother pig.'
(Victor, oai:scholarspace.manoa.hawaii.edu: NL1-035, 00:00:23.0-00:00:25.0)

(248) **Itu** bangkuang pun tak bergerak.
that turnip also NEG move
'That turnip also does not move.'
(Victor, oai:scholarspace.manoa.hawaii.edu: NL1-034, 00:01:20.0-00:01:22.2)

(249) Budak **ini** sangat kechik lah.
child **this** very small EMP
'This child is very small.'
(Peter Wee, oai:scholarspace.manoa.hawaii.edu: NL1-022, 00:03:23.5-00:03:25.3)

(250) Sekarang dia tolak bicycle **itu**.
now 3SG push **that**
'Now he is pushing that bicycle.'
(Peter Wee, oai:scholarspace.manoa.hawaii.edu: NL1-022, 00:04:34.6-00:04:36.3)

Sini 'here' and *sana* 'there' are also to be interpreted deictically, based on context. Examples (251) to (254) demonstrate the uses of *sini* and *sana*.

(251) Kita **sini** tak-a[60] pokok.
1PL **here** NEG-have tree
'We do not have the tree here.'
(Peter Wee, oai:scholarspace.manoa.hawaii.edu: NL1-022, 00:00:35.5-00:00:36.9)

---

60 Note that the shortened version of *tak ada* 'NEG have' is *tak -a*.

(252) Lama   tak   jalan **sini**.
      Long.time NEG   walk **here**
      '(I have) not walked here (for) a long time.'
      (Jane Quek, oai:scholarspace.manoa.hawaii.edu: NL1-142, 00:00:06.5-00:00:08.3)

(253) Pusing **sini** pusing **sana**.
      turn   **here** turn   **there**
      'Turns here and turns there.'
      (Jane Quek, oai:scholarspace.manoa.hawaii.edu: NL1-044, 00:22:09.8-00:22:11.6)

(254) Dia tau **sana** ada   orang.
      3SG know **there** EXIST people
      'He knows there is someone (there).'
      (Victor, oai:scholarspace.manoa.hawaii.edu: NL1-142, 00:02:23.1-00:02:24.8)

4.5.3 Numerals

Two sets of cardinal numbers are used. One set is derived from Malay, while the other from Hokkien. In general, the Malay terms for numbers are used. Hokkien numerical terms are used specifically with lunar calendar dates and kinship terms.

Table 32 lists the set of Malay-derived numbers used in Baba Malay. Note that *se-* is short for *satu* 'one', and *satu* is the only numeral that has its own contracted prefix version.

Table 32: Baba Malay numerals derived from Malay.

Numeral	Use	Numeral	Use
satu	1	se-belas	11
dua	2	dua-belas	12
tiga	3	tiga-belas	13
empat	4	dua-puloh	20
lima	5	tiga-puloh	30
enam	6	empat-puloh	40
tujoh	7	empat-puloh satu	41
lapan	8	se-ratus	100
semilan	9	dua-ratus	200
se-puloh	10	se-ribu	1000

Examples (255) and (256) show how these Malay-derived general numerals are used.

(255) Ada **satu** orang tua lah.
EXIST **one** person old EMP
'There is an old person.'
(Victor, oai:scholarspace.manoa.hawaii.edu: NL1-028, 00:00:21.5-00:00:24.0)

(256) Ada **tiga** ékor beruang.
EXIST **three** CLF.animal bear
'There are three bears.'
(Victor, oai:scholarspace.manoa.hawaii.edu: NL1-032, 00:00:25.2-00:00:27.3)

On the other hand, the Hokkien-derived numbers are only used for particular domains that are discussed using Hokkien terms. These include kinship and lunar calendar dates (see sections 7.1.2 and 7.1.3 respectively). The lunar system is used in particular for keeping track of Chinese festivities, which are traditionally important to the Peranakans. Note that there are fifteen days to the lunar month, thus Hokkien numbers used in Baba Malay do not usually exceed fifteen. Table 33 lists the relevant numerals that have been derived from Hokkien.

Table 33: Baba Malay numerals derived from Hokkien.

Numeral	Use	Numeral	Use
it	1	gau	9
ji	2	chap	10
sa	3	chap-it	11
si	4	chap-ji	12
gor	5	chap-sa	13
lak	6	chap-si	14
chit	7	chap-gor	15
puay	8		

Examples (257) and (258) show how these Hokkien-derived numerals are used.

(257) **Ji** pék.
two father's.elder.brother
'Second uncle (who is older than one's father).'
(Jane Quek, oai:scholarspace.manoa.hawaii.edu: NL1-132, 00:07:50.6-00:07:52.0)

(258) *Bila   chuay   it   chap-go gua pi sohio.*
      when beginning.lunar.month **one** **fifteen** 1SG go burn.incense
      'I will go burn incense on the first and the fifteenth of the lunar month.'
      (Victor, oai:scholarspace.manoa.hawaii.edu: NL1-171, 00:09:53.9-00:09:56.8)

4.5.3.1 Other numerical expressions

Odd-numbered items are referred to as *ganjil*, while a collection of even-numbered items is referred to as being in a pair or *pasang*.

(259) *Bila   kita tangkap gambair,*
      when 1PL   capture picture
      *kita tak suka **ganjil**,   mesti ber-pasang.*[61]
      1PL NEG like **odd.number** must POSS-pair
      'when we take photographs, we do not like odd numbers, (we) must have pairs.'
      (Peter Wee, oai:scholarspace.manoa.hawaii.edu: NL1-148, 00:12:02.8-00:12:09.8)

While *ganjil* cannot be used to count, *pasang* can be used for counting items.

(260) *Se-**pasang** gelang   tangan.*
      one-**pair**   bracelet hand
      'One pair of hand bracelets.'
      (Peter Wee, oai:scholarspace.manoa.hawaii.edu: NL1-148, 00:09:56.6-00:10:06.7)

(261) *Se-**pasang** kasot   manék*
      one-**pair**   shoes bead
      'One pair of beaded shoes.'
      (Peter Wee, oai:scholarspace.manoa.hawaii.edu: NL1-148, 00:08:24.0-00:08:31.3)

Pasang can also be used to refer to two items that may not form natural pairs such as shoes or bracelets.[62] What this means is that in an example such as (262), the speaker is referring to two pairs of pants when he uses the term *se-pasang*, and not a single pair (according to the Western concept of what a pair of pants comprises).

---

61 Only instance where *ber-* appears to indicate some notion of possession.
62 The Peranakan bride wears one on each hand.

(262) Se-***pasang*** suluair.
one-**pair**   pants
'one pair of pants (technically two pants).'
(Peter Wee, oai:scholarspace.manoa.hawaii.edu: NL1-148, 00:08:54.3-
00:08:56.4)

Other numerical expressions include *satu-satu* (one by one), *dua-dua* (two by two), and so on and so forth. An example of such use can be found in (263).

(263) ***Satu-satu,*** budak   masok-kan.
one-one   child   put.in-TR
'One by one, children put in (the pears).'
(Peter Wee, oai:scholarspace.manoa.hawaii.edu: NL1-022, 00:05:51.4-
00:05:42.3)

4.5.4 Quantifiers

Quantifiers in Baba Malay include these terms: *sumua* 'all', *manyak* 'many', *berapa* 'some', and *sikit* 'little'. These quantifiers can be used on their own as nouns, or be used to modify other nouns and adjectives (see section 5.3.6 for information on the modification of adjectival phrases). The following examples demonstrate how they are used in Baba Malay. Example (264) shows how the quantifier can be used as a noun on its own. Examples (265), (266) and (267) show how these typically modify nouns, and example (268) demonstrates how quantifiers can modify adjectives too.

(264) ***Sumua*** kata sedap.
all   say delicious
All say (it's) delicious.
(Jane Quek, oai:scholarspace.manoa.hawaii.edu: NL1-142, 00:10:04.8-
00:10:05.8)

(265) Kita ***sumua*** ada   chakap sama tu   dua budak.
1PL **all**   PROG   talk   with that two child
'All of us are talking to the two boys.'
(Victor, oai:scholarspace.manoa.hawaii.edu: NL1-071, 00:16:41.5-00:16:49.8)

(266) Makan ikan ***manyak***.
eat   fish **many**
'Eat a lot of fish.'
(Lilian, oai:scholarspace.manoa.hawaii.edu: NL1-079, 00:03:44.4-00:03:46.6)

(267) *Tu   dua budak chakap sama kita **berapa** orang.*
      that two child talk   with 1SG   **some** people
      'Those two children talked to some of us.'
      (Victor, oai:scholarspace.manoa.hawaii.edu: NL1-071, 00:18:06.8-00:18:09.3)

(268) *Asien-asin   **sikit.***
      somewhat.salty **little**
      'A little salty.'
      (Jane Quek, oai:scholarspace.manoa.hawaii.edu: NL1-142, 00:11:18.0-00:11:20.8)

4.6 Prepositions

Prepositions here refer to a closed set of lexical items that occur before the noun phrase complement. Adverbial phrases which modify main predicates are formed when prepositions are used in conjunction with these noun phrase complements. Prepositions in Baba Malay include general prepositions *dekat* and *di*, *dalam* 'inside', *dari* 'from', *sampay* 'until' and *sama* 'with'. Other prepositions include those that specifically concern location, such as *depan* 'front', *se-belah* 'beside (literally: one-side)', *belakang* 'behind', *atas* 'top', and *bawah* 'bottom'. General prepositions *dekat* and *di* can precede the use of these prepositions for locations). Table 34 provides a list of all prepositions found in Baba Malay.

Table 34: List of prepositions in Baba Malay.

Prepositions	Uses
dekat	general prepositions
di	at, in, to, on
dalam (dekat dalam, di dalam)	inside
depan (dekat depan, di depan)	front
se-belah (dekat se-belah, di se-belah)	beside (literally: one-side)
belakang (dekat belakang, di belakang)	behind
atas (dekat atas, di atas)	top
bawah (dekat bawah, di bawah)	bottom
dari	from
sampay	until
sama	with

Among these, *dekat* (contracted version: *kat*) has the literal meaning of 'near', as shown by its use in example (269). Its use as a general preposition is a product of grammaticalization. It is used to denote the concepts of *at*, as demonstrated by examples (270) and (271), *in*, as with example (272), *to*, as with example (273), and *on*, as with example (274).

(269) *Kupukupu trebang **di** dekat itu mia anjing.*
butterfly fly **PREP** near that REL dog
'The butterfly flew near that dog.'
(Peter Wee, oai:scholarspace.manoa.hawaii.edu: NL1-030, 00:01:36.8-00:01:41.7)

(270) *Dia tarok **kat** depan.*
3SG put **PREP** front
'He put (it) in front.'
(Peter Wee, oai:scholarspace.manoa.hawaii.edu: NL1-022, 00:03:05.0-00:03:06.4)

(271) ***Dekat** dia nia kebun.*
PREP 3SG POSS garden
'At his garden.'
(Victor, oai:scholarspace.manoa.hawaii.edu: NL1-034, 00:00:22.0-00:00:23.4)

(272) *Se-kali dia angkat tulang itu **dekat** mulot dia.*
one-time 3SG lift bone that **PREP** mouth 3SG
'Once it lifted that bone in its mouth.'
(Peter Wee, oai:scholarspace.manoa.hawaii.edu: NL1-030, 00:02:46.5-00:02:48.6)

(273) *Dia salin-kan **dekat** bakol.*
3SG transfer-TR **PREP** basket
'He transferred (the pears) to the basket.'
(Peter Wee, oai:scholarspace.manoa.hawaii.edu: NL1-022, 00:00:50.8-00:00:55.4)

(274) *Satu couple ada tarok dia mia kain **dekat** rumpot.*
one PROG put 3SG POSS cloth **PREP** grass
'One couple is putting their cloth on the grass.'
(Jane Quek, oai:scholarspace.manoa.hawaii.edu: NL1-088, 00:05:36.3-00:05:41.3)

Di is another general preposition in Baba Malay, whose use is derived from Malay, in which it is used to indicate 'at'. It is used in sentences where *dekat* is already used to denote 'near', as with examples (275) and (276). Example (269) is replicated here as example (275). *Di* can also be used in a more general sense, and not precede other prepositions, as with examples (277) and (278). *Di* is much less frequently used than *dekat*, and may be a later development in Baba Malay, as speakers begin to borrow more from Malay.

(275) Kupukupu trebang **di** dekat itu mia anjing.
butterfly fly **PREP** near that REL dog
'The butterfly flew near that dog.'
(Peter Wee, oai:scholarspace.manoa.hawaii.edu: NL1-030, 00:01:36.8-00:01:41.7)

(276) Kerekot **di** dekat panjang.
bent.and.curled.up **PREP** near bed
'Bent and curled up on the bed.'
(Lilian, oai:scholarspace.manoa.hawaii.edu: NL1-079, 00:04:26.2-00:04:28.5)

(277) Datang **di** tepi sunggay.
come **PREP** side river
'Came to the side of the river.'
(Peter Wee, oai:scholarspace.manoa.hawaii.edu: NL1-030, 00:02:14.1-00:02:17.3)

(278) Tulang **di** mulot, buang **di** sunggay.
bone **PREP** mouth throw **PREP** river
'Bone in the mouth, thrown into the river.'
(Peter Wee, oai:scholarspace.manoa.hawaii.edu: NL1-030, 00:02:14.1-00:02:17.3)

Another preposition in Baba Malay is *dalam* 'inside'. It can be used on its own, as with example (279), and it can also be used together with the general preposition *dekat*, as demonstrated by examples (280) and (281).

(279) Dia-orang punggot itu buah pear masok **dalam** bakol.
3-PL pick.up that CLF.fruit enter **inside** basket
'They picked up those pears (and) put (them) inside the basket.'
(Victor, oai:scholarspace.manoa.hawaii.edu: NL1-028, 00:03:56.1-00:03:58.5)

(280) Dia tarok bunga **kat** dalam kepok.
3SG put flower **PREP** inside box
'He put flowers inside the box.'
(Jane Quek, oai:scholarspace.manoa.hawaii.edu: NL1-088, 00:04:07.9-00:04:09.9)

(281) Dia   mia   kodok **kat**   **dalam**   sana.
      3SG   POSS   frog   **PREP**   **inside** there
      'His frog (is) inside there.'
      (Jane Quek, oai:scholarspace.manoa.hawaii.edu: NL1-088, 00:09:50.3-00:09:52.8)

Depan is used to indicate 'front'. Similarly, *depan* can be used independently of other prepositions, as with examples (282) and (283). Other prepositions such as *di* and *dekat (kat)* may also precede *depan*, as with examples (284) and (285).

(282) **Depan** carpark ada   ini   kebun   bunga.
      front   EXIST   this   garden flower
      'In front of the carpark there is this flower garden.'
      (Peter Wee, oai:scholarspace.manoa.hawaii.edu: NL1-107, 00:07:32.8-00:07:38.7)

(283) Kebun   bunga   **depan** carpark.
      garden flower **front** carpark
      'The flower garden is in front of the carpark.'
      (Peter Wee, oai:scholarspace.manoa.hawaii.edu: NL1-107, 00:07:51.2-00:07:54.6)

(284) **Di**   **depan** carpark nanti jumpa satu kebun   bunga.
      PREP **front** carpark later meet   one   garden flower
      'In front of the carpark (you) will see one flower garden.'
      (Peter Wee, oai:scholarspace.manoa.hawaii.edu: NL1-107, 00:08:12.0-00:08:17.2)

(285) Dia   tarok **kat**   **depan**.
      3SG   put   PREP   front
      'He puts (it) in front.'
      (Peter Wee, oai:scholarspace.manoa.hawaii.edu: NL1-022, 00:03:04.4-00:03:06.4)

Se-belah, literally 'one-side' is used to indicate 'besides.' It can used independently as with examples (286) and (287). *Se-belah* can also be used with a preceding general preposition, as demonstrated by example (288).

(286) **Se-belah**   park   satu   keday   kopi.
      one-side   one   shop   coffee
      'Beside the park (is) one coffee shop.'
      (Victor, oai:scholarspace.manoa.hawaii.edu: NL1-103, 00:11:30.9-00:11:34.1)

(287) Lu   mesti seberang sempang   se-belah supermarket.
      2SG   must   cross   traffic.junction **one-side**
      'You must cross the junction beside the supermarket.'
      (Victor, oai:scholarspace.manoa.hawaii.edu: NL1-103, 00:14:22.6-00:14:27.1)

(288) **Di   se-belah,** dia   ketok   apa?
      PREP   one-side 3SG   knock   what
      'Beside, they are knocking what?'
      (Jane Quek, oai:scholarspace.manoa.hawaii.edu: NL1-043, 00:14:31.8-00:14:33.5)

Belakang is used to denote 'behind', as demonstrated by examples (289) to (291).

(289) Tempat buang ayé   **belakang** restaurant sair.
      place   throw water **behind**   CONF
      'The toilet is behind the restaurant indeed.'
      (Victor, oai:scholarspace.manoa.hawaii.edu: NL1-103, 00:13:29.4-00:13:33.5)

(290) **Belakang** restaurant tu   ada   chiwan.
      behind   that   EXIST   toilet
      'Behind that restaurant there is a toilet.'
      (Peter Wee, oai:scholarspace.manoa.hawaii.edu: NL1-107, 00:05:29.4-00:05:34.2)

(291) Anjing utan   kejair **belakang** dia.
      dog   jungle chase   **behind**   3SG
      'The wolf chased behind him.'
      (Victor, oai:scholarspace.manoa.hawaii.edu: NL1-035, 00:04:22.3-00:04:23.9)

Atas is used to indicate 'top', as shown in examples (292) to (293).

(292) Dia   naik   tangga   **atas** pokok.
      3SG   ascend   ladder   **top**   tree
      'He climbs a ladder to the top of the tree.'
      (Peter Wee, oai:scholarspace.manoa.hawaii.edu: NL1-022, 00:01:08.6-00:01:12.1)

(293) Rumah-rumah   **atas** bukit.
      house-PL   **top**   mountain
      'The houses are on top of the mountain.'
      (Peter Wee, oai:scholarspace.manoa.hawaii.edu: NL1-030, 00:03:58.2-00:04:00.6)

(294) Kodok **dekat atas** itu yacht senang.
 frog **PREP top** that relax
 'The frog is on top of that yacht relaxing.'
 (Jane Quek, oai:scholarspace.manoa.hawaii.edu: NL1-088, 00:00:53.5-00:00:56.4)

Bawah is used to denote 'bottom', as with example (295).

(295) Dia dudok **bawah** pokok.
 3SG sit **bottom** tree
 'He sat at the bottom of the tree.'
 (Peter Wee, oai:scholarspace.manoa.hawaii.edu: NL1-022, 00:01:34.9-00:01:37.1)

The notion 'from' is expressed by the preposition *dari*, as with examples (296) to (298).

(296) Si sa ko **dari** mana?
 PERSON three paternal.aunt **from** where
 'Third paternal aunt from where?'
 (Lilian, oai:scholarspace.manoa.hawaii.edu: NL1-079, 00:08:49.3-00:08:53.2)

(297) Dia jatoh **dari** ranjang.
 3SG fall **from** bed
 'She fell from the bed.'
 (Victor, oai:scholarspace.manoa.hawaii.edu: NL1-028, 00:08:29.1-00:08:31.3)

(298) **Dari** tempat letak keréta, lu mesti seberang satu sempang.
 from place park car 2SG must cross one traffic.junction
 'From the car park, you must cross one junction.'
 (Victor, oai:scholarspace.manoa.hawaii.edu: NL1-103, 00:11:02.0-00:11:05.1)

Sampay has undergone grammaticalization. Its original meaning that is also retained in Baba Malay is 'reach' while the preposition it forms is 'until', a related notion. *Sampay* can be used to indicate 'until' with regard to place, as with example (300), time, as with example (301), and state, as with example (302). Example (299) shows how *sampay* is used to mean 'reach'.

(299) Apa macham gua boléh **sampay** sana?
 what like 1SG can **reach** there
 'How can I reach there?'
 (Victor, oai:scholarspace.manoa.hawaii.edu: NL1-103, 00:18:27.4-00:18:31.7)

(300) Gua   sudah   jalan **sampay** sini.
      1SG   already   walk   **until**   here
      'I already walked until here.'
      (Lilian, oai:scholarspace.manoa.hawaii.edu: NL1-079, 00:16:04.9-00:16:07.3)

(301) Dudok **sampay** pukol   lima.
      sit   **until**   strike five
      'Sit until five o'clock.'
      (Victor, oai:scholarspace.manoa.hawaii.edu: NL1-142, 00:03:03.3-00:03:05.6)

(302) Dia   dudok   bicycle   chepat   pulak   **sampay**
      3SG   sit   fast   instead   **until**
      dia   nia   buah   pear   jatoh.
      3SG   POSS   CLF.fruit   fall
      'He rode the bicycle fast instead, until his pears fell.'
      (Victor, oai:scholarspace.manoa.hawaii.edu: NL1-028, 00:03:11.6-00:03:13.0)

Besides being used literally to mean 'same', and as a conjunction (see section 4.7), *sama* is also used as a preposition, denoting 'with'. The general use of *sama* is demonstrated in examples (303) to (306).

(303) Orang   itu   pukol   kuching   **sama**   kayu.
      person   that   hit   cat   **with**   stick
      'That person hit the cat with the stick.'
      (Victor, oai:scholarspace.manoa.hawaii.edu: NL1-009, 00:40:58.1-00:41:00.2)

(304) Ini   kawan,   dia   datang   **sama**   apa?
      this   friend   3SG   come   **with**   what
      'This friend, he came with what?'
      (Peter Wee, oai:scholarspace.manoa.hawaii.edu: NL1-022, 00:01:34.9-00:01:37.1)

(305) Pi   masak   **sama**   dia.
      go   cook   **with**   3SG
      'Go cook with it (fish).'
      (Jane Quek, oai:scholarspace.manoa.hawaii.edu: NL1-142, 00:12:43.3-00:12:45.2)

(306) Dia   chakap   **sama**   dia.
      3SG   speak   **with**   3SG
      'He is talking to him.'
      (Peter Wee, oai:scholarspace.manoa.hawaii.edu: NL1-022, 00:02:44.4-00:02:46.0)

Sama is also used in comparatives, as demonstrated by example (307) (refer to section 5.3.1 for more details and examples).

(307) Dia   tinggi **sama** ngko   dia.
       3SG   tall   **with**   older.brother 3SG
       'He is as tall as his brother.'
       (Victor, oai:scholarspace.manoa.hawaii.edu: NL1-009, 00:10:31.5-00:10:33.6)

Additionally, *sama* is used to connect a verb with its object noun phrase, as compared to the obliques in examples (304) to (307). This is demonstrated in examples (309) to (311). Example (308) shows that this is optional for transitive verbs, when compared to example (309). Inserting *sama* is also a way of making an intransitive verb transitive, as example (311) demonstrates.

(308) Dia   sumua halo   tu   mia anjing.
       3SG   all   chase that REL dog
       'They all chased that dog.'
       (Peter Wee, oai:scholarspace.manoa.hawaii.edu: NL1-030, 00:04:32.1-00:04:34.1)

(309) Halo   **sama** budak ini.
       chase.away **with**   boy   this
       'Chase away this boy.'
       (Peter Wee, oai:scholarspace.manoa.hawaii.edu: NL1-030, 00:06:02.5-00:06:04.6)

(310) Rindu **sama** gua.
       miss   **with**   1SG
       'Miss me.'
       (Jane Quek, oai:scholarspace.manoa.hawaii.edu: NL1-043, 00:29:51.9-00:29:54.3)

(311) Senyum **sama** gua.
       smile   **with**   1SG
       'Smile at me.'
       (Jane Quek, oai:scholarspace.manoa.hawaii.edu: NL1-142, 00:18:07.3-00:18:08.7)

Interestingly, what becomes apparent here is that while the *sama* form can be used with non-animate items such as *kayu* 'stick' in (303), more often than not, it appears with an animate object, usually of a higher order, such as with humans and personal pronouns. Semantically, the usages of *sama* in examples (303) to (311) appear to correspond with differential object marking, a feature that is found in the region. Papia Kristang, a Portuguese based creole found in the Malay Archipelago uses *ku/kung/kong* (lexically derived from the Portuguese preposition *com*) for this purpose. More strikingly, Bossong (2021) points out that the root of differential object marking in Papia Kristang may be found in *sama* in Bazaar Malay, which may in turn have been derived from the Hokkien particle *kăp*, as in the sentence *guà kăp î khuă* 'literally: 1SG with 3SG see' (example sentence from Bossong 2021). That Baba Malay and Bazaar Malay are both influenced heavily by Hokkien as a substratal language suggests that *sama* in Baba Malay may possibly be interpreted as differential object marking. There is however one crucial difference. While differential object marking is usually obligatory on higher order animate objects such as personal pronouns and proper names, *sama* in Baba Malay is optional on these higher order animate objects, albeit more likely to occur with these than with lower order animate objects. For example, *rindu sama gua* 'miss with 1SG' in (310) can also be expressed as *rindu gua* 'miss 1SG'.

4.7 Conjunctions

Table 35 lists the conjunctions that are commonly used in Baba Malay.

Table 35: List of conjunctions in Baba Malay.

Conjunction	Use
sama	and
habi/abi	finish
ka	or
tapi	but
pasal/ pasair	because
kalu	if
bila	when
sunggu pun	although (literally 'really also')

The following example sentences show how the various conjunctions are used. Examples (312) to (314) demonstrate the use of coordinating conjunctions. These are used to conjoin similar phrases, or clauses at the same level. In example (315), the subject noun is unexpressed in the second clause (see section 5.6.2), and both components being conjoined are clauses. Constituents involved in conjunction are presented in parentheses.

(312) [Ini kupukupu] **sama** [anjing ni].
this butterfly **and** dog this
'This butterfly and this dog'
(Peter Wee, oai:scholarspace.manoa.hawaii.edu: NL1-030, 00:01:48.0-00:01:50.4)

(313) [Mak pegi pasair], **habis** tu [dia pegi kopitiam].
mother go market **finish** that 3SG go coffee.shop
'Mother went to the market. After that she went to the coffeeshop.'
(Peter Wee, oai:scholarspace.manoa.hawaii.edu: NL1-110, 00:01:23.4-00:01:29.3)

(314) Gua rasa ini [anak dia] **ka** [chuchu dia].
1SG think this child 3SG **or** grandchild 3SG
'I think this is his child or grandchild.'
(Peter Wee, oai:scholarspace.manoa.hawaii.edu: NL1-022, 00:02:13.0-00:02:15.0)

(315) [Gua mia adék bikin kék] **tapi** [tak sedap].
1SG POSS sibling make cake **but** NEG delicious
'My sister baked a cake but it was not delicious.'
(Jane Quek, oai:scholarspace.manoa.hawaii.edu: NL1-117, 00:14:38.9-00:14:44.6)

Examples (316) to (319) show the use of subordinating conjunctions. These ones link subordinate clauses to main clauses. The subordinate clauses in the following examples are presented in parentheses. Example (317) is specifically a conditional expression.

(316) Tiga minggu macham, dia balék
three week like.that 3SG return
'(For) about three weeks, she returns

[**pasair** dia tinggal Singapore].
because 3SG live Singapore
because she lives in Singapore.'
(Jane Quek, oai:scholarspace.manoa.hawaii.edu: NL1-142, 00:04:03.8-00:04:09.2)

(317) [**Kalo** gua tau lu mo datang],
if 1SG know 2SG want come
'If I knew you were coming,

gua tentu jumpa lu dekat airport.
1SG definite meet 2SG PREP
I (would) definitely meet you at the airport.'
(Victor, oai:scholarspace.manoa.hawaii.edu: NL1-053, 00:13:32.1-00:13:37.9)

(318) [**Bila** bahru gua balék rumah],
      When just 1SG   return home
      'When I just returned home,

   bahru gua dapat tau   pasair tu   accident.
   just 1SG get   know matter that
   I just got to know (about) that accident.'
   (Victor, oai:scholarspace.manoa.hawaii.edu: NL1-053, 00:02:22.8-00:02:26.3)

(319) [**Sunggu.pun** dia tak standard],
      although   3SG NEG
      'Although he (is of) no standard,

   dia dapat ini kreja.
   3SG get   this work
   he got this work.'
   (Victor, oai:scholarspace.manoa.hawaii.edu: NL1-053, 00:20:53.4-00:20:57.2)

More details on the different types of conjunctions and their syntactic patterns can be found in section 5.6.8. Conditionals are discussed in section 5.6.7.

4.8 Discourse elements

Baba Malay discourse is characterized by the speakers' use of interjections and particles.

4.8.1 Interjections

In this grammar, interjections whose main functions are emotive, refer to both single word and short two word utterances that can be used independently, or right at the beginning of sentences. Interjections are characteristic of daily conversations in Baba Malay, with participants engaging in *mincharok*, or the use of curse words. While there is usually little illocutionary force in *mincharok*, and hence no intent on the speaker's part to curse her or his interlocutor or to wish bad things upon them, it is considered *kasar* 'coarse' to engage in *mincharok*. It is also less appropriate for younger speakers to use *mincharok* with older speakers, although it is normal for older speakers to use it with peers and younger speakers regardless of occasion. Note that not all interjections are forms of *mincharok* 'curse'. A list of common interjections is given in the Table 36, some of which are *mincharok*.

Table 36: List of common interjections in Baba Malay.

Interjection	Use
aiyo	exclamation of irritation
ala	exclamation of regret
ayi	exclamation of surprise
alamak	exclamation of dismay
éh	exclamation in a jibing manner
amboey	exclamation of surprise
adoey	exclamation of pain
kus semangat	exclamation of shock (literal: cry to a dead spirit)
mati	die
mampus	dead
chilaka	cursed one

The following examples in (320) to (323) demonstrate how some of these interjections are used. Close translations are provided in the instances where these interjections cannot be directly translated into English.

(320) **éh,** ho mia lah lu.
 EXCLAM.JIBE good life EMP 2SG
 'Hey, you have a good life.' (said in a jibing manner)
 (Jane Quek, oai:scholarspace.manoa.hawaii.edu: NL1-044, 00:26:20.3-00:26:22.9)

(321) **Ayi** mampus kambing dia kuat sekali.
 EXCLAM.SURPRISE dead goat 3SG strong very
 'Surprising, goodness, the goat it (is) very strong.'
 (Peter Wee, oai:scholarspace.manoa.hawaii.edu: NL1-022, 00:01:52.8-00:01:54.6)

(322) **Amboey** dia kasi-kan kopiah.
 EXCLAM.surprise 3SG give-TR hat.
 'Surprising. He gave (him) the hat.'
 (Peter Wee, oai:scholarspace.manoa.hawaii.edu: NL1-052, 00:05:06.6-00:05:10.2)

(323) **Alamak,** **chilaka,** kepala gua sakit.
 EXCLAM.DISMAY cursed.one head 1SG sick
 'Goodness, cursed one, my head hurts.'
 (Peter Wee, oai:scholarspace.manoa.hawaii.edu: NL1-052, 00:05:45.8-00:05:47.8)

4.8.2 Particles

While interjections can be used on their own, and at the beginning of sentences, particles in Baba Malay are used at the end of sentences. These discourse particles do not change the meaning of the utterances they are attached to, but rather have emotive value. The two most commonly used particles are *lah* and *sair*.

Lah, usually accompanied with a falling pitch is used emphatically. Emphatic *lah* can be attributed to Hokkien influence, just as *lah* in Colloquial Singapore English (a contact language with a Hokkien substrate) is said to have been derived from Hokkien (Platt and Ho 1989). Semantically, the insertion of this pragmatic particle does not change the meanings in these utterances. The usage of *lah* is shown in examples (324) to (329). In these examples, the insertion of *lah* at the end of the utterances emphasizes the value of what has been said in the utterance. For example, in (324), *lah* emphasizes that the person the interlocutor is talking about became furious, and in (325), that the child was guarding his sheep.

(324) Abi   dia   naik   geram   **lah.**
      finish 3SG   ascend   furious **EMP**
      'After that he became furious.'
      (Peter Wee, oai:scholarspace.manoa.hawaii.edu: NL1-030, 00:03:00.2-00:03:02.0)

(325) Budak ni   ada   jaga   dia   mia   kambing **lah.**
      child this PROG   guard 3SG   POSS   sheep   **EMP**
      'This child is guarding his sheep.'
      (Peter Wee, oai:scholarspace.manoa.hawaii.edu: NL1-030, 00:04:00.6-00:04:03.4)

(326) Dia-orang sumua marah   dia   **lah.**
      3-PL   all   angry   3SG   **EMP**
      'They all (were) angry (at) him.'
      (Peter Wee, oai:scholarspace.manoa.hawaii.edu: NL1-030, 00:04:37.9-00:04:40.0)

(327) Chakiak orang   putéh **lah.**
      clogs   person white **EMP**
      'Western-style clogs.'
      (Peter Wee, oai:scholarspace.manoa.hawaii.edu: NL1-030, 00:07:15.6-00:07:17.5)

(328) Tak   mo   **lah.**
      NEG   want   **EMP**
      '(I) don't want to.'
      (Jane Quek, oai:scholarspace.manoa.hawaii.edu: NL1-142, 00:06:17.9-00:06:19.1)

(329) Sini   masak   nia   sedap   **lah.**
      here   cook   REL   delicious   **EMP**
      '(The food) that is cooked here (is) delicious.'
      (Jane Quek, oai:scholarspace.manoa.hawaii.edu: NL1-142, 00:06:45.8-00:06:48.1)

The other particle that is commonly used is *sair*, which has been analysed as being derived from *sekali* 'very' (Gwee 1998, Gwee 2006). This particle is usually accompanied with a rising pitch. Gwee translates *sair* as 'indeed', and in line with this, *sair* appears to have the effect of confirming the utterance itself, that what is being said is indeed the case. It is glossed as a confirmative particle in this grammar. As a discourse particle, *sair* does not significantly affect the meanings of the utterances to which it is attached. The usage of *sair* is demonstrated by examples (330) to (335). Note that the *sair* particle is not the same lexical item as *sair* in *apa sair*, which is the contracted form of the refined *apa pasair* 'why, literally: what reason?' (coarse form: *apa pasal*). Example (220) is replicated below as example (331).

(330) Panas   **sair.**
      hot   **CONF**
      'hot indeed.'
      (Victor, oai:scholarspace.manoa.hawaii.edu: NL1-009, 00:02:25.1-00:02:26.3)

(331) Taukay   kebun   ni   kiam   **sair.**
      boss   garden   this   miserly   **CONF**
      'This boss (of the) garden is miserly indeed.'
      (Victor, oai:scholarspace.manoa.hawaii.edu: NL1-028, 00:01:03.7-00:01:05.8)

(332) Dia   chakap   Peranakan   lanchang   **sair.**
      3SG   speak   fluent   **CONF**
      'He speaks Peranakan fluently indeed.'
      (Victor, oai:scholarspace.manoa.hawaii.edu: NL1-028, 00:19:18.8-00:19:22.4)

(333) Tapi   bukan   anak   **sair.**
      but   NEG   child   **CONF**
      'but (it is) not the children indeed.'
      (Jane Quek, oai:scholarspace.manoa.hawaii.edu: NL1-142, 00:09:54.0-00:09:56.2)

(334) *Jangan bising **sair**.*
do.not noisy **CONF**
'do not (be) noisy indeed.'
(Jane Quek, oai:scholarspace.manoa.hawaii.edu: NL1-142, 00:15:21.3-00:15:23.9)

(335) *Suay **sair**.*
unlucky **CONF**
'Unlucky indeed.'
(Jane Quek, oai:scholarspace.manoa.hawaii.edu: NL1-142, 00:15:55.6-00:15:56.5)

5 Syntax

As an isolating language, Baba Malay utilizes word order predominantly in expressing syntactic relations. This chapter concerns the syntax of noun phrases, verb phrases, adjectival phrases, adverbial phrases, as well as more complex clauses. Overall, Baba Malay is neither predominantly head-initial nor head-final, as the examples in this chapter will demonstrate.

5.1 Noun phrases

The noun phrase (NP) in Baba Malay comprises pronoun or a noun phrase and optional modifiers that both precede and follow the noun head. Modifiers include demonstratives, person marker, numerals, quantifiers, and adjectives. Modifiers may also come in the form of genitive clauses as well as relative clauses. Examples (336) to (350) demonstrate the different types of noun phrases found in Baba Malay.

(336) Pronoun
Dia tolak.
3SG push
'He pushed.'
(Victor, oai:scholarspace.manoa.hawaii.edu: NL1-028, 00:04:27.7-00:04:28.7)

(337) Noun without modifier
Anjing sudah mangun.
dog already wake.up
'The dog has already woken up.'
(Jane Quek, oai:scholarspace.manoa.hawaii.edu: NL1-088, 00:00:17.1-00:00:18.7)

(338) Noun with preceding demonstrative
Dia-orang tolong itu budak.
3-PL help that child
'They helped that child.'
(Victor, oai:scholarspace.manoa.hawaii.edu: NL1-028, 00:04:09.1-00:04:11.1)

(339) Noun with following demonstrative
Budak ini sangat kechik.
child this very small
'This (is) very small.'
(Peter Wee, oai:scholarspace.manoa.hawaii.edu: NL1-022, 00:03:23.5-00:03:25.3)

(340) Noun with preceding person marker
Si tua.
PERSON old
'That old person.'
(Peter Wee, oai:scholarspace.manoa.hawaii.edu: NL1-022, 00:04:10.4-00:04:10.8)

(341) Noun with preceding numeral
Satu bakol sudah ilang.
one basket already lost
'One basket has gone missing.'
(Peter Wee, oai:scholarspace.manoa.hawaii.edu: NL1-022, 00:05:47.1-00:05:48.9)

(342) Noun with preceding demonstrative, numeral and classifier
Ayi dia jumpa **tiga ékor budak.**
EXCLAM.surprise 3SG meet **three CLF.animal child**
'Surprising he met three children.'
(Peter Wee, oai:scholarspace.manoa.hawaii.edu: NL1-022, 00:05:52.6-00:05:54.5)

(343) Noun with preceding quantifier
Sumua orang sekarang tak tau chakap.
all person now NEG know speak
'Everyone now does not know (how to) speak.'
(Victor, oai:scholarspace.manoa.hawaii.edu: NL1-002, 00:07:37.8-00:07:40.9)

(344) Noun with following quantifier
Angkat **changkay changkay sumua** pegi belakang.
carry **cup cup all** go behind
'Carry all the cups (and) go to the back.'
(Jane Quek oai:scholarspace.manoa.hawaii.edu: NL1-043, 00:06:47.4-00:06:50.1)

(345) Noun with preceding adjective
Cherita-kan gua **betol** mia cherita.
story-TR 1SG **true** REL story
'Tell me a true story.'
(Jane Quek oai:scholarspace.manoa.hawaii.edu: NL1-100, 00:02:56.4-00:03:00.5)

(346) Noun with following adjective
Babi kechik chakap.
pig small speak
'The small pig spoke.'
(Victor, oai:scholarspace.manoa.hawaii.edu: NL1-035, 00:03:44.7-00:03:45.9)

(347) Noun with preceding genitive
Gong-ma mia gambar.
grandfather-grandmother POSS picture
'Grandparents' photographs.'
(Victor, oai:scholarspace.manoa.hawaii.edu: NL1-002, 00:10:57.8-00:10:59.0)

(348) Noun with following genitive
Bini dia sama anjing.
wife 3SG with dog
'His wife and the dog.'
(Victor, oai:scholarspace.manoa.hawaii.edu: NL1-034, 00:01:31.8-00:01:33.3)

(349) Noun with preceding relative clause
[Dia diri-kan] nia bicycle.
3SG stand-TR REL
'The bicycle that he (made) stand up.'
(Victor, oai:scholarspace.manoa.hawaii.edu: NL1-028, 00:02:44.9-00:02:46.0)

(350) Noun with following relative clause
Ini sumua dia mia kawan [nang jaga kambing].
This all 3SG POSS friend REL guard sheep
'These (are) all his friends that guard the sheep.'
(Peter Wee, oai:scholarspace.manoa.hawaii.edu: NL1-030, 00:05:58.2-00:06:00.8)

The examples show that most types of noun phrases have both head-initial and head-final structures, except for person marker, numerals and noun classifiers that obligatorily occur before the noun head. This pattern of modification is shown in examples (341) and (342). The following sections introduce the different types of noun phrases in more detail. Relative clauses are discussed later in section 5.6.3.

5.1.1 Genitive

Case is not overtly expressed or marked in Baba Malay, and the genitive relationship between possessor and possessed is not expressed by the genitive case. Instead, there are two ways of expressing possession. The first of which is by using the lexical items *mia* and *nia*, which are contracted forms of *punya*.[63] It is notable that *punya* is also used as a relative clause marker (see section 5.6.3). In this instance, the noun phrase is head-final. The second method, a head-initial way of expressing possession is by possessed-possessor word order. Examples (351) to (356) demonstrate the use of *punya* and its other contracted forms, with (18) replicated here as (351).

(351) Peter **punya** bapak.
    POSS father
'Peter's father.'
(Victor, oai:scholarspace.manoa.hawaii.edu: NL1-009, 00:45:01.7-00:45:06.9)

(352) William **nia** bapak.
    POSS father
'William's father.'
(Victor, oai:scholarspace.manoa.hawaii.edu: NL1-009, 00:45:06.9-00:45:09.7)

(353) Asam gugol **mia** kulit
tamarind dried.fruit **POSS** skin
'The dried tamarind's skin'
(Jane Quek, oai:scholarspace.manoa.hawaii.edu: NL1-142, 00:11:51.6-00:11:54.0)

(354) Kita **mia** orang
1PL **POSS** people
'Our people'
(Victor, oai:scholarspace.manoa.hawaii.edu: NL1-035, 00:05:49.3-00:05:50.4)

(355) Dia **mia** nama
3SG **POSS** name
'Its name'
(Peter Wee, oai:scholarspace.manoa.hawaii.edu: NL1-079, 00:00:37.9-00:00:41.4)

(356) Dia **mia** kawan
3SG **POSS** friend
'His friend'
(Peter Wee, oai:scholarspace.manoa.hawaii.edu: NL1-030, 00:05:58.2-00:05:59.0)

---

63 *Pia* is also said to exist as a contracted form of *punya*, but the item is not found in grammar's corpus.

While expressions using *punya* as a possessive marker can be used to mark genitive relations between a proper noun, common noun or a pronoun and the possessed noun, only pronouns can function as possessor in the possessed-possessor structures. There are no instances of non-pronouns functioning as the possessor in utterances of the following sort. Note that third person pronoun *dia* occasionally occurs as *nia*, but these are forms that are etymologically and functionally unrelated. Examples (357) to (361) illustrate the possessed-possessor genitive structure.

(357) *Badan lu.*
body 2SG
'Your body.'
(Lilian, oai:scholarspace.manoa.hawaii.edu: NL1-079, 00:11:33.1-00:11:36:1)

(358) *Kambing dia*
sheep 3SG
'His sheep'
(Peter Wee, oai:scholarspace.manoa.hawaii.edu: NL1-030, 00:05:47.9-00:05:48.0)

(359) *Bini dia.*
wife 3SG
'His wife.'
(Victor, oai:scholarspace.manoa.hawaii.edu: NL1-034, 00:01:32.0-00:01:33.3)

(360) *Mata dia*
eye 3SG
'His eyes'
(Peter Wee, oai:scholarspace.manoa.hawaii.edu: NL1-030, 00:00:23.9-00:00:24.5)

(361) *Rumah gua.*
house 1SG
'my house.'
(Victor, oai:scholarspace.manoa.hawaii.edu: NL1-035, 00:02:41.9-00:02:43.0)

In all, as *punya* constructions have more functionality than possessed-possessor constructions (which can only express genitive relations where pronouns are concerned), Baba Malay's more dominant word order where nouns and genitives are concerned is GEN N, rather than N GEN.

5.1.2 Noun phrases with determiners

Determiners in this grammar refer to demonstratives, person marker, numerals, classifiers and quantifiers, these items co-occurring with nouns to express semantic contrasts, for example, distance and quantity. These determiners have different distributions. In general, demonstratives as well as quantifiers can precede or follow nouns, while numerals and classifiers precede nouns.

In addition, it is important to note that there are no determiners that express a definite-indefinite contrast. Context is largely used to determine if a noun is definite or indefinite. Example (110) is replicated here as (362), and example (337) as (363).

(362) First mention of a noun
 Orang   panjat   pokok.
 person climb   tree
 'A person climbs a tree.'
 (Victor, oai:scholarspace.manoa.hawaii.edu: NL1-028, 00:00:15.6-00:00:17.6)

(363) Subsequent mention of a noun
 Anjing sudah   mangun.
 dog   already   wake.up
 'The dog has already woken up.'
 (Jane Quek, oai:scholarspace.manoa.hawaii.edu: NL1-088, 00:00:17.1-00:00:18.7)

Both *orang* 'person' and *anjing* 'dog' in the above examples do not co-occur with any determiner, yet *orang* is interpreted as indefinite, and *anjing*, as definite. This is due to the contexts in which they occur. Where (362) is specifically concerned, *orang* is the first utterance in a narrative and there is no precedent. The word is hence interpreted as indefinite. In the case of (363), *anjing* has been mentioned prior to this occurrence, and it is therefore understood by the listener as definite.

5.1.2.1 Noun phrases with demonstratives

While there is no definite-indefinite contrast in Baba Malay, definite determiners can be contrasted based mainly on distance or space. The demonstratives *ini* 'this' and *itu* 'that' encode deixis. *Ini* is proximal, co-occurring with nouns that are typically close to the speaker or the action taking place, while *itu* is distal, co-occurring with nouns that are typically further away from the speaker or the action taking place. There is no preferred word order for noun phrases comprising a demonstrative and noun. Note that the shortened versions of *ini* and *itu* are *ni* and *tu* respectively. Examples (364) to (368) show how the demonstrative can be used before the noun it modifies.

(364) **Ini** kebun.
       this garden
       'this garden.'
       (Peter Wee, oai:scholarspace.manoa.hawaii.edu: NL1-022, 00:00:32.0-00:00:32.8)

(365) **Ini** rumah-rumah.
       this house-PL
       'these houses.'
       (Peter Wee, oai:scholarspace.manoa.hawaii.edu: NL1-030, 00:03:52.6-00:03:53.2)

(366) **Ni** orang.
       this person
       'This person.'
       (Peter Wee, oai:scholarspace.manoa.hawaii.edu: NL1-022, 00:00:29.0-00:00:30.0)

(367) **Tu** budak perompuan.
       that child female
       'That girl.'
       (Victor, oai:scholarspace.manoa.hawaii.edu: NL1-028, 00:03:28.0-00:03:29.2)

(368) **Itu** kopiah.
       that hat
       'That hat.'
       (Victor, oai:scholarspace.manoa.hawaii.edu: NL1-028, 00:04:37.0-00:04:38.5)

Examples (369) to (373) show the opposite – that demonstratives can follow nouns. Example (369) replicates (132).

(369) Budak **ini**
       child **this**
       'This child.'
       (Peter Wee, oai:scholarspace.manoa.hawaii.edu: NL1-022, 00:03:23.5-00:03:24.0)

(370) Anjing hutan **ini**.
       dog jungle **this**
       'This wolf.'
       (Peter Wee, oai:scholarspace.manoa.hawaii.edu: NL1-030, 00:04:24.7-00:04:26.6)

(371) *Anjing* **tu.**
 dog that
 'That dog.'
 (Peter Wee, oai:scholarspace.manoa.hawaii.edu: NL1-030, 00:01:41.7-00:01:42.3)

(372) *Kuching.belanda* **tu.**
 rabbit that
 'That rabbit.'
 (Peter Wee, oai:scholarspace.manoa.hawaii.edu: NL1-030, 00:01:18.0-00:01:19.4)

(373) *Si tua* **tu.**
 PERSON old that
 'That old person.'
 (Peter Wee, oai:scholarspace.manoa.hawaii.edu: NL1-022, 00:04:10.4-00:04:11.0)

In addition, *demonstratives* may occur together with *punya*, as demonstrated in the following examples of (374) and (375). In these examples, the function of *punya* appears to be similar to when it is a relative clause marker (see section 5.6.3), a relative clause being a subordinate clause that modifies the head noun. The subordinate clauses contain deictic information in these examples. For these constructions, the demonstrative always occurs before noun.

(374) **Ini** *mia budak.*
 this REL child
 'This child here.'
 (Peter Wee, oai:scholarspace.manoa.hawaii.edu: NL1-030, 00:03:49.0-00:03:50.0)

(375) **Tu** *mia anjing.*
 that REL dog
 'That dog there.'
 (Peter Wee, oai:scholarspace.manoa.hawaii.edu: NL1-030, 00:03:32.3-00:04:34.1)

Although demonstrative precedes noun in the *punya* construction, this is not the most basic type of noun phrase that features a demonstrative. Both DEM-NP and NP-DEM orders are equally common in Baba Malay and there is no preferred word order.

5.1.2.2 Noun phrases with person marker

Noun phrases featuring the person marker *si* always have the order *si*-NP. Examples (376) to (379) demonstrate this structure. Example (242) is replicated as (377).

(376) ***Si*** *Mary.*
     PERSON
     'Mary.'
     (Victor, oai:scholarspace.manoa.hawaii.edu: NL1-037, 00:01:07.1-00:01:08.2)

(377) ***Si*** *sa ko bongsu.*
     PERSON third paternal.aunt youngest.child
     'Youngest third paternal aunt.'
     (Lilian, oai:scholarspace.manoa.hawaii.edu: NL1-079, 00:09:01.2-00:09:02.9)

(378) ***Si*** *tua tu.*
     PERSON old that
     'That old person.'
     (Peter Wee, oai:scholarspace.manoa.hawaii.edu: NL1-022, 00:04:10.4-00:04:11.0)

(379) ***Si*** *ano ni?*
     PERSON anonymous this
     'This anonymous person?'
     (Peter Wee, oai:scholarspace.manoa.hawaii.edu: NL1-107, 00:12:13.5-00:12:15.2)

5.1.2.3 Noun phrases with numerals, noun classifiers and partitives

Similar to noun phrases comprising the person marker, noun phrases are head-final when they comprise numerals or numerals and classifiers. Examples (380) to (384) illustrate noun phrases comprising numerals without classifiers, and examples (385) to (389) illustrate noun phrases comprising numerals with classifiers. It is interesting to note that the classifier used for animals can also be used with young children. The relevant examples are (385) and (389).

(380) ***Satu*** *anjing.*
     one dog
     '**One** dog.'
     (Peter Wee, oai:scholarspace.manoa.hawaii.edu: NL1-030, 00:02:57.0-00:02:57.9)

(381) **Satu** tulang.
 one bone
 'One bone.'
 (Peter Wee, oai:scholarspace.manoa.hawaii.edu: NL1-030, 00:02:55.0-00:02:55.8)

(382) **Empat ratus** taon.
 four hundred year
 'Four hundred years.'
 (Victor, oai:scholarspace.manoa.hawaii.edu: NL1-051, 00:13:45.4-00:13:47.0)

(383) **Dua** bulan.
 two month
 'Two months.'
 (Victor, oai:scholarspace.manoa.hawaii.edu: NL1-051, 00:03:33.6-00:03:35.0)

(384) Ni **empat** minggu.
 this **four** week
 'These four weeks.'
 (Victor, oai:scholarspace.manoa.hawaii.edu: NL1-051, 00:16:55.0-00:16:56.5)

(385) **Se-kor** kambing.
 one-CLF.animal goat
 'One goat.'
 (Victor oai:scholarspace.manoa.hawaii.edu: NL1-022, 00:01:32.4-00:01:34.7)

(386) **Dua bijik** pear.
 two CLF.small.round
 'Two pears.'
 (Peter Wee, oai:scholarspace.manoa.hawaii.edu: NL1-022, 00:05:04.5-00:05:05.4)

(387) **Satu bijik** timun.
 one CLF.small.round cucumber
 'One cucumber.'
 (Jane Quek, oai:scholarspace.manoa.hawaii.edu: NL1-149, 00:03:17.8-00:03:19.4)

(388) **Se-kuntum** bunga
 one-CLF.bloom flower
 'One flower'
 (Victor, oai:scholarspace.manoa.hawaii.edu: NL1-160, 00:01:59.2-00:02:00.7)

(389) *Ni   tiga   ékor   budak.*
      this **three CLF.animal** children
      'These three children.'
      (Peter Wee, oai:scholarspace.manoa.hawaii.edu: NL1-022, 00:05:53.5-00:05:54.5)

Partitive phrases can also be considered here. Whereas noun classifiers here are used for counting individuated items, partitives here are used to refer to a part of or a quantity of a mass, unindividuated noun. These are syntactically similar to noun classifiers, with a modifier preceding head. Examples (390) to (394) illustrate the use of partitive phrases in Baba Malay. In examples (393) and (394), contracted forms of the relative clause marker *punya* mediate between partitive and noun.

(390) ***Satu   botol***   *susu.*
      one   bottle   milk
      'One bottle of milk.'
      (Peter Wee, oai:scholarspace.manoa.hawaii.edu: NL1-148, 00:21:05.5-00:21:08.5)

(391) ***Satu   changkay***   *ayé.*
      one   cup   water
      'One cup of water.'
      (Peter Wee, oai:scholarspace.manoa.hawaii.edu: NL1-148, 00:21:41.5-00:21:42.6)

(392) ***Satu   kepéng***   *ayam.*
      one   piece   chicken
      'One piece of chicken.'
      (Peter Wee, oai:scholarspace.manoa.hawaii.edu: NL1-148, 00:21:16.8-00:21:17.9)

(393) ***Satu   éla***   *mia   kain.*
      one   sheet   REL   cloth
      'One sheet of cloth.'
      (Peter Wee, oai:scholarspace.manoa.hawaii.edu: NL1-148, 00:23:27.5-00:23:28.5)

(394) ***Satu   baldi***   *mia   ayé.*
      one   pail   REL   water
      'One pail of water.'
      (Peter Wee, oai:scholarspace.manoa.hawaii.edu: NL1-148, 00:21:42.7-00:21:44.7)

Noun phrases in Baba Malay can thus comprise NUM-NP, NUM-CLF-NP, and NUM-PART-NP sequences, all of these being head-final in nature.

5.1.2.4 Noun phrases with quantifiers

Noun phrases may also have quantifiers as modifiers. In these instances, the modifier may precede or follow the head noun. The use of quantifiers with noun phrases is illustrated in examples (395) to (400).

(395) **Sumua**   adék-beradék.
     all   sibling-PL
     'All siblings.'
     (Victor, oai:scholarspace.manoa.hawaii.edu: NL1-002, 00:07:37.9-00:07:38.5)

(396) Orang orang **sumua.**
     people people **all**
     'All people.'
     (Jane Quek, oai:scholarspace.manoa.hawaii.edu: NL1-142, 00:01:23.6-00:01:24.6)

(397) **Manyak** orang.
     many   people
     'Many people.'
     (Jane Quek, oai:scholarspace.manoa.hawaii.edu: NL1-142, 00:00:24.0-00:00:25.5)

(398) Dagin putéh **manyak.**
     meat   white **many**
     'A lot of white meat.'
     (Lilian, oai:scholarspace.manoa.hawaii.edu: NL1-079, 00:03:52.5-00:03:53.6)

(399) **Berapa** orang.
     some   people
     'Some people.'
     (Victor, oai:scholarspace.manoa.hawaii.edu: NL1-071, 00:18:08.3-00:18:09.3)

(400) Umor **sikit.**
     age   **little**
     'Little age.'
     (Victor, oai:scholarspace.manoa.hawaii.edu: NL1-002, 00:06:23.0-00:06:24.1)

Other than noun phrases that are made up of nouns and quantifiers in either phrase-initial or phrase-final positions (Quantifier-NP, NP-Quantifier), it is also possible for quantifiers to take the position of the noun itself, as with examples (401) to (403).

(401) **Manyak** tak sama.
 many NEG same
 'Many are not the same.'
 (Victor, oai:scholarspace.manoa.hawaii.edu: NL1-002, 00:02:13.0-00:02:14.1)

(402) **Sumua** bising.
 all noisy
 'All are noisy.'
 (Jane Quek, oai:scholarspace.manoa.hawaii.edu: NL1-142, 00:01:33.9-00:01:34.5)

(403) Dia minum **sikit**.
 3SG drink **little**
 'He drinks a little.'
 (Victor, oai:scholarspace.manoa.hawaii.edu: NL1-053, 00:22:41.0-00:44:42.7)

The only quantifier that has not been observed to replace the noun itself is *berapa* 'some'. Note that *berapa* is also an interrogative, meaning 'how much'. In this case, only context can help differentiate if *berapa* is meant as a quantifier or as an interrogative.

5.1.3 Noun phrases with adjectival modifiers

Adjectival modifier in Baba Malay can either follow or precede the head in a noun phrase. The more basic noun phrase structure comprises a noun followed by an adjective. Examples of these are listed from (404) to (408).

(404) Dagin **mérah**.
 meat **red**
 'Red meat.'
 (Lilian, oai:scholarspace.manoa.hawaii.edu: NL1-079, 00:03:50.7-00:03:51.7)

(405) Kepok **kosong**.
 box **empty**
 'Empty box.'
 (Lilian, oai:scholarspace.manoa.hawaii.edu: NL1-079, 00:12:56.5-00:12:57.7)

(406) *Beruang* **besair.**
      bear   big
      'Big bear.'
      (Victor, oai:scholarspace.manoa.hawaii.edu: NL1-032, 00:04:24.7-00:04:27.2)

(407) *Kayu* **panjang.**
      wood long
      'Long wood.'
      (Jane Quek, oai:scholarspace.manoa.hawaii.edu: NL1-045, 00:01:20.3-00:01:22.4)

(408) *Pintu* **chanték.**
      door   beautiful
      'Beautiful door.'
      (Victor, oai:scholarspace.manoa.hawaii.edu: NL1-035, 00:01:55.7-00:01:56.8)

Adjectives may also precede nouns in adjectival noun phrases, when the relative clause marker *punya* is used, as with examples (409) to (413). These examples feature the contracted form of *punya*, *mia*. In these, the adjectives and *punya* function as a subordinate clause that provides information about the head noun, so that an example such as (409) *betol mia cherita*, may be interpreted as 'a story that is real'. Example (16) is replicated here as example (409).

(409) **betol** **mia** *cherita.*
      real   REL   story
      'Real story.'
      (Jane Quek, oai:scholarspace.manoa.hawaii.edu: NL1-028, 00:03:24.8-00:03:26.0)

(410) **sekarang** **mia** *orang*
      now   REL   people
      'Modern people'
      (Jane Quek, oai:scholarspace.manoa.hawaii.edu: NL1-142, 00:06:52.9-00:06:54.2)

(411) **dulu**   **mia** *lauk.*
      long.ago   REL   cook.food
      'Old-fashioned dishes.'
      (Jane Quek, oai:scholarspace.manoa.hawaii.edu: NL1-142, 00:09:47.6-00:09:48.5)

(412) **Bising mia** pasair.
    noisy REL matter
    'Noisy matters.'
    (Jane Quek, oai:scholarspace.manoa.hawaii.edu: NL1-142, 00:01:34.1-00:01:35.5)

(413) **Betol mia** nasik lemak.
    real REL rice   cooked.in.coconut.milk
    'Real rice cooked in coconut milk (a dish).'
    (Jane Quek, oai:scholarspace.manoa.hawaii.edu: NL1-142, 00:08:10.0-00:08:11.5)

In effect, while both NP-A and A-NP orders are possible in Baba Malay, the basic form of the adjectival noun phrase is NP-A, since it does not require the use of an additional relative clause marker, even though the A-*punya*-NP structure is also commonly used.

5.1.4 Negation of noun phrases

Noun phrases can be negated by inserting *bukan* before the noun phrase that is to be negated. This is akin to the use of 'not' in English, rather than 'no' in these instances.

(414) **Bukan** anak.
    NEG   children
    'Not children.'
    (Jane Quek, oai:scholarspace.manoa.hawaii.edu: NL1-142, 00:09:54.5-00:09:56.0)

(415) **Bukan** bawang.
    NEG   onion
    'Not onions.'
    (Lilian, oai:scholarspace.manoa.hawaii.edu: NL1-079, 00:10:59.7-00:11:00.0)

(416) **Bukan** saya.
    NEG   1SG
    'Not me.'
    (Jane Quek, oai:scholarspace.manoa.hawaii.edu: NL1-018, 00:03:56.7-00:03:57.3)

(417) **Bukan** Singapore.
    NEG
    'Not Singapore.'
    (Peter Wee, oai:scholarspace.manoa.hawaii.edu: NL1-022, 00:02:19.0-00:02:22.0)

(418) **Bukan** [chakiak kita china mia].
    NEG   clogs   1PL Chinese POSS
    'Not our Chinese(-style) clogs.'
    (Peter Wee, oai:scholarspace.manoa.hawaii.edu: NL1-030, 00:07:17.5-00:17:19.3)

Note that existence of nouns can only be negated when a verb phrase containing the existential marker, *ada*, is negated using a separate negative marker *tak*. *Tak-a* is the contracted version of *tak ada* (refer to section 5.2.8 for more details and examples of the *tak* verbal phrase negation strategy).

(419) **Tak-a**   pokok.
    NEG-EXIST   tree
    'There are no trees.'
    (Peter Wee, oai:scholarspace.manoa.hawaii.edu: NL1-022, 00:00:36.0-00:00:36.9)

In general, as far as the word order of noun phrases is concerned, *bukan* is used in a *bukan*-NP sequence. *Bukan* can also be used to negate statements (see section 5.6.10.2).

5.1.5 Order of elements in noun phrases

It would be simplifying matters to state if the noun phrase is strictly head-final or head-initial. Demonstratives as well as quantifiers may precede or follow the main noun phrase. Adjectival modifiers are observed to precede and follow nouns, although the default word order appears to be noun followed by adjective, since a relative clause marker, *punya*, is required to link adjective to noun when the adjective precedes the noun (see section 5.1.3). However, there is also support for the preference of a head-final noun phrase, considering that numerals, noun classifiers and partitives, the person marker *si*, as well as the negative noun marker *bukan* strictly precede the main noun phrase. Overall, it cannot be concluded that there is either a general preference for the modifier to precede head or for the head to precede the modifier. More discussion on noun phrase word order ensues in the section on relative clauses (see section 5.6.3).

5.2 Verb phrases

A verb phrase (VP) comprises verb, verb and complement(s), or a sequence of more than one verb. Auxiliaries may precede the main verb phrase when they are used to express passivization, modality, or tense and aspect. Verb phrases may also be made up of more than one main verb in the case of serial verb constructions. Modifiers include negation markers and other adverbs. The different types of verb phrases found in Baba Malay are listed from examples (420) to (428).

(420) Intransitive verb
Dia **dudok**.
3SG **sits**
'He sits.'
(Jane Quek, oai:scholarspace.manoa.hawaii.edu: NL1-088, 00:00:46.8-00:00:48.4)

(421) Transitive verb with direct object complement
Bukak **pakay** *baju*.
boy **wear** clothes
'The boy puts on his clothes.'
(Jane Quek, oai:scholarspace.manoa.hawaii.edu: NL1-044, 00:00:59.2-00:01:01.8)

(422) Transitive verb with direct and indirect object complements
Dia **kasi** dia dua bijik pear.
3SG **give** 3SG two CLF.small.round
'He gave him two pears.'
(Peter Wee, oai:scholarspace.manoa.hawaii.edu: NL1-022, 00:05:04.0-00:05:05.4)

(423) Causative verb with clause complement
Yauguai, lu **kasi** gua *terperanjat sekali*.
demon 2SG **cause** 1SG be.shocked very
'Demon, you shocked me.'
(Jane Quek, oai:scholarspace.manoa.hawaii.edu: NL1-043, 00:040:26.2-00:40:28.2)

(424) Auxiliary verb and verb
Sumua **boléh** chakap Peranakan.
all **can** speak
'All can speak Peranakan.'
(Victor, oai:scholarspace.manoa.hawaii.edu: NL1-002, 00:06:12.2-00:16:14.9)

(425) Adverb and verb
Dia **lekair** senyum.
3SG **quick** smile
'He quickly smiled.'
(Jane Quek, oai:scholarspace.manoa.hawaii.edu: NL1-088, 00:06:17.5-00:06:18.6)

(426) Verb and adverb
 Lu   mesti mo   chobak dulu.
 2SG   must   want taste   first
 'You must taste it first.'
 (Jane Quek, oai:scholarspace.manoa.hawaii.edu: NL1-043, 00:21:46.0-
 00:21:48.3)

(427) Serial verb construction
 Dia   dudok   téngok.
 He   sit   look
 'He was sitting and looking.'
 (Jane Quek, oai:scholarspace.manoa.hawaii.edu: NL1-088, 00:00:50.0-
 00:00:51.0)

(428) Negation marker and verb
 Tu   bangkuang pun   tak   begerak.
 that turnip   also NEG   move
 'That turnip also did not move.'
 (Peter Wee, oai:scholarspace.manoa.hawaii.edu: NL1-034, 00:01:34.8-
 00:01:37.7)

The examples show that verb phrases are head-initial and head-final. The following sections provide further details.

5.2.1 Copula constructions

Copulas refer to verbs that link the subject and a complement. In Baba Malay, there are two types of copula constructions. The copula verb *ada* can be utilized. It is used as a regular copula, and it may be used in tag interrogatives, as with examples (429) and (430) (see section 5.6.10.2). However, in most instances, the copula verb is omitted.

(429) **Ada** baik tak-a?
 COP good NEG-COP
 'Are (you) well or not?'
 (Jane Quek, oai:scholarspace.manoa.hawaii.edu: NL1-022, 00:00:09.2-
 00:00:11.2)

(430) Rumah gua   **ada** chanték   tak?
 house   1SG   **COP** beautiful NEG
 'My house is beautiful or not?'
 (Victor, oai:scholarspace.manoa.hawaii.edu: NL1-035, 00:02:41.9-00:02:43.7)

The following examples show typical copula constructions, wherein the copula verb is omitted. In the instances of examples (431) to (435), these copula constructions, by virtue of their word order (subject before complement), associate subjects with complements ranging from adjectival phrases to prepositional phrases.

(431) *Gua lapair.*
 1SG hungry
 'I (am) hungry.'
 (Victor, oai:scholarspace.manoa.hawaii.edu: NL1-009, 00:14:16.4-00:14:17.5)

(432) *Itu barang mentah.*
 that thing unripe
 'That thing (is) unripe.'
 (Victor, oai:scholarspace.manoa.hawaii.edu: NL1-009, 00:22:15.6-00:22:17.1)

(433) *Kemantin chanték.*
 bride beautiful
 'The bride (is) beautiful.'
 (Victor, oai:scholarspace.manoa.hawaii.edu: NL1-009, 00:24:57.7-00:24:58.8)

(434) [*Dia mia barang*] *mahal.*
 3SG POSS thing expensive
 'Its things (are) expensive.'
 (Jane Quek, oai:scholarspace.manoa.hawaii.edu: NL1-142, 00:02:32.9-00:02:33.8)

(435) *Rumah rumah atas bukit.*
 house house top mountain
 'The houses (are) on top of the mountain.'
 (Peter Wee, oai:scholarspace.manoa.hawaii.edu: NL1-030, 00:03:58.2-00:04:00.6)

5.2.2 Modality

Verb phrases may also comprise an auxiliary verb preceding the predicate. There are several functions of auxiliaries, including modality, passivization, and aspect marking. This section is concerned with the structures that expresses modality. Modality is associated with the semantic expression of beliefs, attitudes, obligations and ability. While there are differing opinions as to what deontic modality covers (Traugott 1989), it usually concerns will, permission and obligation (Lyons 1977, Traugott 1989). Epistemic modality, on the other hand, expresses one's belief state or attitude towards a certain proposition (Traugott 1989), while dynamic modality concerns one's capacity to do something (Nuyts 2006). The potential mood as used here indicates that there is a high probability that an action will take place, in the opinion of the speaker. As with other languages, the same auxiliary may have overlapping functions.

The following examples show that the auxiliary verb *boléh* 'can' express all three modalities. In examples (436) and (437), the speakers are discussing the abilities of the agents to perform a particular task. Dynamic modality is expressed by placing *boléh* before the main verb phrase. Example (424) is replicated here as example (436).

(436) Sumua **boléh** [chakap Peranakan].
all   **can**   speak   Peranakan
'All can speak Peranakan.'
(Victor, oai:scholarspace.manoa.hawaii.edu: NL1-002, 00:06:12.2-00:16:14.9)

(437) Kita **boléh** [masak].
1PL **can**   cook
'We can cook.'
(Jane Quek, oai:scholarspace.manoa.hawaii.edu: NL1-142, 00:10:21.0-00:10:22.0)

In the next example of (438), epistemic modality is expressed. The speaker is saying that something may be eaten with rice, and thus expressing a belief about a particular subject.

(438) Ini   sumua **boléh** [makan sama nasik].
This all   **can**   eat   with   rice
'All this (you) can eat with rice.'
(Jane Quek, oai:scholarspace.manoa.hawaii.edu: NL1-142, 00:08:46.5-00:08:48.1)

Boléh can also be used to express deontic modality. In examples (439) and (440), the speakers are not questioning the ability of the agents to perform particular tasks, but asking them if they are willing to perform them. In (439), the speaker is asking if his interlocutor is willing to speak Peranakan, and in (440), the speaker is asking if her mother is willing to prepare a particular dish. Such interpretations require context, given that these sentences could be interpreted as expressing dynamic or epistemic modalities as well.

(439) Lu   **boléh** [chakap Peranakan] tak?
2SG **can**   speak   Peranakan   NEG
'Will you speak Peranakan?'
(Victor, oai:scholarspace.manoa.hawaii.edu: NL1-037, 00:51:13.1-00:51:17.7)

(440) Mak, **boléh** [masak ini] tak?
mother **can** cook this NEG
'Mother, will you cook this?'
(Jane Quek, oai:scholarspace.manoa.hawaii.edu: NL1-142, 00:09:28.4-00:09:29.8)

Mesti 'must' on the other hand, has two uses. *Mesti* can be used to express epistemic modality. In examples (441) and (442), the speakers express certain beliefs they have about the world, and what they have observed. In (441), the speaker says that cats must indeed eat fish, and in (442), the speaker expresses his observation that the person he is talking about must have crashed and fallen down.

(441) Kuching itu **mesti** makan ikan.
cat that **must** eat fish
'That cat must eat fish.'
(Victor, oai:scholarspace.manoa.hawaii.edu: NL1-009, 00:43:41.4-00:43:43.6)

(442) Dia **mesti** ter-langgair.
3SG **must** ACC-crash
'He must have crashed.'
(Peter, oai:scholarspace.manoa.hawaii.edu: NL1-022, 00:03:32.5-00:03:34.1)

Mesti can also be used to express the deontic modality. In the following two examples of (443) and (444), the speaker talks about his group's obligations to carry out particular tasks. In (443), the speaker expresses that Peranakans are obliged to learn the Peranakan language, Baba Malay. In (444), the same speaker expresses that he is obliged to call any elder male acquaintance *engko* 'older brother' in accordance to Peranakan customs.

(443) Kita orang mia Peranakan, kita **mesti** [belajair].
1PL people POSS Peranakan 1PL **must** learn
'Our people's Peranakan, we must learn.'
(Victor, oai:scholarspace.manoa.hawaii.edu: NL1-037, 00:51:13.1-00:51:17.7)

(444) Gua **mesti** [panggay engko].
1SG **must** call older.brother
'I must call (a male acquaintance) older brother.'
(Victor, oai:scholarspace.manoa.hawaii.edu: NL1-037, 00:05:25.7-00:05:27.3)

Similarly, *mo* 'want' as an auxiliary verb can expresses two functions of modality, more specifically the deontic and potential moods, as demonstrated by (445) to (447).

(445) Dia **mo** [piléh].
　　　 3SG **want** choose
　　　 'He wants (to) choose.'
　　　 (Peter Wee, oai:scholarspace.manoa.hawaii.edu: NL1-022, 00:01:19.3-
　　　 00:01:20.0)

(446) Gua **mo** pegi itu kebun bunga.
　　　 1SG **want** go that garden flower
　　　 'I want (to) go (to) that flower garden.'
　　　 (Peter Wee, oai:scholarspace.manoa.hawaii.edu: NL1-107, 00:12:32.0-
　　　 00:12:33.7)

(447) Gua **mo** pi belakang.
　　　 1SG **want** go behind
　　　 'I want to go to the back.'
　　　 (Peter Wee, oai:scholarspace.manoa.hawaii.edu: NL1-052, 00:17:37.6-
　　　 00:17:39.6)

In (445), the speaker is talking about the interloctor's ability to choose, therefore expressing the deontic. In (446) and (447), the speaker is talking about the high probability that he will carry out a particular action in his opinion.

In Baba Malay, it is notable that the notion of *mesti*, whether as an epistemic or deontic auxiliary, can be reinforced and emphasized by the form *mesti mo*, literally translated as 'must want'. *Mesti mo* appears to have been calqued directly from the Hokkien form *beh ai* (literal translation: 'must want', see Pakir 1986). In examples (448) and (449), the speaker is saying that she believes this is what has to happen when a person grows old, thus expressing epistemic modality. In examples (450) and (451), the speakers are expressing that the interlocutors have obligations to carry out particular tasks, thus expressing the deontic modality. In (450), the speaker states that the interlocutor has to remember her when she is gone, and in (451), the speaker states that if one is older, one is obliged to take care of herself or himself. While all speakers translate *mesti mo* as 'want', it is as though by adding volitional *mo* to *mesti*, the speaker believes strongly that the predicated proposition must be what is desired, whether it is part of their belief system (epistemic) or something that they want instilled in someone else's belief system (deontic).

(448) Makan **mesti mo** [orang suap].
　　　 eat **must want** person feed
　　　 '(When this person) eats, there must be a person to feed (him).
　　　 (Lilian, oai:scholarspace.manoa.hawaii.edu: NL1-079, 00:05:01.1-00:05:02.4)

(449) Kenching orang **mesti mo** [jaga apa].
urinate person **must want** take.care what
'(When this person) urinates, a person must take care of whatever it is.'
(Lilian, oai:scholarspace.manoa.hawaii.edu: NL1-079, 00:05:02.4-00:05:04.3)

(450) **Mesti mo** [ingat-kan gua].
must want remember-TR 1SG
'(You) must remember me.'
(Jane Quek, oai:scholarspace.manoa.hawaii.edu: NL1-045, 00:06:26.0-00:06:27.4)

(451) Kalu sudah tua, **mesti mo** [jaga badan].
if already old **must want** take.care body
'If (you are) already old, (you) must take care of (your)body.'
(Lilian, oai:scholarspace.manoa.hawaii.edu: NL1-079, 00:04:49.6-00:04:53.6)

In general, *boléh* 'want', *mesti* 'must', *mo* 'want', and *mesti mo* 'must want' are auxiliaries that express modalities when they precede the main verb phrase (Aux VP).

5.2.3 Passivization

Passivization here refers to the process that promotes the object NP into the subject position. In Baba Malay, there are two patterns of passivization, the first of which uses the passive verb *kena*, and the other uses the ditransitive and causative verb *kasi* 'give' (see section 5.2.4 for more details of ditransitive and causative constructions). The form of passivization that is more commonly found and used is the *kena* passivization. When the passive verb *kena* is used, the logical subject is not expressed in the utterance. Examples (452) and (454) are the active counterparts of the passive sentences in examples (453) and (455).

(452) Orang itu pukol kuching.
person that hit cat
'That person hit the cat.'
(Victor, oai:scholarspace.manoa.hawaii.edu: NL1-009, 00:42:26.0-00:42:27.8)

(453) Itu kuching **kena** pukol.
that cat **PASS** hit
'That cat was hit.'
(Victor, oai:scholarspace.manoa.hawaii.edu: NL1-009, 00:42:37.0-00:42:38.8)

(454) Itu   kuching makan ikan.
      that   cat   eat   fish
      'That cat eats fish.'
      (Victor, oai:scholarspace.manoa.hawaii.edu: NL1-009, 00:37:23.2-00:37:25.5)

(455) Itu   ikan   sudah   **kena**   makan.
      That   fish   already **PASS**   eat
      'That fish has been eaten.'
      (Victor, oai:scholarspace.manoa.hawaii.edu: NL1-009, 00:38:17.8-00:38:19.9)

It is important to note that *kena* is an adversative passive, and is semantically incompatible with sentences that have non-adversative connotations. *Kena* is derived from Malay, where it had meant 'to hit' originally. The passive meaning is not inherent in the original Malay term, which requires that a prefix *ter-* be utilized for it to become a passive marker with the form *terkena* (see Tan, Musa and Seaton 2007). The adversative passive meaning that Baba Malay *kena* takes is a result of Hokkien influence, where passives are adversative. The term that *kena* adopts its functions from is the Hokkien adversative *tio?* (Lim 1988: 55). Note that besides being a passive marker, *kena* is also used as a non-volitional verb meaning 'subjected to', this particular non-volitional function is said to have been derived from the Hokkien passive *tio?* (Lim 1988). The following examples in (456) and (457) show how non-volitional *kena* is used.

(456) Tapi lu   ada **kena**   kaki   chaukah,   alamak.
      but   2SG PFV **subjected.to** friend bad.sport EXCLAM.dismay
      'But if you have been subjected to friends who are bad sports, oh no.'
      (Jane Quek, oai:scholarspace.manoa.hawaii.edu: NL1-142, 00:15:12.8-00:15:15.9)

(457) Mak   **kena**   masak.
      mother **subjected.to** cook
      'Mother was made to cook.'
      (Jane Quek, oai:scholarspace.manoa.hawaii.edu: NL1-142, 00:06:55.0-00:06:58.0)

As illustrated by example (456), a noun can follow *kena* when *kena* is used as a non-volitional verb, as compared to instances of *kena* passivization where the logical subject is not expressed, as with examples (453) and (455). It is thus important to differentiate between examples of non-volitional *kena* which is the auxiliary verb that precedes the main VP in (456) and (457), from true instances of passivization, where the object NP is promoted to subject position.

Whereas the oblique is not kept in passive *kena* sentences, it is maintained in *kasi* passives. *Kasi* literally means 'give', except that there is no volition involved when *kasi* is used as a passive on the part of the patient or the subject of the passive that undergoes the event. These passives are also adversative passives, and are most likely derived from Hokkien. In *kasi* passives (but not *kena* passives), the original object or semantic patient of the active sentence is promoted to subject in the passive sentence, and the logical subject becomes the subject of embedded clause. The sentence in example (459) is the passivized counterpart of the active sentence in example (458). Examples (460) and (461) are two other examples that utilize *kasi* passivization, which allows for the oblique or the original logical subject to be kept in the passive sentences. Examples (26) and (27) are replicated as (458) and (459).

(458) Mary bunoh dia.
      kill 3SG
 'Mary killed him.'
 (Victor, oai:scholarspace.manoa.hawaii.edu: NL1-037, 00:39:17.1-00:39:18.8)

(459) Dia **kasi** [Mary bunoh].
      3SG **PASS** Mary kill
 'He was killed by Mary.'
 (Victor, oai:scholarspace.manoa.hawaii.edu: NL1-037, 00:40:01.8-00:40:14.9)

(460) Orang **kasi** [embok-embok chakap].
      person **PASS** traditional.Peranakan.elders talk
 People were talked about by the traditional Peranakan elders.
 (Lilian, oai:scholarspace.manoa.hawaii.edu: NL1-079, 00:07:59.1-00:08:01.0)

(461) Siapa **kasi** [si Mary bunoh]?
      who **PASS** PERSON Mary kill
 'Who was killed by Mary?'
 (Victor, oai:scholarspace.manoa.hawaii.edu: NL1-037, 00:39:39.8-00:39:43.2)

5.2.4 Ditransitive, causative and benefactive constructions

Ditransitive, as well as causative and benefactive constructions are highly interconnected in Baba Malay. The typical ditransitive construction features the verb *kasi* 'give' which is also used for causative and benefactive constructions.

5.2.4.1 Ditransitive constructions

The typical ditransitive verb, *kasi* 'give' takes two arguments. In its complete form, the ditransitive verb phrase comprises the *kasi* verb, and a sequence comprising an indirect object (the semantic beneficiary) and a direct object NP (the semantic theme).

Examples (462) to (466) illustrate the *kasi* ditransitive construction. Example (422) is replicated below as (462).

(462) Dia **kasi** [dia] [dua bijik pear].
 3SG **give** 3SG two CLF.fruit pear
 'He gave him two pears.'
 (Peter Wee, oai:scholarspace.manoa.hawaii.edu: NL1-022, 00:05:04.0-00:05:05.4)

(463) Dia **kasi** [dia] [tiga].
 3SG **give** 3SG three
 'He gave him three.'
 (Peter Wee, oai:scholarspace.manoa.hawaii.edu: NL1-022, 00:05:20.9-00:05:22.6)

(464) Mak sudah **kasi** [gua] [duit].
 mother already **give** 1SG money
 'Mother already gave me money.'
 (Peter Wee, oai:scholarspace.manoa.hawaii.edu: NL1-094, 00:01:24.0-00:01:25.4)

(465) Mak.ko ada gula-gula mo **kasi** [lu] [dua].
 eldest.paternal.uncle's.wife have sweet-sweet want **give** 2SG two
 'Eldest paternal uncle's wife has sweets that she wants to give you two.'
 (Peter Wee, oai:scholarspace.manoa.hawaii.edu: NL1-094, 00:06:31.0-00:06:48.1)

(466) Dia **kasi** [gua] [itu lauk].
 3SG **give** 1SG that cooked.food
 'He gave me that cooked food.'
 (Jane Quek, oai:scholarspace.manoa.hawaii.edu: NL1-045, 00:17:42.3-00:17:45.0)

Other common ditransitive verbs include *ajair* 'teach', *pinjam* 'lend', and *tunjok* 'show'. Note that the substrate language, Hokkien, uses the same lexeme for both notions of lend and borrow, while the lexifier language, Malay, uses *pinjam* for borrow and *memberi pinjam* 'give borrow' for the concept of 'lending'. In Baba Malay, 'lend' is ditransitive, while 'borrow' is simply transitive, as demonstrated by examples (467) and (468). Example (469) shows how *tunjok* 'show' is used ditransitively.

(467) Lu **pinjam** [gua] [lu mia bég].
2SG **lend** 1SG 2SG REL bag
'You lend me your bag.'
(Jane Quek, oai:scholarspace.manoa.hawaii.edu: NL1-089, 00:28:07.5-00:28:10.0)

(468) Gua **pinjam** [lu mia bég kechik].
1SG **borrow** 2SG POSS bag small
'I borrow your small bag.'
(Jane Quek, oai:scholarspace.manoa.hawaii.edu: NL1-089, 00:28:16.1-00:28:18.5)

(469) Gua **tunjok** [lu] [keday].
1SG **show** 2SG shop
'I showed you the shop.'
(Jane Quek, oai:scholarspace.manoa.hawaii.edu: NL1-043, 00:38:38.1-00:38:39.7)

In general, in ditransitive instances where the verb takes an additional argument, the ditransitive verbs precede the beneficiary (an indirect object NP) and the theme (a direct object NP) in that order. Also, it is possible for either indirect object or direct object to not be expressed. In the ditransitive construction in (470), the indirect object is expressed, whereas in (471), the indirect object is not expressed. In (472), the direct object is not expressed. Example (468) is replicated as (470).

(470) Gua **pinjam** [lu mia bég kechik].
1SG **borrow** 2SG POSS bag small
'I borrow your small bag.'
(Jane Quek, oai:scholarspace.manoa.hawaii.edu: NL1-089, 00:28:16.1-00:28:18.5)

(471) Gua mo **kasi** [angpau].
1SG want **give** red.packet.of.monetary.gift
'I want to give a red packet.'
(Victor, oai:scholarspace.manoa.hawaii.edu: NL1-037, 00:44:51.2-00:44:52.4)

(472) Lu boléh **ajair** gua lah.
2SG can **teach** 1SG EMP
'You can teach me.'
(Peter Wee, oai:scholarspace.manoa.hawaii.edu: NL1-052, 00: 18:04.8-00:18:06.3)

5.2.4.2 Causative and benefactive constructions

Causatives in Baba Malay can also be formed with the verb *kasi*. These causatives have been identified in previous literature as being highly similar to a Hokkien construction that utilizes a corresponding lexical item *hor* 'give' (Pakir 1986; Shih 2009). In effect, the causative construction is similar to the ditransitive *kasi* construction, except that the indirect object NP does not necessarily benefit positively, and that the direct object theme is a verb phrase that represents the caused event which affects the indirect object NP. The indirect object NP and the verb phrase constitute an embedded clause, similar to the *kasi* passive construction (see section 5.2.3). The following sentences in examples (473) and (474) feature the causative construction using the verb *kasi*. Example (423) is replicated here as example (473).

(473) Yauguai, **kasi** [gua terperanjat sekali].
      demon   **cause** 1SG be.shocked   very
      'Demon, you made me be very shocked.'
      (Jane Quek, oai:scholarspace.manoa.hawaii.edu: NL1-043, 00:040:26.2-00:40:28.2)

(474) Dia **kasi** [gua marah sekali].
      3SG **cause** 1SG angry very
      'She made me very angry.'
      (Jane Quek, oai:scholarspace.manoa.hawaii.edu: NL1-043, 00:39:42.7-00:39:45.4)

Other than *kasi*, the verb *paksa* 'force' can also be used in causative constructions, such as with example (475).

(475) John **paksa** [Mary lupa-kan si   Peter].
           force   forget-TR PERSON Peter
      'John forced Mary (to) forget Peter.'
      (Victor, oai:scholarspace.manoa.hawaii.edu: NL1-057, 00:07:04.2-00:07:10.4)

There are also instances where the indirect object benefits from the particular event predicated by the embedded verb phrase. These are benefactive constructions. Note that *paksa* 'force' cannot be used in benefactive constructions. Only *kasi* 'give' can be used in these instances, such as with examples (476) to (478).

(476) Mak   **kasi** [gua pinjam satu ratus].
      mother **let** 1SG borrow one hundred
      'Mother let me borrow one hundred.'
      (Peter Wee, oai:scholarspace.manoa.hawaii.edu: NL1-094, 00:00:40.5-00:00:46.0)

(477) Saya ada satu lagu mo **kasi** [lu dengar].
　　　1SG have one song want **let** you hear
　　　'I have a song that I want to let you hear.'
　　　(Peter Wee, oai:scholarspace.manoa.hawaii.edu: NL1-094, 00:01:05.4-
　　　00:01:12.7)

(478) Jangan **kasi** [dia dengair ini pekara].
　　　do.not **let** 3SG hear this matter
　　　'Do not let him hear about this matter.'
　　　(Peter Wee, oai:scholarspace.manoa.hawaii.edu: NL1-094, 00:05:39.4-
　　　00:05:48.2)

5.2.5 Aspect and tense

Baba Malay utilizes an optional system that combines tense, aspect and mood, with its aspectual system (focusing on the unfolding of events) being the most complex. Figure 29 represents the tense, aspect and mood system of Baba Malay. The only tense that is available in Baba Malay is the future tense. The future tense can be expressed by using the adverbs *belom* 'not yet' and *nanti* 'later'. All of these indicate that the event in question has not taken place as of current time, but will take place later, or that it is highly probable that an event will take place in the opinion of the speaker. The aspectual system comprises the adverb *sudah* 'already', which has a perfective meaning, and the auxiliary verb *ada* 'have', which is used to indicate several aspects, including the perfective, the progressive, experiential perfect and habitual (all of these are relexified versions of its substrate counterpart, Hokkien *u*, see Lee 2009), the adverb *baru*, which has a recent perfect meaning, and the adverb *pernah* 'ever', which is also used to indicate the experiential perfect aspect. Tentative aspect is signaled by reduplication (see section 3.2.1). On the whole, the use of tense, aspect and mood markers is optional in Baba Malay, especially when there is enough context provided for the interlocutor to discern if the event has been completed, is ongoing, or will happen in the future. More details on how sentences can be modified with adverbial phrases that provides information of this sort can be found in section 5.6.6.1. Note also that most aspect markers are glossed in accordance to their literal meanings, because they contribute to the understanding of the particular aspect they are used for, except for *ada*. *Ada*, which is used to denote multiple aspects, has been glossed according to the list of linguistic abbreviations provided in section 1.3.2.

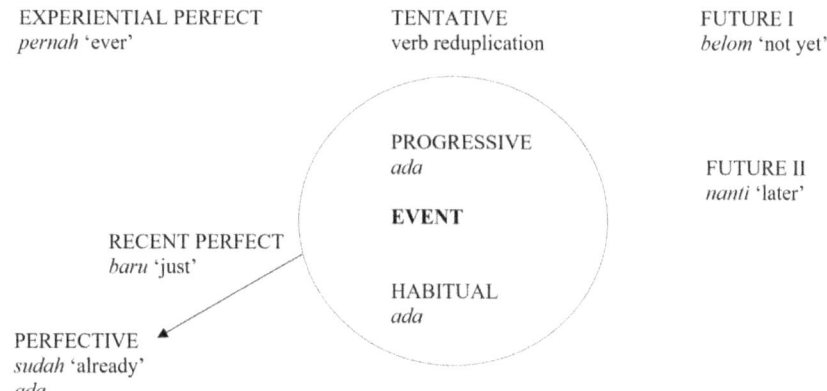

Figure 29: Tense and aspect system of Baba Malay.

5.2.5.1 Perfective aspect

Where aspect is concerned, Baba Malay differentiates between the perfective and the imperfective. The perfective, as used in this grammar, indicates a perspective of the event as an individuated whole, and is associated with completed action (see Comrie 1976:16). In Baba Malay, there are two ways to indicate the perfective aspect. These include the use of the adverb *sudah* and the auxiliary verb *ada*. While *sudah* (contracted version: *sua*) literally means 'already', *ada* has the lexical meaning of the verb 'have' and can also be used as an existential marker, a copula, a progressive marker, and a habitual marker. Examples (479) to (481) show how *ada* can be used to express the perfective aspect, and examples (482) to (484) show how *sudah* can be used for the same purpose.

(479) Dia **ada** beli   apple, bukan?
      3SG **PFV** bought   no
      'She bought an apple, no?'
      (Victor, oai:scholarspace.manoa.hawaii.edu: NL1-051, 00:40:03.5-00:40:06.9)

(480) **Ada** tukar   itu   burong.
      PFV change that bird
      '(It) changed (into) that bird.'
      (Jane Quek, oai:scholarspace.manoa.hawaii.edu: NL1-088, 00:04:15.0-00:04:18.0)

(481) Gua **ada** tutop.
      1SG **PFV** close
      'I closed (the door).'
      (Jane Quek, oai:scholarspace.manoa.hawaii.edu: NL1-043, 00:22:15.8-00:22:16.7)

(482) Gua **sudah** kata lu, betol?
1SG **already** tell 2SG correct
'I told you, right?'
(Peter Wee, oai:scholarspace.manoa.hawaii.edu: NL1-022, 00:03:38.0-00:03:39.6)

(483) Lu **sudah** jatoh lu mia kopiah.
2SG **already** dropped 2SG POSS hat
'You dropped your hat.'
(Peter Wee, oai:scholarspace.manoa.hawaii.edu: NL1-022, 00:04:55.5-00:04:57.5)

(484) Gua **sudah** tau.
1SG **already** know
'I knew.'
(Jane Quek, oai:scholarspace.manoa.hawaii.edu: NL1-043, 00:19:80.1-00:19:19.4)

5.2.5.2 Recent perfect aspect

Baru is used as an adverb to indicate the recent perfect, *baru* also being an adjective that has the literal meaning of 'new'. As an adverb, *baru* marks a situation as being recently completed. The completed situation usually still affects the current moment of speech. This is demonstrated by examples (485) and (486).

(485) Dia **baru** datang.
3SG **just** come
'He just came.'
(Victor, oai:scholarspace.manoa.hawaii.edu: NL1-051, 00:30:58.1-00:30:59.2)

(486) Dia **baru** dapat tau.
3SG **just** receive know
'He just got to know.'
(Jane Quek, oai:scholarspace.manoa.hawaii.edu: NL1-096, 00:00:24.2-00:00:25.8)

Note that in a separate construction, *baru* may also modify the cause that follows it, *baru* in this instance meaning 'just then', or just at that moment. This use is shown in examples (487) and (488).

(487) Lagik satu minggu, **baru**   dia   rasa baik
      more one   week   **just.then** 3SG feel good
      'One more week, just then he felt better.'
      (Victor, oai:scholarspace.manoa.hawaii.edu: NL1-051, 00:29:33.9-00:29:36.4)

(488) **Baru**   masok buah   paya
      just.then enter CLF.fruit papaya
      'Just then (you) put in papaya.'
      (Jane Quek, oai:scholarspace.manoa.hawaii.edu: NL1-142, 00:12:45.7-00:12:48.0)

5.2.5.3 Experiential perfect aspect

The perfect aspect, as used in this grammar, relates a particular state of event to a preceding situation (see Comrie 1976:52). The experiential perfect specifically indicates that a situation has happened some time during the past leading up to the present (see Comrie: 1976:58). In a sense, this combines both time and event, and hence relates to both tense and aspect. The experiential perfect in Baba Malay is expressed by the adverb *pernah* 'ever'. Both *pernah* 'ever' and *tak pernah* 'never' are commonly used in Baba Malay.

(489) Dia **pernah** jumpa gua.
      3SG **ever**   meet 1SG
      'He has met me before.'
      (Victor, oai:scholarspace.manoa.hawaii.edu: NL1-037, 00:03:37.0-00:03:38.2)

(490) John rasa dia **pernah** jumpa Mary.
           think 3SG **ever**   meet
      John thinks that he has met Mary before.'
      (Victor, oai:scholarspace.manoa.hawaii.edu: NL1-037, 00:42:23.6-00:42:25.7)

(491) Dia **tak** **pernah** bikin ini sumua.
      3SG **NEG** **ever**   do   this all
      'She never did this all.'
      (Victor, oai:scholarspace.manoa.hawaii.edu: NL1-037, 00:42:23.6-00:42:25.7)

5.2.5.4 Progressive aspect

The progressive aspect is imperfective, which focuses on the internal structure of a situation, or provides an inward perspective of the event in question (see Comrie 1976:24). As a specific type of imperfective aspect, the progressive refers to a temporary, continuous state (Comrie 1976). The progressive aspect in Baba Malay is expressed by using *ada* as an auxiliary verb. As *ada* expresses both the imperfective as well as the perfective (see section 5.2.5.1), context is usually required to differentiate both uses. Examples (492) to (494) illustrate the use of *ada* as a progressive aspect marker.

(492) Itu   perompuan **ada**   bacha magic book.
      that woman   **PROG**   read
      'That woman is reading a magic book.'
      (Jane Quek, oai:scholarspace.manoa.hawaii.edu: NL1-088, 00:08:46.5-00:08:49.1)

(493) Mak   tu   **ada**   bacha lagik.
      mother   that   **PROG**   read   more
      'That mother is reading more.'
      (Jane Quek, oai:scholarspace.manoa.hawaii.edu: NL1-088, 00:08:54.3-00:08:57.0)

(494) Lu   **ada**   bikin apa?
      2SG   **PROG**   make   what
      'You are making what?'
      (Peter Wee, oai:scholarspace.manoa.hawaii.edu: NL1-042, 00:12:50.2-00:12:51.8)

5.2.5.5 Habitual aspect

Another imperfective aspect in Baba Malay is the habitual, which is used to indicate that a situation is characteristic of an extended period of time (Comrie 1976:27–28). Again, *ada* can be used as an auxiliary verb that expresses the habitual aspect, so context is required to differentiate its use as a habitual aspect marker from its uses as a perfective and progressive aspect marker. Examples (495) to (497) illustrate *ada*'s use as a marker of habitual aspect.

(495) **Ada**   pegi.
      HAB   go
      '(I) usually go.'
      (Jane Quek, oai:scholarspace.manoa.hawaii.edu: NL1-142, 00:00:40.0-00:00:41.0)

(496) Nampak   gua   dia   **ada**   senyum.
      see   1SG   3SG   **HAB**   smile
      '(when she) sees me she usually smiles.'
      (Jane Quek, oai:scholarspace.manoa.hawaii.edu: NL1-043, 00:19:32.2-00:19:33.9)

(497) Tak   senang, gua **ada** masak
      NEG   free   1SG **HAB** cook
      'Not free, I usually cook.'
      (Jane Quek, oai:scholarspace.manoa.hawaii.edu: NL1-043, 00:02:07.6-
      00:02:09.7)

5.2.5.6 Tentative aspect

Tentative aspect is expressed in Baba Malay by verb reduplication (see section 3.2.1 for more details). Examples (498) and (499) illustrate tentative aspect reduplication. In these instances, there is no particular goal or purpose expressed, and the action that is predicated is meant to take place for a short duration of time. It has been claimed that the tentative aspect is a type of perfective aspect, since it represents a closed situation of short duration and relative unimportance (Smith 1991). Verbal reduplication that expresses tentative aspect is commonly found in Sinitic languages, such as Baba Malay's substrate, Hokkien (Tsao 2004).

(498) Jalan jalan
      walk   walk
      'Take a walk.'
      (Jane Quek, oai:scholarspace.manoa.hawaii.edu: NL1-142, 00:02:13.1-
      00:02:14.6)

(499) Téngok téngok
      look   look
      'Take a look.'
      (Jane Quek, oai:scholarspace.manoa.hawaii.edu: NL1-142, 00:02:14.6-
      00:02:16.2)

5.2.5.7 Future tense

Future tense is indicated in two ways in Baba Malay, through the use of the adverbs *belom* 'not yet' and *nanti* 'later'. In examples (500) to (502), *belom* 'not yet' is used to mark the future tense. In examples (503) to (505), *nanti* 'later' is used to do the same. In all these instances, the future tense adverbs precede the main verb phrase.

(500) Saya **belom**   kasi tau   mak.
      1SG   **not.yet** let   know   mother
      'I have not let mother know.'
      (Peter Wee, oai:scholarspace.manoa.hawaii.edu: NL1-094, 00:02:03.4-
      00:02:05.1)

(501) Dia **belom** habis.
3SG **not.yet** finish
'He has not finished.'
(Jane Quek, oai:scholarspace.manoa.hawaii.edu: NL1-142, 00:15:29.2-00:15:30.3)

(502) Budak-budak **belom** pegi.
child-PL **not.yet** go
'The children have not gone.'
(Jane Quek, oai:scholarspace.manoa.hawaii.edu: NL1-100, 00:11:33.1-00:11:37.1)

(503) John **nanti** belajar dua jam kat library
later study two hour PREP library
'John will study (for) two hours at the library.'
(Victor, oai:scholarspace.manoa.hawaii.edu: NL1-051, 00:28:40.5-00:28:50.1)

(504) Gua **nanti** tidor sampay bésok
1SG **later** sleep until tomorrow
'I will sleep until tomorrow.'
(Peter Wee, oai:scholarspace.manoa.hawaii.edu: NL1-058, 00:05:51.3-00:05:53.7)

(505) Gua **nanti** tak makan sampay dia masak ayam
1SG **later** NEG eat until 3SG cook chicken
'I will not eat until she cooks chicken.'
(Peter Wee, oai:scholarspace.manoa.hawaii.edu: NL1-058, 00:06:36.8-00:06:41.5)

Note that both *belom* 'not yet' and *nanti* 'later' are also adverbs that can modify the entire clause when placed in front of the clause. Examples (506) and (507) demonstrate how these adverbs modify the clauses that they precede.

506 **Belom** [dia pulang], gua sudah dapat tau.
before 3SG return.home 1SG already get know
'Before she returned home, I already got to know.'
(Jane Quek, oai:scholarspace.manoa.hawaii.edu: NL1-096, 00:03:17.4-00:03:40.4)

(507) **Nanti** [Mary tinggair dekat Singapore sampay January].
later stay PREP until
'Later Mary (will) stay in Singapore until January.'
(Victor, oai:scholarspace.manoa.hawaii.edu: NL1-051, 00:18:24.3-00:18:27.8)

5.2.6 Serial verb constructions

The notion of serial verbs that this grammar employs follows that of Sebba (1987) and Aikenvald (2005). There is neither clause boundary nor conjunction between the two verbs in a serial verb construction, and both verbs are lexical verbs that are interpreted to share the same categories of tense, aspect, and mood (Sebba 1987). Each component in the serial verb construction must also be able to occur on its own, which is not the case with periphrastic constructions (Aikhenvald 2005). In the case of Baba Malay, serial verb constructions also have to be differentiated from compound verbs such as *buang buang* (literally 'throw throw', meaning 'exorcise') or *naik geléték* (literally 'ascend tickle', meaning 'to be up to mischief'). Examples (508) to (515) show the use of serial verb constructions in Baba Malay. Note that serial verb constructions comprising three verbs are also possible, as in example (510).

(508) Dia [*turun*]   [*masok*].
    3SG **descend enter**
    'He descended and entered.'
    (Victor, oai:scholarspace.manoa.hawaii.edu: NL1-035, 00:05:37.3-00:05:39.8)

(509) Kodok [*turun*]   [*kuluair*].
    frog   **descend go.out**
    'The frog gets down and out.'
    (Jane Quek, oai:scholarspace.manoa.hawaii.edu: NL1-088, 00:08:31.4-00:08:33.3)

(510) Gua mo   [*kuluair*] [*pi*] [*jalan*].
    1SG want **go.out   go   walk**
    'I want to go out, and go and walk.'
    (Victor, oai:scholarspace.manoa.hawaii.edu: NL1-088, 00:53:39.7-00:53:41.8)

(511) Mama   gua mo   [*pi*] [*buang-ayé*].
    grandmother 1SG want **go   throw –water**
    'Grandmother I want to go urinate.'
    (Victor, oai:scholarspace.manoa.hawaii.edu: NL1-037, 00:48:25.8-00:48:27.5)

(512) [***Dudok***] [***téngok***] TV.
    sit   watch
    'Sit and watch the television.'
    (Jane Quek, oai:scholarspace.manoa.hawaii.edu: NL1-142, 00:03:17.1-00:03:19.0)

(513) Kodok tu [*naik*] [*panjat*].
frog that **ascend** **climb**
'The frog is ascending and climbing.'
(Jane Quek, oai:scholarspace.manoa.hawaii.edu: NL1-088, 00:07:37.3-
00:07:41.3)

(514) Kawan -kawan dia [*datang*] [*tolong*].
friend -friend 3SG **come** **help**
'His friends came and helped.'
(Peter Wee, oai:scholarspace.manoa.hawaii.edu: NL1-022, 00:03:58.4-
00:04:00.9)

(515) Kawan dia [*datang*] [*angkat satu kambing*].
friend 3SG **come** **hold** **one** **goat**
'His friend comes holding one goat.'
(Peter Wee, oai:scholarspace.manoa.hawaii.edu: NL1-022, 00:01:41.8-
00:01:44.8)

All instances of serial verb constructions in Baba Malay appear to involve a sequence of dynamic verbs and not stative ones. Speakers also state that it is unnatural for verb sequences to be broken up by conjunctions – serial verb constructions in Baba Malay involve an uninterrupted VP-VP sequence.

5.2.7 Verb phrases with adverbial modifiers

Verb phrases may also be modified by adverbs. Earlier examples of this are seen in section 5.2.5, where adverbs may precede verbs to express tense and aspect. Examples (516) to (525) show the use of other adverbs that may precede or follow the verb phrase.

(516) ***Itu*** bangkuang ***pun*** tak bergerak.
that turnip **also** NEG move
'That turnip also does not move.'
(Victor, oai:scholarspace.manoa.hawaii.edu: NL1-034, 00:01:20.0-00:01:22.2)

(517) Aunty Jane ***selalu*** ketawa-kan gua.
always laugh-TR 1SG
'Aunty Jane always laughs at me.'
(Jane Quek, oai:scholarspace.manoa.hawaii.edu: NL1-043, 00:18:03.5-
00:18:06.4)

(518) Dia **langsong** tidor.
 3SG **straightaway** sleep
 'She slept straightaway.'
 (Victor, oai:scholarspace.manoa.hawaii.edu: NL1-032, 00:06:54.0-00:06:55.8)

(519) Gua **terus** lari.
 1SG **straight** run
 'I ran straight.'
 (Lilian, oai:scholarspace.manoa.hawaii.edu: NL1-079, 00:00:56.7-00:00:57.5)

(520) Dia **pelan-pelan** makan kurang.
 3SG **slow-slow** eat less
 'They slowly eat less.'
 (Lilian, oai:scholarspace.manoa.hawaii.edu: NL1-079, 00:03:42.6-00:03:44.4)

(521) Lu dudok **diam-diam**.
 2SG sit **quiet-quiet**
 'You sit quietly.'
 (Jane Quek, oai:scholarspace.manoa.hawaii.edu: NL1-045, 00:19:50.0-00:19:52.8)

(522) Ingat **baik-baik**.
 remember good-good
 'Remember well.'
 (Jane Quek, oai:scholarspace.manoa.hawaii.edu: NL1-043, 00:21:20.1-00:21:22.7)

(523) Boléh lu tolong gua masak **lagik?**
 can 2SG help 1SG cook **again**
 'Can you help me cook again?'
 (Jane Quek, oai:scholarspace.manoa.hawaii.edu: NL1-045, 00:13:30.1-00:13:34.1)

(524) Dia lalu **pulak**.
 3SG pass **instead**
 'He passed by instead.'
 (Victor, oai:scholarspace.manoa.hawaii.edu: NL1-028, 00:02:14.0-00:02:15.1)

(525) Masak **sahja**
 cook only
 '(I) cook only.'
 (Jane Quek, oai:scholarspace.manoa.hawaii.edu: NL1-142, 00:05:55.9-00:05:57.1)

Of the possible adverbs in Baba Malay, functional adverbs have fixed positions. Some may always precede the verb phrase while others always follow the verb phrase. Table 37 provides a list of commonly used functional adverbs that modify verb phrases, and their positions in relation to the verb phrase.

Table 37: List of commonly used functional adverbs that modify verb phrases and their distributions.

Functional adverb	Use	Position
pun/kun	also	_ VP
selalu	always	_ VP
baru	just	_ VP
balék	again, back	VP _
dulu	first (before doing something else)	VP _
lagik	still, more, again	VP _
pulak	instead	VP _
sahja	only	VP _
jugak	also	VP _

There is no preferred position for the adverb that modifies the verb phrase, a verb phrase comprising Adv VP, or VP Adv. Both are equally common.

5.2.8 Negation of verb phrases

There are a couple of ways in which a verb can be negated, the most general negative marker being *tak*. This marker precedes the verb phrase that it negates. Examples (526) to (530) demonstrate how *tak* is used to negate the verb phrase.

(526) **Tak** jadi.
 NEG happen
 '(It) did not happen.'
 (Peter Wee, oai:scholarspace.manoa.hawaii.edu: NL1-022, 00:02:55.0-00:02:56.3)

(527) *Gua* **tak** *reti.*
 1SG **NEG** understand
 'I do not understand.'
 (Victor, oai:scholarspace.manoa.hawaii.edu: NL1-053, 00:16:31.2-00:16:32.0)

(528) Dia **tak** pi.
 3SG **NEG** go
 'She does not go.'
 (Jane Quek, oai:scholarspace.manoa.hawaii.edu: NL1-142, 00:04:50.5-00:04:51.2)

(529) Itu kambing, gua **tak** tau perompuan ka jantan.
 That goat 1SG **NEG** know female or male
 'That goat, I don't know (if it is) female or male.'
 (Peter Wee, oai:scholarspace.manoa.hawaii.edu: NL1-022, 00:01:47.3-00:01:49.8)

(530) Gua rasa pear tu **tak** boléh makan
 1SG think that **NEG** can eat
 'I think that pear cannot be eaten.'
 (Peter Wee, oai:scholarspace.manoa.hawaii.edu: NL1-022, 00:05:24.3-00:05:25.7)

Commonly used negated forms of verbs have also been developed by contracting negative marker and verb. These contracted forms are *tak-a*, from *tak ada* 'NEG have', and *toksa*, from *tok usa* 'NEG need'. Examples (531) and (532) demonstrate the use of *tak-a*, while (533) to (535) demonstrate the use of *toksa*.

(531) **Tak-a Tak-a**
 NEG-PFV
 '(Did) not.'
 (Jane Quek, oai:scholarspace.manoa.hawaii.edu: NL1-043, 00:22:14.8-00:22:15.8)

(532) Kita sini **tak-a** pokok.
 1PL here **NEG-have** tree
 'Here we do not have trees.'
 (Peter Wee, oai:scholarspace.manoa.hawaii.edu: NL1-022, 00:00:35.5-00:00:36.9)

(533) **Toksa.**
 NEG.need
 'No need.'
 (Lilian, oai:scholarspace.manoa.hawaii.edu: NL1-079, 00:15:25.0-00:15:25.5)

(534) ***Toksa***   *tanya.*
NEG.need   ask
'(Do) not need to ask.'
(Victor, oai:scholarspace.manoa.hawaii.edu: NL1-037, 00:47:31.6-00:47:33.4)

(535) ***Toksa***   *marah*[64]
NEG.need   angry
'(Do) not need to be angry.'
(Jane Quek, oai:scholarspace.manoa.hawaii.edu: NL1-022, 00:40:02.6-00:40:01.0)

Other than *tak*, *jangan* is also used in the negation of verb phrases. Specifically, *jangan* is used in imperatives or commands. More details on non-negative imperatives can be found in section 5.6.11. Examples (536) to (539) show how *jangan* is used in negative imperatives.

(536) ***Jangan***   *raba.*
do.not   touch
'Do not touch.'
(Jane Quek, oai:scholarspace.manoa.hawaii.edu: NL1-043, 00:21:17.3-0021:18.7)

(537) ***Jangan***   *rindu*   *gua.*
do.not   miss   1SG
'Do not miss me.'
(Jane Quek, oai:scholarspace.manoa.hawaii.edu: NL1-043, 00:29:30.0-00:29:32.4)

(538) ***Jangan***   *nangis.*
do.not   cry
'Do not cry.'
(Jane Quek, oai:scholarspace.manoa.hawaii.edu: NL1-043, 00:29:32.4-00:29:33.7)

(539) ***Jangan***   *marah.*
do.not   angry
'Do not (be) angry.'
(Jane Quek, oai:scholarspace.manoa.hawaii.edu: NL1-043, 00:40:08.1-00:40:09.9)

---

64 The copula is optional in Baba Malay.

All negative markers precede the main verb phrase, and negative verb phrases share the structure NEG-VP.

5.2.9 Order of elements in verb phrases

The verb phrase in Baba Malay is not strictly head-final, as adverbs may precede or follow verbs. However, there is still a head-final tendency, considering that both adverbs of tense and aspect, as well as auxiliary verbs strictly precede verbs. Negative markers also precede verbs. Where the main verb phrase is concerned, a verb phrase can comprise an intransitive verb, a transitive verb with direct object, a ditransitive verb with a direct object and indirect object, or a sequence of verbs in the manner of serial verb constructions. It is also possible for the object of a verb to comprise an entire clause, as with causative constructions.

5.3 Adjectival phrases

Adjectival phrases in Baba Malay include comparatives, comparatives of equality, comparatives of similarity, and expressions of excessive degree. Notions of superlatives are expressed by relative clauses, given the appropriate context. Adjectival phrases can also feature adverbs that precede or follow the adjective. Whereas noun phrases are negated by *bukan*, and general verb phrases by *tak*, adjectives have no direct negators. Adjectives are negated as part of a larger verbal phrase negation. A range of different adjectival phrases are featured in examples (540) to (546), including the comparative and superlative in examples (540) to (543), an expression of excessive degree in (544), and adverb-modified adjective phrases in (545) and (546). The negation of a verb phrase featuring an adjective is featured in example (547).

(540) Comparative
Ini   apple lagik manis lagik itu   apple.
this   more   sweet more   that
'This apple (is) sweet than that one.'
(Victor, oai:scholarspace.manoa.hawaii.edu: NL1-009, 00:35:27.2-00:35:29.8)

(541) Comparison of equality
Dia tinggi sama ngko.
3SG tall   same older.brother
'He (is) tall like older brother.'
(Victor, oai:scholarspace.manoa.hawaii.edu: NL1-009, 00:10:16.2-00:10:17.5)

(542) Comparison of similarity
Kerair begi batu.
hard like rock
'Hard like a rock.'
(Peter Wee, oai:scholarspace.manoa.hawaii.edu: NL1-022, 00:05:25.7-00:05:25.9)

(543) Superlative (relative clause)
Ini apple yang manis sekali.
this REL sweet very
'This (is the) apple that (is) very sweet.'
(Victor, oai:scholarspace.manoa.hawaii.edu: NL1-009, 00:35:46.0-00:35:47.8)

(544) Excessive degree
Terlalu sejok.
too cold
'Too cold.'
(Victor, oai:scholarspace.manoa.hawaii.edu: NL1-032, 00:04:42.3-00:04:43.6)

(545) Adverb and Adjective
Budak ini **sangat kechik** *lah.*
child this **very small** EMP
'This child (is) very small.'
(Peter Wee, oai:scholarspace.manoa.hawaii.edu: NL1-022, 00:03:23.5-00:03:25.3)

(546) Adjective and Adverb
Kambing dia **kuat sekali**.
goat 3SG **strong very**
'His goat (is) very strong.'
(Peter Wee, oai:scholarspace.manoa.hawaii.edu: NL1-022, 00:01:53.3-00:01:54.6)

(547) Negation of Verb Phrase with Adjective
Barang **tak hak** *tak beli lah.*
thing **NEG suitable** NEG buy EMP
'The thing (is) not suitable, (we) do not buy.'
(Jane Quek, oai:scholarspace.manoa.hawaii.edu: NL1-142, 00:02:18.5-00:02:20.2)

Note in example (547), that while it appears as though the negative marker *tak* precedes the adjective directly, copulas are usually unexpressed in Baba Malay, and that *tak* negates the verb phrase that comprises *hak* as its complement. Verb phrase negation is covered in section 5.2.8.

5.3.1 Comparatives

Comparatives in Baba Malay are expressed by the structure *lagik*-AP-*lagik*, *lagik*-AP and AP-*lagik*, as shown in the following examples (also see Lee 1999). *Lagik* has the literal meaning of 'more' in these instances.[65] Examples (548) to (553) demonstrate comparative expressions that exist in Baba Malay. The noun phrase that follows the comparative expression is an oblique, as shown by (552) and (553). Example (540) is replicated here as (548).

(548) Ini apple **lagik** manis **lagik** itu apple.
 this **more** sweet **more** that
 'This apple (is) sweet than that one.'
 (Victor, oai:scholarspace.manoa.hawaii.edu: NL1-009, 00:35:27.2-00:35:29.8)

(549) Ini budak panday **lagik** itu budak.
 this child clever **more** that child
 'This child (is) more clever than that child.'
 (Jane Quek, oai:scholarspace.manoa.hawaii.edu: NL1-009, 00:34:17.0-00:34:22.7)

(550) Rumah batu **lagik** bagus **lagik** rumah yang lain.
 house rock **more** good **more** house REL other
 'The rock house (is) better than the house that (is) the other.'
 (Victor, oai:scholarspace.manoa.hawaii.edu: NL1-035, 00:03:16.9-00:03:27.0)

(551) Rumah kayu **lagik** bagus **lagik** rumah rumpot kering.
 house wood **more** good **more** house grass dry
 'The wooden house (is) better than the hay house.'
 (Victor, oai:scholarspace.manoa.hawaii.edu: NL1-035, 00:02:46.1-00:02:50.2)

(552) **Lagik** senang.
 more easy
 '(It is) easier.'
 (Jane Quek, oai:scholarspace.manoa.hawaii.edu: NL1-142, 00:12:50.4-00:12:50.9)

---

65 *Lagik* also means 'still, later, and again.'

(553) Ini **lagik** shiok[66]   kan?[67]
       this **more** satisified.feeling no
       'It feels better, no?'
       (Lilian, oai:scholarspace.manoa.hawaii.edu: NL1-079, 00:07:24.0-00:07:25.7)

The expression of comparative always follows the noun phrase that it modifies. Again the copula is non-obligatory.

5.3.2 Comparison of equality

It is also possible in Baba Malay to express equality using the structure in the following examples of (554) to (556), where *sama* is used to link the adjective with the noun phrase the subject is being compared to. The *sama NP* sequence functions as an adverb that modifies the adjective preceding it. Example (541) is replicated as (554) here.

(554) *Tapi dia tinggi **sama** ngko.*
       But   3SG tall   **same** older.brother
       'But he (is) tall like older brother.'
       (Victor, oai:scholarspace.manoa.hawaii.edu: NL1-009, 00:10:16.2-00:10:17.5)

(555) *Derek tinggi **sama** ngko   dia.*
              tall   **same** older.brother 3SG
       'Derek (is) tall like his older brother.'
       (Victor, oai:scholarspace.manoa.hawaii.edu: NL1-009, 00:10:31.5-00:10:33.6)

(556) *Panday **sama** anak dia.*
       clever **same** son   3SG
       'Clever like her son.'
       (Victor, oai:scholarspace.manoa.hawaii.edu: NL1-009, 00:08:10.1-00:08:12.1)

Again, the main noun phrase precedes the adjectival phrase, except for example (556), where the subject is dropped. Subjects are optional in Baba Malay (see section 5.6.2).

---

66 This is the only word where ʃ is found, hence *shiok* [ʃoʔ] is not part of the stable consonant inventory. The word itself may have been derived from Punjabi *shauk* [ʃjawʔ], which is an exclamation that is akin to 'great'.

67 *Kan* in this instance is a contracted version of *bukan* 'no'.

5.3.3 Comparison of similarity

Another type of comparison in Baba Malay is that of similarity. These expressions are akin to stating that the subject in question is similar to something else, but not completely alike. For these expressions, *begitu* or *macham* are used, both meaning 'like'. The contracted form of *begitu* is *begi*. Similar to comparatives of equality, *begi* NP and *macham* NP function as adverbs that modify the adjectives or verbs they follow, except for examples (560) and (562) where they modify the noun phrases that they follow. Note that many of these expressions featuring *begitu* or *macham* are idiomatic, as with examples (558), (559), (561), and (562). Example (542) is replicated here as example (557).

(557) Kerair **begi** batu
 hard **like** rock
 'Hard like a rock.'
 (Peter Wee, oai:scholarspace.manoa.hawaii.edu: NL1-022, 00:05:25.7-00:05:25.9)

(558) Dia-orang seronoh **begi** kain lipat
 3-PL proper **like** cloth fold
 'They (are) proper like a folded cloth.'
 (Peter Wee, oai:scholarspace.manoa.hawaii.edu: NL1-052, 00:03:03.8-00:03:13.0)

(559) Dia chakap **begi** lidah tak-a tulang.
 3SG speak **like** tongue NEG-have bone
 'He speaks like a tongue without bone (uncontrollable).'
 (Peter Wee, oai:scholarspace.manoa.hawaii.edu: NL1-104, 00:13:51.4-00:13:53.8)

(560) Itu **macham** Chettiar Melaka
 that **like**
 'That (is) like the Chettiars in Malacca (known for being moneylenders)'
 (Lilian, oai:scholarspace.manoa.hawaii.edu: NL1-079, 00:02:21.7-00:02:23.4)

(561) Orang ni panday sekali **macham** gauchaytian
 person this clever very **like** monkey.god
 'This person (is) very clever like the monkey god.'
 (Peter Wee, oai:scholarspace.manoa.hawaii.edu: NL1-104, 00:22:36.7-00:22:40.8)

(562) Dia **macham** kain lipat
      3SG **like**   cloth fold
      'He (is) like a folded cloth (very proper).'
      (Peter Wee, oai:scholarspace.manoa.hawaii.edu: NL1-052, 00:03:28.7-00:03:21.3)

5.3.4 Superlatives

There is no actual grammatical construction in Baba Malay that is strictly a superlative. In fact, the interpretation of the notion of a superlative depends on the given context, and superlatives take the form of relative clauses (see section 5.6.3). For example, the speaker produces (563) and (564) after giving examples about what constitutes comparatives, the earlier example (548) being the comparative counterpart of these sentences. Similarly, example (565) is produced in this speaker's retelling of Grimm's *The Three Little Pigs*, and after producing this utterance, he says in English, "the youngest". Example (543) is replicated here as (563).

(563) Ini   apple **yang** manis sekali.
      this   **REL**   sweet very
      'This is the apple that is very sweet (the sweetest apple)'.
      (Victor, oai:scholarspace.manoa.hawaii.edu: NL1-009, 00:35:46.0-00:35:47.8)

(564) Ni   **yang** manis sekali.
      this **REL**   sweet very
      'This is that which is very sweet (this which is the sweetest).'
      (Victor, oai:scholarspace.manoa.hawaii.edu: NL1-009, 00:35:43.0-00:35:43.7)

(565) Si   babi **yang** kechik.
      PERSON   pig   **REL**   small
      'The pig that is small (the pig that is the smallest)'
      (Victor, oai:scholarspace.manoa.hawaii.edu: NL1-035, 00:01:12.0-00:01:17.0)

These sentences that are to be interpreted as superlatives are essentially relative clauses that post-modify the noun phrase head. Lee (1999) also interprets similar constructions to be superlatives, although she does not identify these as relative clauses. More information on relative clauses can be found in section 5.6.3.

5.3.5 Excessive degree

Excessive degree is expressed in Baba Malay by pre-modifying the adjective concerned with the adverb *terlalu* 'too'. In Malay, *ter-* forms the superlative when attached to an adjective. However, in Baba Malay, *ter-* is attached to the verb *lalu* which means to 'pass something or someone by', and the resulting adverb expresses the notion of 'too', or to an excessive degree. The prefix *ter-* is otherwise not productive, the other unrelated *ter-* prefix being used to express that a verb is accidental or involves movement (see section 4.2.1.1). Examples (566) to (571) show utterances that express excessive degree.

(566) *Itu   kuéh-kuéh   **terlalu**   manis.*
      that   cake-PL   **too**   sweet
      'Those cakes (are) too sweet.'
      (Victor, oai:scholarspace.manoa.hawaii.edu: NL1-053, 00:05:50.4-00:05:54.5)

(567) *Tu   kuéh   rasa   **terlalu**   manis.*
      that cake   feel   **too**   sweet
      'That cake (I) feel (is) too sweet.'
      (Victor, oai:scholarspace.manoa.hawaii.edu: NL1-053, 00:06:27.6-00:06:30.3)

(568) *Itu   bubor   **terlalu**   panas.*
      that   porridge   **too**   hot
      'That porridge (is) too hot.'
      (Victor, oai:scholarspace.manoa.hawaii.edu: NL1-032, 00:04:27.2-00:04:30.6)

(569) *Itu   kerosi   **terlalu**   keras.*
      that   chair   **too**   hard
      'That chair (is) too hard.'
      (Victor, oai:scholarspace.manoa.hawaii.edu: NL1-032, 00:05:19.8-00:05:21.4)

(570) *Kerosi   tu   **terlalu**   lembéh.*
      chair   that   **too**   soft
      'That chair (is) too soft.'
      (Victor, oai:scholarspace.manoa.hawaii.edu: NL1-032, 00:05:29.2-00:05:31.8)

(571) *Itu   pun   **terlalu**   tinggi.*
      that   also   **too**   tall
      'That (is) also too tall.'
      (Victor, oai:scholarspace.manoa.hawaii.edu: NL1-032, 00:06:34.1-00:06:35.7)

Where expressions of excessive degree are concerned, the adjectival phrase is head-final, with preceding modifier *terlalu* 'too'.

5.3.6 Adjectival phrases with adverbial modifiers

In general, adverbs may precede or follow the main adjectival phrase. Examples (572) to (574) show adverbs preceding the adjective while examples (575) to (577) show adverbs following the adjective. Example (545) is replicated below as example (572).

(572) **Sunggu** chukop
really enough
'Just nice.'
(Victor, oai:scholarspace.manoa.hawaii.edu: NL1-032, 00:05:50.8-00:05:52.3)

(573) Budak ini **sangat** kechik lah.
child this **very** small EMP
'This child (is) very small.'
(Peter Wee, oai:scholarspace.manoa.hawaii.edu: NL1-022, 00:03:23.5-00:03:25.3)

(574) **Manyak** panas, dia tak boléh tahan.
Many hot 3SG NEG can withstand
'(It is) very hot, she cannot stand (it).'
(Jane Quek, oai:scholarspace.manoa.hawaii.edu: NL1-142, 00:04:28.6-00:04:30.6)

(575) Mahal **sikit**
expensive **little**
'A little expensive.'
(Jane Quek, oai:scholarspace.manoa.hawaii.edu: NL1-142, 00:02:48.7-00:02:50.0)

(576) Chanték **sekali**
beautiful **very**
'Very beautiful.'
(Jane Quek, oai:scholarspace.manoa.hawaii.edu: NL1-142, 00:02:35.7-00:02:37.2)

(577) Dulu dia jahat **sikit**.
long.ago 3SG evil **little**
'Long ago he (was) a little evil.'
(Jane Quek, oai:scholarspace.manoa.hawaii.edu: NL1-142, 00:02:35.7-00:02:37.2)

There is no preference for the adjectival phrase to be either head-initial or head-final. Both are observed to be equally common in Baba Malay.

5.3.7 Order of elements in adjectival phrases

The different types of adjectival phrases covered in this section are general comparatives, comparatives of equality, comparatives of similarity, superlatives (in the form of relative clauses), and expressions of excessive degree, as well as simple adjectival phrases that are either pre-modified or post-modified by adverbs. In many instances (such as with the different comparatives), the modifiers mostly follow the head adjective. However, it is also common to have modifiers preceding the adjectives, as with expressions of excessive degree and general modifications of the simple adjectival phrase. Note that adverbs may also precede or follow basic adjectival phrases. In general, similar to dealing with the noun phrase, it is inaccurate to state that the adjectival phrase has a preference for being head-initial or head-final.

5.4 Adverbial phrases

In earlier sections, adverbs have been shown to modify verbs and adjectives in Baba Malay. This section shows how the adverbial phrase may provide more information on matters of time, location, manner, intensity, and degree. These adverbial phrases are not strictly limited to phrases containing adverbs. They may also be noun phrases, prepositional phrases, or adjectival phrases that function as modifiers of verb phrases and other adjectival phrases. These adverbial phrases also have to be differentiated from adverbial clauses that modify other clauses (see section 5.6.6). Examples (578) to (580) demonstrate the use of different adverbial phrases.

(578) Temporal
Mary   nanti   tinggair   Melaka   dua   minggu.
              later   live   two   week
'Mary will stay in Malacca for two weeks.'
(Victor, oai:scholarspace.manoa.hawaii.edu: NL1-051, 00:28:06.4-00:28:12.4)

(579) Location
Mary   beli   apple   kat   pasair.
              buy   PREP   market
'Mary bought the apple at the market.'
(Victor, oai:scholarspace.manoa.hawaii.edu: NL1-051, 00:33:27.0-00:33:32.4)

(580) Manner
Kuching.belanda   lari   chepat   sekali
rabbit   run   fast   very
'The rabbit ran very fast.'
(Peter Wee, oai:scholarspace.manoa.hawaii.edu: NL1-030, 00:00:51.0-00:00:55.1)

5.4.1 Temporal adverbial phrases

Adverbial phrases may be used to indicate information regarding time. In Baba Malay, it is common to have noun phrase or preposition phrase functioning as an adverbial phrase that modifies the verb phrase. Examples (581) to (583) demonstrate ways in which the noun phrase and preposition phrase can modify the verb phrase. Example (578) is replicated below as example (581).

(581) Mary   nanti   tinggair   Melaka   **dua   minggu.**
               later   live   **two   week**
       'Mary will stay in Malacca for two weeks.'
       (Victor, oai:scholarspace.manoa.hawaii.edu: NL1-051, 00:28:06.4-00:28:12.4)

(582) John   nanti   belajar   **dua   jam   kat**   library.
               later   study   **two   hour PREP**
       'John will study for two hours at the library.'
       (Victor, oai:scholarspace.manoa.hawaii.edu: NL1-051, 00:28:40.5-00:28:50.1)

(583) Kukus   tu   sayor   **dalam   se-puloh   minit.**
       steam   that   vegetable   **inside one-ten   minute**
       'Steam those vegetables for ten minutes.'
       (Victor, oai:scholarspace.manoa.hawaii.edu: NL1-051, 00:27:29.9-00:27:36.5)

Adverbial phrases regarding time usually follow the verb phrases that they modify instead of preceding them. A sentence may also have more than one adverbial phrase, as with example (582), which has two adverbial phrases, the first one following the verb phrase expressing time, and the second one expressing location.

5.4.2 Location adverbial phrases

Adverbial phrases in Baba Malay that usually comprise prepositional phrases are used to convey information regarding location. Examples (584) to (587) illustrate this use. Example (295) is replicated here as (584), (275) appears here as (585), and (582) appears here as (586).

(584) Dia   dudok   **bawah   pokok.**
       3SG   sit   **bottom   tree**
       'He sat at the bottom of the tree.'
       (Peter Wee, oai:scholarspace.manoa.hawaii.edu: NL1-022, 00:01:34.9-00:01:37.1)

(585) Kupukupu trebang **di**   **dekat** itu   mia anjing.
butterfly fly   **PREP** **near** that REL dog
'The butterfly flew near that dog.'
(Peter Wee, oai:scholarspace.manoa.hawaii.edu: NL1-030, 00:01:36.8-00:01:41.7)

(586) John nanti belajar dua jam   **kat**   library.
later study   two hour **PREP**
'John will study for two hours at the library.'
(Victor, oai:scholarspace.manoa.hawaii.edu: NL1-051, 00:28:40.5-00:28:50.1)

(587) Ada   gui   **kat**   **sana.**
PROG kneel **PREP** **there**
'(They) are kneeling there.'
(Jane Quek, oai:scholarspace.manoa.hawaii.edu: NL1-088, 00:05:43.6-00:05:45.8)

Again, these adverbial phrases that modify the verb phrase usually follow rather than precede it. A verb phrase may also be modified by more than one adverbial phrase, as with example (586). There is no preference for any specific order where these adverbial phrases are concerned. The temporal adverbial phrase may precede location adverbial phrase, or vice versa.

5.4.3 Manner adverbial phrases

Adverbial phrases may also be used to indicate the manner in which something is done. Adverbial phrases can comprise adjectives used as adverbs, as with examples (588) and (589). Adverbial phrases expressing manner may also comprise preposition phrases featuring *sama* 'with',[68] as in examples (590) and (591). Example (580) is replicated here as (588).

(588) Kuching.belanda lari **chepat** **sekali.**
rabbit   run **fast**   **very**
'The rabbit ran very fast.'
(Peter Wee, oai:scholarspace.manoa.hawaii.edu: NL1-030, 00:00:51.0-00:00:55.1)

---

68 *Sama* is also used as the general conjunction marker, equivalent to 'and'.

(589) *Labi.labi main **pelan** sair.*
 tortoise play **slow** CONF
 'The tortoise played slowly indeed.'
 (Peter Wee, oai:scholarspace.manoa.hawaii.edu: NL1-030, 00:00:58.4-00:01:00.6)

(590) *Lu boléh bukak itu pintu **sama ini** konchi.*
 2SG can open that door **with this** key
 'You can open that door with this key.'
 (Victor, oai:scholarspace.manoa.hawaii.edu: NL1-123, 00:05:30.3-00:05:33.8)

(591) *Dia pinjak itu kachua **sama dia mia** kasot.*
 3SG step.on that cockroach **with 3SG POSS** shoe
 'He stepped on that cockroach with his shoe.'
 (Victor, oai:scholarspace.manoa.hawaii.edu: NL1-123, 00:06:06.1-00:06:09.8)

5.4.4 Order of elements in adverbial phrases

While single-word adverbs may precede or follow the verb phrase, more complex adverbial phrases like the ones in this section usually follow the verb instead of preceding it. These adverbial phrases expressing time, location, and manner are mostly head-initial, with the modifiers (mainly complements) following the heads, rather than preceding them.

5.5 Summary of word order at the phrase level

Table 38 sums up the different types of word order at the phrase level, and the default order of individual phrases, if any.

Table 38: List of phrases, their word orders and general tendency.

NP	DEM N / N DEM	No dominant tendency
	A *punya* N / N A (basic)	
	GEN *punya* N (basic) / N GEN	
	(only when possessor is a pronoun)	
	PERSON N	
	NUM N	
	CLF N	
	NEG N	

Table 38 (continued)

VP	AUX V ADV V (strictly so for tense and aspect) V ADV NEG V	Modifier-head tendency
AP	ADV A A ADV	No dominant tendency
AdvP	ADV COMP	Head-modifier tendency
Prepositions		

The observed word orders in Baba Malay are interesting for being different from the common parameters postulated for SVO languages (Greenberg 1963), especially with the lack of dominant tendencies for NPs and APs. Also, while VPs have a modifier-head tendency, AdvP are the opposite, with a head-modifier tendency.

5.6 Clauses

While the preceding sections focused on phrase-internal structures, this section focuses on order at the higher clause level. Essentially, these sections are concerned with what phrases constitute a clause (or what some may refer to as a sentence), and what more complex clauses (such as relative clauses, complement clauses, among others) comprise.

5.6.1 Word order at the clause level

Clauses are generally predicate-final, the verb functioning as the predicate in most instances. This is demonstrated by examples (592) and (593). Example (24) is shown below as (592).

(592) *Budak tu* **senyum**
child that **smile**
'That child smiles.'
(Jane Quek, oai:scholarspace.manoa.hawaii.edu: NL1-088, 00:00:35.9-00:00:37.7)

(593) Budak **pakay** baju
child **wear** clothes
'The child puts on clothes.'
(Jane Quek, oai:scholarspace.manoa.hawaii.edu: NL1-088, 00:00:59.4-00:01:01.8)

Sentences featuring adjectives like the ones that follow in examples (594) and (595), can be interpreted to have an unexpressed copula predicate. For the purpose of comparison, example (596) features an expressed copula, copulas being optional in Baba Malay.

(594) Ini orang **kiamsiap** sair.
this person **miserly** CONF
'This person (is) miserly indeed.'
(Jane Quek, oai:scholarspace.manoa.hawaii.edu: NL1-105, 00:02:06.1-00:02:07.5)

(595) Ini orang **tuakang sekali**.
this person **generous very**
'This person (is) very generous.'
(Jane Quek, oai:scholarspace.manoa.hawaii.edu: NL1-105, 00:01:29.8-00:01:32.5)

(596) Ini piso **ada** tajam.
this knife **COP** sharp
'This knife is sharp.'
(Jane Quek, oai:scholarspace.manoa.hawaii.edu: NL1-105, 00:03:58.5-00:03:59.9)

Similarly, sentence-final predicates can include noun phrases, as with examples (597) and (598). Again, the copula is not expressed in these cases. Example (146) is replicated as (597) here.

(597) Ini **buah** pear.
this **CLF.FRUIT**
'These (are) pears.'
(Peter Wee, oai:scholarspace.manoa.hawaii.edu: NL1-022, 00:00:27.9-00:00:28.9)

(598) Peter punya bapak sama William punya bapak **adék-beradék**.
POSS father and POSS father **sibling-PL**
'Peter's father and William's father (are) siblings.'
(Victor, oai:scholarspace.manoa.hawaii.edu: NL1-009, 00:45:01.7-00:45:06.9)

In general, the word order of basic clauses in Baba Malay is NP-VP, when subjects are expressed. Again, it is possible for subjects to not be expressed (see section 5.6.2). However, as section 5.6.9 shows, this general order may be disrupted when topicalization occurs, as it commonly does in Baba Malay.

5.6.2 Grammatical relations and alignment

Baba Malay is a SVO (subject verb object) language. In Baba Malay, the subject NP is not marked differently from the object NP. Instead, in most instances, the subject of a clause can be determined by word order. The syntactic subject precedes the main verb phrase. This is demonstrated by examples (599) to (601). Example (602) shows that the subject is not always overtly expressed in Baba Malay, the language being null-subject. Example (199) is replicated here as (601).

(599) **Beruang kechik** ada mangkok kechik
 bear small POSS bowl small
 'The small bear has a small bowl.'
 (Victor, oai:scholarspace.manoa.hawaii.edu: NL1-032, 00:01:20.9-00:01:24.5)

(600) **Beruang kechik** dudok kerosi kechik
 bear small sit chair small
 'The small bear sits on a small chair.
 (Victor, oai:scholarspace.manoa.hawaii.edu: NL1-032, 00:01:44.0-00:01:46.8)

(601) **Tu bangkuang** tak bergerak
 that turnip NEG move
 'That turnip does not move.'
 (Victor, oai:scholarspace.manoa.hawaii.edu: NL1-034, 00:01:00.5-00:01:03.3)

(602) Ada satu tukang kebun, sama bini dia,
 EXIST one labourer garden and wife 3SG
 tanam bangkuang
 plant turnip
 'There was a gardener, and his wife, (who) planted turnips.'
 (Victor, oai:scholarspace.manoa.hawaii.edu: NL1-034, 00:00:15.9-00:00:22.0)

In terms of grammatical relations, it is also possible for the object to undergo passivization with the use of passive marker, *kena*, so that the object is promoted to subject. The logical subject is not expressed (also see section 5.2.3 on passivization). Examples (603) and (604) illustrate an active sentence and its passive counterpart, wherein the object from (603) is promoted to the subject position of (604), and the logical subject is then dropped in this passive sentence.

(603) **Orang itu   pukol kuching.**
      person that hit   cat
      'That person hit the cat.'
      (Victor, oai:scholarspace.manoa.hawaii.edu: NL1-009, 00:42:26.0-00:42:27.8)

(604) **Itu   kuching kena pukol.**
      that cat   PASS hit
      'That cat was hit.'
      (Victor, oai:scholarspace.manoa.hawaii.edu: NL1-009, 00:42:37.0-00:42:38.8)

In terms of alignment, Baba Malay is a clear nominative-accusative language. The subject of the intransitive verb is treated equivalently to the agent of the transitive verb. This is demonstrated by examples (605) and (606). The subject of the intransitive verb, as with *kuching tu* 'that cat' in (605), and the agent of the transitive verb, as with *anjing* 'dog' in (606), always precede the verb, whereas the object of the transitive verb always follows the verb.

(605) **Kuching tu   lompat.**
      cat   that jump
      'That cat jumped.'
      (Jane Quek oai:scholarspace.manoa.hawaii.edu: NL1-043, 00:10:58.0-00:10:59.8)

(606) **Anjing ambék bakol.**
      dog   take   basket
      'The dog takes the basket.'
      (Jane Quek oai:scholarspace.manoa.hawaii.edu: NL1-088, 00:01:19.6-00:01:21.9)

There are no overt coding devices that reflect the nominative-accusative alignment in Baba Malay. There are also no other coding devices found on nouns or verbs to indicate alignment, agreement or cross-referencing, and syntactic relations are expressed mainly by word order.

5.6.3 Relative clauses

Relative clauses here refer to subordinate clauses that modify a noun phrase. In Baba Malay, there are two relative clause markers (Lee 2012). One of the relative clause markers is *yang* (or sometimes *nang*), which post-modifies the noun phrase head, as it does in Malay, the language from which it is derived. The other relative clause is *punya* (contracted forms: *mia*, *nia*, and *pia*), which is used in its basic lexical form to indicate possession (see section 5.1.1 on genitives). That *punya* is also used for relative clauses may be attributed to influence from the substrate Hokkien relative clause marker *e*, which is also used to indicate possession (see Lee 2012). Note that *punya* is also used to indicate possession in other varieties of Malay, including Jakarta Malay, Manado Malay, and Moluccan Malay. Whereas *yang* relative clauses post-modify noun heads, *punya* relative clauses pre-modify noun heads.

The subject of the subordinate clause can be relativized using both *yang* and *punya* constructions. Examples (607) and (608) illustrate how *yang* introduces relative clauses postnominally, while examples (609) and (610) show how the prenominal relative clause marker *punya* is used. Example (22) is replicated here as example (610).

(607) Subject
Ini budak [***nang*** ter-teriak wolf].
this child **REL** ACD-call.out
'This boy that accidentally cried wolf.'
(Peter Wee, oai:scholarspace.manoa.hawaii.edu: NL1-030, 00:03:34.9-00:03:37.3)

(608) Ini sumua dia mia kawan [***nang*** jaga kambing].
this all 3SG POSS friend **REL** guard sheep
'These are all his friends who guard sheep.'
(Peter Wee, oai:scholarspace.manoa.hawaii.edu: NL1-030, 00:03:34.9-00:03:37.3)

(609) [téngok saya ***punya***] kuda punya kaki sudah patah
look 1SG **REL** horse POSS leg already snap
'The horse that was looking at me had one of its legs already snapped.'
(Lee 2012)

(610) [Anak perompuan ***nia***] satu.
child female **REL** one
'The one that is a girl.'
(Jane Quek, oai:scholarspace.manoa.hawaii.edu: NL1-142, 00:00:44.8-00:00:47.0)

Both *yang* and *punya* can also be used to relativize the direct object of the relative clause, as shown in examples (611) to (614). Examples (611) and (612) illustrate how *yang* is used for postnominal relativization, while examples (613) and (614) illustrate how *punya* is used for prenominal relativization.

(611) Direct object
 Itu kerosi kechik [**yang** dia pechah].
 this chair small **REL** 3SG break
 'That chair that she broke.'
 (Victor, oai:scholarspace.manoa.hawaii.edu: NL1-032, 00:06:03.1-00:06:05.6)

(612) Ini [**yang** dia kejar].
 This **REL** 3SG chase
 'This that he chased.'
 (Peter Wee, oai:scholarspace.manoa.hawaii.edu: NL1-030, 00:02:06.0-00:02:07.5)

(613) Gua nampak [orang tarék **punya**] chia
 1SG see person pull **REL** car
 'I saw the car (rickshaw) that the man pulled.'
 (Lee 2012)

(614) [Satu orang masak **mia**].
 one person cook **REL**
 '(The one) that one person cooked.'
 (Jane Quek, oai:scholarspace.manoa.hawaii.edu: NL1-142, 00:11:08.5-00:11:09.6)

Yang and *punya* may also be used to relativize indirect object. *Yang* is used as a postnominal relative clause marker in example (615), and *punya* is used as a prenominal relative clause marker in example (616).

(615) Indirect object
 Itu perompuan [**yang** mak kasi lauk], sudah balék.
 that female **REL** mother give cook.food already return
 'That female that mother gave cooked food to, has returned.'
 (Lee 2012)

(616) Saya nampak [saya kasi kuéh **punya**] orang.
 1SG see 1SG give cake **REL** person
 'I saw the man whom I gave the cake to.'
 (Lee 2012)

The only position that *yang* can relativize, but not *punya*, is the possessor. This function of *yang* is illustrated by examples (617) and (618). The reason that *punya* cannot be used to relativize possessor might be because it is already used as a lexical verb to indicate possession (see section 5.1.1), hence making it confusing if it is also used to relativize the possessor. The sentence in (619) is constructed and presented to speakers, who judged it to be ungrammatical. They state that it is not possible to construct a sentence using *punya* to express 'that person whose friends hit me' (Lee 2012).

(617) Possessor
Saya kenal satu anjing [**yang** ada lima anak kechik].
1SG know one dog REL POSS five child small
'I know a dog that has five small children.'
(Lee 2012)

(618) [**Yang** ada umor sikit].
REL have age little
'(Those that) have a little age /Those that are a little old.'
(Victor, oai:scholarspace.manoa.hawaii.edu: NL1-002, 00:06:22.4-00:06:24.1)

(619) *itu (orang) punya kawan-kawan pukol gua **punya** orang.
that (person) possess friend-friend hit 1SG REL person
'that person whose friends hit me.'
(Lee 2012)

Overall, the two relative clause markers, *yang* and *punya* have different patterns of use. While *yang* modifies a head noun phrase postnominally, *punya* modifies a head noun phrase prenominally. Speakers can use *yang* to relativize subject, direct object, indirect object, and possessor, while they can use *punya* to relativize subject, direct object, and indirect object, but not possessor. Both relative clause structures use the gap-type strategy, where there is no overt indication of role of the head within the relative clause (see Comrie 1989).

5.6.4 Complement clauses

In Baba Malay, complement clauses can be predicated by a verb or an adjective. In a sense, the complement clause is required to complete the meaning of the verb or adjective. The zero strategy is used for the complement clause, with the main clause and subordinate clause being juxtaposed against each other. These are shown from examples (620) to (627).

(620) John **rasa** [dia pernah jumpa Mary].
think 3SG ever meet
John thinks that he has met Mary before.
(Victor, oai:scholarspace.manoa.hawaii.edu: NL1-037, 00:42:23.6-00:42:25.7)

(621) Gua **rasa** [pear tu tak boléh makan].
 1SG **think** that NEG can eat
 'I think that pear cannot be eaten.'
 (Peter Wee, oai:scholarspace.manoa.hawaii.edu: NL1-022, 00:05:24.3-00:05:25.7)

(622) Gua **rasa** [ni orang ada peték buah pear].
 1SG **think** this person PROG pluck CLF.fruit
 'I think this person is plucking pears.'
 (Peter Wee, oai:scholarspace.manoa.hawaii.edu: NL1-022, 00:00:28.9-00:00:31.2)

(623) Gua **tau** [lu mo datang].
 1SG **know** 2SG want come
 I know you want to come.'
 (Victor, oai:scholarspace.manoa.hawaii.edu: NL1-053, 00:13:49.3-00:13:50.8)

(624) Mak dia **harap** [dia balék siang].
 mother 3SG **hope** 3SG return early
 'His mother hopes he returns early.'
 (Victor, oai:scholarspace.manoa.hawaii.edu: NL1-090, 00:05:46.0-00:05:58.6)

(625) Gua tak **pikay** [gua pernah jumpa lu].
 1SG NEG **think** 1SG ever meet 2SG
 'I do not think I have ever met you.'
 (Jane Quek, oai:scholarspace.manoa.hawaii.edu: NL1-096, 00:52:09.0-00:52:11.3)

(626) Tak **sangka** [boléh jumpa orang Peranakan].
 NEG **expect** can meet person
 '(I) did not expect (I) could meet Peranakans.'
 (Victor, oai:scholarspace.manoa.hawaii.edu: NL1-002, 00:04:31.4-00:04:33.7)

(627) Gua **tentu** [jumpa lu dekat airport].
 1SG **definite** meet 2SG PREP
 'I (am) definite (I would) meet you at the airport.'
 (Victor, oai:scholarspace.manoa.hawaii.edu: NL1-053, 00:13:34.1-00:13:37.9)

In instances where the subject is not expressed in the subordinate clause, the unexpressed subject always shares the same referent as the subject of the main clause, as with examples (626) and (627). These are instances of subject control, whereas the rest of the examples, (620) to (624), are instances of object control. Object control occurs when the object of the main verb is also the subject of the verb in the subordinate clause. It is also possible for the subject to be overtly expressed in the subordinate clause in cases of subject control (where the subject of main clause has the same referent as the subject of the subordinate clause). This is demonstrated by example (625). However, this is less frequently observed, possibly due to the efficiency of dropping subjects and the preference for null-subject in Baba Malay.

5.6.5 Direct and indirect speech

In Baba Malay, the zero strategy is used for both direct and indirect speech. There is very little difference between direct and indirect speech, except that the pronoun used within the subordinate clause changes accordingly. In examples (628) to (630), the speakers are using direct speech, either reporting what they said themselves, or what others have said in its original form. In instances such as these, the subordinate clause usually involves first person or second person pronouns.

(628) Gua **kata,** [gua sudah lama kun tak makan].
1SG **say,** 1SG already long.time also NEG eat
'I said, "I also have not eaten (this) for a long time."'
(Lilian, oai:scholarspace.manoa.hawaii.edu: NL1-079, 00:00:52.3-00:00:55.7)

(629) Mama sumua **chakap,**
grandmother all **speak**
[amek gua mia aloji kuluair].
take 1SG POSS small.clock out
'Grandmothers all said, "Take my small clock out."'
(Jane Quek, oai:scholarspace.manoa.hawaii.edu: NL1-142, 00:10:19.5-00:10:21.4)

(630) Tony gua **chakap,** [oh lu Catholic ada chutsi eh]?[69]
1SG **speak** 2SG have rebirth Q
'My Tony said, "Oh you Catholics have the concept of rebirth?"'
(Jane Quek, oai:scholarspace.manoa.hawaii.edu: NL1-142, 00:06:05.7-00:06:10.8)

Where indirect speech is concerned, the zero strategy is also used, and the only difference between direct and indirect speech is that third person pronouns are usually used in indirect speech. Examples (631) and (632) show instances of indirect speech.

---

[69] Intended as a joke.

(631) Bill **chakap**, [dia sudah pi France].
      speak   3SG already go
      'Bill said, he has already been to France.'
      (Victor, oai:scholarspace.manoa.hawaii.edu: NL1-053, 00:09:59.6-00:10:02.8)

(632) Dia **kata**, [lama dia tak makan].
      3SG **say** long.time 3SG NEG eat
      'She said she has not eaten (this) for a long time.'
      (Lilian, oai:scholarspace.manoa.hawaii.edu: NL1-079, 00:00:31.2-00:00:33.5)

5.6.6 Adverbial clauses

The adverbial clause functions as a modifier of the larger component clause. The adverbial clause is an adjunct and optional, the main clause being grammatical on its own in the absence of the adverbial clause. However, it is often indispensable, offering additional information on time, location, and to some extent, manner. Examples of the different types of adverbial clauses are shown here from (633) to (635).

(633) Temporal
      [Dulu minggu], Mary jatoh sakit.
      before week   fall sick
      'Last week Mary fell sick.'
      (Victor, oai:scholarspace.manoa.hawaii.edu: NL1-051, 00:04:39.2-00:04:43.8)

(634) Location
      [Se- lepas restaurant itu], lu nanti jumpa satu cake shop.[70]
      one- after   that 2SG later see   one
      'Immediately after that restaurant, you will see a cake shop.'
      (Peter Wee, oai:scholarspace.manoa.hawaii.edu: NL1-107, 00:13:51.3-00:13:57.8)

(635) Manner
      Dia menangis sedéh sedéh [bila dia kuluair rumah].
      3SG cry   sad   sad   when 3SG go.out house
      'She cried sadly when she left the house.'
      (Victor, oai:scholarspace.manoa.hawaii.edu: NL1-053, 00:04:52.8-00:04:45.7)

---

[70] It is possible for *se-* 'one' to be prefixed to *lepas* 'after', to denote immediacy, or that an event took place one moment after another did. Similarly, it is possible for *se-* 'one' to be prefixed to *belom*, to denote that an event took place immediately before another.

5.6.6.1 Temporal adverbial clauses

One of the most important functions of adverbial clauses is to indicate information regarding time, considering that Baba Malay has a more elaborate system of aspect than of tense. Tense is hence often implied through the use of adverbial clauses. The following examples show how past, present and future are implied through the use of adverbial clauses. These clauses usually precede the main clause, although they may also follow it. The events in examples (636) to (638) are to be interpreted as having happened in the past, the events in examples (639) to (641) are current, and those in examples (642) to (644) in the future.

(636) [*Empat puloh taon lepas*],
Four ten years after
Tan nia chepuat tinggair dekat Katong.
REL family live PREP
'Forty years ago, the Tan family lived in Katong.'
(Victor, oai:scholarspace.manoa.hawaii.edu: NL1-051, 00:00:38.5-00:00:54.5)

(637) [*Dua bulan lepas*], *Mary beli rumah dekat Katong.*
four month after buy house PREP
'Four months ago, Mary bought a house in Katong.'
(Victor, oai:scholarspace.manoa.hawaii.edu: NL1-051, 00:03:33.6-00:03:35.4)

(638) *Ini cherita jadi dia* [*lima ratus taon lepas*].
this story happen 3SG five hundred year after
'This story happened five hundred years ago.'
(Victor, oai:scholarspace.manoa.hawaii.edu: NL1-051, 00:01:42.4-00:01:46.5)

(639) [*Sekarang*] *tak tau chakap.*
now NEG know speak
'Now, (people) do not know how to speak.'
(Victor, oai:scholarspace.manoa.hawaii.edu: NL1-002, 00:07:39.2-00:07:40.9)

(640) [*Ini ari*], *Mary lu mo pegi mana?*
this day 2SG want go where
'Today, where do you want to go, Mary?'
(Peter Wee, oai:scholarspace.manoa.hawaii.edu: NL1-042, 00:02:28.1-00:02:30.6)

(641) [*Hari ini*], *Mary jumpa Jane dekat pasair.*
day this meet PREP market
'Today, Mary is meeting Jane at the pasair.'
(Victor, oai:scholarspace.manoa.hawaii.edu: NL1-051, 00:07:20.9-00:07:25.3)

(642) [Bésok], Mary pi pasair.
tomorrow go market
'Tomorrow, Mary will go to the market.'
(Victor, oai:scholarspace.manoa.hawaii.edu: NL1-051, 00:22:27.0-00:22:29.4)

(643) [Lain minggu], Mary pi Melaka.
another week go
'Next week Mary will go to Malacca.'
(Victor, oai:scholarspace.manoa.hawaii.edu: NL1-051, 00:25:03.5-00:25:06.3)

(644) [Lagik bulan], Mary pi Melaka.
More month go
'A month later, Mary will go to Malacca.'
(Victor, oai:scholarspace.manoa.hawaii.edu: NL1-051, 00:26:17.6-00:26:20.9)

It is interesting to note that the word *lepas* which is literally interpreted as an adverb meaning 'after', is used in conjunction with noun phrases that indicate a quantity of time, to denote the past and not the future. This is seen in examples (636) to (638). However, its counterpart *belom* 'before' is not used to indicate the future. Instead, the future is expressed when *lagik* 'more, precedes the relevant noun phrases, as with example (644). *Lain* 'another', as shown in example (643) has a more limited function of expressing next day, week, month or year. A list of words concerning time and date can be found in section 7.1.3.

5.6.6.2 Location adverbial clauses

Location can also be expressed by adverbial clauses. These also usually precede the main clause, but may also follow. Location adverbial phrases are shown in examples (645) to (650). Example (634) is replicated here as (645), and example (288) is replicated here as (646).

(645) [Se-lepas restaurant itu], lu nanti jumpa satu cake shop.
one-after that 2SG later see one
'Immediately after that restaurant, you will see a cake shop.'
(Peter Wee, oai:scholarspace.manoa.hawaii.edu: NL1-107, 00:13:51.3-00:13:57.8)

(646) [Di se-belah], dia ketok apa?
PREP one-side 3SG knock what
'Beside, they are knocking what?'
(Jane Quek, oai:scholarspace.manoa.hawaii.edu: NL1-043, 00:14:31.8-00:14:33.5)

(647) [Depan carpark], ada ini kebun bunga.
front EXIST this garden flower
'In front of the carpark, there is a flower garden.'
(Peter Wee, oai:scholarspace.manoa.hawaii.edu: NL1-107, 00:07:32.8-00:07:38.7)

(648) [Di tepi library] ada satu keday jual kuéh.
PREP side EXIST one shop sell cake
'At the side of the library, there is a shop selling cake.'
(Peter Wee, oai:scholarspace.manoa.hawaii.edu: NL1-107, 00:08:41.5-
00:08:45.0)

(649) Anjing sudah mangun, [dekat dalam basket].
dog already wake.up PREP inside
'The dog had already woken up, inside the basket.'
(Jane Quek, oai:scholarspace.manoa.hawaii.edu: NL1-088, 00:00:17.1-
00:00:21.7)

(650) Itu budak main itu speedboat, [dekat itu laut sana].
that child play that PREP that pond there
'That child is playing with that speedboat, at that pond over there.'
(Jane Quek, oai:scholarspace.manoa.hawaii.edu: NL1-088, 00:05:22.1-
00:05:27.0)

Note that in examples (649) and (650), the adverbial clause modifies the entire clause. They are not adverbial phrases that modify only the verb phrase, as evidenced by the pause between both clauses.

5.6.6.3 Manner adverbial clauses

Adverbial clauses may also be used to modify other clauses to express the manner in which something is done, as shown in examples (651) to (653). Example (506) is replicated here as (653).

(651) Dia menangis sedéh sedéh [bila dia kuluair rumah].
3SG cry sad sad when 3SG go.out house
'She cried sadly when she left the house.'
(Victor, oai:scholarspace.manoa.hawaii.edu: NL1-053, 00:04:52.8-00:04:45.7)

(652) [Lepas makan pagi bahru], dia pi kreja.
after eat morning just 3SG go work
'After just eating breakfast, she goes to work.'
(Victor, oai:scholarspace.manoa.hawaii.edu: NL1-051, 00:32:20.1-00:32:22.8)

(653) [Belom dia pulang],   gua sudah dapat tau.
      before 3SG return.home 1SG already get   know
      'Before she returned home, I already got to know (about something).'
      (Jane Quek, oai:scholarspace.manoa.hawaii.edu: NL1-096, 00:03:17.4-
      00:03:40.4)

Thus far, the examples discussed in these sections show that subordinate clauses may precede or follow the main clause, although there appears to be a stronger preference for subordinate clause to precede main clause. More adverbial clauses are discussed in the section on subordinating conjunctions (see section 5.6.8.2).

5.6.7 Conditional

Kalu (alternative form: kalo) 'if' is used to connect clauses that semantically express conditionals or *if-then* constructions (see Traugott et al. 1986), where in a simplified sense, a proposition is implied to be true if the conditions of another are fulfilled. Examples (654) to (657) illustrate the use of conditionals in Baba Malay. *Kalu* can also be used for counterfactuals with imagined states, as with example (656). It is typically used at the beginning of the first clause that describes the antecedent. The second clause describes the consequence if the antecedent conditions are met. Although this is rare, *kalu* and its antecedent can also form the second clause, with the consequent clause fronted, as with example (657). Example (191) is replicated here as example (655).

(654) [**Kalo** gua   tau   lu   mo   datang],
      if   1SG   know   2SG   want   come
      gua   tentu   jumpa   lu   dekat   airport
      1SG   definite meet   2SG   PREP
      'If I knew you were coming, I am definite (I would) meet you at the airport.'
      (Victor, oai:scholarspace.manoa.hawaii.edu: NL1-053, 00:13:32.1-00:13:37.9)

(655) [**Kalu** mo   kechik-kan   badan],   kurang-kan   roti.
      if   want   small-TR   body   less-TR   bread
      'If (you) want to make your body smaller, lessen (your intake of) bread.'
      (Victor, oai:scholarspace.manoa.hawaii.edu: NL1-053, 00:12:27.5-00:12:32.0)

(656) [**Kalu** chutsi], gua   tak   mo   angkat   pot.
      if   rebirth   1SG   NEG   want   carry
      'If there is rebirth I do not want to carry a pot (out into this world).'
      (Jane Quek, oai:scholarspace.manoa.hawaii.edu: NL1-053, 00:05:51.6-
      00:05:53.4)

(657) Gua bésok datang, [**kalu** Anne mo gua datang].
      1SG tomorrow come   **if**   want 1SG come
      'I will come tomorrow if Anne wants me to come.'
      (Victor, oai:scholarspace.manoa.hawaii.edu: NL1-053, 00:14:56.9-00:15:03.4)

5.6.8 Conjunctions

There are two types of conjunctions, as mentioned in section 4.7, these being coordinating conjunctions and subordinating conjunctions.

5.6.8.1 Coordinating conjunctions

Coordinating conjunctions are used to conjoin a phrase with another phrase, or a clause with another clause. The four coordinating conjunction markers in Baba Malay are *sama* 'and', *habis* 'finish', *ka* 'or', and *tapi* 'but'.

In general, *sama* 'and' can be used to conjoin noun phrase to noun phrase or adjective phrase to adjective phrase. Examples (658) and (659) show how *sama* acts as a link between noun phrases, while (660) to (661) demonstrate how *sama* 'and' is used between adjective phrases.

(658) [Mak]   **sama** [ko]   pegi pasair.
      mother   **and**   paternal.aunt go   market
      'Mother and paternal aunt went to market.'
      (Peter Wee, oai:scholarspace.manoa.hawaii.edu: NL1-110, 00:00:17.4-
      00:00:20.1)

(659) Mak   masak [iték   tim],   [babi buah   keluak]
      mother   cook   duck   double.boil   pig   CLF.fruit Pangium.edule
      sama   [sambal   petay].
      and   chili.paste   flat.bean
      'Mother cooked double boiled duck, pork cooked with Pangium edule, and chili with flat beans.'
      (Peter Wee, oai:scholarspace.manoa.hawaii.edu: NL1-110, 00:06:51.5-
      00:06:57.2)

(660) Dia   kasi   mak   [marah] **sama** [sedéh].
      3SG   cause   mother   angry   **and**   sad
      'She made mother angry and sad.'
      (Peter Wee, oai:scholarspace.manoa.hawaii.edu: NL1-110, 00:10:46.5-
      00:10:53.1)

(661) Ini   ari   [panas] **sama** [melekat].
      this   day   hot   **and**   sticky
      'Today (is) hot and sticky.'
      (Peter Wee, oai:scholarspace.manoa.hawaii.edu: NL1-110, 00:13:24.5-00:13:26.3)

It is rarer to find *sama* 'and' being used to conjoin verb phrases. Speakers state that it is not possible to do two things at once, and prefer to use *habis* 'finish' to link two separate clauses together sequentially. Contracted versions of the word *habis* are *habi* and *abi*. The following examples in (662), (663), and (664) show how *habis* is used to link separate clauses. Example (313) is replicated here as (662).

(662) [Mak   pegi   pasair], **habis** tu   [dia pegi kopitiam].
      mother   go   market   finish   that 3SG   go   coffee.shop
      'Mother went to the market. After that she went to the coffeeshop.'
      (Peter Wee, oai:scholarspace.manoa.hawaii.edu: NL1-110, 00:01:23.4-
      00:01:29.3)

(663) [Mak   bikin   kuéh], **habis** tu   [dia siram ayé   pokok bunga].
      mother make   cake   finish   that 3SG   flush water tree   flower
      'Mother baked cake. After that she watered the plants.'
      (Peter Wee, oai:scholarspace.manoa.hawaii.edu: NL1-110, 00:03:41.6-
      00:03:57.2)

(664) [Jalan   jalan] **habi**,   [dudok kopi   house].
      walk   walk   **finish**, sit   coffee
      'After taking a walk, (I) sit (in the) coffee house.'
      (Jane Quek oai:scholarspace.manoa.hawaii.edu: NL1-142, 00:02:53.8-
      00:02:56.1)

Ka 'or' is used to connect any type of phrase to its equivalent type of phrase, or any clause to another clause. Example (665) shows how it connects noun phrases, example (666), verb phrases, example (667), proper nouns, and example (668), preposition phrases. Example (314) is replicated here as (665).

(665) Gua   rasa   ini   [anak   dia]   **ka** [chuchu   dia].
      1SG   think   this   child   3SG   **or** grandchild   3SG
      'I think this is his child or grandchild.'
      (Peter Wee, oai:scholarspace.manoa.hawaii.edu: NL1-022, 00:02:13.0-
      00:02:15.0)

(666) [Mandi] **ka** [bikin apa]?
      bathe   **or** do   what
      'Bathe or do what?'
      (Jane Quek, oai:scholarspace.manoa.hawaii.edu: NL1-045, 00:07:54.8-
      00:07:56.5)

(667) [Terang bulan] **ka** [di   tanjong katong]   ka.
      Bright moon   **or** PREP cape   uncertain or
      'Bright moon or at the uncertain cape or (both are names of songs) or'
      (Jane Quek, oai:scholarspace.manoa.hawaii.edu: NL1-043, 00:08:27.8-
      00:08:31.0)

(668) [Dekat longkang] **ka** [dekat kopi   tiam ka],
      PREP drain   **or** PREP   coffee shop or,
      'At the drain or at the coffee shop or,'

Tapi 'but' is used between two clauses, as in examples (669) to (671). Example (315) is replicated below as example (669).

(669) [Gua mia adék   bikin kék]   **tapi** [tak sedap].
      1SG REL sibling make   cake   **but**   NEG   delicious
      'My sister baked a cake but it was not delicious.'
      (Jane Quek, oai:scholarspace.manoa.hawaii.edu: NL1-117, 00:14:38.9-
      00:14:44.6)

(670) [Mary pi sekolah] **tapi** [dia tak suka bacha surat].
            go school   **but**   3SG NEG like read   letter
      'Mary goes to school but she doesn't like to study.'
      (Jane Quek, oai:scholarspace.manoa.hawaii.edu: NL1-117, 00:16:26.0-
      00:16:29.5)

(671) [Bunga tu   chanték]   **tapi** [mak   gua tak suka].
      flower that beautiful **but**   mother 1SG NEG like
      'That flower is beautiful but my mother does not like (it).'
      (Jane Quek, oai:scholarspace.manoa.hawaii.edu: NL1-117, 00:16:50.9-
      00:16:53.7)

5.6.8.2 Subordinating conjunctions

Subordinating conjunctions are used to conjoin subordinate clause to main clause. In these instances, the subordinate clauses are usually also adverbial clauses, functioning as modifiers of the main clause. Two commonly used subordinating conjunctions are *pasal* (refined form: *pasair*) 'because', *bila* 'when', and *sunggu pun* (literally: really also) 'although'.

Pasal, which literally means 'matter, reason', is grammaticalized, becoming 'because'. *Pasal* 'because' is typically used between different clauses, where the first clause describes the outcome, and the second clause describes the reason behind the outcome. Examples (672) to (674) show how *pasal* is used, example (672) being a replication of (316). Note that the *pasal* construction is the only subordinate clause that usually follows the main clause, rather than precede it (see section 5.6.6 for more examples of subordinate clauses preceding main clauses).

(672) Tiga   minggu   macham   dia   balék   [***pasair***   dia
      three week   like.that 3SG   return **because**   3SG
      tinggal Singapore].
      live   Singapore
      'For about three weeks, she returns because she lives in Singapore.'
      (Jane Quek, oai:scholarspace.manoa.hawaii.edu: NL1-142, 00:04:03.8-00:04:09.2)

(673) [***Pasair***   orang   tau].
      because   person   know
      'Because people know.'
      (Jane Quek, oai:scholarspace.manoa.hawaii.edu: NL1-142, 00:09:41.1-00:09:43.0)

(674) Kita   kena   masak   [***pasair***   kita   tau   masak].
      1PL   PASS   cook   **because**   1PL   know   cook
      'We are made to cook because we know how to cook.'
      (Jane Quek, oai:scholarspace.manoa.hawaii.edu: NL1-142, 00:09:49.5-00:09:54.0)

While most Baba Malay speakers use *pasal* for 'because', individual variation is also observed in the corpus, where the Malay form *kerana* 'because' is used, as in example (675).

(675) Gua   angkat   manyak   tissue   [***kerana***   gua   séisema]
      1SG   carry   many   **because**   1SG   have.a.cold
      'I carry a lot of tissue because I have a cold.'
      (Victor, oai:scholarspace.manoa.hawaii.edu: NL1-053, 00:17:19.4-00:17:25.9)

Bila 'when', which is also used as an interrogative (see sections 4.1.3.4 and 5.6.10.1), can be used as a conjunction between a main clause and an adverbial clause. It is more common for the main clause to follow the adverbial clause, as with examples (676) and (677) rather than precede it, as with example (678).

(676) [**Bila** baru gua balék rumah], baru gua dapat tau
      when just 1SG return home just 1SG get know
      pasair tu accident.
      matter that
      'When I just returned home, I just got to know (about) that accident.'
      (Victor, oai:scholarspace.manoa.hawaii.edu: NL1-053, 00:02:22.8-00:02:26.3)

(677) [**Bila** gua senang], gua jalan jalan lah.
      when 1SG free 1SG walk walk EMP
      'When I (am) free, I take walks.'
      (Jane Quek, oai:scholarspace.manoa.hawaii.edu: NL1-142, 00:01:50.1-
      00:01:52.2)

(678) Gua dapat tau pasair tu accident [**bila** gua jumpa dia].
      1SG get know matter that **when** 1SG meet 3SG
      'I got to know (about) that accident when I met her.'
      (Victor, oai:scholarspace.manoa.hawaii.edu: NL1-053, 00:00:30.5-00:00:36.0)

Sunggu pun (literally 'really also') functions as subordinating conjunction 'although'. The subordinate clause it introduces usually precedes the main clause, although it is also acceptable for the subordinate clause to follow the main clause. The use of *sunggu pun* 'although' is demonstrated in examples (679), (680) and (681). Example (319) is replicated here as (679).

(679) [**Sunggu.pun** dia tak standard], dia dapat ini kreja.
      although 3SG NEG 3SG get this work
      'Although he (is of) no standard, he got this work.'
      (Victor, oai:scholarspace.manoa.hawaii.edu: NL1-053, 00:20:53.4-00:20:57.2)

(680) [**Sunggu.pun** lu tak suka dia], lu mesti perama.
      although 2SG NEG like 3SG 2SG must polite
      'Although you do not like him, you must be polite.'
      (Victor, oai:scholarspace.manoa.hawaii.edu: NL1-053, 00:23:21.7-00:23:25.2)

(681) Dia boléh buang krejar, [**sunggu.pun** dia minum sikit].
      3SG can throw work **although** 3SG drink little
      'He can lose his job although he drinks little.'
      (Victor, oai:scholarspace.manoa.hawaii.edu: NL1-053, 00:22:38.1-00:22:42.7)

Similar to observations made in section 5.6.6, most of subordinate clauses usually precede the main clause, the only exceptions being sentences featuring *pasal* 'because'.

5.6.9 Topicalization

Topicalization occurs when a particular constituent is fronted in a clause so that it is the most prominent component of the clause. Topicalization is commonly used in Baba Malay, and speakers topicalize the elements they believe to be most important. In an earlier description of Baba Malay as it was spoken in Malacca, Lim (1988) suggests that Baba Malay has a basic sentence structure of topic followed by comment. He alludes to Li and Thompson (1976) who suggest that many Asian languages have Topic-Comment as their basic structure, instead of subject and predicate. Baba Malay, having derived its characteristics from substrate Hokkien, could have had adopted its Topic-Comment structure. However, one hesitates to state that Baba Malay is more Topic-Comment than it is Subject-Predicate, simply because there are a number of instances of Subject-Predicate examples, such as with the recently discussed examples (679) to (681). Instead, it is preferable to assert that topicalization often happens in Baba Malay.

The different constituents that can be fronted through topicalization include noun phrase object, adjectival phrase, adverbial phrase and also adverbial clause. Verb phrases usually do not have to be topicalized, since it is common for subjects to not be explicitly expressed, leaving verb phrases to already front the clause. Note that commas may be provided in some of the examples below to help in the parsing of these clauses, even though the speakers do not pause between the constituent being topicalized and the rest of the clause in some instances.

Examples (682) to (684) demonstrate topicalization of the object noun phrase.

(682) [*Kerosi*], *dudok, belom panas, sudah jalan.*
chair, sit not.yet hot already walk
'That chair is not yet hot from sitting, (and you) already are going.'
(Lilian, oai:scholarspace.manoa.hawaii.edu: NL1-079, 00:15:11.8-00:15:14.3)

(683) [*Ikan kuning*], *tarok asam.*
fish yellow put tamarind
'Yellow fish, put tamarind (on it).'
(Jane Quek, oai:scholarspace.manoa.hawaii.edu: NL1-142, 00:07:29.4-00:07:32.2)

(684) [*Teloh*], *goréng.*
egg fry
'The egg, fry (it).'
(Jane Quek, oai:scholarspace.manoa.hawaii.edu: NL1-142, 00:07:44.8-00:07:47.5)

While the noun phrase is topicalized in the preceding examples, the following ones in examples (685) to (687) demonstrate topicalization of adjectives. It is necessary to eliminate the possibility that the verb phrase is being topicalized, considering that there is very little use of the copula verb *ada* in Baba Malay. It is not possible to make presumptions about whether *ada* should also be fronted, since no such data exists. However, it is interesting to note that there is no other instance of verb phrase fronting. In most instances, when verb phrases occur at the beginning of the clause, the clause carries no explicit subject, whereas in the examples that follow, the subject remains, albeit no longer in the sentence-initial position. Thus, these examples demonstrate the topicalization of something other than the verb phrase, more likely, the adjectival phrase.

(685) [*Samplang*], dia.
promiscuous 3SG
'Promiscuous, he is.'
(Peter Wee, oai:scholarspace.manoa.hawaii.edu: NL1-052, 00:02:57.4-00:02:58.5)

(686) [*Betol*], ini mas
real this gold
'Real, this gold is.'
(Jane Quek, oai:scholarspace.manoa.hawaii.edu: NL1-100, 00:52:54.1-00:52:55.1)

(687) [*Senyap*], satu rumah.
silent one house
'Silent, the one house'
(Victor, oai:scholarspace.manoa.hawaii.edu: NL1-037, 00:03:00.6-00:03:03.5)

It is also possible for adverbial phrases and adverbial clauses to be fronted, although adverbial phrases modifying time, location and manner usually follow the verb phrase rather than precede it (see section 5.4). Instances of adverbial phrase topicalization are much rarer, as with example (688). On the other hand, it is very common for adverbial clauses to be topicalized, adverbial clauses having been observed to occur at both the beginning and the end of sentences (see section 5.6.6). Examples (633) and (634) are replicated as examples (689) and (690).

(688) [*Betol lawa*], dia pakay.
real stylish 3SG wear
'Really stylish, he dresses.'
(Jane Quek, oai:scholarspace.manoa.hawaii.edu: NL1-101, 00:06:22.8-00:06:27.3)

(689) [*Dulu minggu*], Mary jatoh sakit.
     before week   fall   sick
     'Last week Mary fell sick.'
     (Victor, oai:scholarspace.manoa.hawaii.edu: NL1-051, 00:04:39.2-00:04:43.8)

(690) [*Se-lepas restaurant itu*], lu   nanti jumpa satu cake shop.
     one-after   that 2SG later see   one
     'Immediately after that restaurant, you will see a cake shop.'
     (Peter Wee, oai:scholarspace.manoa.hawaii.edu: NL1-107, 00:13:51.3-00:13:57.8)

5.6.10 Questions

The types of questions in Baba Malay can be divided into two kinds, content questions and tag questions.

5.6.10.1 Content questions

The interrogative pronouns and adverbs of Baba Malay are summarized in Table 39 (also see sections 4.1.3.4 and 4.4.2).

Table 39: List of interrogative pronouns and adverbs in Baba Malay.

apa	what	Interrogative pronouns
siapa	who	
siapa punya/ mia/ nia	whose	
berapa	how many	
mana	which	
bila	when	Interrogative adverbs
mana	where	
apa pasal/ pasair/ sair	why 'what reason'	
apa macham/ cham	how 'what like'	
mana ada	rhetorical 'where EXIST'	

Interrogatives can either be fronted or remain *in situ*. Note that questions may occur with *ah* as an optional question particle.

    Apa literally means what', and it can replace a noun phrase in a sentence. *Apa* can be fronted, as with example (691). Example (693) shows how questions with *apa* are usually answered. Example (171) is replicated here as (692).

(691) **Apa** ini ah?
　　　what that Q
　　　'What is this?'
　　　(Peter Wee, oai:scholarspace.manoa.hawaii.edu: NL1-042, 00:08:32.1-
　　　00:08:33.4)

(692) Ini **apa?**
　　　This **what**
　　　'This (is) what?'
　　　(Victor, oai:scholarspace.manoa.hawaii.edu: NL1-037, 00:23:11.1-00:23:12.5)

(693) Ini hospital.
　　　this
　　　'This (is) a hospital.'
　　　(Victor, oai:scholarspace.manoa.hawaii.edu: NL1-103, 00:01:01.4-00:01:03.6)

Siapa 'who' is also an interrogative pronoun, and may replace noun phrases in utterances, as demonstrated by examples (694) to (696). Example (696) demonstrates how questions with *siapa* may be answered. Example (172) is replicated as (694).

(694) **Siapa** itu?
　　　who that
　　　'Who (is) that?'
　　　(Peter Wee, oai:scholarspace.manoa.hawaii.edu: NL1-042, 00:23:11.1-
　　　00:23:12.5)

(695) Mary ini **siapa?**[71]
　　　　　　 this **who**
　　　'This Mary (is) who?'
　　　(Peter Wee, oai:scholarspace.manoa.hawaii.edu: NL1-042, 00:23:11.1-00:23:12.5)

(696) Ini anak dia.
　　　this child 3SG
　　　'This (is) his child.'
　　　(Peter Wee, oai:scholarspace.manoa.hawaii.edu: NL1-022, 00:02:13.5-
　　　00:02:14.4)

The notion of 'whose' is expressed when *siapa* is used together with possessive *punya*, as with examples (697) and (698). The short versions of *punya* are *mia* and

---

[71] Where *siapa* 'who' and the second person pronoun *lu* are concerned, it is generally more polite to ask "*Lu siapa?*" rather than "*siapa lu?*".

nia (see section 5.1.1), although there are no instances of *siapa nia* recorded. Due to place assimilation to *p*, the onset of the second syllable in *siapa* 'who', *siapa punya* and *siapa mia* may be preferred over *siapa nia*. Inadvertently, the answers to these questions are utterances that replace *siapa* with a noun phrase, indicating who the possessor is, as with example (699). Example (173) is replicated here as (697).

(697) **Siapa punya** bubor itu?
 who POSS porridge that
 'Whose porridge (is) that?'
 (Victor, oai:scholarspace.manoa.hawaii.edu: NL1-032, 00:04:10.1-00:04:12.1)

(698) Ini rumah **siapa mia**?
 this house who POSS
 'This house (is) whose?'
 (Jane Quek, oai:scholarspace.manoa.hawaii.edu: NL1-092, 00:02:01.1-00:02:03.9)

(699) Gua mia ngkua mia.
 1SG POSS father-in-law POSS
 'My father-in-law's.'
 (Jane Quek, oai:scholarspace.manoa.hawaii.edu: NL1-092, 00:03:03.0-00:03:06.3)

Berapa denotes 'how many' (recall that it can also be used to mean 'some', see section 5.1.2.4). *Berapa* can be used with noun classifiers and nouns, as with (700), or on its own, as with (701). The default meaning of the utterance concerns how much something costs, but with the appropriate context, noun classifiers and nouns can be used to further define what is being asked. Example (702) replicates (387), and shows how questions with *berapa* may be answered.

(700) **Berapa** bijik itu lémo kat sana?
 how.many CLF.fruit that lemon PREP there
 'How many lemons (are) there?'
 (Jane Quek, oai:scholarspace.manoa.hawaii.edu: NL1-093, 00:27:14.8-00:27:17.8)

(701) Itu lémo **berapa**?
 that lemon **how.many**
 'That lemon (is) how much?'
 (Jane Quek, oai:scholarspace.manoa.hawaii.edu: NL1-093, 00:27:05.5-00:27:07.9)

(702) *Satu bijik timun*
 one CLF.small.round cucumber
 'One cucumber.'
 (Jane Quek, oai:scholarspace.manoa.hawaii.edu: NL1-149, 00:03:17.8-00:03:19.4)

Mana has two functions, one of which is 'which' and the other is 'where' ('where' examples are discussed later). *Mana* is usually used when an interlocutor is presented more than one option to choose from, and asked to make a particular choice. There is some individual variation. In addition to *mana*, as with example (703), a speaker also uses *apa* to indicate 'which', as demonstrated by example (705). Example (704) replicates (175), and example (706) shows how these *mana*-type questions can be answered.

(703) ****Mana**** *satu lu suka?*
 which one 2SG like
 'Which one do you like?'
 (Jane Quek, oai:scholarspace.manoa.hawaii.edu: NL1-089, 01:03:17.5-01:03:18.7)

(704) ****Mana**** *baik,* ****mana**** *satu tak baik?*
 which good **which** one NEG good
 'Which (is) good, which one (is) not good?'
 (Peter Wee, oai:scholarspace.manoa.hawaii.edu: NL1-022, 00:01:23.2-00:01:26.3)

(705) ****Apa**** *colour?*
 what
 'What colour?'
 (Jane Quek, oai:scholarspace.manoa.hawaii.edu: NL1-089, 01:03:44.8-01:03:47.0)

(706) *Gua suka mérah.*
 1SG like red
 'I like red.'
 (Jane Quek, oai:scholarspace.manoa.hawaii.edu: NL1-089, 01:04:17.2-01:04:19.4)

Whereas the above examples show uses of interrogative pronouns, the following examples demonstrate how interrogative adverbs are used. These may substitute adverbial clauses. In most instances, *bila* questions take the form of (707) rather than (708), even though both are well-formed to speakers. Example (641) is replicated as

(709), and shows how *bila* interrogatives may be answered. Answers usually reflect some kind of temporal information.

(707) **Bila** lu mo datang?
when 2SG want come
'When (do) you want to come?'
(Jane Quek, oai:scholarspace.manoa.hawaii.edu: NL1-093, 00:05:24.3-00:05:26.5)

(708) Dia nia sehjit **bila?**
3SG POSS birthday **when**
'Her birthday (is) when?'
(Victor, oai:scholarspace.manoa.hawaii.edu: NL1-037, 00:43:10.9-00:43:13.6)

(709) hari ini, Mary jumpa Jane dekat pasair.
day this meet PREP market
'Today, Mary is meeting Jane at the pasair.'
(Victor, oai:scholarspace.manoa.hawaii.edu: NL1-051, 00:07:20.9-00:07:25.3)

Other than being used to mean 'which', *mana* primarily functions to mean 'where'. The following examples show how *mana* is used to mean 'where'. Again, *mana* usually occurs fronted as with (710). Example (711) is a rare instance of *mana* occurring *in situ*. Example (237) is replicated here as example (710), and example (712) shows a typical answer to *mana* interrogatives. Answers to *mana* interrogatives in this sense usually indicate a particular location.

(710) **Mana** pi si Mary?
where go PERSON
'Where goes Mary?'
(Victor, oai:scholarspace.manoa.hawaii.edu: NL1-037, 00:08:42.2-00:08:43.5)

(711) Lu pakay chanték mo pi **mana?**
2SG wear beautiful want go **where**
'You dress beautifully to go where?'
(Victor, oai:scholarspace.manoa.hawaii.edu: NL1-042, 00:07:01.5-00:07:03.6)

(712) Mary pi sekolah.
go school
'Mary goes to school.'
(Jane Quek, oai:scholarspace.manoa.hawaii.edu: NL1-117, 00:16:26.0-00:16:27.5)

Apa pasal (refined form: *pasair*, short refined form *sair*) literally means 'what reason', and corresponds to 'why'. Note that *apa pasal* is always fronted as in examples (713) and (714), and it has not been observed at the end of utterances. Example (715) show how these questions are usually answered, where *pasal/ pasair/ sair* occurs as a grammaticalized 'because' (see section 5.6.8.2).

(713) **Apa pasal** lu marah?
 what reason 2SG angry
 'Why (are) you angry?'
 (Jane Quek, oai:scholarspace.manoa.hawaii.edu: NL1-093, 00:23:43.8-00:23:45.1)

(714) **Apa sair** si Mary bikin kuéh?
 what reason PERSON make cake
 'Why (is) Mary baking a cake?'
 (Victor, oai:scholarspace.manoa.hawaii.edu: NL1-037, 00:01:06.7-00:01:09.1)

(715) **Pasal** dia jahat, macham hantu.
 because 3SG evil, like ghost
 'Because he (is) evil, like a ghost.'
 (Jane Quek, oai:scholarspace.manoa.hawaii.edu: NL1-093, 00:26:21.2-00:26:27.0)

Apa macham (short form: *cham*), literally 'what like', is used to indicate 'how' in Baba Malay. The expression usually occurs fronted, as with example (716). The only instances where it does not occur right at the beginning of the utterance are instances wherein other elements have been fronted, as demonstrated by example (717). *Apa macham* questions can be answered by simple statements, as demonstrated by example (718).

(716) **Apa macham** pi bank?
 what like go
 'How (do I) go to the bank?'
 (Victor, oai:scholarspace.manoa.hawaii.edu: NL1-103, 00:13:54.5-00:13:56.7)

(717) Bésok, si Mary, **apa cham** mo balék sekolah?
 tomorrow PERSON **what like** want return school
 'How (does) Mary want to return to school tomorrow?'
 (Victor, oai:scholarspace.manoa.hawaii.edu: NL1-037, 00:41:02.5-00:41:04.8)

(718) Dia   mo   dudok   bus.
      3SG   want   sit   bus
      'She wants to take the bus.'
      (Peter Wee, oai:scholarspace.manoa.hawaii.edu: NL1-052, 00:09:14.8-
      00:09:18.0)

Whereas the previous interrogatives are used for the purpose of seeking an answer, *mana ada* 'where EXIST' is used as a rhetorical question. *Mana ada* always occurs at the beginning of utterances. The expression is used in response to an interlocutor's statement or question, to imply the negative. For example, (719) follows an interlocutor's question about where a knife is, and it denies the existence of said knife. (720) on the other hand, is a response to an interlocutor's statement, that a particular person is clever. It does not give one's opinion directly, and is akin to asking, "How is he clever?" There is an inherent implicature that the speaker does not share the same opinion as the interlocutor. Note that this structure is essentially derived from Hokkien. For example, the Hokkien equivalent of example (720) is *dolo u lihai*, which shares the same literal translation: 'where EXIST clever', free translation 'How is he clever', and implication (that the person being spoken about is not clever). Example (240) is replicated as (719).

(719) **Mana   ada   piso?**
      where   EXIST   knife
      'Where is the knife (implying there is no knife)?
      (Victor, oai:scholarspace.manoa.hawaii.edu: NL1-037, 00:21:02.8-00:21:05.6)

(720) **Mana   ada   panday?**
      where   EXIST   clever
      'How is he clever (implying he is not)?
      (Jane Quek, oai:scholarspace.manoa.hawaii.edu: NL1-093, 00:21:32.7-
      00:21:34.2)

In summary, whereas interrogative pronouns can occur fronted, or *in situ*, there is a preference for interrogative adverbs to be fronted. This is in line with the nature of adverbial clauses, which tend to be fronted in Baba Malay (see section 5.6.6).

5.6.10.2 Tag questions
Other than questions that feature interrogative pronouns and adverbs, tag questions are also commonly used in Baba Malay. Tag questions are essentially declaratives that have been converted into interrogatives with the insertion of a tag at the end of the sentence. Tags are usually negative in nature, and common ones include adverb,

belom 'not yet' (see section 5.2.5.7), noun negation marker, *bukan* (see section 5.1.4) and verb negation marker, *tak* (see section 5.2.8). Another tag is the *tak* VP *tak* option.

Belom 'not yet' is used at the end of sentences featuring *sudah* 'already' to ask if an event has already taken place. Examples (721) to (723) show how the *belom* tag is used, and examples (724) and (725) demonstrate typical answers to questions with *belom*. The positive answer would comprise *sudah* 'already' VP, while the negative answer uses *belom* 'not yet' VP.

(721) Itu kuéh sudah jadi **belom?**
that cake already become **not.yet**
'Has that cake formed yet?'
(Peter Wee, oai:scholarspace.manoa.hawaii.edu: NL1-098, 00:19:55.5-00:19:57.7)

(722) Itu mia lauk sudah siap **belom?**
that REL cooked.food already prepared **not.yet**
'Has that cook food been prepared yet?
(Peter Wee, oai:scholarspace.manoa.hawaii.edu: NL1-099, 00:18:12.8-00:18:16.5)

(723) Lu sudah siap **belom?**
2SG already prepared **not.yet**
'Are you prepared yet?'
(Jane Quek, oai:scholarspace.manoa.hawaii.edu: NL1-100, 00:10:36.4-00:10:39.0)

(724) Itu mia lauk sumua sudah siap.
that REL food all already prepared
'That cooked food is all prepared already.'
(Peter Wee, oai:scholarspace.manoa.hawaii.edu: NL1-099, 00:18:51.2-00:18:53.9)

(725) Mary belom siap.
not.yet prepared
'Mary is not prepared yet.'
(Peter Wee, oai:scholarspace.manoa.hawaii.edu: NL1-099, 00:20:11.5-00:20:13.9)

Another negative tag in Baba Malay is *bukan* (contracted form: *kan*[72]). The following examples in (726) to (728) show how the *bukan* tag is used. Earlier, the use of *bukan* to negate noun phrases was noted (see section 5.1.4). In these instances, *bukan* is used to negate the clause. Essentially, the speaker has a view and seeks confirmation. Typical replies to these questions will comprise *ya* 'yes', or *bukan* 'no'. These are demonstrated by examples (729) and (730).

(726) Dia   ada   beli   apple   **bukan**?
      3SG   PFV   buy   no
      'He bought apples, no?'
      (Victor, oai:scholarspace.manoa.hawaii.edu: NL1-051, 00:40:03.6-00:40:07.2)

(727) Dia   pi   sekolah   **bukan**?
      3SG   go   school   no
      'He goes to school, no?'
      (Victor, oai:scholarspace.manoa.hawaii.edu: NL1-051, 00:40:24.4-00:40:27.4)

(728) Lu   mo   bukak   pintu   **kan**?
      2SG   want   open   door   no
      'You want to open the door, no?'
      (Jane Quek, oai:scholarspace.manoa.hawaii.edu: NL1-044, 00:20:58.3-00:21:00.1)

(729) Ya   lah.   Lama   tak   jalan   sini.
      yes   EMP   long.time   NEG   walk   here
      'Yes. (I have) not walked here for a long time.'
      (Jane Quek, oai:scholarspace.manoa.hawaii.edu: NL1-142, 00:00:05.1-00:00:08.3)

(730) Bukan.   Terima.
      no   accept
      'No. Accept (it).'
      (Jane Quek, oai:scholarspace.manoa.hawaii.edu: NL1-045, 00:17:57.8-00:17:59.7)

While *bukan* negates the entire clause (and noun phrase), *tak* has been noted to negate verb phrase (see section 5.2.8). When *tak* is used as a tag marker, the speaker seeks information with no particular presupposed stance, as demonstrated by examples (731) to (735). Compare (726) to (731), and (727) to (732). In (726), the speaker is

---

72 This is not to be confused with transitive marker *–kan*.

questioning the *notion* of the agent having bought apples, thinking that the agent has most probably bought apples, whereas in (731), the speaker is questioning whether the agent bought apples or not, without presuming that the agent has bought apples. Similarly, in (727), the speaker questions the *notion* of whether the agent goes to school, presuming that the agent goes to school, whereas in (732), the speaker questions whether the agent goes to school, without any strong presumptions about whether the agent goes to school. Example (430) is replicated as (735).

(731) Mary ada beli apple **tak**?
   PFV buy **NEG**
   'Did Mary buy the apples?'
   (Victor, oai:scholarspace.manoa.hawaii.edu: NL1-051, 00:39:15.5-00:39:17.9)

(732) Dia pi sekolah **tak**?
   3SG go school **NEG**
   'Does he go to school?'
   (Victor, oai:scholarspace.manoa.hawaii.edu: NL1-051, 00:40:17.5-00:40:18.6)

(733) Lu jaga chuchu **tak**?
   2SG take.care grandchildren **NEG**
   'Do you take care of grandchildren?'
   (Jane Quek, oai:scholarspace.manoa.hawaii.edu: NL1-142, 00:00:50.8-00:00:52.5)

(734) Lu boléh tunjok-kan jalan **tak**?
   2SG can show-TR walk **NEG**
   'Can you show the way?'
   (Victor, oai:scholarspace.manoa.hawaii.edu: NL1-083, 00:19:58.2-00:20:01.9)

(735) Rumah gua ada chanték **tak**?
   house 1SG COP beautiful **NEG**
   'My house is beautiful or not?'
   (Victor, oai:scholarspace.manoa.hawaii.edu: NL1-035, 00:02:41.9-00:02:43.7)

Other than the tag *tak*, it is also possible to form questions in the VP *tak* VP form. These have the same function as the basic *tak* tag and can be thought of as more fully developed versions of the basic *tak* questions. Examples (736) to (740) show how the VP *tak* VP form is used. Note that (739) and (740) appear as AP *tak* AP on the surface, but they are versions of VP where the copula is not expressed, unlike in (736), where the copula is fully expressed. Example (736) replicates (429).

(736) Ada baik **tak** -a?
 COP good **NEG** -COP
 'Are (you) well or not?'
 (Jane Quek, oai:scholarspace.manoa.hawaii.edu: NL1-142, 00:00:09.2-00:00:11.2)

(737) Lu perchaya **tak** perchaya?
 2SG trust **NEG** trust
 'Do you trust or not trust (this news)?'
 (Peter Wee, oai:scholarspace.manoa.hawaii.edu: NL1-125, 00:02:09.2-00:02:11.8)

(738) Lu setuju **tak** setuju?
 2SG agree **NEG** agree
 'Do you agree or not agree?'
 (Peter Wee, oai:scholarspace.manoa.hawaii.edu: NL1-125, 00:02:14.3-00:02:16.6)

(739) Chanték **tak** chanték?
 beautiful **NEG** beautiful
 'Beautiful or not beautiful?'
 (Peter Wee, oai:scholarspace.manoa.hawaii.edu: NL1-091, 00:03:41.3-00:03:43.9)

(740) Lain minggu, John tak tentu senang **tak** senang.
 another week NEG certain free **NEG** free
 'Next week, John is not sure if he is free or not free.'
 (Peter Wee, oai:scholarspace.manoa.hawaii.edu: NL1-091, 00:27:52.6-00:27:57.9)

The following examples demonstrate how *tak* and VP *tak* VP questions may be answered. Example (741) is a response to (739), while example (742) answers the question in example (733). Note that while *ya* is still used to mean 'yes', *bukan* 'no' is not used as a response to these questions (unlike the *bukan* questions). Instead, *tak ada* (short: *tak a*) 'NEG EXIST' is used to indicate a negative response. It is possible also for answers to be given without *ya* or *tak ada*. Declarative statements like those in examples (743) and (744) are also common responses to *tak* questions.

(741) Ya. kasot ini chanték.
 yes shoe this beautiful
 'Yes. These shoes (are) beautiful.'
 (Peter Wee, oai:scholarspace.manoa.hawaii.edu: NL1-091, 00:04:06.2-00:04:10.1)

(742) Tak   a   lah. Tak gitu   lah.
      NEG EXIST   EMP   NEG like.that EMP
      'No. (It is) not like that.'
      (Jane Quek oai:scholarspace.manoa.hawaii.edu: NL1-142, 00:00:52.5-00:00:53.8)

(743) Suka lah.
      Like EMP
      '(I) like (response to whether or not the agent likes to play mahjong).'
      (Jane Quek oai:scholarspace.manoa.hawaii.edu: NL1-142, 00:15:07.7-00:15:09.4)

(744) Tak   boléh.
      NEG   can
      'Cannot (response to whether something can or cannot be done).'
      (Jane Quek oai:scholarspace.manoa.hawaii.edu: NL1-043, 00:05:14.9-00:05:15.4)

Besides the above two main types of tag questions, other tags also exist, such as the ones listed in examples (745) to (748).

(745) Asam   gugol   mia   kulit ya?
      tamarind dried.fruit POSS   skin, yes
      'The dried tamarind's skin, yes?'
      (Jane Quek, oai:scholarspace.manoa.hawaii.edu: NL1-142, 00:11:51.6-00:11:54.4)

(746) Gua mia   favourite ah?
      1SG POSS   Q
      'My favourite?'
      (Jane Quek, oai:scholarspace.manoa.hawaii.edu: NL1-142, 00:10:37.2-00:10:39.5)

(747) oh lu   Catholic ada   chutsi eh?[73]
         2SG   have rebirth Q
      'Oh you Catholics have the concept of rebirth?'
      (Jane Quek, oai:scholarspace.manoa.hawaii.edu: NL1-142, 00:06:08.2-00:06:10.8)

---

[73] Intended as a joke.

(748) Gua   lapair   tau?
      1SG   hungry   know
      'I (am) hungry, (you) know?'
      (Victor, oai:scholarspace.manoa.hawaii.edu: NL1-002, 00:17:16.3-00:17:17.3)

The responses to these questions depend on whether the speaker has an intended answer (in which case the appropriate responses are *ya* 'yes' and *bukan* 'no'), or whether the speaker is genuinely enquiring for information (in which case the appropriate responses are *ya* 'yes' and *tak* VP). In the above questions, only (745) can be answered with *bukan*, since it is the notion of the clause that is being questioned.

It is useful here to recall that both content questions and tag questions differ in intonation (see section 3.7.3) Whereas content questions are accompanied by a rise-fall when the interrogative occurs in utterance-initial position, and a rise at the end of question when the interrogative occurs in utterance-final position, tags always occur at the end of the utterance, hence tag questions are always accompanied by a rise at the end of the utterance.

5.6.11 Imperatives

Verb phrases function as imperatives on their own, except for negative imperatives that are essentially verb phrases made up of *jangan* 'do not' and the main verb phrase (see section 5.2.8). Examples of non-negative imperatives are shown in (749) to (753).

(749) Pi   buang   ayé   kechik.
      Go   throw   water   small
      'Go urinate.'
      (Peter Wee, oai:scholarspace.manoa.hawaii.edu: NL1-052, 00:18:51.7-00:18:53.9)

(750) Pegi   lah.
      Go   EMP
      'Go.'
      (Victor, oai:scholarspace.manoa.hawaii.edu: NL1-037, 00:50:25.1-00:50:26.4)

(751) Pegi   buang   ayé   baik-baik.
      go   throw   water   good-good
      'Go urinate well.'
      (Victor, oai:scholarspace.manoa.hawaii.edu: NL1-037, 00:52:15.4-00:52:17.0)

(752) *Belajar chakap.*
learn speak
'Learn to speak'
(Jane Quek, oai:scholarspace.manoa.hawaii.edu: NL1-043, 00:32:04.1-00:32:05.8)

(753) *Tutop pintu.*
close door
'Close the door.'
(Jane Quek, oai:scholarspace.manoa.hawaii.edu: NL1-043, 00:23:01.3-00:23:02.8)

By and large, it is considered impolite to use these imperatives as well as the negative imperatives discussed in section 5.2.8, with speakers who have more seniority than oneself. Requests have to be couched in questions together with the appropriate terms of address. For more information on interrogatives, please refer to section 5.6.10.

6 Differences between Baba Malay Spoken in Singapore and Malacca

While this grammar is based on the variety of Baba Malay that is mainly spoken in Singapore, it is useful to consider the ways in which the Singapore variety differs from that spoken in Malacca (Malaysia). This chapter aims to highlight some areas of divergence between the varieties spoken in Singapore and in Malacca, as well as selected areas of similarities where they exist.

The differences between Singapore Baba Malay and Malacca Baba Malay are systematic and by nature, phonetic and phonological (Lee 2014), as well as morphological and syntactic (Lee 2018). The variety of Baba Malay in Singapore is more influenced by its substrate, Hokkien, and the variety that is spoken in Malacca is more influenced by its lexifier, Malay. These differences can be attributed to the specific ecologies at both locations – Malay influence is notable in Malacca, whereas Hokkien is consequential in Singapore (see section 2.3 for more details).

6.1 Phonetic and phonological differences

Phonetically, Malacca Baba Malay is different from Singapore Baba Malay in that Malacca Baba Malay speakers do not produce the vowel [ɔ], whereas Singapore Baba Malay speakers do. Phonologically, where words end with [e] and [o] in the Singapore variety, they may end with [aj] and [aw] in the Malacca variety, making the latter more alike Malay.

6.1.1 Vowel [ɔ]

The main difference between the two varieties of Baba Malay is the lack of the vowel [ɔ] in the Malacca variety. The vowels of a proficient male Malacca Baba Malay speaker in his sixties are measured for their first and second formants. The tokens are extracted from twelve hours' worth of interview sessions, from sections where speech is naturally-occurring. The same methodology was adopted for measuring vowels of Singapore Baba Malay, with the speaker selected for matching age and gender (see section 3.8) The following vowel chart in Figure 30 shows the vowel space of this speaker of the Malacca variety, in which [ɔ] is missing.

The vowel space of the Malacca Baba Malay speaker can be compared with the vowel space of a proficient Singapore Baba Malay speaker, also a male in his sixties. The vowel space of the Singapore Baba Malay speaker, featured earlier as figure 25, is replicated here as Figure 31. The Singapore Baba Malay speaker is observed to produce the vowel [ɔ], whereas the Malacca Baba Malay speaker does not do so.

https://doi.org/10.1515/9783110745061-006

6.1 Phonetic and phonological differences — 231

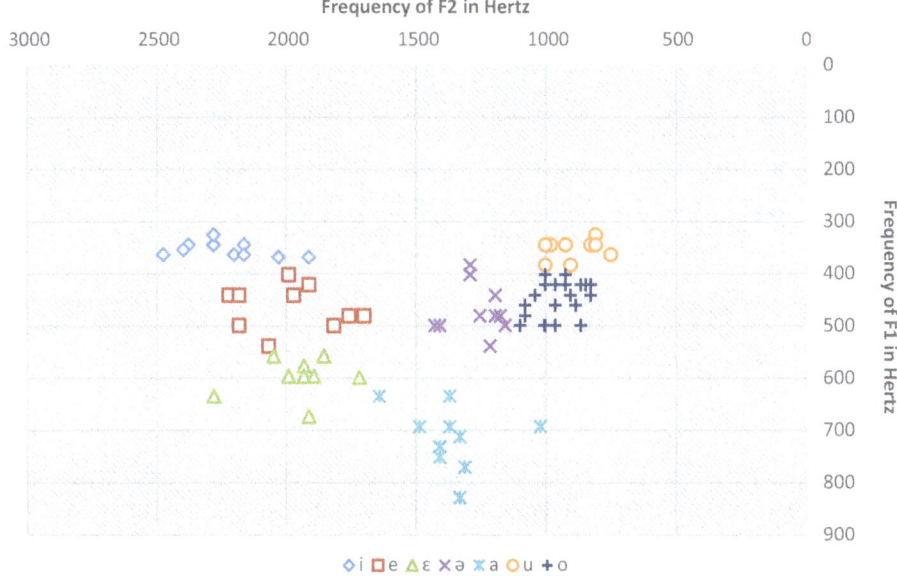

Figure 30: Vowel space of a Malacca Baba Malay speaker.

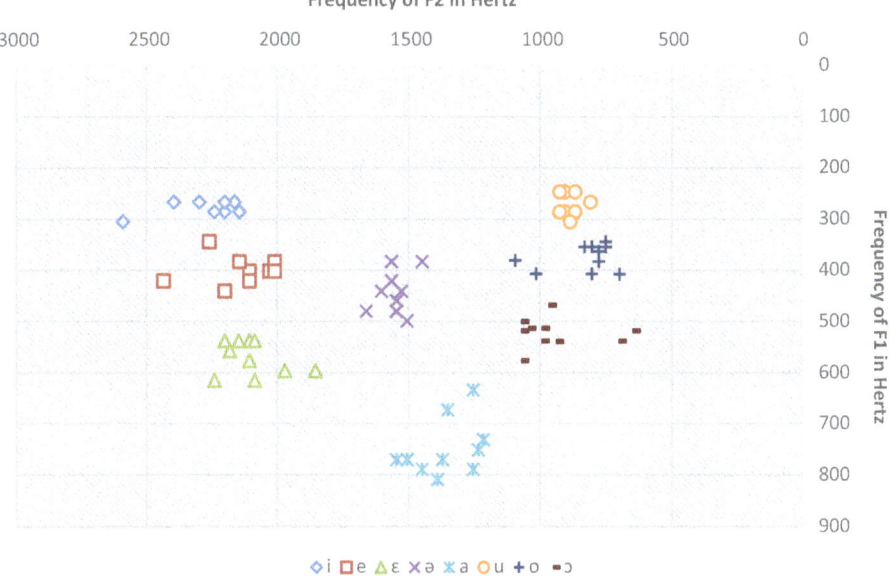

Figure 31: Vowel space of a Singapore Baba Malay speaker.

The vowel space of Malacca Baba Malay can be represented by the vowel chart in Table 40.

Table 40: Vowel chart of Malacca Baba Malay.

	Front	Central	Back
	Non-rounded	Non-rounded	Rounded
Close	i		u
Close-mid	e	ə	o
Open-mid	ɛ		
Open		a	

Where consonants are concerned, Malacca Baba Malay has the exact same consonant inventory as Singapore Baba Malay. The consonants in the Malacca variety can be represented by the following chart in Table 41.

Table 41: Consonant chart of Malacca Baba Malay.

		Labial	Alveolar	Post-alveolar	Velar	Glottal
Plosives	Voiceless	p	t		k	ʔ
	Voiced	b	d		g	
Affricates	Voiceless			tʃ		
	Voiced			dʒ		
Fricatives	Voiceless		s			h
Nasals		m	n	ɲ	ŋ	
Lateral			l			
Flap			r			

Glides: w (voiced labiovelar); j (voiced palatal)

6.1.2 [e], [o] versus [aj], [aw]

As discussed in the chapter on phonology (see section 3.3), words that end with [aj] and [aw] in Malay end with [e] and [o] respectively in Singapore Baba Malay. Malacca Baba Malay is similar to both Malay and Singapore Baba Malay, in that both [aj] and [aw], as well as [e] and [o] endings can be observed. Again, it is not accurate to generate [e] and [o] from a hypothetical monophthongization of [aj] and [aw] since [aj] and [aw] appear to be a later development due to the influence of Malay. Examples (754) and (755) demonstrate the use of [e] word-finally in the Malacca variety, whereas examples (756) and (757) show the use of [aj] word-finally in the same variety. Comparing Malacca Baba Malay directly with Malay, Sharif (1981) notes that [e] replaces [aj] word-finally in this variety (he represents [aj] as [ai]),[74] and he provides example (757) from his transcripts as a counterpoint, stating that this may be due to "a considerable amount of exposure to the Malay society" (Sharif 1981:106).

(754) [dja **pake** matʃam kawboj].
 3SG **wear** like cowboy
 'He wore (it) like a cowboy.'
 (Albert Ku, oai:scholarspace.manoa.hawaii.edu: NL1-046, 00:01:12.3-00:01:14.3)

(755) [kaki taʔ **sampe**].
 leg NEG **reach**
 'Legs do not reach.'
 (Albert Ku, oai:scholarspace.manoa.hawaii.edu: NL1-046, 00:02:52.6-00:02:54.0)

(756) [təpoʔ **pandaj pandaj**].
 clap **clever clever**
 'Clap cleverly.'
 (Albert Ku, oai:scholarspace.manoa.hawaii.edu: NL1-024, 00:15:38.3-00:15:39.4)

(757) [**pakaj**]
 use
 'Use'
 (Sharif 1981: 106)

Similarly, word-final [aw] and [o] both occur in Malacca Baba Malay, whereas word-final [aw] occurs in Malay, but not in Singapore Baba Malay, and word-final [o] occurs in Singapore variety but not in Malay. In the current corpus, *piso* 'knife' is the only item that shows up with word-final [o], as with example (758). Examples (759) to (763) demonstrate the use of word-final [aw].

(758) [**piso** mana]?
 knife where
 'Where (is) the knife?'
 (Albert Ku, oai:scholarspace.manoa.hawaii.edu: NL1-048, 00:14:07.8-00:14:08.6)

---

[74] Sharif (1981) represents these as phones instead of phonemes.

(759) [**kalaw** bole]
     if   can
     'If possible'
     (Albert Ku, oai:scholarspace.manoa.hawaii.edu: NL1-003, 00:02:09.2-00:02:10.2)

(760) [oraŋ **kalaw** tʃakap terus teraŋ]
     people **if**   speak straight bright
     'People, if (they) speak straight-forwardly'
     (Albert Ku, oai:scholarspace.manoa.hawaii.edu: NL1-003, 00:04:13.7-00:04:16.5)

(761) [**maw** aŋkat tu]
     want carry that
     'Want (to) carry that'
     (Albert Ku, oai:scholarspace.manoa.hawaii.edu: NL1-046, 00:02:33.1-00:02:33.5)

(762) [**kalaw**]
     if
     'If'
     (Sharif 1981: 26)

(763) [mesti **maw**]
     must **want**
     'must'
     (Sharif 1981: 20)

The best explanation again for the phonological difference identified between both varieties may be that Peranakans in Malacca are consistently exposed to Standard Malay compared to those in Singapore, since word-final [aj] and [aw] occur in Standard Malay, but not word-final [e] and [o].

6.2 Morphological differences

In terms of morphology, the Malacca variety differs only slightly from the Singapore variety. At first glance, Malacca Baba Malay appears to take on more affixes than Singapore Baba Malay.

6.2.1 *Ke- -an* nominalizing circumfix

In other varieties of Malay such as Bahasa Melayu and Bahasa Indonesia, the circumfix *ke-* and *-an* may be added to adjectives and verbs to form nouns of an abstract nature. In the Singapore Baba Malay corpus utilized for this grammar, there is no occurrence of this circumfix, whereas in the corresponding Malacca Baba Malay corpus, the circumfix occurs with the word *banyak* 'many' so that it becomes a noun, as with examples (764) and (765). This is also observed to occur in Sharif (1981)'s transcripts of Malacca Baba Malay, as with example (766). Also, while 'many' in Singapore Baba Malay is *manyak*, the corresponding word is *banyak* in these observed Malacca Baba Malay instances, making the Malacca variety more alike the Standard Malay varieties.

(764) **Ke-banyak-an** chakap saya
NMZ-many-NMZ speak 1SG
'Many say *saya* (for I).'
(Albert Ku, oai:scholarspace.manoa.hawaii.edu: NL1-003, 00:01:06.1-00:01:08.2)

(765) Anjing itu **ke-punya-an** Mary.
dog that **NMZ-possess-NMZ**
'That dog (is) Mary's possession.'
(Albert Ku, oai:scholarspace.manoa.hawaii.edu: NL1-010, 00:36:11.7-00:36:15.5)

(766) **Ke-banyak-an** orang tongsan
NMZ-many-NMZ people China
'Many (were) Chinese'
(Sharif 1981: 41)[75]

However, note that *ke-* may also be omitted in Malacca Baba Malay, as with example (767) and (768). In fact, *-an* in (767) appears as a regular nominalizer that is also used for non-abstract items, as with *chakap -an* 'speech' in (768). The general *-an* nominalizer is also found in Singapore Baba Malay (see section 4.1.1.1).

(767) Orang bahasa China **banyak-an**
person language China **many-NMZ**
'Many of the Chinese speakers'
(Albert Ku, oai:scholarspace.manoa.hawaii.edu: NL1-003, 00:04:18.2-00:04:20.4)

(768) **Chakap-an** Baba
speak-NMZ Baba
'The speech of the Babas.'
(Albert Ku, oai:scholarspace.manoa.hawaii.edu: NL1-003, 00:04:10.3-00:04:11.4)

---

[75] Sharif's transcripts (1981) are transcribed phonetically, but they are presented here orthographically.

6.2.2 Other affixes

Similar to Singapore Baba Malay, affixes in Malacca Baba Malay are not always meaningful. For example, in (770) and (772), Malay middle voice marker makes no difference to the interpretation of the word it is attached to. These can be compared to the unaffixed versions in examples (769) and (771).

(769) **bawak** datang kuéh itu.
 carry come cake that
 'Carry that cake here.'
 (Albert Ku, oai:scholarspace.manoa.hawaii.edu: NL1-013, 00:15:52.9-00:15:55.1)

(770) Dia pegi jalan jalan **berbawak** satu jarring.
 3SG go walk walk **carry** one net
 'He went walking carrying one net.'
 (Albert Ku, oai:scholarspace.manoa.hawaii.edu: NL1-047, 00:00:54.8-00:00:56.9)

(771) Dia **gonchang** botol itu.
 3SG **shake** bottle that
 'He shook that bottle.'
 (Albert Ku, oai:scholarspace.manoa.hawaii.edu: NL1-025, 00:09:39.8-00:09:42.1)

(772) **Bergonchang.**
 Shake
 'Shake (something).'
 (Albert Ku, oai:scholarspace.manoa.hawaii.edu: NL1-025, 00:09:36.9-00:09:38.7)

In addition to nominalizer -*an*, other commonly used productive affixes in Malacca Baba Malay are the ones that are also used in Singapore Baba Malay, these being transitive marker -*kan* and accidental and movement prefix *ter*- (see section 4.2.1.1). Examples (773) to (775) show usage of the transitive marker, examples (776) to (778) demonstrate how the accidental prefix is used, and examples (779) and (780) show usage of the uncontrolled movement prefix.

(773) **pechah-kan**
 break-TR
 'break (something).'
 (Albert Ku, oai:scholarspace.manoa.hawaii.edu: NL1-024, 01:12:17.0-01:12:18.6)

(774) Lu **jatoh-kan** barang.
 2SG **fall-TR** thing
 'You dropped something.'
 (Albert Ku, oai:scholarspace.manoa.hawaii.edu: NL1-025, 00:05:13.8-00:05:15.9)

(775) **Sandah-kan** itu tangga.
 lean-TR that ladder
 'Lean that ladder (against something).'
 (Albert Ku, oai:scholarspace.manoa.hawaii.edu: NL1-025, 00:03:22.2-00:03:26.5)

(776) Dia **ter-tendang** depan dia.
 3SG **ACD-kick** front 3SG
 'He accidentally kicked in front of him.'
 (Albert Ku, oai:scholarspace.manoa.hawaii.edu: NL1-047, 00:01:23.7-00:01:25.7)

(777) **ter-langgair.**
 ACD-crash
 'Accidentally crash.'
 (Albert Ku, oai:scholarspace.manoa.hawaii.edu: NL1-046, 00:03:33.0-00:03:33.6)

(778) Dia mia kopiah **ter-tinggal.**
 3SG POSS hat **ACD-stay**
 'His hat accidentally left behind.'
 (Albert Ku, oai:scholarspace.manoa.hawaii.edu: NL1-046, 00:04:39.0-00:04:40.9)

(779) **ter-pusing.**
 MVT-whirl
 'Whirl around.'
 (Albert Ku, oai:scholarspace.manoa.hawaii.edu: NL1-046, 00:03:35.0-00:03:38.5)

(780) keréta tu **ter-balék.**
 car that **MVT-return**
 'That car turned upside down.'
 (Albert Ku, oai:scholarspace.manoa.hawaii.edu: NL1-046, 00:04:06.1-00:04:10.8)

Note that while derivational morphology is limited in both varieties of Baba Malay, Malacca Baba Malay speakers are mostly aware of other derivational affixes used in Standard Malay and are able to use these. For example, while Malacca Baba Malay speakers interviewed state that there is no person prefix in Baba Malay, this prefix is observed in earlier data (Sharif 1981). This is likely due to the fact that the speaker was being interviewed by a speaker of Standard Malay.

(781) **pe-kerja** dia
 PERSON-work 3SG
 'His worker.'
 (Sharif 1981: 45)

In general, while Malacca Baba Malay speakers may be aware of other derivational affixes in Malay due to their exposure to Standard Malay as a dominant language in their environment, the ones that are considered by them to be Baba Malay are the abstract nominalizer circumfix *ke- -an*, general nominalizer *-an*, transitive marker *-kan*, and accidental and uncontrolled movement prefix *ter-*. Singapore Baba Malay speakers, on the other hand, have different levels of awareness of Standard Malay affixes if these occur solely in Standard Malay, depending on whether they have learnt Standard Malay formally, informally, or not at all.

6.3 Syntactic differences

In terms of syntax, several differences can be noted between the two varieties of Baba Malay, including word order within the noun phrase, and lexical choice of function words.

6.3.1 Noun phrase

With regard to the noun phrase, Malacca Baba Malay and Singapore Baba Malay are mostly similar. The only major difference concerning the noun phrase is the order of demonstrative determiners and nouns in both varieties.

6.3.1.1 Demonstrative determiners

While demonstrative determiners are observed to both precede and follow the main noun phrase in Singapore Baba Malay, the Malacca Baba Malay data recorded show that determiners follow the main noun phrase rather than precede it, as with examples (782) to (787). This appears to be a newer development considering that the older transcripts of Lim (1981, 1988) and Sharif (1981) show both word orders.

(782) *Barang*   **ini**   *banyak.*
       thing   **this**   many
       'These things (are) many.'
       (Albert Ku, oai:scholarspace.manoa.hawaii.edu: NL1-003, 00:07:00.0-00:07:01.3)

(783) *Peték*   *buah*   **tu**
       pluck   fruit   **that**
       'Pluck that fruit.'
       (Albert Ku, oai:scholarspace.manoa.hawaii.edu: NL1-046, 00:00:36.5-00:00:38.0)

(784) Dia   pakay kopiah **itu**
      3SG   wear   hat   **that**
      'He wears that hat.'
      (Albert Ku, oai:scholarspace.manoa.hawaii.edu: NL1-046, 00:02:49.9-00:02:50.8)

(785) Tangkap kodok **tu**
      capture frog   **that**
      'Captured that frog.'
      (Albert Ku, oai:scholarspace.manoa.hawaii.edu: NL1-046, 00:01:19.2-00:01:20.2)

(786) Anjing **itu**   pun   jatoh
      dog   **that** also fall
      'That dog also fell.'
      (Albert Ku, oai:scholarspace.manoa.hawaii.edu: NL1-046, 00:01:42.6-00:01:44.2)

(787) Kawin   **itu**.
      marriage **that**
      'That marriage.'
      (Uncle Chan, oai:scholarspace.manoa.hawaii.edu: NL1-008, 00:04:54.0-00:04:56.1)

The finding that determiner follows noun in Malacca Baba Malay, differs from that of Lim (1991, 1998) and Sharif (1988). It is notable that while they state that determiner precedes noun, their transcripts show that both word orders are common, as with examples (788) to (793).

(788) **Ini**   orang   pegi mintak.
      this person go   ask
      'This person goes and asks.'
      (Lim 1988: 53)

(789) **Itu**   orang.
      that person
      'That person.'
      (Sharif 1981: 17)

(790) **Itu**   kuéh.
      that cake
      'That cake.'
      (Sharif 1981: 22)

(791) Anak **itu** dua taon.
child **that** two year
'That child (is) two years old.'
(Lim 1988: 54)

(792) Malam **ini** mesti mau sambod.
tonight **this** must want pray
'Tonight (we) must pray.'
(Sharif 1981: 18)

(793) Macham kuéh pau **tu**
like cake bun **that**
'Like that cake bun (a type of food)
(Sharif 1981: 21)

Malacca Baba Malay has lost its determiner noun word order within the last thirty years or so, noting that that Sharif's and Lim's fieldwork was carried out before 1981. A plausible explanation may be that Baba Malay speakers are coming into contact with Malay speakers more extensively in Malacca. Residential areas are mixed, and it is also no longer the case that most Chinese settlers would be located in the area around the Malacca River, while the local Malay population live mostly in the rural areas (see Lim 1988:16). In contrast, Malay is less dominant in Singapore, and the determiner noun word order may be maintained due to the fact that the determiner noun word order occurs in English, which is the dominant language in Singapore (see section 2.3 for more information on the different language environment of Malacca and Singapore).

6.3.2 Verb phrase

Where the verb phrase is concerned, there are lexical differences in the aspectual systems of Malacca Baba Malay and Singapore Baba May.

6.3.2.1 Progressive aspect

In Singapore Baba Malay, the progressive aspect is expressed with the use of auxiliary verb *ada* (see section 5.2.5.4), which literally means 'possess', and is also an existential marker, a copula, and a perfective marker. In Malacca Baba Malay, *tengah* functions as a progressive marker in addition to *ada*. *Tengah* literally translates to 'middle', and is also used in Standard Malay to express the progressive. Another progressive marker in Standard Malay that is not found in Baba Malay is *sedang*. It is surprising that *tengah* occurs in Malacca Baba Malay but not *sedang*, since *tengah* has been noted to be more formal than *sedang* (see Mintz 1994). Note that while Sharif (1981) indicates *tengah* as being the progressive marker, his transcripts also demonstrate *ada* being used as a progressive marker. This is shown in examples (797) and (798). Examples (794) and (795) concern the use of *tengah* as a progressive marker, while examples (796) to (798) show *ada* being used for the same function.

(794) Budak ini **tengah** mandi sama anjing.
child this **PROG** bathe with dog
'This child is bathing with the dog.'
(Albert Ku, oai:scholarspace.manoa.hawaii.edu: NL1-047, 00:03:34.0-00:03:36.9)

(795) Kita **tengah** bikin.
1PL **PROG** make
'We are making (something).'
(Sharif 1981: 53)

(796) Dia **ada** ingat.
3SG **PROG** think
'He is thinking.'
(Albert Ku, oai:scholarspace.manoa.hawaii.edu: NL1-046, 00:05:09.0-00:05:10.9)

(797) Kita **ada** semayang Tuapékong
1PL **PROG** pray (name of a deity)
'We are praying (to) Tuapekong.'
(Sharif 1981: 20)

(798) Dia **ada** kerja
3SG **PROG** work
'He is working.'
(Sharif 1981: 51)

6.3.2.2 Perfective aspect

Similar to the Singapore variety, the perfective aspect in the Malacca variety can be expressed using either *sudah* 'already' or *ada* (see section 5.2.5.1). There is no difference between the two varieties, except that *dah* appears as the contracted form of *sudah* in Malacca Baba Malay. Note that *dah* is also used as the contracted form of *sudah* in general colloquial Malay. This differs from the Singapore Baba Malay contracted form, *sua*. Examples (799) to (801) demonstrate this usage of *dah*, example (802) shows *sudah* used in its complete form, while (803) to (805) show how *ada* can also be used to express the perfective aspect.

(799) Hari pun **dah** petang.
　　　day also **already** evening
　　　'The day has already (become) evening.'
　　　(Albert Ku, oai:scholarspace.manoa.hawaii.edu: NL1-047, 00:03:02.2-00:03:04.3)

(800) Buah tu **dah** jatoh
　　　fruit that **already** fall
　　　'That fruit already fell.'
　　　(Albert Ku, oai:scholarspace.manoa.hawaii.edu: NL1-046, 00:00:58.0-00:01:00.9)

(801) Military tu **dah** mati
　　　　　　　　that **already** die
　　　'That military (man) already died.'
　　　(Sharif 1981: 40)

(802) Kita **sudah** jadi orang besar lah.
　　　1PL **already** become person big EMP
　　　'We already became adults.'
　　　(Sharif 1981: 29)

(803) Barang **ada** pechah.
　　　thing **PFV** break
　　　'That thing broke.'
　　　(Albert Ku, oai:scholarspace.manoa.hawaii.edu: NL1-024, 01:12:40.5-01:12:42.8)

(804) Jepun **ada** chakap
　　　Japanese **PFV** talk
　　　'The Japanese talked.'
　　　(Sharif 1981: 40)

(805) **Ada** ikot Melayu dulu dulu.
　　　PFV follow Malay old old
　　　'They followed the old Malays.'
　　　(Sharif 1981: 26)

6.3.3 Adjectival and adverbial phrases

There are also slight differences in specific types of adjectival and adverbial phrases between the two varieties of Baba Malay. Differences are found in the structures of comparatives and in the form of *dengan* 'with' adverbial phrases.

6.3.3.1 *Daripada* comparatives

With regard to comparatives, while Singapore Baba Malay speakers use the form *lagik* AP *lagik* (*lagik* literally means 'more' in this instance, see section 5.3.1), Malacca Baba Malay speakers mostly use the Standard Malay form *lebéh* AP *daripada*, as with examples (806) to (808). *Lebéh* translates to 'more' and *daripada* 'from'.[76] Note that *lebéh* is also used to indicate 'more' in Singapore Baba Malay, but it is not used in comparatives. A separate but related form is *kurang* AP *daripada*, *kurang* meaning 'less'. This usage is demonstrated in example (809). There is no corresponding form in the Singapore variety.

(806) Apple mérah **lebéh** manis   **daripada** apple ijo.
             red   **more**   sweet   **than**   green
      'The red apple is sweeter than the green apple.'
      (Albert Ku, oai:scholarspace.manoa.hawaii.edu: NL1-005, 00:30:38.9-00:30:45.9)

(807) Apple ini **lebéh** manis   **daripada** apple itu
             this   **more**   sweet   **than**   that
      'This apple is sweeter than that apple.'
      (Albert Ku, oai:scholarspace.manoa.hawaii.edu: NL1-005, 00:30:33.0-00:30:37.5)

(808) Di sini **lebéh** banyak apple **daripada** sana
           PREP   here   **more**   many   **than**   there
      'Here (there are) more apples than there.'
      (Albert Ku, oai:scholarspace.manoa.hawaii.edu: NL1-005, 00:31:18.6-00:31:22.1)

(809) Apple ini **kurang** banyak **daripada** sana
             here   **less**   many   **than**   there
      '(There are) less apples here than there.'
      (Albert Ku, oai:scholarspace.manoa.hawaii.edu: NL1-005, 00:31:54.0-00:32:09.8)

6.3.3.2 *Dengan* 'with' adverbial phrase

Adverbial phrases of manner in Malacca Baba Malay can be introduced with *dengan* in addition to *sama*. Their Singapore Baba Malay equivalents are introduced by *sama*, which is also the general conjunction marker in that variety (adverbial phrases of manner that use *sama* are covered in section 5.4.3). This use of *dengan* (also found in Malay) is very rarely found in Singapore Baba Malay. The following examples show how *dengan* 'with' is used to introduce adverbial phrases in the Malacca variety. It is interesting to note that neither *suka hati* in example (810) nor *gembira* in (812) are

---

[76] *Daripada* can be further analysed in Malay as containing preposition *dari* 'from' and *pada* 'on'.

used in Singapore Baba Malay to mean 'happy'. In Singapore Baba Malay, the same notion is expressed by Hokkien term *huahi*. Examples (810) to (814) demonstrate the use of *dengan*, while example (815) demonstrates the use of *sama*.

(810) Orang itu   pukol kuching **dengan** kayu.
      person that hit   cat   **with**   stick
      'That person hit the cat with the stick.'
      (Albert Ku, oai:scholarspace.manoa.hawaii.edu: NL1-010, 00:21:35.6-00:21:38.1)

(811) Gua sangat suka.hati   gua   chakap **dengan** lu.
      1SG very   like.heart 1SG   speak   **with**   2SG
      'I (am) very happy I am speaking with you.'
      (Albert Ku, oai:scholarspace.manoa.hawaii.edu: NL1-005, 00:46:12.1-00:46:14.4)

(812) Dia makan apple manis **dengan** gembira.
      3SG eat   sweet **with**   happy
      'He ate the sweet apple happily.'
      (Albert Ku, oai:scholarspace.manoa.hawaii.edu: NL1-005, 00:36:33.0-00:36:41.0)

(813) Ini   ada satu cherita réka –an   sahja
      this COP one   story   invent-NMZ   only
      dengan se-orang   budak.
      with   one-person child
      'This is only one invented story with one child.'
      (Albert Ku, oai:scholarspace.manoa.hawaii.edu: NL1-047, 00:00:15.7-00:00:18.9)

(814) **Dengan** Santali
      with   (company name)
      'With Santali.'
      (Sharif 1981: 41)

(815) Budak ini   tengah mandi **sama** anjing.
      child this PROG   bathe **with** dog
      'This child is bathing with the dog.'
      (Albert Ku, oai:scholarspace.manoa.hawaii.edu: NL1-047, 00:03:34.0-00:03:36.9)

6.3.4 Conjunctions

Two conjunctions in Malacca Baba Malay differ lexically from those used in Singapore Baba Malay.

6.3.4.1 Dan/sama 'and' coordinating conjunction

While Singapore Baba Malay speakers use *sama* to indicate general conjunction 'and' (see section 5.6.8.1), Malacca Baba Malay speakers use *sama* and *dan*. *Dan* has the same function in Standard Malay, while *sama* is used to indicate 'with' in that language. The Malacca variety is more influenced by Standard Malay than the Singapore variety. Examples (816) and (817) demonstrate the usage of *dan*, and example (818) demonstrates the usage of *sama* by the same speaker. Example (819) shows that *sama* cannot be used for sequential relations. Sequential relations in both Malacca Baba Malay and Singapore Baba Malay are expressed by entirely separate clauses that can be mediated with the use of *habi* (see section 5.6.8.1).

(816) Satu ékor anjing **dan** jugak satu ékor kodok.
one CLF.animal dog **and** also one CLF.animal frog
'One dog and also one frog.'
(Albert Ku, oai:scholarspace.manoa.hawaii.edu: NL1-047, 00:00:23.2-00:00:28.2)

(817) Budak jantan ini **dan** anjing balék
Child male this **and** dog return
'This boy and dog returned.'
(Albert Ku, oai:scholarspace.manoa.hawaii.edu: NL1-047, 00:03:16.2-00:03:18.6)

(818) Apal sal budak ini **sama** anjing ini mo ni?
what reason child this **and** dog this want this
'Why do this child and this dog want this?'
(Albert Ku, oai:scholarspace.manoa.hawaii.edu: NL1-047, 00:03:27.7-00:03:30.6)

(819) Dia chakap chakap **sama** nangis.
3SG speak speak **and** cry
'He was speaking and crying.'
(Lim1988: 37)

6.3.4.2 Atau/ ka 'or' coordinating conjunction

While Singapore Baba Malay speakers use *ka* to indicate 'or', Malacca Baba Malay speakers use *atau*. The usage of *ka* in Singapore Baba Malay is explained in section 5.6.8.1. Unsurprisingly, considering that Malacca Baba Malay speakers come into much more contact with Standard Malay than speakers of the Singapore variety, *atau* is derived from Malay. *Ka* on the other hand is derived from Hokkien. *Ka* is found in earlier documentations of Malacca Baba Malay, but appears to have fallen out of usage. Examples (820) and (821) show the usage of Malay-derived *atau* 'or', while example (822) shows an earlier usage of Hokkien-derived *ka*. Example (823), which has been taken out of Sharif's (1981) transcripts, is interesting, because it shows the use of both *ka* and *atau* in the same sentence, establishing that both lexical items were available to the speaker of the Malacca variety in the 1980s.

(820) Sekarang mia   murid-murid **atau** budak-budak sekolah.
      now   REL   disciple-PL **or**   child-PL   school
      'The current disciples or school children.'
      (Albert Ku, oai:scholarspace.manoa.hawaii.edu: NL1-003, 00:01:22.7-00:01:27.0)

(821) Dia   mo   buat   kawan   sama   dia   **atau** mo   tangkap
      3SG   want   make   friend with   3SG   **or**   want   capture
      gua   makan.
      1SG   eat
      'He wanted to make friends with him or capture me to eat.'
      (Albert Ku, oai:scholarspace.manoa.hawaii.edu: NL1-003, 00:01:22.7-00:01:27.0)

(822) Lu   suka   chakap   Melayu   **ka**   suka   chakap   English?
      2SG   like   speak   Malay   **or**   like   speak   English
      'Do you like to speak Malay or do (you) like to speak English?'
      (Lim1988: 38)

(823) Chuchu   ada   empat   **ka**   **atau** lima
      grandchild   have   four   **or**   **or**   five
      'Grandchildren (I) have four or five.'
      (Sharif 1981: 36)

6.4 Diverging ecologies

Current-day Malacca Baba Malay and Singapore Baba Malay differ in a number of ways, pervading areas of phonetics and phonology (Lee 2014), morphology and syntax (Lee 2018). Singapore Baba Malay speakers have an additional [ɔ] vowel in their inventory that is possibly derived from Hokkien (see section 3.8) and utilize features that may be attributed to Hokkien influence, such as the demonstrative noun order and the use of the coordinating conjunction *ka* 'or'. Malacca Baba Malay is significantly more influenced by Standard Malay. In terms of phonology, words ending with [aj] and [aw] are permissible in the Malacca variety (as with Standard Malay). Where morphology is concerned, the Standard Malay abstract nominalizer *ke- -an* is also used by Malacca Baba Malay speakers. Other Standard Malay syntactic features that Malacca Baba Malay speakers use include the noun demonstrative word order, the progressive marker *tengah*, the contracted perfective *dah*, the *lebéh/kurang* AP *daripada* comparative, the use of *dengan* for adverbial phrases, and the coordinating conjunctions *dan* 'and' and *atau* 'or'. More so than before, it is also clear that the

Malacca variety is losing Hokkien features, such as the determiner noun order, as well as the use of coordinating conjunction *ka* 'or'. Overall, both varieties clearly diverge in whether they are more influenced by Standard Malay or Hokkien.

The observations made above fall in line with the observations made about the current sociological environments that both communities of speakers participate in (see section 2.3, Lee 2018). The dominance of Malay in Malacca is clear, especially with the language being used as the language of administration, commerce, and mainstream education. Even though Malacca Baba Malay speakers often state that they do not speak Malay at home, the fact is that their variety shows signs of being heavily influenced by Malay (Lee 2018: 165). Singapore Baba Malay shows more divergence away from Malay. While English (or a vernacular version of it) is the most dominant language in Singapore and the home language of many Peranakans, its influence is less clear, since English is neither the contact language's substrate nor lexifier. The Hokkien features that characterize Singapore Baba Malay on the other hand, may be reinforced then by the fact that Hokkien is one of the more popular, unofficial Chinese languages spoken in Singapore, and that the Chinese are a significant majority (Lee 2018: 167). The high levels of multilingualism in Singapore and Malacca make their language ecologies complex ones, but in general, the influence of Malay and Hokkien explain how these two varieties of Baba Malay have evolved, and may continue to evolve.

While this chapter does not aim to provide an exhaustive list of Malacca Baba Malay features, it is hoped that users will find the list of differences between both varieties useful as a starting point in the discussion.

7 Appendices

These appendices include various word lists, a set of four spoken texts, as well as 10 *pantun* 'poetry' written by one of the language consultants. Finally, the appendices also contain a Baba Malay-English lexicon as well as an English-Baba Malay reversal index.

7.1 Word lists

The various word lists in this section include a Swadesh 100-word list, a list of kinship terms, and a list of expressions for day, month, and time.

7.1.1 Swadesh 100-word list

The following list in Table 42 is based on Swadesh's (1995) 100-word list.

Table 42: Swadesh 100-word list in Baba Malay.

No.	Word	Gloss	No.	Word	Gloss
1.	saya gua	I (refined) I (coarse)	2.	lu	you
3.	kita	we	4.	ini	this
5.	itu	that	6.	siapa?	who?
7.	apa?	what?	8.	bukan tak	no, negates noun negates verb
9.	sumua	all	10.	manyak	many
11.	satu	one	12.	dua	two
13.	besar besair	big (coarse) big (refined)	14.	panjang	long
15.	kechik	small	16.	perompuan	woman
17.	jantan	man, male	18.	orang	person
19.	ikan	fish	20.	burong	bird
21.	anjing	dog	22.	kutu	louse
23.	pokok	tree	24.	bijik	seed
25.	daoun	leaf	26.	akar akair	root (coarse) root (refined)

Table 42 (continued)

No.	Word	Gloss	No.	Word	Gloss
27.	kulit kayu 'skin wood'	bark	28.	kulit	skin
29.	isi	flesh	30.	darah	blood
31.	tulang	bone	32.	minyak	grease, oil
33.	teloh	egg	34.	tandok	horn
35.	buntot	tail, backside	36.	bulu	feather, fine hair
37.	rambot	hair, coarse hair	38.	kepala	head
39.	kuping	ear	40.	mata	eye
41.	hidong, idong	nose	42.	mulot	mouth
43.	gigi	tooth	44.	lidah	tongue
45.	kuku	fingernail	46.	kaki	foot, leg
47.	lutot	knee	48.	tangan	hand
49.	perot	belly, stomach	50.	léihéi	neck
51.	tétek	breast	52.	hati, ati jantong	heart / heart (when referring to emotions)
53.	hati, ati	liver	54.	minum	drink
55.	makan	eat	56.	gigit	bite
57.	nampak, téngok	see, look	58.	dengar dengair	hear (coarse) / hear (refined)
59.	tau	know	60.	tidor	sleep
61.	mati	die	62.	bunoh	kill
63.	berenang	swim	64.	terbang, trebang	fly
65.	jalan	walk	66.	datang mari	come / come let us do something
67.	baring	lie down	68.	dudok	sit, stay
69.	diri	stand	70.	kasi	give, let, cause, PASS
71.	chakap kata	speak say	72.	mata ari, mata hari 'eye sun'	sun
73.	bulan	moon, month	74.	bintang	star
75.	ayé	water	76.	hujan, ujan	rain

Table 42 (continued)

No.	Word	Gloss	No.	Word	Gloss
77.	batu	stone, rock, cave	78.	paser	sand
79.	tanah	soil, ground, earth	80.	awan	cloud
81.	asap	smoke	82.	api	fire
83.	abu	ash	84.	bakar bakair	burn (coarse) burn (refined)
85.	jalan tengah jalan 'middle path'	path road	86.	bukit gunong	hill mountain
87.	mérah	red	88.	hijo, ijo	green
89.	kuning	yellow	90.	putéh	white
91.	hitam, itam	black	92.	malam	night
93.	panas panair	hot (coarse) hot (refined)	94.	sejok	cold
95.	penoh kerniang	full full (from food)	96.	baru	new
97.	baik bagus	good good (EXCLAM)	98.	bulat	round
99.	kering	dry, hay	100.	nama	name

7.1.2 Kinship terms

Baba Malay has a complex set of kinship terms, that originates mostly from Hokkien, with some use of Malay terms such as *bapak* for 'father' and *besar/besair* (literally meaning 'big') denoting 'eldest'. Some of these terms are used together with Hokkien and Malay- derived numerals (see section 4.5.3 for a list of relevant numerals), also to denote one's position among others. *Sa-hia*, derived entirely from Hokkien (literally meaning 'three-elder.brother'), would denote third eldest brother, as would *hia numbor tiga* 'elder.brother number three'. *Numbor tiga* in the latter instance is derived from Malay. A list of kinship terms is presented in Table 43. The term 'cousin' as used in this list, refers to the child of a parent's sibling.

Table 43: Kinship terms in Baba Malay.

No.	Kinship term	Gloss	No.	Kinship term	Gloss
1.	mak nya-nya	mother	2.	bapak baba	father
3.	mak-yi 'mother-mother's sister'	second mother [in the case of a second marriage or a clash in astrological signs (popular astrology)]	4.	tio-tio 'parent's.eldest. sister's husband' eng-chék 'honorific-father's younger.brother'	second father [in the case of a second marriage or a clash in astrological signs (popular astrology)]
5.	nya besar/besair 'Nyonya-big'	eldest daughter	6.	ba-tengah 'Baba-middle'	middle son
7.	nya bongsu 'Nyonya-youngest'	youngest daughter	8.	ba-chik 'Baba-small'	youngest son
9.	bini	wife	10.	laki	husband
11.	chingkay	parent-in-law, father-in-law (indirect address)	12.	chay.em	mother-in-law (indirect address)
13.	kua eng-kua 'honorific-father.in.law'	father-in-law (direct address)	14.	nio	mother-in-law (direct address)
15.	tachi	elder sister, also used for cousins	16.	hia	elder brother, also used for cousins
17.	tachi besar/besair 'elder.sister big'	eldest sister	18.	hia besar/besair 'elder.brother big' tua-hia 'big-elder.brother'	eldest brother
19.	tachi numbor dua 'elder.sister number two'	second elder sister	20.	hia numbor dua 'elder.brother number two' ji-hia 'two-elder.brother'	second elder brother
21.	tachi numbor tiga 'elder.sister number three'	third elder sister	22.	hia numbor tiga 'elder.brother number three' sa-hia 'three-elder.brother'	third elder brother

Table 43 (continued)

No.	Kinship term	Gloss	No.	Kinship term	Gloss
23.	adék	sibling, younger sibling	24.	adék-beradék 'sibling-PL'	siblings, younger siblings
25.	adék perompuan 'younger.sibling female'	younger sister	26.	adék jantan 'younger.sibling male'	younger brother
27.	adék numbor satu 'younger.sibling number one'	eldest younger sibling	28.	adék bongsu 'sibling youngest'	youngest sibling
29.	pangkat adék-beradék 'rank sibling-PL'	cousins	30.	kopiau	paternal cousins
31.	chau	elder sister's husband	32.	so eng-so 'honorific-elder.brother's.wife'	elder brother's wife
33.	yi	mother's sister	34.	ku eng-ku 'honorific-mother's.brother'	mother's brother
35.	tio eng-tio 'honorific-mother's.sister's.husband'	mother's sister's husband	36.	kim eng-kim 'honorific-mother's.brother's.wife'	mother's brother's wife
37.	yi-yi	mother's eldest sister	38.	ku-ku	mother's eldest brother
39.	tio-tio	mother's eldest sister's husband	40.	kim-kim	mother's eldest brother's wife
41.	ji-yi 'two-mother's.sister'	mother's second sister	42.	ji-tio 'two-mother's.sister's.husband'	mother's second sister's husband
43.	ji-ku 'two-mother's.brother'	mother's second brother	44.	ji-kim 'two-mother's.brother's wife'	mother's second brother's wife

Table 43 (continued)

No.	Kinship term	Gloss	No.	Kinship term	Gloss
45.	ko	father's sister	46.	pék eng-pék 'honorific-father's.elder.brother'	father's elder brother
47.	tio eng-tio 'honorific-father's.sister's.husband'	father's sister's husband (also mother's sister's husband)	48.	em	father's elder brother's wife
49.	mak-ko 'mother-father's.sister'	father's eldest sister	50.	pék-pék	father's eldest brother
51.	tio-tio	father's eldest sister's husband (also mother's eldest sister's husband)	52.	mak-em 'mother-father's.elder.brother's.wife'	father's eldest brother's wife
53.	chék eng-chék 'honorific-father's.younger.brother'	father's younger brother	54.	chim eng-chim 'honorific-father's.younger.brother's.wife	father's younger brother's wife
55.	ji-ko 'two-father's.elder.sister'	father's second sister	56.	ji pek 'two-father's.elder.brother'	father's second elder brother
57.	ji-chék 'two-father's.younger.brother'	father's second younger brother	58.	ji-chim 'two-father's.younger.brother's.wife'	father's second younger brother's wife
59.	gong	grandparent, also grandfather	60.	cho	great-grandparent, also great-grandmother
61.	mamak	grandmother	62.	gong.gong	grandfather
63.	mak-cho 'mother-great.grandparent' cho-cho	great-grandmother	64.	cho-gong 'great-grandfather'	great-grandfather

Table 43 (continued)

No.	Kinship term	Gloss	No.	Kinship term	Gloss
65.	po em-po 'honorific-grandaunt'	grand-aunt	66.	chék-gong 'father's.younger.brother-grandparent'	grandfather's younger brother
67.	ku-gong-cho 'mother's.brother-grandparent-great.grandparent'	great-grandmother's brother	68.	cho-po 'great.grandparent-grandaunt'	great-grandaunt
69.	gong-cho 'grandparent/great.grandparent'	ancestors	70.	chuchu	grandchild
71.	chichi	great-grandchild	72.	onéng.onéng	great-great grandchild

7.1.3 Expressions for day, month and time

The days of the week are indicated by the word for day (*ari* or *hari*), followed by a number that represents a specific day of the week. This is with the exception of Sunday – *ari minggu* literally means 'day week'. The system for days of the week in Baba Malay is similar to the Hokkien system, where a number is assigned to each day; Tuesday corresponds to 'two', and Sunday corresponds to 'week'. For example, Tuesday in Hokkien is *lépài jī* 'week two', while Sunday is *lépài jit* 'week day'. This is different from Malay, where Tuesday is *Selasa* and Sunday is *Ahad*. Table 44 lists the days of the week in Baba Malay.

Table 44: Days of the week in Baba Malay.

No.	Day	Gloss	No.	Day	Gloss
1.	ari satu 'day one'	Monday	2.	ari dua 'day two'	Tuesday
3.	ari tiga 'day three'	Wednesday	4.	ari empat 'day four'	Thursday
5.	ari lima 'day five'	Friday	6.	ari enam 'day six'	Saturday
7.	ari minggu 'day week'	Sunday			

Similarly, the months of the year are formed by combining the word for month (*bulan*) and a number that represents a specific month. Again, this is closer to the Hokkien system, where specific numbers represent specific months, although the word for month occurs after the numeral in Hokkien, instead of before. For instance, February is *jī guek*, literally 'two month' in Hokkien, as compared to *bulan dua* 'month two' in Baba Malay. These expressions may also refer to the lunar month. Table 45 lists expressions to do with the month in Baba Malay.

Table 45: Months in Baba Malay.

No.	Day	Gloss	No.	Day	Gloss
1.	*bulan satu* 'month one'	January	2.	*bulan dua* 'month two'	February
3.	*bulan tiga* 'month three'	March	4.	*bulan empat* 'month four'	April
5.	*bulan lima* 'month five'	May	6.	*bulan enam* 'month six'	June
7.	*bulan tujoh* 'month seven'	July	8.	*bulan lapan* 'month eight'	August
9.	*bulan semilan* 'month nine'	September	10.	*bulan puloh* 'month ten'	October
11.	*bulan se-belas/belair* 'month one-ten (coarse/refined)'	November	12.	*bulan dua-belas/belair* 'month two-ten (coarse/refined)'	December
13.	*bulan tujoh satu* 'month seven one'	first of July	14.	*bulan empat lima* 'month four five'	fourth of May

Although the expressions in Table 45 can be used to denote the lunar month, Peranakans also use Hokkien forms to indicate important days on the lunar calendar, as listed in Table 46.

Table 46: Important dates on the lunar calendar in Baba Malay.

No.	Day	Gloss	No.	Day	Gloss
1.	*chay-it* 'beginning. of.lunar.calendar-one'	first day of the lunar month; new year's day	2.	*chay-gau* 'beginning.of.lunar. calendar-nine' *ti-gong séh* 'sky-deity birth'	ninth day of the lunar month, birth of Jade Emperor (ninth day of first lunar month)
3.	*chap-gor* 'ten-five	fifteenth day of lunar month; lovers' day	4.	*chap-gor méh* 'ten-five night'	night of the fifteenth day of the lunar;

Table 46 (continued)

No.	Day	Gloss	No.	Day	Gloss
5.	chit guék 'seven month'	seventh month; Hungry Ghost month	6.	puay guék chap-gor 'eight month ten-five'	fifteenth day of the eighth lunar month; Mid-autumn festival
7.	tangchék	Winter Solstice	8.	lun-guék intercalary-month	intercalary month, in the year that an extra month occurs
9.	lun-chit-guék 'intercalary-seven-month'	intercalary seventh month, in the year that there are two seventh months	10.	ji-gau méh 'two-nine night'	night of the twenty-ninth day of the twelfth lunar month; night of new year's eve

General diurnal expressions are listed in Table 47.

Table 47: General diurnal expressions in Baba Malay.

No.	Time expression	Gloss	No.	Time expression	Gloss
1.	pagi	morning	2.	hari/ari	day
3.	tengah hari/ari 'middle day'	midday	4.	petang	evening
5.	sinjakala	dusk	6.	malam	night
7.	siang hari/ari 'day'	daytime	8.	siang malam 'night day'	night time
9.	se-malam 'one-night'	yesterday	10.	ini hari/ ini ari/ ni ari 'this day'	today
11.	besok	tomorrow	12.	rusak	day after tomorrow

The expressions for specific time are similar to those in Malay. These are listed in Table 48. The words *pagi* 'morning' or *petang* 'evening' follow these expressions to indicate if the event takes place before midday or after midday.

Table 48: Specific time in Baba Malay.

No.	Time	Gloss	No.	Day	Gloss
1.	pukol satu 'strike one'	one o'clock	2.	pukol dua 'strike two'	two o'clock
3.	pukol tiga 'strike three'	three o'clock	4.	pukol empat 'strike four'	four o'clock
5.	pukol lima 'strike five'	five o'clock	6.	pukol enam 'strike six'	six o'clock

Table 48 (continued)

No.	Time	Gloss	No.	Day	Gloss
7.	pukol tujoh 'strike seven'	seven o'clock	8.	pukol lapan 'strike eight'	eight o'clock
9.	pukol semilan 'strike nine'	nine o'clock	10.	pukol puloh 'strike ten'	ten o'clock
11.	pukol se-belas/ belair 'strike one-ten (coarse/refined)'	eleven o'clock	12.	pukol dua-belas/ belair 'strike two-ten (coarse/refined)'	twelve o'clock
13.	pukol se-belas puloh pagi 'strike one-ten ten morning'	ten minutes past eleven in the morning	14.	pukol lima lapan petang 'strike five eight evening'	eight minutes past five in the evening

7.2 Texts

The texts in this section of the appendix include four spoken texts and a collection of ten written *pantun* 'poetry'. The four spoken texts are *Cherita Pear sama Peter Wee* (Pear Story with Peter Wee), *Anjing sama Tulang sama Peter Wee* (The Dog and the Bone with Peter Wee), *Bangkuang Besair sama Victor* (The Enormous Turnip with Victor), and *Chakapan sama Aunty Jane* (Conversation with Aunty Jane). It should be noted that it is particularly common for older Peranakans to have been familiar with Western fables and tales such as the ones listed here.

The spoken texts are transcribed using a system that is modelled after Du Bois et al's (2012) Discourse Transcription conventions. Each line on the transcript represents one intonation unit. The interpretation of transitions between intonation units are based on Baba Malay intonation patterns (see section 3.7.3. on sentence level intonation). Table 49 provides the list of conventions used in the texts. These conventions are indicated in the top tiers that represent intonation units.

Table 49: Transcription conventions for texts.

No.	Symbol	Use
1.	IU	Intonation unit
1.	.	Final intonation boundary, usually associated with fall in overall pitch contour in Baba Malay
2.	,	Continuing intonation boundary, usually associated with a rise at the end of the intonation unit in Baba Malay

Table 49 (continued)

No.	Symbol	Use
3.	?	Appeal intonation boundary, associated with overall rise-fall for WH-questions, and rise at the end of the intonation unit for tag questions in Baba Malay
4.	...	Noticeable pause between 0.3 to 0.6 seconds
5.	=	Lengthening on preceding segment
6.	@	Pulse of laughter
7.	#	Indecipherable syllable
8.	(2.1)	Pause of 2.1 seconds. Numbers in brackets represent duration in seconds. Pauses which are longer than 0.6 seconds are indicated by this convention.

7.2.1 Cherita Pear sama Baba Peter Wee

((NL1-022:Pear Story[77] with Peter Wee: 0.00-379.00))

PETER WEE;

1.
Baba Malay IU	*Ah ini dekat mana ini?*
Baba Malay words	*ah ini dekat mana*
English gloss	filler this PREP where
English free translation	Ah what country (is) this?

2.
(2.7)

3.
Baba Malay IU	*Ini tempat pokok,*
Baba Malay words	*ini tempat pokok*
English gloss	this place tree
English free translation	This is an orchard,

4.
(1.1)

---

[77] Chafe, Wallace (ed.), *The Pear Stories: Cognitive, Cultural, and Linguistic Aspects of Narrative Production*. Norwood, New Jersey: Ablex (1980).

5.
Baba Malay IU	*Ini buah pear,*
Baba Malay words	*Ini buah pear*
English gloss	this fruit
English free translation	These are pears,

6.
Baba Malay IU	*Gua rasa orang ni orang ada peték buah pear.*
Baba Malay words	*gua rasa ni orang ada peték buah pear.*
English gloss	1SG think this person PROG pluck fruit
English free translation	I think the person is plucking pears.

7.
Baba Malay IU	*Masok ini kebun,*
Baba Malay words	*Masok ini kebun*
English gloss	enter this garden
English free translation	Enter this garden,

8.
Baba Malay IU	*Kebun dekat Europe ini.*
Baba Malay words	*Kebun dekat Europe ini*
English gloss	garden PREP this
English free translation	This garden (is) in Europe.

9.
Baba Malay IU	*Ada pear.*
Baba Malay words	*Ada pear*
English gloss	EXIST
English free translation	There (are) pears.

10.
Baba Malay IU	*Kita sini tak-a tak-a pokok.*
Baba Malay words	*Kita sini tak a tak a pokok*
English gloss	1PL here NEG have NEG have tree
English free translation	We here, do not have trees.

11.
Baba Malay IU	*Pear tau?*
Baba Malay words	*Pear tau*
English gloss	know
English free translation	Pear (trees you) know?

12.
Baba Malay IU	*Oh betol betol. . .oh satu sudah jatoh.*
Baba Malay words	Oh betol betol oh satu sudah jatoh
English gloss	Filler true true Filler one already fall
English free translation	Oh true enough, one fell.

13.
(2.6)

14.
Baba Malay IU	*Buah pear bukan?*
Baba Malay words	Buah pear bukan
English gloss	fruit no
English free translation	It (is) pear, no?

15.
(1.0)

16.
Baba Malay IU	*Mata gua tak gitu betol,*
Baba Malay words	Mata gua tak gitu betol
English gloss	eye 1SG NEG like.this correct
English free translation	My eyes (are) not accurate,

17.
Baba Malay IU	*gua nampak begi buah paya hijo.*
Baba Malay words	gua nampak begi buah paya hijo
English gloss	1SG see like.that fruit papaya green
English free translation	(they) look like green papayas (to) me.

18.
Baba Malay IU	*Bukan lah ini sumua pear=.*
Baba Malay words	Bukan lah ini sumua pear
English gloss	no EMP this all
English free translation	No these are all pears.

19.
Baba Malay IU	*Dia sudah dia sudah punggot punggot dia mia pear . . .*
Baba Malay words	Dia sudah dia sudah punggot punggot dia mia pear
English gloss	3SG already 3SG already pick.up pick.up 3SG POSS
English free translation	He picked up his pears

20.

Baba Malay IU	*dia salin-kan dekat bakol.*
Baba Malay words	dia salin-kan dekat bakol
English gloss	3SG transfer-TR PREP basket
English free translation	(and) transferred (them) to a basket.

21.
(2.4)

22.

Baba Malay IU	*Tu ini dia mia buah pear ini,*
Baba Malay words	Tu ini dia mia buah pear ini
English gloss	that this 3SG POSS fruit this
English free translation	Those pears of his,

23.

Baba Malay IU	*Kalu mesti mo angkat tangan*
Baba Malay words	Kalu mesti mo angkat tangan tarok
English gloss	if must want hold hand put
English free translation	If you want (you) put (your) hand (there),

24.

Baba Malay IU	*kalu tak-a jatoh kan dia,*
Baba Malay words	kalu tak a tak a jatoh-kan dia
English gloss	if NEG EXIST NEG EXIST drop-TR 3SG
English free translation	if not (you will) drop it,

25.

Baba Malay IU	*Dia sumua pichah.*
Baba Malay words	Dia sumua pichah
English gloss	3PL all break
English free translation	They all break.

26.
(1.9)

27.

Baba Malay IU	*Mesti angkat baik baik,*
Baba Malay words	Mesti angkat baik baik
English gloss	must hold good good
English free translation	Must hold them well,

28.
(1.9)

29.
Baba Malay IU	*Itu ada tangga dia naik tangga atas pokok.*
Baba Malay words	*Itu ada tangga dia naik tangga atas pokok*
English gloss	that COP ladder 3SG climb ladder top tree
English free translation	That is a ladder, he climbs the ladder up the tree.

30.
Baba Malay IU	*Sekarang dia mo apa?*
Baba Malay words	*Sekarang dia mo apa*
English gloss	now 3SG want what
English free translation	Now what (does) he want (to do)?

31.
Baba Malay IU	*Satu satu dia mo apa bikin tu?*
Baba Malay words	*Satu satu dia mo apa bikin tu*
English gloss	one one 3SG want what make that
English free translation	One by one, what (is) he doing?

32.
(2.3)

33.
Baba Malay IU	*Dia mo piléh gua rasa.*
Baba Malay words	*Dia mo piléh gua rasa*
English gloss	3SG want choose 1SG think
English free translation	He wants to choose, I think.

34.
(2.1)

35.
Baba Malay IU	*Dia mo piléh mana baik...*
Baba Malay words	*Dia mo piléh mana baik*
English gloss	3SG want choose which good
English free translation	He wants to choose which (is) good...

36.
Baba Malay IU	*Mana satu tak baik.*
Baba Malay words	mana satu tak baik
English gloss	which one NEG good
English free translation	which one (is) not good.

37.
Baba Malay IU	*Mana sudah terbantot,*
Baba Malay words	Mana sudah terbantot
English gloss	which already unripe
English free translation	which has not ripened.

38.
Baba Malay IU	*Mana sudah masak,*
Baba Malay words	mana sudah masak
English gloss	which already ripe
English free translation	which (is) already ripe,

39.
Baba Malay IU	*Mana belom masak,*
Baba Malay words	Mana belom masak
English gloss	which not.yet ripe
English free translation	which (is) not yet ripe.

40.
Baba Malay IU	*Ayé dia naik,*
Baba Malay words	Ayé dia naik
English gloss	EXCLAM.surprise 3SG climb
English free translation	Aye he is going up,

41.
Baba Malay IU	*Naik tangga pi peték lagik.*
Baba Malay words	Naik tangga pi peték lagik
English gloss	climb ladder go pluck more
English free translation	Climbing the ladder to go pluck more.

42.
Baba Malay IU	*Ini kawan dia datang sama apa?*
Baba Malay words	Ini kawan dia datang sama apa
English gloss	this friend 3SG come with what
English free translation	These friends are coming with what?

43.

Baba Malay IU	*Sama donkey eh #sama goat.*
Baba Malay words	*Sama donkey eh sama goat*
English gloss	with filler with
English free translation	With a donkey, (no) with a goat.

44
(1.2)

45.

Baba Malay IU	*Kambing=,*
Baba Malay words	*Kambing*
English gloss	goat
English free translation	Goat,

46.

Baba Malay IU	*Kawan dia datang angkat satu kambing.*
Baba Malay words	*Kawan dia datang angkat satu kambing*
English gloss	friend 3SG come hold one goat
English free translation	His friend comes holding a goat.

47.

Baba Malay IU	*Kambing dia ada locheng.*
Baba Malay words	*Kambing dia ada locheng*
English gloss	goat 3SG have bell
English free translation	His goat has a bell.

48.

Baba Malay IU	*Itu kambing gua tak tau perompuan ka jantan.*
Baba Malay words	*itu kambing gua tak tau perompuan ka jantan*
English gloss	that goat 1SG NEG know female or male
English free translation	I don't know if that goat (is) male or female.

49.
(3.2)

50.

Baba Malay IU	*Ayé mampus. . .kambing dia kuat sekali.*
Baba Malay words	*Ayé mampus kambing dia kuat sekali*
English gloss	EXCLAM.surprise dead goat 3SG strong very
English free translation	Oh this goat is so strong!

51.
Baba Malay IU	*Tarék dia.*
Baba Malay words	*Tarék dia*
English gloss	pull 3SG
English free translation	Pulling it.

52.
Baba Malay IU	*Ayé ini dia peték lagik lah.*
Baba Malay words	*Ayé ini dia peték lagik lah*
English gloss	EXCLAM.surprise this 3SG pluck again EMP
English free translation	Ah he plucks again.

53.
(2.4)

54.
Baba Malay IU	*Buah pear. . .pear tree.*
Baba Malay words	*Buah pear pear tree*
English gloss	fruit
English free translation	Pear tree.

55.
(2.3)

56.
Baba Malay IU	*Ala orang dia mia mungka bukan main,*
Baba Malay words	*Ala orang dia mia mungka bukan main*
English gloss	EXCLAM.regret people 3SG POSS face NEG play
English free translation	This person's face, (he is) not to be trifled with,

57.
Baba Malay IU	*garang sekali,*
Baba Malay words	*garang sekali*
English gloss	fierce very
English free translation	(he is) very fierce,

58.
Baba Malay IU	*Kus semangat.*
Baba Malay words	*Kus semangat*
English gloss	EXCLAM.cry.to.a.dead.spirit
English free translation	Oh my goodness

59.
(3.0)

60.
Baba Malay IU	*Ini ada bicycle=,*
Baba Malay words	Ini ada bicycle
English gloss	this EXIST
English free translation	There is a bicycle.

61.
Baba Malay IU	*Gua rasa ini anak dia ka chuchu dia,*
Baba Malay words	Gua rasa ini anak dia ka chuchu dia
English gloss	1SG feel this child 3SG or grandchild 3SG
English free translation	I think this (is) his child or his grandchild,

62.
Baba Malay IU	*pi charék dia mia gonggong. . .gua rasa.*
Baba Malay words	pi charék dia mia gonggong gua rasa
English gloss	go find 3SG POSS grandfather 1SG think
English free translation	goes to find his grandfather, I think.

63.
Baba Malay IU	*Ini mia tempat bukan Singapore lah. . .*
Baba Malay words	Ini mia tempat bukan Singapore lah
English gloss	this REL place NEG EMP
English free translation	This place (is) not Singapore,

64.
Baba Malay IU	*bukan this region. . .*
Baba Malay words	bukan this region
English gloss	NEG
English free translation	Not this region. . .

65.
Baba Malay IU	*gua rasa ini sumua Mediterranean.*
Baba Malay words	gua rasa ini sumua Mediterranean
English gloss	1SG feel this all
English free translation	I think this (is) all Mediterranean.

66.
(3.3)

67.
Baba Malay IU	*Ala panas sair pakay kopiah dia.*
Baba Malay words	Ala panas sair pakay kopiah dia
English gloss	EXCLAM.regret hot indeed wear hat 3SG
English free translation	Goodness, it (is) hot indeed, (the child) is wearing his hat.

68.
Baba Malay IU	*Ah ini anak dia ka chuchu,*
Baba Malay words	Ah ini anak dia ka chuchu
English gloss	filler this child 3SG or grandchild
English free translation	Ah this child or his grandchild,

69.
Baba Malay IU	*dia panggay dia mia gonggong.*
Baba Malay words	dia panggay dia mia gonggong
English gloss	3SG call 3SG POSS grandfather
English free translation	He (is) calling his grandfather.

70.
(5.0)

71.
Baba Malay IU	*Apa dia buat?*
Baba Malay words	Apa dia buat
English gloss	what 3SG do
English free translation	What (is) he doing?

72.
(2.7)

73.
Baba Malay IU	*Dia chakap sama dia.*
Baba Malay words	Dia chakap sama dia
English gloss	3SG speak with 3SG
English free translation	He is speaking with him.

74.
(2.5)

75.

Baba Malay IU	*Ah dia mo angkat.*
Baba Malay words	Ah dia mo angkat
English gloss	filler 3SG want lift
English free translation	Oh he wants to lift,

76.

Baba Malay IU	*Oh dia mo angkat tarok mana tarok dia mia,*
Baba Malay words	Oh dia mo angkat tarok mana tarok dia mia
English gloss	filler 3SG want carry put where put 3SG POSS
English free translation	Oh he wants to carry and put where, put on his

77.

Baba Malay IU	*Bicycle.*
Baba Malay words	Bicycle
English gloss	
English free translation	

78.
(1.0)

79.

Baba Malay IU	*Eh tak jadi.*
Baba Malay words	Eh tak jadi
English gloss	filler NEG happen
English free translation	Ey it didn't happen.

80.
(5.5)

81.

Baba Malay IU	*Ala…mia berat.*
Baba Malay words	Ala mia berat
English gloss	EXCLAM.regret REL heavy
English free translation	Goodness, (this) heavy.

82.

Baba Malay IU	*Jatoh lah=.*
Baba Malay words	Jatoh lah
English gloss	fall EMP
English free translation	(He will) fall (for certain).

83.
Baba Malay IU	*Amcam. . .oh dia tarok kat depan.*
Baba Malay words	Amcam oh dia tarok kat depan
English gloss	how filler 3SG put PREP front
English free translation	How? Oh he is putting (it) in front.

84.
(2.9)

85.
Baba Malay IU	*Téngok budak anak itu kechik,*
Baba Malay words	téngok budak anak itu kechik
English gloss	look child child that small
English free translation	Look at that small child,

86.
Baba Malay IU	*Sudah boléh pakay bicycle.*
Baba Malay words	Sudah boléh pakay bicycle
English gloss	already can use
English free translation	Already can use a bicycle.

87.
(2.5)

88.
Baba Malay IU	*Ayé jatoh lagik.*
Baba Malay words	Ayé jatoh lagik
English gloss	EXCLAM.surprise fall again
English free translation	Ah (he) fell again.

89.
(1.0)

90.
Baba Malay IU	*Gua sudah kata nanti jatoh lu téngok.*
Baba Malay words	Gua sudah kata nanti jatoh lu téngok
English gloss	1SG already say later fall 2SG see
English free translation	I told you (he) would fall later you see.

91.
(0.9)

92.
Baba Malay IU   Mesti jatoh.
Baba Malay words   Mesti   jatoh
English gloss   must   fall
English free translation Must fall.

93.
Baba Malay IU   Budak ini... sangat kechik lah.
Baba Malay words   Budak   ini   sangat   kechik   lah
English gloss   child   this very   small   EMP
English free translation This boy (is) so small.

94.
(3.4)

95.
Baba Malay IU   Ah jumpa kawan dia.
Baba Malay words   Ah   jumpa   kawan   dia
English gloss   filler meet   friend 3SG
English free translation Ah (he) met his friends.

96.
Baba Malay IU   Gua rasa mesti ter-langgair tau?
Baba Malay words   Gua   rasa   mesti   ter-langgair   tau
English gloss   1SG   think   must   ACD-crash   know
English free translation I think (there) must be a crash (you) know.

97.
(2.0)

98.
Baba Malay IU   Ah dia téngok dia habis.
Baba Malay words   Ah   dia   téngok   dia   habis
English gloss   filler 3PL   see   3SG   finish
English free translation Ah they see him finish.

99.
Baba Malay IU   Tu... gua sudah kata lu betol,
Baba Malay words   Tu   gua   sudah   kata   lu   betol,
English gloss   that   1SG   already say   2SG   correct
English free translation That I already told you, correct,

100.
(1.0)

101.
Baba Malay IU	*Ala,*
Baba Malay words	*Ala*
English gloss	EXCLAM.regret
English free translation	Goodness,

102.
Baba Malay IU	*Habis... dia mia buah pear sumua,*
Baba Malay words	*Habis dia mia buah pear sumua*
English gloss	finish 3SG POSS fruit all
English free translation	(In the) end, his pears all

103.
Baba Malay IU	*Ter-lambong,*
Baba Malay words	*Ter-lambong*
English gloss	ACD-toss
English free translation:	were tossed,

104.
Baba Malay IU	*Bicycle jatoh,*
Baba Malay words	*Bicycle jatoh*
English gloss	fall
English free translation	The bicycle fell,

105.
Baba Malay IU	*Budak jatoh,*
Baba Malay words	*Budah jatoh*
English gloss	child fall
English free translation	The child fell,

106.
Baba Malay IU	*Buah pear dia sumua sudah,*
Baba Malay words	*Buah pear dia sumua sudah*
English gloss	fruit 3PL all already
English free translation	The pears they all had

107.
Baba Malay IU   *Sudah jatoh.*
Baba Malay words   *Sudah   jatoh*
English gloss   already   fall
English free translation   Had fallen.

108.
(1.0)

109.
Baba Malay IU   *Ah kaki dia sudah kena.*
Baba Malay words   *Ah   kaki   dia   sudah   kena*
English gloss   filler leg   3SG   already PASS
English free translation   Ah his foot was affected.

110.
(3.0)

111.
Baba Malay IU   *Ah siapa ni apa ni?*
Baba Malay words   *Ah   siapa ni   apa   ni*
English gloss   filler who   this what this
English free translation   Ah who (is) this (and) what (is) this?

112.
Baba Malay IU   *Ah kawan-kawan dia datang tolong.*
Baba Malay words   *Ah   kawan kawan dia   datang tolong*
English gloss   filler friend friend 3SG   come   help
English free translation   Ah his friends come to help.

113.
(2.5)

114.
Baba Malay IU   *Sumua tolong dia lah.*
Baba Malay words   *Sumua   tolong dia   lah*
English gloss   all   help   3SG   EMP
English free translation   All (are) helping him.

115.
Baba Malay IU   *Punggot dia mia buah pear,*
Baba Malay words   *Punggot   dia   mia   buah   pear*
English gloss   pick.up   3SG   POSS   fruit   enter-TR
English free translation Picking his pears,

116.
Baba Malay IU   *masok-kan bakol dia*
Baba Malay words   *masok-kan   bakol   dia*
English gloss   enter-TR   basket   3SG
English free translation entering (them into) his basket.

117.
Baba Malay IU   *Ayé dia ini lambong-kan.*
Baba Malay words   *Ayé   dia   ini   lambong-kan*
English gloss   EXCLAM.surprise   3SG   this   toss-TR
English free translation He is throwing (it).

118.
(1.0)

119.
Baba Malay IU   *Si tua tu pelan-pelan,*
Baba Malay words   *Si   tua   tu   pelan   pelan*
English gloss   PERSON   old   that   slow   slow
English free translation The old man slowly,

120.
Baba Malay IU   *Angkat satu-satu,*
Baba Malay words   *Angkat   satu-satu*
English gloss   take   one-one
English free translation Taking (them) one by one,

121.
Baba Malay IU   *Tak mo ini budak-budak amék-kan sumua.*
Baba Malay words   *Tak   mo   ini   budak-budak   amék-kan   sumua*
English gloss   NEG   want   this   child-PL   take-TR   all
English free translation Don't want these children (to) take all.

122.

Baba Malay IU	*Sudah lambong.*
Baba Malay words	*Sudah lambong*
English gloss	already throw
English free translation	Thrown (them).

123.

Baba Malay IU	*Gua rasa dia mia pear ini kerair.*
Baba Malay words	*Gua rasa dia mia pear ini kerair*
English gloss	1SG think 3PL POSS this hard
English free translation	I think their pears (are) hard.

124.

Baba Malay IU	*Belom masak=.*
Baba Malay words	*Belom masak*
English gloss	not.yet ripe
English free translation	Not yet ripe.

125.

Baba Malay IU	*Tu sudah masak dia bikin macam habis nua.*
Baba Malay words	*Tu sudah masak dia bikin macam habis nua*
English gloss	that already ripe 3SG make like finish smashed.up
English free translation	That (is) already ripe (and) he makes it smashed up.

126.
(3.1)

127.

Baba Malay IU	*Ah ni apa ni?*
Baba Malay words	*Ah ni apa ni*
English gloss	filler this what this
English free translation	Ah what (is) this?

128.
(1.1)

129.

Baba Malay IU	*Budak ini buat buat main main lah.*
Baba Malay words	*Budak ini buat buat main main lah*
English gloss	child this do do play play EMP
English free translation	The children are playing.

130.
(3.1)

131.
Baba Malay IU	*Mmm=,*
Baba Malay words	*Mmm*
English gloss	
English free translation	

132.
Baba Malay IU	*Sudah sudah habis ter-jalan balék.*				
Baba Malay words	*Sudah*	*sudah*	*habis*	*ter-jalan*	*balék*
English gloss	already	already	finish	MVT-walk	back
English free translation	(when it is) already finished, he returns.				

133.
Baba Malay IU	*Ah sekarang dia tolak bicycle itu.*					
Baba Malay words	*Ah*	*sekarang*	*dia*	*tolak*	*bicycle*	*itu*
English gloss	filler	now	3SG	push		that
English free translation	Ah now he is pushing that bicycle.					

134.
(1.5)

135.
Baba Malay IU	*Dia mia dua. . . dia mia kawan.*					
Baba Malay words	*Dia*	*mia*	*dua*	*dia*	*mia*	*kawan*
English gloss	3SG	POSS	two	3SG	POSS	friend
English free translation	His two . . . his friends.					

136.
(0.8)

137.
Baba Malay IU	*Dia jalan lain tempat dia jalan lain tempat.*						
Baba Malay words	*Dia*	*jalan*	*lain*	*tempat*	*dia*	*jalan*	*lain*	*tempat*
English gloss	3SG	walk	another	place	3PL	walk	another	place
English free translation	He walks to another place, they walk to another place.						

138.
(2.1)

139.
Baba Malay IU	*Ah dia ni punggot apa ini.*
Baba Malay words	*Ah dia ni punggot apa ni*
English gloss	filler 3SG this pick.up what this
English free translation	Ah what (is) he picking up?

140.
Baba Malay IU	*Oh dia punggot kopiah dia.*
Baba Malay words	*Oh dia punggot kopiah dia*
English gloss	filler 3SG pick.up hat 3SG
English free translation	Oh he (is) picking up his hat.

141.
Baba Malay IU	*Kopiah dia sudah jatoh.*
Baba Malay words	*Kopiah ada sudah jatoh*
English gloss	hat PFV already fall
English free translation	The hat had fallen.

142.
Baba Malay IU	*Dia teriak dia,*
Baba Malay words	*Dia teriak dia*
English gloss	3SG call.out 3SG
English free translation	He calls out to him.

143.
Baba Malay IU	*Oi?*
Baba Malay words	*Oi*
English gloss	
English free translation	(calling out)

144.
(2.0)

145.
Baba Malay IU	*Ah. . .lu sudah jatoh lu mia kopiah.*
Baba Malay words	*Ah lu sudah jatoh lu mia kopiah*
English gloss	filler 2SG already drop 2SG POSS hat
English free translation	You dropped your hat.

146.
(1.6)

147.
Baba Malay IU   *Ada angkat-kan kasi-kan dia balék,*
Baba Malay words   Ada   angkat-kan   kasi-kan   dia   balék
English gloss   PFV   pick.up-TR   give-TR   3SG   back
English free translation (He) picked (it) up (and) returned it back to him.

148.
Baba Malay IU   *Habi dia kasi dia dua bijik pear.*
Baba Malay words   Habi   dia   kasi   dia   dua   bijik   pear
English gloss   finish 3SG   give   3SG   two   CLF.small.round
English free translation Then he gave him two pears.

149.
(1.0)

150.
Baba Malay IU   *Amboi,*
Baba Malay words   Amboi
English gloss   EXCLAM.surprise
English free translation Suprising,

151.
(1.5)

152.
Baba Malay IU   *Dia kasi-kan kopiah,*
Baba Malay words   Dia   kasi-kan   kopiah
English gloss   3SG   give-TR   hat
English free translation He gave (him) the hat.

153.
Baba Malay IU   *Dia dapat dua bijik pear balék huh,*
Baba Malay words   Dia   dapat   dua   bijik   pear   balék   huh
English gloss   3SG   receive two   CLF.small.round   back
English free translation He received two pears back huh,

154.
Baba Malay IU   *Happy dia.*
Baba Malay words   Happy dia
English gloss   3SG
English free translation He (is) happy.

155.
Baba Malay IU	*Ayé-,*
Baba Malay words	*Ayé-*
English gloss	EXCLAM.surprise
English free translation	Surprising,

156.
Baba Malay IU	*Ah dia kasi-kan kawan dia.*				
Baba Malay words	*Ah*	*dia*	*kasi-kan*	*kawan*	*dia*
English gloss	filler	3SG	give-TR	friend	3SG
English free translation	Ah he gave it to his friends.				

157.
(2.0)

158.
Baba Malay IU	*Ah tu lah kasi-kan kawan dia,*					
Baba Malay words	*Ah*	*tu*	*lah*	*kasi-kan*	*kawan*	*dia*
English gloss	filler	that	EMP	give-TR	friend	3SG
English free translation	Ah that (he) gave to his friends.					

159.
(0.9)

160.
Baba Malay IU	*Oh dia kasi dia tiga.*				
Baba Malay words	*Oh*	*dia*	*kasi*	*dia*	*tiga*
English gloss	filler	3SG	give	3PL	three
English free translation	Oh he gave them three.				

161.
Baba Malay IU	*Oh sekarang budak-budak ini makan,*					
Baba Malay words	*Oh*	*sekarang*	*budak*	*budak*	*ini*	*makan*
English gloss	filler	now	child	child	this	eat
English free translation	Oh now these children are eating,					

162.
Baba Malay IU	*Gua rasa pear tu tak boléh makan lah,*						
Baba Malay words	*Gua*	*rasa*	*pear*	*tu*	*tak*	*boléh*	*makan*	*lah*
English gloss	1SG	think		that	NEG	can	eat	EMP
English free translation	I think those pears cannot be eaten.							

163.
Baba Malay IU   *Kerair begi batu.*
Baba Malay words   Kerair   begi   batu
English gloss   hard   like.that rock
English free translation Hard like rocks.

164.
(1.0)

165.
Baba Malay IU   *Tak masak mentah=.*
Baba Malay words   Tak   masak   mentah
English gloss   NEG   ripe   raw
English free translation Not ripe (still) raw.

166.
(2.0)

167.
Baba Malay IU   *Ah ni si tua dia.*
Baba Malay words   Ah   ni   si   tua   dia
English gloss   filler this   PERSON   old   3SG
English free translation Ah this the old man he

168.
(0.8)

169.
Baba Malay IU   *Turun tangga.*
Baba Malay words   turun   tangga
English gloss   descend   ladder
English free translation goes down the ladder.

170.
(1.0)

171.
Baba Malay IU   *Téngok si tua peték dia mia pear,*
Baba Malay words   Téngok   si   tua   peték   dia   mia   pear
English gloss   look   PERSON   old   pluck   3SG   POSS
English free translation Look at the old man pluck his pear

172.

Baba Malay IU	*Berapa sayang.*
Baba Malay words	*Berapa sayang*
English gloss	how.many care
English free translation	How much care.

173.

Baba Malay IU	*Pelan-pelan=,*
Baba Malay words	*Pelan pelan*
English gloss	slow slow
English free translation	Slowly,

174.

Baba Malay IU	*Satu-satu=,*
Baba Malay words	*Satu satu*
English gloss	one one
English free translation	One by one,

175.

Baba Malay IU	*Budak masok-kan.*
Baba Malay words	*Budak masok-kan*
English gloss	child enter-TR
English free translation	The boys enter.

176.
(3.0)

177.

Baba Malay IU	*Ayé mati sekair mana gua mia pear?*
Baba Malay words	*Ayé mati sekair mana gua mia pear*
English gloss	EXCLAM.surprise die indeed where 1SG POSS
English free translation	Oh goodness, die, where (are) my pears?

178.

Baba Malay IU	*Oh satu bakol sudah ilang.*
Baba Malay words	*Oh satu bakol sudah ilang*
English gloss	filler one basket already lost
English free translation	Oh one basket has gone missing.

179.
(4.0)

180.

Baba Malay IU	*Ayé dia jumpa ini tiga ékor budak.*
Baba Malay words	Ayé　　　　　　dia　jumpa　ini　tiga　ékor
English gloss	EXCLAM.surprise　3SG　meet　this　three　CLF.animals
	budak
	child
English free translation	Aye he meets these three children.

181.
(2.5)

182.

Baba Malay IU	*Ada makan pear.*
Baba Malay words	Ada　makan　pear
English gloss	PROG　eat
English free translation	Eating pear.

183.
(6.0)

184.

Baba Malay IU	*Oh sudah si tua ini heran,*
Baba Malay words	Oh　sudah　si　　　tua　ini　héran
English gloss	filler　already　PERSON　old　this　wonder
English free translation	Oh already this old man wonders,

185.

Baba Malay IU	*Mana budak ini dapat pear #makan?*
Baba Malay words	Mana　budak　ini　dapat　pear　makan
English gloss	where　child　this　get　　　　　eat
English free translation	Where did these children get the pears to eat (from)?

186.
(2.0)

187.

Baba Malay IU	*Ada lagik eh?*
Baba Malay words	Ada　lagik　eh
English gloss	EXIST　more　Q
English free translation	Is there more?

188.
Baba Malay IU   *Sumua habis.*
Baba Malay words   *Sumua   habis*
English gloss   all   finish
English free translation All finished.

189.
(3.0)

190.
Baba Malay IU   *Habis.*
Baba Malay words   *Habis*
English gloss   finish
English free translation the end.

<T=379.00>

7.2.2 Anjing Sama Tulang sama Baba Peter Wee

((NL1-030: Three stories based loosely on Aesop's Fables[78] with Peter Wee: 94.00-215.00))

PETER WEE;

1.
Baba Malay IU   *Anjing ini sama ni apa?*
Baba Malay words   *anjing ini   sama   apa*
English gloss   dog   this   with   what
English free translation The dog (is) with the what?

2.
Baba Malay IU   *Ini nampak begi butterfly.*
Baba Malay words   *Ini   nampak begi   butterfly*
English gloss   this   look   like
English free translation This looks like a butterfly.

---

[78] The story of The Dog and the Bone is based loosely on The Dog and its Reflection in one of Aesop's Fables (133 on the Perry Index).

3.
Baba Malay IU	*Itu kita panggay kupu-kupu.*
Baba Malay words	Itu kita panggay kupu-kupu
English gloss	this 1PL call butterfly
English free translation	This we call "butterfly".

4.
Baba Malay IU	*Kupu-kupu trebang,*
Baba Malay words	kupu-kupu trebang,
English gloss	butterfly fly
English free translation	The butterfly flew,

5.
Baba Malay IU	*Di dekat anjing.*
Baba Malay words	Di dekat anjing
English gloss	PREP near dog
English free translation	Near the dog.

6.
Baba Malay IU	*Anjing mo main main,*
Baba Malay words	Anjing mo main main
English gloss	dog want play play
English free translation	The dog wants to play,

7.
Baba Malay IU	*sama ni nia kupu-kupu lah.*
Baba Malay words	sama ni nia kupu-kupu lah
English gloss	with this REL butterfly EMP
English free translation	'with this butterfly.'

8.
(1.1)

9.
Baba Malay IU	*Dia lompat sini,*
Baba Malay words	Dia lompat sini
English gloss	3SG jump here
English free translation	It jumps here,

10.

Baba Malay IU	*dia lompat sana,*
Baba Malay words	dia lompat sana
English gloss	3SG jumps there
English free translation	it jumps there,

11.

Baba Malay IU	*Ini kupu-kupu sama anjing ni,*
Baba Malay words	Ini kupu-kupu sama anjing ni
English gloss	this butterfly and dog this
English free translation	This butterfly and this dog,

12.
(1.6)

13.

Baba Malay IU	*Begi buat kawan lah.*
Baba Malay words	Begi buat kawan lah
English gloss	like.that make friend EMP
English free translation	Seems that (they) became friends.

14.
(2.2)

15.

Baba Malay IU	*So dia buat buat main sama dia lah.*
Baba Malay words	So dia buat buat main sama dia lah
English gloss	3SG make make play with 3SG EMP
English free translation	So they played with each other.

16.
(3.4)

17.

Baba Malay IU	*So dia main lah.*
Baba Malay words	So dia main lah
English gloss	3SG play EMP
English free translation	So they played.

18.
Baba Malay IU   *Yeah then they chakap,*
Baba Malay words   Yeah then they chakap
English gloss   speak
English free translation Yeah then they chatted,

19.
Baba Malay IU   *Sama satu sama lain.*
Baba Malay words   sama   satu   sama   lain
English gloss   with   this   with   that
English free translation With one another.

20.
(2.5)

21.
Baba Malay IU   *Ini dia kejar dia.*
Baba Malay words   Ini   dia   kejar   dia
English gloss   this   3SG   chase   3SG
English free translation This chased it.

22.
(1.3)

23.
Baba Malay IU   *Ter-kejar ni mia apa?*
Baba Malay words   Ter-kejar   ni   mia   apa
English gloss   MVT-chase   this   REL   what
English free translation (It) chased this what (do you call that)?

24.
Baba Malay IU   *Butterfly.*

25.
Baba Malay IU   *Kupu-kupu.*
Baba Malay words   Kupu-kupu
English gloss   butterfly
English free translation Butterfly.

26.

Baba Malay IU	*Se-kali kejar kejar kejar,*
Baba Malay words	*Se-kali kejar kejar kejar*
English gloss	this-time chase chase chase
English free translation	Once (it) chased chased chased,

27.

Baba Malay IU	*Datang di tepi sunggay.*
Baba Malay words	*Datang di tepi sunggay*
English gloss	come PREP side river
English free translation	(It) came to the side of the river.

28.
(0.5)

29.

Baba Malay IU	*Habis dia nampak satu,*
Baba Malay words	*Habis dia nampak satu*
English gloss	finish 3SG see one
English free translation	Then (it) saw one,

30.
(4.2)

31.

Baba Malay IU	*Satu apa?*
Baba Malay words	*Satu apa*
English gloss	one what
English free translation	One what (is that)?

32.
Baba Malay IU   What's the word huh?

33.
(2.5)

34.

Baba Malay IU	*Satu=,*
Baba Malay words	*Satu*
English gloss	one
English free translation	One=,

35.
(2.1)

36.
Baba Malay IU	*Gua sudah lupa nanti,*
Baba Malay words	*Gua sudah lupa nanti,*
English gloss	1SG already forget wait
English free translation	I forgot, wait (let me think),

37.
Baba Malay IU	*Let me think.*

38.
Baba Malay IU	*Bone ah,*

39.
Baba Malay IU	*Satu tulang.*
Baba Malay words	*Satu tulang*
English gloss	one bone
English free translation	One bone.

40.
Baba Malay IU	*Tak tau apa tulang itu.*
Baba Malay words	*Tak tau apa tulang itu*
English gloss	NEG know what bone it
English free translation	(I) don't know what bone it (is).

41.
Baba Malay IU	*Tulang babi ka tulang,*
Baba Malay words	*Tulang babi ka tulang*
English gloss	bone pig or bone
English free translation	Bone of pig or bone (of),

42.
(1.0)

43.
Baba Malay IU	*Tulang apa,*
Baba Malay words	*Tulang apa*
English gloss	bone what
English free translation	What bone,

44.

Baba Malay IU	*Se-kali dia angkat tulang itu dekat mulot dia,*
Baba Malay words	*Se-kali dia angkat tulang itu dekat mulot dia*
English gloss	one-time 3SG carry bone that PREP mouth 3SG
English free translation	Once it carried that bone in its mouth,

45.

Baba Malay IU	*Dia jalan tepi sunggay,*
Baba Malay words	*Dia jalan tepi sunggay*
English gloss	3SG walk side river
English free translation	It walked (to the) side of the river,

46.

Baba Malay IU	*Dia nampak dia mia bayang.*
Baba Malay words	*Dia nampak dia mia bayang*
English gloss	3SG see 3SG REL shadow
English free translation	It saw its reflection.

47.
(1.1)

48.

Baba Malay IU	*Dia nampak dia bayang,*
Baba Malay words	*Dia nampak dia bayang*
English gloss	3SG see 3SG shadow
English free translation	It saw its reflection,

49.

Baba Malay IU	*Dia kata éh . . . ada lagik satu tulang.*
Baba Malay words	*Dia kata éh ada lagik satu tulang*
English gloss	3SG say EXCLAM EXIST more one bone
English free translation	It said, hey there (is) one more bone.

50.
(0.9)

51.

Baba Malay IU	*Nampak lagik satu anjing lah.*
Baba Malay words	*Nampak lagik satu anjing lah*
English gloss	see more one dog EMP
English free translation	(It) saw another dog.

52.
Baba Malay IU   *Ini ada @ lagik satu tulang.*
Baba Malay words   Ini   ada   @   lagik   satu   tulang
English gloss   this   POSS   more   one   bone
English free translation   It had another bone.

53.
Baba Malay IU   *Abi dia naik geram lah.*
Baba Malay words   Abi   dia   naik   geram   lah
English gloss   finish 3SG   ascend   furious EMP
English free translation   It became furious.

54.
(1.2)

55.
Baba Malay IU   *Dia naik geram dia mo,*
Baba Malay words   Dia   naik   geram   dia   mo
English gloss   3SG   ascend   furious 3SG   want
English free translation   It (was) furious it wanted,

56.
Baba Malay IU   *Tangkap @@lagik satu tulang,*
Baba Malay words   Tangkap @@   lagik   satu   tulang
English gloss   capture   more   one   bone
English free translation   (to) capture this other bone,

57.
Baba Malay IU   *Jatoh-ken dia sendiri mia*
Baba Malay words   jatoh-ken   dia   sendiri   mia
English gloss   fall-TR   3SG   self   GEN
English free translation   (It) fell (itself) its own

58.
Baba Malay IU   *Habis ilang habis.*
Baba Malay words   Habis   ilang   habis
English gloss   finish   lost   finish
English free translation   (It's) finished, lost.

59.

Baba Malay IU	*Satu kun tak a.*
Baba Malay words	*Satu kun tak a*
English gloss	one also NEG POSS
English free translation	(It) doesn't (even) have one.

60.
(1.1)

61.

Baba Malay IU	*Habi dia,*
Baba Malay words	*Habi dia*
English gloss	finish 3SG
English free translation	Then it,

62.

Baba Malay IU	*Hati dia sudah sakit.*
Baba Malay words	*Hati dia sudah sakit*
English gloss	heart 3SG already sick
English free translation	It (was) already sad.

63.

Baba Malay IU	*Satu pun tak ada.*
Baba Malay words	*Satu pun tak ada*
English gloss	one also NEG POSS
English free translation	(It) doesn't (even) have one.

64.

Baba Malay IU	*Sua ilang dia mia tulang.*
Baba Malay words	*Sua ilang dia mia tulang*
English gloss	already lost 3SG GEN bone
English free translation	(It) already lost its bone.

65.
(1.8)

66.

Baba Malay IU	*Habis kupu-kupu datang,*
Baba Malay words	*Habis kupu-kupu datang*
English gloss	then butterfly come
English free translation	Then the butterfly came,

67.
Baba Malay IU	*Kacho dia balék.*
Baba Malay words	*Kacho dia balék.*
English gloss	disturb 3SG again
English free translation	(To) disturb it again.

68.
(1.9)

69.
Baba Malay IU	*Sua dia sudah ilang.*
Baba Malay words	*Sua dia sudah ilang*
English gloss	already 3SG already lost
English free translation	It already lost.

70.
Baba Malay IU	*Sumua apa dia ada sumua sua ilang.*
Baba Malay words	*Sumua apa dia ada sumua sua ilang*
English gloss	all what 3SG POSS all already lost
English free translation	All that it had it already lost.

71.
(1.0)

72.
Baba Malay IU	*Tulang di mulot,*
Baba Malay words	*Tulang di mulot*
English gloss	bone PREP mouth
English free translation	The bone in the mouth,

73.
Baba Malay IU	*Buang di sunggay.*
Baba Malay words	*Buang di sunggay*
English gloss	throw PREP river
English free translation	Thrown into the river.

<T=121.00>

7.2.3 Bangkuang Besair sama Baba Victor Goh

((NL1-034:The Enormous Turnip[79] with Victor: 0.00-183.00))

VICTOR;

1.
Baba Malay IU	*Ada satu hari,*
Baba Malay words	*Ada satu hari*
English gloss	EXIST one day
English free translation	One day,

2.
Baba Malay IU	*Ada satu tukang kebun,*
Baba Malay words	*Ada satu tukang kebun*
English gloss	EXIST one laborer garden
English free translation	There was a gardener,

3.
Baba Malay IU	*Sama bini dia,*
Baba Malay words	*Sama bini dia*
English gloss	and wife 3SG
English free translation	And his wife,

4.
Baba Malay IU	*Tanam,*
Baba Malay words	*Tanam*
English gloss	plant
English free translation	(they) were planting,

5.
Baba Malay IU	*Bangkuang.*
Baba Malay words	*Bangkuang*
English gloss	turnip
English free translation	Turnip.

---

[79] The turnip story told here is a retelling of Alexander Afanasyev's The Enormous Turnip, published in 1863. See Афанасьев, А. Н. (1863)1984. Репка: Сказка N 89. Фундаментальная электронная библиотека: Русская литература и фольклор.

6.
Baba Malay IU	*Dekat dia nia,*
Baba Malay words	Dekat dia nia
English gloss	at 3PL POSS
English free translation	At their,

7.
(1.8)

8.
Baba Malay IU	*Kebun.*
Baba Malay words	Kebun
English gloss	garden
English free translation	Garden.

9.
Baba Malay IU	*Ada satu. . .bangkuang dia téngok betol besair.*
Baba Malay words	Ada satu bangkuang dia téngok betol besair
English gloss	EXIST one turnip 3PL see really big
English free translation	There was one turnip they saw (that was) really big.

10.
(2.9)

11.
Baba Malay IU	*Tukang kebun chakap,*
Baba Malay words	Tukang kebun chakap
English gloss	laborer garden speak
English free translation	The gardener spoke,

12.
Baba Malay IU	*Gua mo cha=bot itu bangkuang besair sekarang.*
Baba Malay words	gua mo chabot itu bangkuang besair sekarang
English gloss	1SG want pull.out that turnip big now
English free translation	I want to pull out that big turnip now.

13.
(1.4)

14.
Baba Malay IU	*Lepas itu,*
Baba Malay words	*Lepas itu*
English gloss	after that
English free translation	After that,

15.
Baba Malay IU	*Kita boléh…buat,*
Baba Malay words	*Kita boléh buat*
English gloss	1PL can make
English free translation	We can make,

16.
(2.1)

17.
Baba Malay IU	*Sup bangkuang.*
Baba Malay words	*Sup bangkuang*
English gloss	soup turnip
English free translation	Turnip soup

18.
Baba Malay IU	*Untok[80] makan malam.*
Baba Malay words	*untok makan malam*
English gloss	for eat night
English free translation	for dinner.

19.
Baba Malay IU	*Dia nia bini chakap.*
Baba Malay words	*Dia nia bini chakap.*
English gloss	3SG POSS wife speak
English free translation	His wife spoke.

20.
(1.6)

---

80 The usage of *untok* is Malay. Its usage is rare but observed in the Baba Malay speech of those who speak Malay.

21.
Baba Malay IU	*Tukang kebun,*
Baba Malay words	Tukang kebun
English gloss	labourer garden
English free translation	The gardener,

22.
(1.1)

23.
Baba Malay IU	*Tarék itu,*
Baba Malay words	Tarék itu
English gloss	pull that
English free translation	Pulled that

24.
Baba Malay IU	*Tarék itu,*
Baba Malay words	Tarék itu
English gloss	pull that
English free translation	Pulled that

25.
Baba Malay IU	*Bangkuang.*
Baba Malay words	Bangkuang
English gloss	turnip
English free translation	Turnip.

26.
Baba Malay IU	*Tapi tu bangkuang. . .tak bergerak.*
Baba Malay words	Tapi tu bangkuang tak bergerak
English gloss	but that turnip NEG move
English free translation	But that turnip did not move.

27.
(1.6)

28.
Baba Malay IU	*Tukang kebun,*
Baba Malay words	Tukang kebun
English gloss	laborer garden
English free translation	The gardener,

29.
Baba Malay IU	*Ta=rék itu bangkuang lagik,*
Baba Malay words	Tarék itu bangkuang lagik
English gloss	pull that turnip again
English free translation	Pulled that turnip again,

30.
Baba Malay IU	*Tu bangkuang,*
Baba Malay words	Tu bangkuang
English gloss	that turnip
English free translation	That turnip,

31.
Baba Malay IU	*Pokok bangkuang...tak bergerak.*
Baba Malay words	Pokok bangkuang tak bergerak
English gloss	tree turnip NEG move
English free translation	The turnip did not move.

32.
(1.8)

33.
Baba Malay IU	*Tukang kebun panggay dia nia bini tolong.*
Baba Malay words	Tukang kebun panggay dia nia bini tolong
English gloss	laborer garden call 3SG POSS wife help
English free translation	That gardener called his wife to help.

34.
Baba Malay IU	*Tukang kebun sama bini dia,*
Baba Malay words	Tukang kebun sama bini dia
English gloss	laborer garden and wife 3SG
English free translation	The gardener and his wife,

35.
Baba Malay IU	*Ta=rék itu bangkuang.*
Baba Malay words	Tarék itu bangkuang
English gloss	pull that turnip
English free translation	Pulled that turnip.

36.
Baba Malay IU	*Itu bangkuang pun. . .tak bergerak.*
Baba Malay words	*Itu bangkuang pun tak bergerak*
English gloss	that turnip also NEG move
English free translation	That turnip also did not move.

37.
(3.1)

38.
Baba Malay IU	*Tukang kebun mia bini,*
Baba Malay words	*Tukang kebun mia bini*
English gloss	laborer garden POSS wife
English free translation	The gardner' wife,

39.
Baba Malay IU	*Panggay anjing dia tolong.*
Baba Malay words	*Panggay anjing dia tolong*
English gloss	call dog 3PL help
English free translation	Called their dog to help.

40.
Baba Malay IU	*Tukang kebun,*
Baba Malay words	*Tukang kebun*
English gloss	laborer garden
English free translation	The gardener,

41.
Baba Malay IU	*Bini dia sama anjing,*
Baba Malay words	*Bini dia sama angjing*
English gloss	wife 3SG and dog
English free translation	his wife and the dog,

42.
Baba Malay IU	*Ta=rék tu bangkuang.*
Baba Malay words	*Tarék tu bangkuang*
English gloss	pull that turnip
English free translation	Pulled that turnip.

43.
Baba Malay IU   *Tu bangkuang,*
Baba Malay words   Tu   bangkuang
English gloss   that   turnip
English free translation   That turnip,

44.
Baba Malay IU   *Pun=tak bergerak.*
Baba Malay words   pun   tak   bergerak
English gloss   also NEG   move
English free translation   also did not move.

45.
(1.7)

46.
Baba Malay IU   *Tu anjing,*
Baba Malay words   Tu   anjing
English gloss   that   dog
English free translation   That dog,

47.
(1.5)

48.
Baba Malay IU   *Menyalap.*
Baba Malay words   *Menyalap*
English gloss   howl
English free translation   howled.

49.
Baba Malay IU   *Panggay kuching tolong,*
Baba Malay words   Panggay   kuching   tolong
English gloss   call   cat   help
English free translation   called the cat to help,

50.
Baba Malay IU   *Gonggong ... #*
Baba Malay words   *Gonggong*
English gloss   ONOMATOPOEIA.bark
English free translation   Barked...

51.
Baba Malay IU	*Anjing tu gonggong.*
Baba Malay words	*Anjing tu gonggong*
English gloss	dog that ONOMATOPOEIA.bark
English free translation	That dog barked.

52.
Baba Malay IU	*Sama,*
Baba Malay words	*Sama*
English gloss	with
English free translation	with,

53.
Baba Malay IU	*Si kuching.*
Baba Malay words	*Si kuching*
English gloss	PERSON cat
English free translation	the cat.

54.
Baba Malay IU	*Mintak tolong.*
Baba Malay words	*Mintak tolong*
English gloss	ask.sincerely help
English free translation	Asking sincerely for help.

55.
Baba Malay IU	*Tukang kebun,*
Baba Malay words	*Tukang kebun*
English gloss	laborer garden
English free translation	The gardener,

56.
Baba Malay IU	*Bini dia,*
Baba Malay words	*bini dia*
English gloss	wife 3SG
English free translation	his wife

57.
Baba Malay IU	*Anjing sama kuching,*
Baba Malay words	*anjing sama kuching*
English gloss	dog and cat
English free translation	dog and cat,

58.

Baba Malay IU	*Tarék tu bangkuang.*
Baba Malay words	*Tarék tu bangkuang*
English gloss	pull that turnip
English free translation	Pulled that turnip.

59.

Baba Malay IU	*Bangkuang tu pun. . . tak bergerak.*
Baba Malay words	*Bangkuang tu pun tak bergarak*
English gloss	turnip that also NEG move
English free translation	That turnip also did not move.

60.
(1.3)

61.

Baba Malay IU	*Tukang kebun chakap,*
Baba Malay words	*Tukang kebun chakap*
English gloss	laborer garden speak
English free translation	The gardener spoke,

62.

Baba Malay IU	*Tak guna lah.*
Baba Malay words	*Tak guna lah*
English gloss	NEG use EMP
English free translation	(It is) no use.

63.

Baba Malay IU	*Ini=,*
Baba Malay words	*Ini*
English gloss	this
English free translation	This,

64.

Baba Malay IU	*Tak guna betol.*
Baba Malay words	*Tak guna betol*
English gloss	NEG use really
English free translation	(It is) no use really.

65.
Baba Malay IU	*Ini bangkuang,*
Baba Malay words	*Ini bangkuang*
English gloss	this turnip
English free translation	This turnip,

66.
(2.0)

67.
Baba Malay IU	*Tak bergerak.*
Baba Malay words	*Tak bergerak*
English gloss	NEG move
English free translation	Does not move.

68.
(1.9)

69.
Baba Malay IU	*Si kuching,*
Baba Malay words	*Si kuching*
English gloss	PERSON cat
English free translation	The cat,

70.
Baba Malay IU	*Panggay,*
Baba Malay words	*Panggay*
English gloss	call
English free translation	called,

71.
Baba Malay IU	*Ah…si burong.*
Baba Malay words	*Ah si burong*
English gloss	filler PERSON bird
English free translation	the bird.

72.
Baba Malay IU	*Pi #tolong mo tolong.*
Baba Malay words	*Pi tolong mo tolong*
English gloss	go help want help
English free translation	Go help (we) want help.

73.
(1.7)

74.
Baba Malay IU	*Tukang kebun...bini dia,*
Baba Malay words	*Tukang kebun bini dia*
English gloss	laborer garden wife 3SG
English free translation	The gardener, his wife,

75.
Baba Malay IU	*Anjing...kuching sama,*
Baba Malay words	*Anjing kuching sama*
English gloss	dog cat and
English free translation	dog, cat and

76.
Baba Malay IU	*Burong,*
Baba Malay words	*Burong*
English gloss	bird
English free translation	bird,

77.
Baba Malay IU	*Ta=rék,*
Baba Malay words	*Tarék*
English gloss	pull
English free translation	Pulled

78.
(1.9)

79.
Baba Malay IU	*Tarék itu bangkuang.*
Baba Malay words	*Tarék itu bangkuang*
English gloss	pull that turnip
English free translation	pulled that turnip.

80.
(1.5)

81.
Baba Malay IU	*Sama sekejab tu bangkuang,*
Baba Malay words	*sama sekejab tu bangkuang*
English gloss	with a.while that turnip
English free translation	After a while that turnip

82.
Baba Malay IU	*Pun=bergerak.*
Baba Malay words	*Pun bergerak*
English gloss	also move
English free translation	Also moved.

83.
(1.0)

84.
Baba Malay IU	*Itu malam…sumua dapat,*
Baba Malay words	*Itu malam sumua dapat*
English gloss	that night all get
English free translation	That night all got,

85.
Baba Malay IU	*Makan,*
Baba Malay words	*Makan*
English gloss	eat
English free translation	to eat,

86.
Baba Malay IU	*Sup bangkuang.*
Baba Malay words	*Sup bangkuang*
English gloss	soup turnip
English free translation	turnip soup.

87.
Baba Malay IU	*Untok makan malam,*
Baba Malay words	*for makan malam*
English gloss	for eat night
English free translation	for dinner,

88.
Baba Malay IU	*Untok makan besok pagi,*
Baba Malay words	Untok makan besok pagi
English gloss	for eat tomorrow morning
English free translation	for breakfast tomorrow,

89.
Baba Malay IU	*Untok makan tengah hari,*
Baba Malay words	Untok makan tengah hari
English gloss	for eat middle day
English free translation	for lunch,

90.
Baba Malay IU	*Untok makan,*
Baba Malay words	Untok makan
English gloss	for eat
English free translation	to eat,

91.
Baba Malay IU	*Minum téh nia jam.*
Baba Malay words	Minum téh nia jam
English gloss	drink tea REL time
English free translation	(for) teatime.

<T=183.00>

7.2.4 Chakapan sama Aunty Jane Quek

((NL1-142: Conversation 2 with Jane Quek: 0.00-372.70))

1.
JQ;
IU   ###,

2.
JQ;
Baba Malay IU	*Ah tachi…apa khabair=?*
Baba Malay words	Ah tachi apa khabair
English gloss	filler elder.sister what news
English free translation	Ah elder sister how are you?

3.
JQ;
Baba Malay IU	*Lama tak jum=pa,*
Baba Malay words	*Lama tak jumpa*
English gloss	long.time NEG meet
English free translation	Haven't met you in a long time,

4.
JQ;
Baba Malay IU	*Ah. . .yah lah,*
Baba Malay words	*Ah yah lah*
English gloss	filler yes EMP
English free translation	Ah yes,

5.
JQ;
Baba Malay IU	*Lama tak. . .jalan sini,*
Baba Malay words	*Lama tak jalan sini*
English gloss	long.time NEG walk here
English free translation	Haven't walked here in a long while,

6.
JQ;
Baba Malay IU	*Tak jumpa lu lu apa macham?*
Baba Malay words	*Tak jumpa lu lu apa macham*
English gloss	NEG meet 2SG 2SG what like that
English free translation	Haven't met you, how are you?

7.
JQ;
Baba Malay IU	*Ada baik tak baik.*
Baba Malay words	*ada baik tak baik*
English gloss	COP good NEG good
English free translation	Are you well or not.

8.
JQ;
Baba Malay IU	*Se – lama ada pi main judi tak?*
Baba Malay words	*se-lama ada pi main judi tak*
English gloss	one-long.time HAB go play gamble NEG
English free translation	Do you still gamble regularly?

9.
JQ;
Baba Malay IU   *Mahjong se-ka se-kali lah=.*
Baba Malay words   *Mahjong se-ka   se-kali   lah*
English gloss   one-time   one-time   EMP
English free translation (I play mahjong) once in a while.

10.
JQ;
Baba Malay IU   *Ada kaki. . .pi main,*
Baba Malay words   *Ada   kaki   pi   main*
English gloss   EXIST friend go   play
English free translation If there are friends (I) go play,

11.
JQ;
Baba Malay IU   *Kalu tak-a orang panggay tak main,*
Baba Malay words   *Kalu   tak-a   orang   panggay   tak   main*
English gloss   if   NEG-EXIST   people   call   NEG   play
English free translation If there is no calling (I) do not play,

12.
JQ;
Baba Malay IU   *Jalan jalan.*
Baba Malay words   *Jalan   jalan*
English gloss   walk   walk
English free translation (I) take walks.

13.
JQ;
Baba Malay IU   *Abi main cherki tak?*
Baba Malay words   *Abi   main   cherki   tak*
English gloss   then   play   Peranakan.card.game   NEG
English free translation Then do you play 'cherki'(card game)?

14.
JQ;
Baba Malay IU   *Cherki pun sama lah.*
Baba Malay words   *Cherki   pun   sama   lah*
English gloss   Peranakan.card.game   also   same   EMP
English free translation 'Cherki' (is) also the same.

15.
JQ;
Baba Malay IU	*Se-lama kun. . .tak manyak orang main cherki.*
Baba Malay words	*Se-lama kun tak manyak orang main cherki*
English gloss	one-long.time also NEG many people play card.game
English free translation	For a long time (now) also, there are not many people playing 'cherki'.

16.
JQ;
Baba Malay IU	*Tak # gitu main cherki lah.*
Baba Malay words	*Tak gitu main cherki lah*
English gloss	NEG like.this play card.game EMP
English free translation	Not like this (I do not) play 'cherki'.

17.
JQ;
Baba Malay IU	*Tak apa pi jalan jalan,*
Baba Malay words	*Tak apa pi jalan jalan*
English gloss	NEG what go walk walk
English free translation	(If there is) nothing (I) go for a walk,

18.
JQ;
Baba Malay IU	*Makan makan=,*
Baba Malay words	*Makan makan*
English glossqq	eat eat
English free translation	Eat (here and there),

19.
JQ;
Baba Malay IU	*Macham lah.*
Baba Malay words	*Macham lah*
English gloss	like.that EMP
English free translation	Like that.

20.
JQ;
Baba Malay IU	*Pass. . .Pass time lah.*
Baba Malay words	*pass pass time lah*
English gloss	EMP
Free translation	Pass time lah.

21.
JQ;
Baba Malay IU *Day by day pass macham lah.*
Baba Malay words day by day pass macham lah
English gloss like.that EMP
English free translation Day by day pass like that.

22.
(1.9)

23.
JQ;
Baba Malay IU *Ada pegi,*
Baba Malay words Ada pegi
English gloss HAB go
English free translation (I do) go,

24.
JQ;
Baba Malay IU *Mana lagik,*
Baba Malay words Mana lagik
English gloss where more
English free translation Where else,

25.
JQ;
Baba Malay IU *Apa macham lu ada berapa manyak chuchu?*
Baba Malay words Apa macham lu ada berapa manyak chuchu
English gloss what like 2SG have how many grandchild
English free translation How are you, how many grandchildren do you have?

26.
JQ;
Baba Malay IU *Ada lah tiga.*
Baba Malay words Ada lah tiga
English gloss have EMP three
English free translation I have three.

27.
JQ;
Baba Malay IU	*Anak prompuan nia satu=,*
Baba Malay words	Anak prompuan nia satu
English gloss	child female REL one
English free translation	One that is a girl,

28.
JQ;
Baba Malay IU	*Anak jantan mia dua=,*
Baba Malay words	Anak jantan mia dua
English gloss	child male REL two
English free translation	Two that are boys,

29.
JQ;
Baba Malay IU	*Ah sudah tiga chuchu lah.*
Baba Malay words	Ah sudah tiga chuchu lah
English gloss	filler already three grandchild EMP
English free translation	There (are) already three grandchildren.

30.
JQ;
Baba Malay IU	*Lu jaga chuchu tak?*
Baba Malay words	Lu jaga chuchu tak
English gloss	2SG take.care grandchild NEG
English free translation	Do you take care of your grandchildren?

31.
JQ;
Baba Malay IU	*Tak a lah tak gitu lah.*
Baba Malay words	Tak-a lah tak gitu lah
English gloss	NEG-EXIST EMP NEG like.this EMP
English free translation	No not like this.

32.
JQ;
Baba Malay IU	*Se-ka se-kali dia orang mo kuluar,*
Baba Malay words	Se-ka se-kali dia-orang mo kuluar
English gloss	one-time one-time 3-PL want go.out
English free translation	Once in a while they want to go out.

33.
JQ;
Baba Malay IU   *Dia panggay. . .mata- mata-kan.*
Baba Malay words   *Dia   panggay   mata-mata -kan*
English gloss   3PL   call   eye-eye-TR
English free translation   They call me to watch over (the grandchildren).

34.
JQ;
Baba Malay IU   *Ah. . .mata-mata-kan lah.*
Baba Malay words   *Ah   mata-mata-kan   lah*
English gloss   filler eye-eye-TR   EMP
English free translation   (I) watch (them).

35.
JQ;
Baba Malay IU   *Satu dua jam macham lah.*
Baba Malay words   *Satu dua   jam   macham   lah*
English gloss   one   two   hour   like.that EMP
English free translation   One (or) two hours like that.

36.
JQ;
Baba Malay IU   *Macham sahja orang tua gitu lah.*
Baba Malay words   *Macham   sahja   orang   tua   gitu   lah*
English gloss   like.this only   people   old   like.this EMP
English free translation   Like this only, old people (do it) like this.

37.
JQ;
Baba Malay IU   *Boléh makan makan=,*
Baba Malay words   *Boléh   makan   makan*
English gloss   can eat   eat
English free translation   (If you) can eat, eat.

38.
JQ;
Baba Malay IU   *Boléh jalan jalan=.*
Baba Malay words   *Boléh   jalan   jalan*
English gloss   can   walk   walk
English free translation   (If you) can walk, walk.

39.
JQ;
IU   Be happy=,

40.
JQ;
Baba Malay IU   *Toksa sikit sikit marah.*
Baba Malay words   Toksa   sikit   sikit   marah
English gloss   do.not.need   little little angry
English free translation (You) don't need to be angry over small things.

41.
JQ;
Baba Malay IU   *Apa sair lu siap-siap maki maid?*
Baba Malay words   apa   sair   lu   siap-siap   maki   maid
English gloss   what   reason 2SG   perpetually   scold
English free translation Why do you perpetually scold the maid?

42.
JQ;
Baba Malay IU   *Maid kun orang jugak.*
Baba Malay words   Maid   kun   orang   jugak
English gloss   also people also
English free translation Maids (are) people also.

43.
JQ;
Baba Malay IU   *Abi gua téngok manyak= sair pi pasar.*
Baba Malay words   Abi   gua   téngok   manyak   sair   pi   pasar
English gloss   then   1SG   see   many   indeed   go   market
English free translation Then I see many going to the market.

44.
JQ;
Baba Malay IU   *Sumua= complain pasair maid.*
Baba Malay words   Sumua   complain   pasair   maid
English gloss   all   matter
English free translation All complaining about maid matters.

45.
JQ;
Baba Malay IU   *Maid kun orang ini lah maid ini lah.*
Baba Malay words   *Maid   kun   orang   ini   lah   maid   itu   lah*
English gloss   also   people this   EMP   that   EMP
English free translation   Maid (are) also people, (maid) this and (maid) that.

46.
JQ;
Baba Malay IU   *Maid itu lah.*
Baba Malay words   *Maid   itu   lah*
English gloss   that   EMP
English free translation   The maid (does) that.

47.
JQ;
Baba Malay IU   *Tak-a satu chakap maid baik.*
Baba Malay words   *Tak-a   satu   chakap maid   baik*
English gloss   NEG-EXIST   one   speak   good
English free translation   Not one says the maid (is) good.

48.
JQ;
Baba Malay IU   *Tak tau apa sair ni orang orang sumua.*
Baba Malay words   *Tak   tau   apa   sair   ni   orang   orang   sumua*
English gloss   NEG   know   what   reason this   people   people   all
English free translation   Don't know why these people all.

49.
JQ;
Baba Malay IU   *Orang orang sumua.*
Baba Malay words   *orang   orang   sumua*
English gloss   people   people   all
English free translation   People all.

50.
JQ;
IU   *Huh?*

51.
JQ;
Baba Malay IU   *Orang maid pun orang human being,*
Baba Malay words   Orang   maid   pun   orang   human   being
English gloss   people   also   people
English free translation The maids (are) also human beings,

52.
JQ;
Baba Malay IU   *Kalu tak-a maid datang sama lu krejar,*
Baba Malay words   Kalu   tak-a   maid   datang   sama   lu   krejar
English gloss   if   NEG-EXIST   come   with   2SG   work
English free translation If there are no maids to come work for you,

53.
JQ;
Baba Malay IU   *Orang chakap lu,*
Baba Malay words   Orang   chakap   lu
English gloss   people   speak   2SG
English free translation People speak about you,

54.
JQ;
Baba Malay IU   *Misti mo ##,*
Baba Malay words   Misti   mo
English gloss   must   want
English free translation Must##,

55.
JQ;
Baba Malay IU   *Lu mia duit manyak besar bayar orang,*
Baba Malay words   Lu   mia   duit   manyak   besar   bayar   orang
English gloss   2SG   POSS   money   many   big   pay   people
English free translation Your money (is) very big (it) pays people,

56.
JQ;
Baba Malay IU   *Su=mua bising=pasair maid.*
Baba Malay words   Sumua   bising   pasair   maid
English gloss   all   noisy   matter
English free translation All make a lot of noise about maid matters.

57.
JQ;
Baba Malay IU   *Dengar pun boring.*
Baba Malay words   *Dengar pun   boring*
English gloss   listen   also
English free translation It is boring to even hear about this.

58.
(13.4)

59.
JQ;
Baba Malay IU   *Bila gua senang gua jalan jalan lah.*
Baba Malay words   *Bila   gua senang gua   jalan jalan   lah*
English gloss   when 1SG   free   1SG walk   walk   EMP
English free translation When I (am) free I take walks.

60.
JQ;
Baba Malay IU   *Jalan pi Parkway Parade,*
Baba Malay words   *Jalan pi   Parkway Parade*
English gloss   walk   go
English free translation Walk to Parkway Parade (shopping mall),

61.
JQ
Baba Malay IU   *Jalan jalan makan,*
Baba Malay words   *Jalan jalan   makan*
English gloss   walk   walk   eat
English free translation Walk a bit and eat,

62.
JQ;
Baba Malay IU   *Téngok baju=,*
Baba Malay words   *Téngok   baju*
English gloss   look   clothes
English free translation Look at clothes,

63.
JQ;
Baba Malay IU   *Ah chanték kita beli satu lay=,*
Baba Malay words   Ah   chanték   kita beli satu   lay
English gloss   filler beautiful 1PL buy one   CLF.piece of fabric or paper
English free translation   (If it is) pretty we buy one piece,

64.
JQ;
Baba Malay IU   *Tak chanték jalan jalan=,*
Baba Malay words   Tak   chanték   jalan jalan
English gloss   NEG   beautiful walk   walk
English free translation   (If it is) not pretty (I) take a walk,

65.
JQ;
Baba Malay IU   *Minum kopi=,*
Baba Malay words   Minum   kopi
English gloss   drink   coffee
English free translation   Drink coffee,

66.
JQ;
Baba Malay IU   *Sama kawan kuluar=,*
Baba Malay words   Sama   kawan   kuluar
English gloss   with   friend go.out
English free translation   Go out with friends,

67.
JQ;
Baba Malay IU   *Ada kali. . .gua mia friend kuluar,*
Baba Malay words   Ada   kali   gua   mia   friend   kuluar
English gloss   EXIST   time   1SG   POSS   go.out
English free translation   There are times my friend go out,

68.
JQ;
Baba Malay IU   *From Australia panggay,*
Baba Malay words   From Australia   panggay
English gloss   call
English free translation   From Australia (she) calls,

69.
JQ;
Baba Malay IU	*Aunty kita pi,*
Baba Malay words	*Aunty kita pi*
English gloss	1PL go
English free translation	Aunty we go,

70.
JQ;
Baba Malay IU	*Pi Takashimaya= Orchard Road side,*
Baba Malay words	*Pi Takashimaya Orchard Road side*
English gloss	go
English free translation	Go to Takashimaya (shopping mall) at Orchard Road,

71.
JQ;
Baba Malay IU	*Jalan jalan=,*
Baba Malay words	*Jalan jalan*
English gloss	walk walk
English free translation	Take walk,

72.
JQ;
Baba Malay IU	*Téngok téngok,*
Baba Malay words	*Téngok téngok*
English gloss	look look
English free translation	Take a look-see,

73.
JQ;
Baba Malay IU	*Kalu téngok barang hak,*
Baba Malay words	*Kalu téngok barang hak*
English gloss	if see thing suitable
English free translation	If (we) see a suitable thing,

74.
JQ;
Baba Malay IU	*Kita beli lah.*
Baba Malay words	*Kita beli lah*
English gloss	1PL buy EMP
English free translation	We buy.

75.
JQ;
Baba Malay IU	*Barang tak hak tak beli lah.*
Baba Malay words	*Barang tak hak tak beli lah*
English gloss	thing NEG suitable NEG buy EMP
English free translation	(If) the thing (is) not suitable we won't buy.

76.
JQ;
Baba Malay IU	*Pegi Isetan,*
Baba Malay words	*Pegi Isetan*
English gloss	go
English free translation	Go to Isetan (departmental store),

77.
JQ;
Baba Malay IU	*Pegi Cold Storage,*
Baba Malay words	*Pegi Cold Storage*
English gloss	go
English free translation	Go to Cold Storage (supermarket),

78.
JQ;
Baba Malay IU	*Gua mia kawan suka pi Isetan nia,*
Baba Malay words	*Gua mia kawan suka pi Isetan nia*
English gloss	1SG POSS friend like go POSS
English free translation	My friend likes to go to Isetan's,

79.
JQ;
IU	*Shopping centre,*

80.
JQ;
Baba Malay IU	*Pasair dia mia meat very fresh.*
Baba Malay words	*pasair dia mia meat very fresh*
English gloss	because 3SG POSS
English free translation	Because its meat (is) very fresh.

81.
JQ;
Baba Malay IU   *Tapi mahal lah.*
Baba Malay words   *Tapi   mahal   lah*
English gloss   but   expensive   EMP
English free translation   But it (is) expensive.

82.
JQ;
Baba Malay IU   *Dia mia barang mahal,*
Baba Malay words   *Dia   mia   barang   mahal*
English gloss   3SG   POSS   thing   expensive
English free translation   Its things (are) expensive,

83.
JQ;
Baba Malay IU   *Tapi dia mia meat betol...fresh.*
Baba Malay words   *Tapi dia   mia   meat betol   fresh*
English gloss   but   3SG   POSS   really
English free translation   But its meat (is) really fresh.

84.
JQ;
Baba Malay IU   *Chanték sekali.*
Baba Malay words   *Chanték   sekali*
English gloss   beautiful   very
English free translation   Very beautiful.

85.
JQ;
Baba Malay IU   *Dia bikin ## steamboat,*
Baba Malay words   *Dia   bikin   steamboat*
English gloss   3SG   make
English free translation   She makes steamboat (hot pot),

86.
JQ;
Baba Malay IU   *Dia selalu pi sana.*
Baba Malay words   *Dia   selalu   pi   sana*
English gloss   3SG   always   go   there
English free translation   She always goes there.

87.
JQ;
Baba Malay IU   *Dia tak beli kita market nia.*
Baba Malay words   Dia   tak   beli   kita   market   nia
English gloss   3SG   NEG   buy   1PL   REL
English free translation   She doesn't buy the ones that are at our markets.

88.
JQ;
Baba Malay IU   *Dia sudah used to it lah.*
Baba Malay words   Dia   sudah   used   to   it   lah
English gloss   3SG   already   EMP
English free translation   She (is) already used to it.

89.
JQ;
IU   My Australia friend is like that,

90.
JQ;
Baba Malay IU   *Tapi ya lah betol betol fresh.*
Baba Malay words   Tapi   ya   lah   betol   betol   fresh
English gloss   but   yes   EMP   really   really
English free translation   But yes it is really really fresh.

91.
JQ;
Baba Malay IU   *Mahal sikit lah.*
Baba Malay words   Mahal   sikit   lah
English gloss   expensive   little EMP
English free translation   A little expensive.

92.
JQ;
Baba Malay IU   *Jalan jalan abi tu makan,*
Baba Malay words   Jalan   jalan   abi   tu   makan
English gloss   walk   walk   finish   that   eat
English free translation   Take a walk and after that eat,

93.
JQ:
Baba Malay IU   Lunch habi,
Baba Malay words   Lunch   habi
English gloss   finish
English free translation   Lunch (is) over,

94.
JQ;
Baba Malay IU   Jalan jalan habi,
Baba Malay words   Jalan   jalan   habi
English gloss   walk   walk   finish
English free translation   After taking a walk,

95.
JQ;
Baba Malay IU   Dudok kopi house,
Baba Malay words   Dudok   kopi   house
English gloss   sit   coffee
English free translation   Sit at the coffee house,

96.
JQ;
Baba Malay IU   Minum kopi lah.
Baba Malay words   Minum   kopi   lah
English gloss   drink   coffee EMP
English free translation   Drink coffee.

97.
JQ;
Baba Malay IU   Cappucino ka=,
Baba Malay words   Cappucino ka
English gloss   or
English free translation   Cappucino or,

98.
JQ;
Baba Malay IU   Latte ka=,
Baba Malay words   Latte ka
English gloss   or
English free translation   Latte or,

99.
JQ;
Baba Malay IU   Makan ## itu pancake share share,
Baba Malay words   Makan   itu   pancake   share   share
English gloss   eat   that
English free translation   Share some pancake,

100.
JQ;
Baba Malay IU   Macham lah.
Baba Malay words   Macham   lah
English gloss   like.that EMP
English free translation   Like that.

101.
JQ;
Baba Malay IU   Dudok= sampay pukol lima,
Baba Malay words   Dudok   sampay   pukol   lima
English gloss   sit   until   strike five
English free translation   Sit until five o'clock,

102.
JQ;
Baba Malay IU   ## Charék makan dinner,
Baba Malay words   Charék   makan   dinner
English gloss   find   eat
English free translation   Find dinner to eat,

103.
JQ;
Baba Malay IU   Abi itu pulang,
Baba Malay words   Abi   itu   pulang
English gloss   finish that   return
English free translation   After that (we) return,

104.
JQ;
Baba Malay IU   Pulang sampay rumah,
Baba Malay words   Pulang   sampay   rumah
English gloss   return   until   house
English free translation   (We) return home,

105.
JQ;
IU   Seven eight or nine,

106.
JQ;
Baba Malay IU   *Pukol lapan pukol semilan*
Baba Malay words   *Pukol   lapan   pukol   semilan*
English gloss   strike   eight   strike   nine
English free translation Eight or night o'clock.

107.
JQ;
Baba Malay IU   *macham lah.*
Baba Malay words   *macham   lah*
English gloss   like.that EMP
English free translation (It is) like that.

108.
JQ;
Baba Malay IU   *Balék rumah mandi=,*
Baba Malay words   *Balék   rumah   mandi*
English gloss   return   house   bathe
English free translation Return home to bathe,

109.
JQ;
Baba Malay IU   *Dudok= téngok tv,*
Baba Malay words   *Dudok   téngok   tv*
English gloss   sit   see
English free translation Sit and watch tv,

110.
JQ;
Baba Malay IU   *TV bagus=,*
Baba Malay words   *TV bagus*
English gloss   good
English free translation If the television show is good,

111.
JQ;
Baba Malay IU	*Téngok satu pukol dua belas.*
Baba Malay words	*Téngok sampay pukol dua belas*
English gloss	see until strike two ten
English free translation	Watch until twelve o'clock.

112.
JQ;
Baba Malay IU	*TV tak bagus,*
Baba Malay words	*TV tak bagus*
English gloss	NEG good
English free translation	(if) the television show (is) not good,

113.
JQ;
Baba Malay IU	*Se-belas tutup.*
Baba Malay words	*Se-belas tutop*
English gloss	one-ten close
English free translation	Turn off at eleven.

114.
JQ;
Baba Malay IU	*Pi tidor.*
Baba Malay words	*Pi tidor*
English gloss	go sleep
English free translation	Go sleep.

115.
JQ;
Baba Malay IU	*Then...pagi sudah mangun.*
Baba Malay words	*Then pagi sudah mangun*
English gloss	morning already wake
English free translation	Then in the morning I already wake up.

116.
JQ;
Baba Malay IU	*Sua tua= tak boléh tidor tau?*
Baba Malay words	*Sudah tua tak boléh tidor tau*
English gloss	already old NEG can sleep know
English free translation	Already old (I am) cannot sleep (you) know?

117.
JQ;
Baba Malay IU	*Kalu apa macham lambat,*
Baba Malay words	*Kalu apa macham lambat*
English gloss	if what like late
English free translation	Even if (I sleep) late,

118.
JQ;
Baba Malay IU	*Tidor pun tak boléh tidor.*
Baba Malay words	*Tidor pun tak boléh tidor*
English gloss	sleep also NEG can sleep
English free translation	(I still) cannot sleep.

119.
JQ;
Baba Malay IU	*Apa macham pukol lima lebéh sudah mangun.*
Baba Malay words	*Apa macham pukol lima lebéh sudah mangun*
English gloss	what like.that strike five more already wake
English free translation	However (late I go to bed, I) wake up slightly after five.

120.
JQ;
Baba Malay IU	*Mata sudah ter-bukak.*
Baba Malay words	*Mata sudah ter-bukak*
English gloss	eye already MVT-open
English free translation	Eyes already opened.

121.
JQ;
Baba Malay IU	*Sudah tak boléh tidor balék.*
Baba Malay words	*Sudah tak boléh tidor balék*
English gloss	already NEG can sleep return
English free translation	Already cannot return to sleep.

122.
JQ;
Baba Malay IU	*Orang kata,*
Baba Malay words	*Orang kata*
English gloss	people say
English free translation	People say,

123.
JQ;
Baba Malay IU   *boléh tidor pukol se-puloh lah.*
Baba Malay words   *boléh   tidor   pukol   se-puloh   lah*
English gloss   can   sleep   strike one-ten   EMP
English free translation (they) can sleep until ten o'clock.

124.
JQ;
Baba Malay IU   *Ayé=,*
Baba Malay words   *Ayé*
English gloss   EXCLAM.surprise,
English free translation Goodness,

125.
JQ;
Baba Malay IU   *Ho mia,*
Baba Malay words   *Ho   mia*
English gloss   good   life
English free translation Good life,

126.
JQ;
Baba Malay IU   *Gua tak boléh. . .pukol se-puloh,*
Baba Malay words   *Gua   tak   boléh   pukol   se-puloh*
English gloss   1SG   NEG   can   strike one-ten
English free translation I cannot (sleep until) ten o'clock,

127.
JQ;
Baba Malay IU   *Amcham pun,*
Baba Malay words   *Amcham   pun*
English gloss   how   also
English free translation However (much I try),

128.
JQ;
Baba Malay IU   *Pukol lima lebéh gua sudah mangun.*
Baba Malay words   *Pukol   lima   lebéh   gua   sudah   mangun*
English gloss   strike five   more   1SG   already   wake
English free translation After five I already wake up.

129.
JQ;
Baba Malay IU	*Dia orang boléh tidor pukol se-puloh.*
Baba Malay words	*Dia-orang boléh tidor pukol se-puloh*
English gloss	3-PL can sleep strike one-ten
English free translation	They can sleep (until) ten o'clock.

130.
JQ;
Baba Malay IU	*Mata ari gemoh pantat pun tak boléh mangun.*
Baba Malay words	*Mata ari gemoh pantat pun tak boléh mangun*
English gloss	eye day sun.dry buttocks also NEG can wake
English free translation	The sun shines on your backside (they) also cannot get up.

131.
(6.0)

132.
NL;
Baba Malay IU	*Australia friend bila dia mo balék?*
Baba Malay words	*Australia friend bila dia mo balék*
English gloss	when 3SG want return
English free translation	When does your friend from Australia want to return?

133.
JQ;
Baba Malay IU	*Bila dia pulang=,*
Baba Malay words	*Bila dia pulang*
English gloss	when 3SG return
English free translation	When she returns,

134.
JQ;
Baba Malay IU	*Tiga minggu…macham dia balék lah.*
Baba Malay words	*Tiga minggu macham dia balék lah*
English gloss	three week like.that 3SG return EMP
English free translation	Three weeks or so she returns.

135.
JQ;
Baba Malay IU   *Because dia Singaporean=.*
Baba Malay words   Because   dia   Singaporean
English gloss   3SG
English free translation Because she (is) Singaporean.

136.
JQ;
Baba Malay IU   *Pasair dia tinggal Singapore,*
Baba Malay words   Pasair   dia   tinggal Singapore
English gloss   because   3SG   live
English free translation Because she lives in Singapore,

137.
JQ;
Baba Malay IU   *Dia kena balék for,*
Baba Malay words   Dia   kena   balék   for
English gloss   3SG   subjected.to   return
English free translation She has to return for,

138.
JQ;
Baba Malay IU   *Ini apa?*
Baba Malay words   Ini   apa
English gloss   this   what
English free translation This what?

139.
JQ;
Baba Malay IU   *Chop kan?*
Baba Malay words   Chop   kan
English gloss   NEG
English free translation The stamp (on the passport) no?

140.
JQ;
Baba Malay IU   *Ah...balék kat Australia lama,*
Baba Malay words   Ah   balék   kat   Australia   lama
English gloss   filler return PREP   long.time
English free translation She returned to Australia for a long time,

141.
JQ;
IU   *Seven eight years.*

142.
JQ;
Baba Malay IU   *Macham lah se-ka se-kali dia kuluair,*
Baba Malay words   *Macham   lah   se-ka   se-kali   dia   kuluair*
English gloss   like.that EMP   one-time   one-time   3SG   go.out
English free translation   Like that once in a while she comes out,

143.
JQ;
Baba Malay IU   *Jalan jalan=,*
Baba Malay words   *jalan   jalan*
English gloss   walk   walk
English free translation   Take a walk,

144.
JQ;
Baba Malay IU   *Dua tiga minggu=,*
Baba Malay words   *Dua   tiga   minggu*
English gloss   two   three   week
English free translation   Two three weeks,

145.
JQ;
Baba Malay IU   *Satu bulan dia pulang lah.*
Baba Malay words   *Satu   bulan   dia   pulang   lah*
English gloss   one   month   3SG   return   EMP
English free translation   (After) one month she returns.

146.
JQ;
Baba Malay IU   *Macham lah.*
Baba Malay words   *Macham   lah*
English gloss   like.that   EMP
English free translation   Like that.

147.
JQ;
Baba Malay IU   *Tapi dia orang tak suka Singapore.*
Baba Malay words   *Tapi   dia-orang   tak   suka   Singapore*
English gloss   but   3-PL   NEG   like
English free translation But she doesn't like Singapore.

148.
JQ;
Baba Malay IU   *Manyak panas dia tak boléh tahan.*
Baba Malay words   *Manyak   panas   dia   tak   boléh   tahan*
English gloss   many   hot   3SG   NEG   can   withstand
English free translation She cannot stand that it is very hot.

149.
NL;
Baba Malay IU   *Dia toksa jaga chuchu ah?*
Baba Malay words   *Dia   toksa   jaga   chuchu   ah*
English gloss   3SG   do.not.need   take.care   grandchild   filler
English free translation She doesn't have to take care of her grandchildren?

150.
JQ;
Baba Malay IU   *Dia tak boléh tahan panas.*
Baba Malay words   *Dia   tak   boléh   tahan   panas*
English gloss   3SG   NEG   can   withstand   hot
English free translation She cannot stand that it is hot.

151.
JQ;
Baba Malay IU   *Dia sendiri pi jalan suka pi aircon.*
Baba Malay words   *Dia   sendiri   pi   jalan   suka   pi   aircon*
English gloss   3SG   self   go   walk   like   go
English free translation She herself likes to go to airconditioned places when she walks.

152.
JQ;
Baba Malay IU   *Makan itu foodcourt,*
Baba Malay words   *Makan   itu   foodcourt*
English gloss   eat   that
English free translation Eat at that foodcourt,

153.
JQ;
Baba Malay IU　　　　　　　*Dekat tengah jalan foodcourt dia tak masok.*
Baba Malay words　　　　　*Dekat　tengah jalan　foodcourt　dia　tak　masok*
English gloss　　　　　　　　PREP　middle walk　　　　　　　3SG　NEG　enter
English free translation　　The foodcourt in the middle of the road she doesn't enter.

154.
JQ;
Baba Malay IU　　　　　　　*Dia pegi # aircon mia foodcourt.*
Baba Malay words　　　　　*Dia　pegi　aircon　mia　foodcourt*
English gloss　　　　　　　　3SG　go　　　　　　　REL
English free translation　　She goes to foodcourts that are air-conditioned.

155.
JQ;
Baba Malay IU　　　　　　　*Foodcourt foodcourt pun dia seldom,*
Baba Malay words　　　　　*Foodcourt　foodcourt　pun　dia　seldom*
English gloss　　　　　　　　　　　　　　　　　　　　also　3SG
English free translation　　She also seldom (even goes to) the foodcourt,

156.
JQ;
Baba Malay IU　　　　　　　*Dia téngok ma=na nia foodcourt.*
Baba Malay words　　　　　*Dia　téngok　mana　nia　foodcourt*
English gloss　　　　　　　　3SG　see　　　which　REL
English free translation　　She sees which foodcourt it is.

157.
JQ;
Baba Malay IU　　　　　　　*Takashimaya nia foodcourt ka apa.*
Baba Malay words　　　　　*Takashimaya　nia　　foodcourt　ka　apa*
English gloss　　　　　　　　　　　　　　　POSS　　　　　　　or　what
English free translation　　Takashimaya's foodcourt or what.

158.
JQ;
Baba Malay IU　　　　　　　*Lain nia dia tak pi.*
Baba Malay words　　　　　*Lain　nia　dia　tak　pi*
English gloss　　　　　　　　other　REL　3SG　NEG　go
English free translation　　Others she does not go.

159.
NL;
Baba Malay IU	*Ada apa tak sama?*
Baba Malay words	Ada apa tak sama
English gloss	EXIST what NEG same
English free translation	What is different?

160.
JQ;
Baba Malay IU	*Hot panas dirty lah.*
Baba Malay words	Hot panas dirty lah
English gloss	hot EMP
English free translation	Hot, dirty.

161.
JQ;
Baba Malay IU	*Tempat tu ko=tor=.*
Baba Malay words	Tempat tu kotor
English gloss	place that dirty
English free translation	That place (is) dirty.

162.
JQ;
Baba Malay IU	*Kuluar nia tak bagus kotor.*
Baba Malay words	kuluar nia tak bagus kotor
English gloss	outside REL NEG good dirty
English free translation	(Those) that are outside are not good, dirty.

163.
JQ;
Baba Malay IU	*Dia orang sudah biasa macham.*
Baba Malay words	Dia-orang sudah biasa macham
English gloss	3-PL already used.to.it like.that
English free translation	She is already used to it like that.

164.
JQ;
Baba Malay IU	*Kita apa court pun ma=sok lah.*
Baba Malay words	Kita apa court pun masok lah
English gloss	1PL what also enter EMP
English free translation	We enter whatever court it is.

165.
JQ;
IU   Small court big court,

166.
JQ;
Baba Malay IU   *Sumua ma=sok lah.*
Baba Malay words   Sumua   masok   lah
English gloss   all   enter   EMP
English free translation All (we) enter.

167.
JQ;
Baba Malay IU   *Ada radat,*
Baba Malay words   Ada   radat
English gloss   EXIST   greed.vulgar
English free translation (We) have greed (vulgar),

168.
JQ;
Baba Malay IU   *Cher=kek sudah cher=kek lah.*
Baba Malay words   Cherkek   sudah   cherkek   lah
English gloss   eat.vulgar   already   eat.coarse   EMP
English free translation Already eaten (we) eat more.

169.
JQ;
IU   @@@@@@@@.

170.
JQ;
Baba Malay IU   *Macham lah apa mo bikin,*
Baba Malay words   Macham   lah   apa   mo   bikin
English gloss   like.that   EMP   what   want   make
English free translation Like that what (do we) want to do,

171.
JQ;

Baba Malay IU	*Human being macham lah.*
Baba Malay words	*Human being macham lah*
English gloss	like.that EMP
English free translation	Human beings are like that.

172.
JQ;
Baba Malay IU	*Dia sudah biasa,*
Baba Malay words	*Dia sudah biasa*
English gloss	3SG already used.to.it
English free translation	She (is) used to it,

173.
JQ;
Baba Malay IU	*From young macham,*
Baba Malay words	*From young macham*
English gloss	like.that
English free translation	From young like that,

174.
JQ;
Baba Malay IU	*Kita ini tak ah kita ini chin=chai lah.*
Baba Malay words	*Kita ini tak ah kita ini chinchai lah*
English gloss	1PL this NEG filler 1PL this not.fussy EMP
English free translation	We (are) not we (are) not fussy.

175.
JQ;
Baba Malay IU	*Ma=na pun dudok ma=kan lah.*
Baba Malay words	*Mana pun dudok makan lah*
English gloss	where also sit eat EMP
English free translation	Anywhere we sit and eat.

176.
JQ;
Baba Malay IU	*Orang panggay makan ma=kan lah.*
Baba Malay words	*Orang panggay makan makan lah*
English gloss	people call eat eat EMP
English free translation	(If) people call us to eat (we) eat.

177.
JQ;
Baba Malay IU	*Ada #...ini saya makan,*
Baba Malay words	*Ada ini saya makan*
English gloss	EXIST this 1SG eat
English free translation	(If) there is this, I (will) eat,

178.
JQ;
Baba Malay IU	*Itu tak tau makan.*
Baba Malay words	*Itu tak tau makan*
English gloss	that NEG know eat
English free translation	That (you) do not know how to eat.

179.
JQ;
Baba Malay IU	*Bodoh mo mampus.*
Baba Malay word	*Bodoh mo mampus*
English gloss	stupid want EXCLAM.dead
English free translation	Stupid (until I) want to die. [humorous intent]

180.
JQ;
Baba Malay IU	*Stupid sekali tak tau makan.*
Baba Malay words	*Stupid sekali tak tau makan*
English gloss	very NEG know eat
English free translation	Very stupid (if you) do not know how to eat. [humorous intent]

181.
JQ;
Baba Malay IU	*Ini tak tau makan,*
Baba Malay words	*Ini tak tau makan*
English gloss	this NEG know eat
English free translation	This (you) do not know how to eat,

182.
JQ;
Baba Malay IU	*Ada kali kawan pun sama,*
Baba Malay words	*Ada kali kawan pun sama*
English gloss	EXIST time friend also same
English free translation	There are times friends (are) also the same,

183.
JQ;
Baba Malay IU	*Nasik ulam dia tak tau makan.*
Baba Malay words	*Nasik.ulam dia tak tau makan*
English gloss	cooked.rice.with.mixed.herbs 3PL NEG know eat
English free translation	Mixed herbs rice with shredded anchovies they do not know how to eat.

184.
JQ;
Baba Malay IU	*Nasik goreng pun tak tau makan.*
Baba Malay words	*Nasik goreng pun tak tau makan*
English gloss	cooked.rice fry also NEG know eat
English free translation	Fried rice too (they) do not know how to eat.

185.
JQ;
Baba Malay IU	*A=pa nia Peranakan?*
Baba Malay words	*Apa nia Peranakan*
English gloss	what REL Peranakan
English free translation	What kind of Peranakan? [humorous intent]

186.
JQ;
Baba Malay IU	*Tak sepekah.*
Baba Malay words	*Tak sepekah*
English gloss	NEG acceptable
English free translation	Not acceptable.

187.
NL;
Baba Malay IU	*Aunty Jane suka masak tak?*
Baba Malay words	*Aunty Jane suka masak tak*
English gloss	like cook NEG
English free translation	Aunty Jane likes to cook?

188.
JQ;
Baba Malay IU	*Su=ka=.*
Baba Malay words	*Suka*
English gloss	like
English free translation	(I) like.

189.
JQ;
Baba Malay IU	*Tapi selalu gua chakap,*
Baba Malay words	*Tapi selalu gua chakap*
English gloss	but always 1SG speak
English free translation	But I always say,

190.
JQ;
Baba Malay IU	*Lain kali kalu gua mati ah,*
Baba Malay words	*Lain kali kalu gua mati ah*
English gloss	other time if 1SG die filler
English free translation	Next time if I die,

191.
JQ;
Baba Malay IU	*Kalu chutsi gua tak mo angkat pot.*
Baba Malay words	*Kalu chutsi gua tak mo angkat pot*
English gloss	if born 1SG NEG want carry
English free translation	If reborn I do not want to carry the pot.

192.
JQ;
Baba Malay IU	*Tak mo angkat pen.*
Baba Malay words	*Tak mo angkat pen*
English gloss	NEG want carry
English free translation	I do not want to carry the pen.

193.
JQ;
Baba Malay IU	*Hari hari tak bikin apa,*
Baba Malay words	*Hari hari tak bikin apa*
English gloss	day day NEG do what
English free translation	Everyday (I) do not do anything,

194.
JQ;
Baba Malay IU	*Ma=sak sahja.*
Baba Malay words	*Masak sahja*
English gloss	cook only
English free translation	Only cook.

195.
NL;
Baba Malay IU	*Angkat pen?*
Baba Malay words	*Angkat pen*
English gloss	carry
English free translation	Carry the pen?

196.
JQ;
Baba Malay IU	*Angkat pot pen sumua tak mo.*
Baba Malay words	*Angkat pot pen sumua tak mo*
English gloss	carry all NEG want
English free translation	Carry the pot pen, I do not want all.

197.
JQ;
Baba Malay IU	*Mo angkat duit kuluar.*
Baba Malay words	*Mo angkat duit kuluar*
English gloss	want carry money out
English free translation	(I) want to carry money out (when I am reborn). [humorous intent]

198.
NL;
IU   @@@@@@.

199.
JQ;
Baba Malay IU	*Tony gua chakap,*
Baba Malay words	*Tony gua chakap*
English gloss	1SG speak
English free translation	My Tony said,

200.
JQ;
Baba Malay IU	*Tony gua chakap,*
Baba Malay words	*Tony gua chakap*
English gloss	1SG speak
English free translation	My Tony said,

201.
JQ;
Baba Malay IU   Oh. . .lu Catholic ada chutsi eh=?
Baba Malay words   Oh   lu   Catholic ada   chutsi   eh
English gloss   Filler 2SG   have   born   filler
English free translation   Oh you Catholic have the concept of rebirth?
                            [humorous intent]

202.
JQ;
Baba Malay IU   @@@@@,

<T=372.70>

7.2.5 Ten Pantuns by Baba Albert Ku

The following set of texts are ten *pantuns* composed by Baba Albert Ku from Malacca. The *pantun* is a traditional Malay verse with a general *abab* rhyme scheme, but the rhyme scheme is not always strictly adhered to. The first two lines are known as the *pembayang* 'shadow', and these lines set the general tone of the poem. The main message of the *pantun*, known as the *maksud* 'meaning', is conveyed in the third and fourth lines. Peranakan pantuns often relate to Peranakan subject matters, although it is interesting that the Malay language is followed closely. Pantuns can be composed on the spot, exchanged between performers (see III in table 50), and sung to a tune called the *dondang sayang* 'melody (of) love'. The art of singing *pantun* to the *dondang sayang* is endangered, but there are still cultural associations such as the Gunong Sayang Association in Singapore that preserve this tradition. The following pantuns in Table 50 were written, and have no recordings associated with them.

Table 50: A list of ten *pantun* by Albert Ku.

No.	Pantun	Interlinear gloss and free translation
I.	Apa ada di gunong api	1. Apa ada di gunong api what EXIST PREP mountain fire
	Nampak api merah menjulang	'What exists on top of fire mountain?'
	Sudah lama gua tabor budi	2. Nampak api merah menjulang see fire red tower
	Emas juga di pandang orang	'See the towering red fire'

Table 50 (continued)

No.	Pantun	Interlinear gloss and free translation
		3. Sudah lama gua tabor budi already long.time.1SG sow character 'I have given my respect for a long time.'
		4. Emas juga di-pandang orang gold also PASS-view people 'Gold is still looked at by people.'
II.	Dari Melaka ka Pulau Daik	5. Dari Melaka ka PulauDaik from Malacca to Island 'From Malacca to Daik Island'
	Mau beli sakati kerang	
	Kalau baka pokok itu baik	6. Mau beli sa-kati kerang want buy one-catty clam 'Wanted to buy one catty of clams'
	Ranting jatoh di pungot orang	
		7. Kalau baka pokok itu baik if lineage tree that good 'If the lineage of that tree is good'
		8. Ranting jatoh di pungot orang branch fall PASS pick.up people 'A fallen branch will be picked up by people.'
III.	Diberi hendak tak hendak	9. Di-beri hendak tak hendak PASS-give want NEG want 'Given something whether you want it or not'
	Walau pun si ayer susu	
	Tahun ini kawinkan anak	10. Walau pun si ayer susu although also PERSON water milk 'Even though it is a person with milk'
	Tahun depan timbang chuchu	
		11. Tahun ini kawin-kan anak year this marry-TR child 'This year (you) marry off your child'
		12. Tahun depan timbang chuchu year front balance grandchild 'Next year (you) balance your grandchild (on your lap.'
	Walau pun si ayer susu	13. Walau pun si ayer susu although also PERSON water milk 'Even though it is a person with milk'
	Susu dibeli rumah chek Ah Tan	
	Tahun depan dapat chuchu	14. Susu di-beli rumah chek Ah Tan Milk PASS-buy house uncle 'Milk bought from the house of Uncle Ah Tan'
	Gua harap chuchu jantan	
		15. Tahun depan dapat chuchu year front get grandchild 'Next year (you) get a grandchild.'
		16. Gua harap chuchu jantan 1SG hope grandchild male 'I hope for a grandson.'

Table 50 (continued)

No.	Pantun		Interlinear gloss and free translation
	Susu dibeli rumah chek Ah Tan	17.	Susu di-beli rumah chek Ah Tan milk PASS-buy house uncle 'Milk bought from the house of Uncle Ah Tan'
	Beli labu buat kua		
	Kalau dapat chuchu jantan	18.	Beli labu buat kua buy pumpkin make gravy 'Buy pumpkin to make gravy'
	Jangan lupa chiah gua		
		19.	Kalau dapat chuchu jantan if get grandchild male 'If you get a grandson'
		20.	Jangan lupa chiah gua do.not forget invite 1SG 'Do not forget to invite me.'
IV.	Apa ada di Gunong Daik	21.	Apa ada di Gunong Daik what EXIST PREP mountain 'What exists on Daik Mountain?'
	Nampak api merah menjulang		
	Jika ada budi yang baik	22.	Nampak api merah menjulang see fire red tower 'See the towering red fire'
	Sampai mati dikenang orang		
		23.	Jika ada budi yang baik if have character REL good 'If (you) have a good character'
		24.	Sampai mati di-kenang orang until die PASS-reminisce people 'Until (you) die you will be remembered by people.'
V.	Bibik Tengah sudah pulang	25.	Bibik Tengah sudah pulang Bibik middle already return 'Middle Bibik has already returned'
	Kena hujan baju basah		
	Apa guna banyak wang	26.	Kena hujan baju basah PASS rain clothes wet '(She) was rained on (so her) clothes are wet'
	Kalau tidak berbudi bahasa		
		27.	Apa guna banyak wang what use many money 'What is the use of a lot of money?'
		28.	Kalau tidak ber-budi bahasa if NEG POSS-character respect 'If (one) does not have a respectable character'
VI.	Kain di ikat dengan benang	29.	Kain di-ikat dengan benang cloth PASS-tie with thread 'Cloth tied with thread'
	Letak mari di kayu Jati		
	Sembilan laut-an dah gua berenang	30.	Letak mari di kayu jati place come PREP wood teak 'Come to the place with the teak wood'
	Belum dapat kehendak hati		

Table 50 (continued)

No.	Pantun		Interlinear gloss and free translation
		31.	Sembilan laut-an dah gua berenang nine sea-NMZ already 1SG swim 'I have swam nine oceans'
		32.	Belum dapat ke-hendak hati not.yet get NMZ-want heart 'I have not gotten what the heart wants'
VII.	Pergi pasar beli manga	33.	Pergi pasar beli manga go market buy mango 'Went to the market to buy mangoes'
	Mangga di beli dari chek Dara		
	Kalau lu dah berumah tangga	34.	Mangga di-beli dari Chek Dara mango PASS-buy from uncle 'Mangoes bought from Uncle Dara'
	Jangan pulak lupa saudara mara		
		35.	Kalau lu dah ber-rumah tangga if 2SG already POSS-house ladder' 'If you get married'
		36.	Jangan pulak lupa saudara mara do.not instead forget relations relatives 'Do not forget (your) relatives instead.'
VIII.	Pergi kedei beli arang	37.	Pergi kedei beli arang go shop buy charcoal 'Went to a shop to buy charcoal'
	Beli juga sa ikat buah	38.	Beli juga sa-ikat buah buy also one-tie fruit 'Also bought a bundle of fruit.'
	Kalau ada di negeri orang		
	Jangan pulak lupa kan gua	39.	Kalau ada di negeri orang if EXIST PREP country people 'If (you) are in (other) people's country'
		40.	Jangan pulak lupa-kan gua do.not instead forget-TR 1SG 'Do not forget me.'
IX.	Sakit jari kena sembilu	41.	Sakit jari kena sembilu pain finger PASS prick 'Pain in the finger from a prick'
	Sembilu kena di Tiang Dua		
	Emak Bapak besar kan lu	42.	Sembilu kena di tiang dua prick PASS PREP pillar two 'Pricked at Pillar Two'
	Jangan berdusta bila besar		
		43.	Emak Bapak besar-kan lu mother father big-TR 2SG '(Your) parents raised you.'
		44.	Jangan berdusta bila besar do.not betray when big 'Do not betray them when you are old'

Table 50 (continued)

No.	Pantun	Interlinear gloss and free translation
X.	Dari Dali ka Tiong Baru Mau beli ikan keli Sekarang ini dunia baru Cinta di hati mulai sekali	45. Dari Dali ka Tiong Baru From to Center New 'From Dali to New Center' 46. Mau beli-kan keli want buy-TR catfish 'Wanted to buy catfish' 47. Sekarang ini dunia baru now this world new 'Now this is a new world' 48. Cinta di hati mulai sekali love PREP heart from very 'Love from the heart is most important.'

7.3 Lexicon and reversal index

This section features a list of Baba Malay-English lexicon and an English- Baba Malay reversal index.[81] The lexicon is based on data collected in Singapore. It contains approximately 1,100 headwords, and information regarding pronunciation, denotation, etymology and variation where relevant.

7.3.1 Baba Malay- English lexicon

A

a [a] var. of **ada**
a'us [a.ʔus] var. of **ha'us**
abi [a.bi] var. of **habis**
abis [a.bis] var. of **habis**
abu [a.bu] (Malay) *n* ash
ada [a.da] (var. **a**) (Malay) *v* 1) have 2) PROG 3) EXIST 4) PFV 5) COP 6) HAB
adék [a.deʔ] (Malay) *n* 1) sibling 2) younger sibling der. **adék beradék**
adék beradék [a.deʔ bə.ra.deʔ] (Malay) (der. of **adék**) *n* 1) siblings 2) younger siblings **pangkat adek beradek**
agak [a.gaʔ] (Malay) *v* estimate **agak agak**

agak agak [a.gaʔ a.gaʔ] (Malay) (**agak**) *adv* roughly
aiya [aj.ja] (Hokkien) EXCLAM annoyance
aiyo [aj.jo] (Hokkien) EXCLAM irritation
ajair [a.dʒɛ] refined var. of **ajar**
ajar [a.dʒar] (var. **ajair**) (Malay) *v* teach (coarse)
akair [a.kɛ] refined var. of **akar**
akar [a.kar] (var. **akair**) (Malay) *n* root (coarse)
ala [a.la] (English) EXCLAM regret
alamak [a.la.maʔ] (English), (Malay) EXCLAM dismay
aloji [a.lo.dʒi] (Portuguese) *n* 1) small clock 2) wrist watch

---

[81] The lexicon and reversal index were created using Fieldworks Language Explorer (version 8.3) and the Pathway add-on, both programmes were developed by SIL International.

amboi [am.boj] source uncertain EXCLAM surprise
ambun [am.bun] (Malay) *n* tapioca
amcham [am.tʃam] var. of **apa macham**
amék [a.meʔ] (Malay) *v* take
ampun [am.pun] (Malay) **1)** *v* forgive **2)** *n* forgiveness
-an [-an] (Malay) Nom
anak [a.naʔ] (Malay) *n* child
ancheng [an.tʃəŋ] (Hokkien) *n* blessing of the marital bed
angin [a.ŋin] (Malay) *n* wind
angkat [aŋ.kat] (Malay) *v* **1)** lift **2)** hold **3)** pick up **4)** carry
angpau [aŋ.paw] (Hokkien) *n* red packet of monetary gift
anjing [an.dʒing] (Malay) *n* dog
ano [a.no] (English) *adj* anonymous
anting-anting [an.tiŋ-an.tiŋ] (Malay) *n* earrings
apa [a.pa] (Malay) *interrog* what **amcham**, comp. **apa cham**, comp. **apa macham**, comp. **apa pasal**, contr. **apa sair**
apa cham [a.pa.tʃam] var. of **apa macham**
apa macham [a.pa ma.tʃam] (var. **apa cham**; var. **amcham**) (Malay) (comp. of **apa, macham**) *interrog* how
apa pasair [a.pa pa.sɛ] refined var. of **apa pasal**
apa pasal [a.pa pa.sal] (var. **apa pasair**) (Malay) (comp. of **apa, pasal**) *interrog* why (coarse)
apa sair [a.pa sɛ] (Malay) (contr. of **apa, sair** 1) *interrog* why (refined)

api [a.pi] (Malay) *n* fire
arap [a.rap] var. of **harap**
arat [a.rat] (Malay) *n* alcohol
arga [ar.ga] var. of **harga**
ari [a.ri] var. of **hari** comp. **mata ari** sun
arimo [a.ri.mo] var. of **harimo**
asam [a.sam] (Malay) **1)** *n* tamarind **2)** *adj* sour
asap [a.sap] (Malay) *n* smoke
asién asin [a.sjen asin] (Malay) (der. of **asin**) *adj* somewhat salty
asin [a.sin] (Malay) *adj* salty comp. **mulot asin**, der. **asién asin atas** [a.tas] (Malay) *prep* top
ati [a.ti] var. of **hati** comp. **ati baik** kind, comp. **ati busok** cruel, comp. **jantong ati** beloved, id. **ati it gor it chap** nervous
ati baik [a.ti bajʔ] (Malay) (comp. of **ati, baik**) *adj* kind
ati busok [a.ti bu.soʔ] (Malay) (comp. of **ati, busok**) *adj* cruel
ati it gor it chap [a.ti it gɔ it tʃap] (Malay), (Hokkien) (id. of **ati, it, gor, chap**) *adj* nervous
auban [aw.ban] (Hokkien) *adj* selfish
awan [a.wan] (Malay) *n* cloud
ayam [a.jam] (Malay) *n* chicken comp. **mulot pantat ayam**
ayé [a.je] (Malay) *n* water **mata ayé**, comp. **buang ayé**, comp. **buang ayé besair**, comp. **buang ayé kechik**
ayi [a.ji] source uncertain EXCLAM surprise

B

ba [ba] (Hokkien) (contr. of **Baba**) *n* son
ba'u [ba.ʔu] (Malay) *n* smell
baba [ba.ba] var. of **bapak**
Baba [ba.ba] (Hokkien) *n* **1)** Peranakan male **2)** son contr. **ba**
babi [ba.bi] (Malay) *n* pig
bacha [ba.tʃa] (Malay) *v* read
badan [ba.dan] (Malay) *n* body
bagi [ba.gi] (Malay) *adv* similar to
bagus [ba.gus] (Malay) *interj* good
bahasa [ba.ha.sa] (Malay) *n* language
bahu [ba.hu] (var. **bau**) (Malay) *n* shoulder
baik [bajʔ] (Malay) *adj* good comp. **ati baik**, comp. **naik baik**
baju [ba.dʒu] (Malay) *n* clothes

bakair [ba.kɛ] refined var. of **bakar**
bakar [ba.kar] (var. **bakair**) (Malay) *v* burn (coarse)
bakol [ba.kol] (Malay) *n* basket
baku [ba.ku] (Malay) *adj* standard
balay-balay [ba.le-ba.le] Indonesian *n* resting platform
baldi [bal.di] (Malay) *n* pail
balék [ba.leʔ] (Malay) **1)** *v* return **2)** *v* turn over **3)** *adv* back **4)** *adv* again
bangkit [baŋ.kit] (Malay) *n* coconut cookie
bangkuang [baŋ.kwaŋ] (Hokkien) *n* turnip
bapak [ba.paʔ] (var. **baba**) (Malay) *n* father **mak bapak**
barang [ba.raŋ] (Malay) *n* thing

baring [ba.riŋ] (Malay) *v* lie down
baru [ba.ru] (Malay) **1)** *adj* new **2)** *adv* just
basi [ba.si] (Malay) *adj* stale
batang [ba.taŋ] (Malay) *clf* long and thin
batu [ba.tu] (Malay) **1)** *n* rock **2)** *n* stone **3)** *n* cave
bau [baw] var. of **bahu**
bawah [ba.wah] (Malay) *prep* under
bawak [ba.waʔ] (Malay) *v* bring
bawang [ba.waŋ] (Malay) *n* onion
bayair [ba.jɛ] refined var. of **bayar**
bayang [ba.jaŋ] (Malay) *n* shadow
bayar [ba.jar] (var. **bayair**) (Malay) *v* pay (coarse)
bedék [bə.deʔ] (Malay) *v* pummel
bédék [be.deʔ] (Malay) *v* tell a lie
bég [beʔ] (English) *n* bag
begi [bə.gi] (Malay) (contr. of **begitu**) *adv* like that
begitu [bə.gi.tu] (var. **gitu**) (Malay) *adv* like that contr. **begi**
belachu [bə.la.tʃu] (Malay) *n* unbleached cotton outfit used for mourning
belah [bə.lah] (Malay) *prep* side
belair [bə.lɛ] refined var. of **belas**
belajair [bə.la.dʒɛ] var. of **belajar**
belajar [bə.la.dʒar] (var. **belajair**) (Malay) *v* learn (coarse)
belakang [bə.la.kaŋ] (Malay) *prep* behind
belanda [bə.lan.da] (Malay) **1)** *n* (Dutch) **2)** *adj* (Dutch) comp. **kuching belanda**
belangkat [bə.laŋ.kat] (Malay) *v* crawl
belanja [bə.lan.dʒa] (Malay) *v* **1)** spend **2)** treat
belas [bə.las] (refined var. **belair**) (Malay) *cardnum* ten (coarse)
beli [bə.li] (Malay) *v* buy
beliak [bə.ljaʔ] (Malay) *v* glare **mata beliak**
belién [bə.ljen] (Malay) *n* diamond
bélok [be.loʔ] (Malay) *v* turn
belom [bə.lom] (Malay) *adv* **1)** not yet **2)** before
benair [bə.nɛ] refined var. of **benal**
benal [bə.nal] (var. **benair**) (Malay) *adj* rational (coarse)
bengis [bə.ŋis] (Malay) **1)** *adj* fierce **2)** *adj* serious
béngok [be.ŋoʔ] (Malay) *adj* twisted comp. **mulot béngok**
bérak [be.raʔ] (Malay) *v* defecate
beramay [bə.ra.me] (Malay) *adj* crowded
berapa [bə.ra.pa] (Malay) **1)** *interrog* how many **2)** *adv* some
berat [bə.rat] (Malay) *adj* heavy comp. **mulot berat**

berenang [bə.rə.naŋ] (Malay) *v* swim
bergerak [bər.gə.raʔ] (Malay) *v* move
bergetair [bər.gə.tɛ] refined var. of **bergetar**
bergetar [bər.gə.tar] (var. **bergetair**) (Malay) *v* tremble (coarse)
berkelay [bər.kə.le] (Malay) *v* quarrel
berléiléi [bər.lej.lej] (Malay) *v* drip
bersi [bər.si] (Malay) *v* clean
bertengkair [bər.təŋ.kɛ] refined var. of **bertengkar**
bertengkar [bər.təŋ.kar] (var. **bertengkair**) (Malay) *v* argue (coarse)
beruang [bə.rwaŋ] (Malay) *n* bear
beruba [bə.ru.ba] (Malay) *v* repent
berus [bə.rus] (English) *v* brush
besair [bə.sɛ] refined var. of **besar** comp. **buang ayé besair** defecate
besar [bə.sar] (var. **besair**) (Malay) *adj* big
besi [bə.si] (Malay) *n* iron
bésok [be.soʔ] (Malay) *adv* tomorrow
betol [bə.tol] (Malay) **1)** *adj* correct **2)** *adj* true **3)** *adv* really
biasa [bja.sa] (Malay) *adj* used to it
bibik [bi.biʔ] (Malay) *n* older Peranakan woman
bijik [bi.dʒiʔ] (Malay) **1)** *clf* small and round **2)** *n* seed comp. **bijik mata**
bijik mata [bi.dʒiʔ ma.ta] (Malay) (comp. of **bijik**, **mata**) *n* favourite child
bikin [bi.kin] Indonesian *v* **1)** make **2)** do
bila [bi.la] (Malay) *adv* when
bilang [bi.laŋ] (Malay) *v* tell
bilék [bi.leʔ] (Malay) *n* room
bilis [bi.lis] (Malay) *n* anchovy
bini [bi.ni] (Malay) *n* wife
binpo [bin.po] (Hokkien) *n* handkerchief
bintang [bin.taŋ] (Malay) *n* star
bising [bi.siŋ] (Malay) *adj* noisy
bocho [bo.tʃo] (Malay) *adj* leaky comp. **mulot bocho**
bodoh [bo.doh] (Malay) *adj* stupid comp. **buat bodoh**
bohong [bo.hoŋ] (Malay) *n* lie
boik [bojk] (Hokkien) *n* socks
bok-bok [boʔ-boʔ] (Hokkien) (contr. of **embok-embok**) *n* traditional Peranakan elder
boléh [bo.leh] (Malay) *v* can **bongsu** [boŋ.su] (Malay) *adj* youngest (only for familial relations)

botak [bo.taʔ] (Malay) *adj* bald
botol [bo.tol] (English) *n* bottle
bresi [bre.si] var. of **bersi**
buah [bwah] (Malay) *n* fruit
buang [bwaŋ] (Malay) *v* throw comp. **buang ayé**, comp. **buang ayé besair**, comp. **buang ayé kechik**, comp. **buang buang**, comp. **buang mata**, comp. **buang mulot**, comp. **buang sebelah**, comp. **buang segan**, comp. **buang tebiét**
buang ayé [bwaŋ a.je] (Malay) (comp. of **buang, ayé**) *v* urinate
buang ayé besair [bwaŋ a.je bə.sɛ] (Malay) (comp. of **buang, ayé, besair**) *v* defecate
buang ayé kechik [bwaŋ a.je kə.chiʔ] (Malay) (comp. of **buang, ayé, kechik**) *v* urinate
buang buang [bwaŋ bwaŋ] (Malay) (comp. of **buang**) *v* exorcise
buang mata [bwaŋ ma.ta] (Malay) (comp. of **buang, mata**) *v* keep an eye on someone or something
buang mulot [bwaŋ mu.lot] (Malay) (comp. of **buang, mulot**) *v* convey by speaking (as opposed to writing)
buang sebelah [bwaŋ sə.bə.lah] (Malay) (comp. of **buang**) *adv* aside from
buang segan [bwaŋ sə.gan] (Malay) (comp. of **buang, segan**) *v* stretch upon waking up
buang tebiét [bwaŋ tə.bjet] (Malay) (comp. of **buang, terbiat**) *v* throw tantrum
buat [bwat] (Malay) *v* **1)** do **2)** make comp. **buat bodoh**, comp. **buat mahal**, comp. **buat malu**, comp. **buat mungka**, comp. **buat suay**, comp. **buat tak dengair**
buat bodoh [bwat bo.doh] (Malay) (comp. of **buat, bodoh**) *v* feign ignorance

buat mahal [bwat ma.hal] (Malay) (comp. of **buat, mahal**) *v* play hard to get
buat malu [bwat ma.lu] (Malay) (comp. of **buat, malu**) *v* cause embarrassment
buat mungka [bwat muŋ.ka] (Malay) (comp. of **buat, mungka**) *v* be sour-faced
buat suay [bwat swe] (Malay), (Hokkien) (comp. of **buat, suay**) *v* cause misfortune
buat tak dengair [bwat taʔ dən.ɛ] (Malay) (comp. of **buat, tak, dengair**) *v* pretend to not hear
bubor [bu.bɔ] (Hokkien) *n* porridge
budak [bu.daʔ] (Malay) *n* child
budi [bu.di] (Malay) *n* character
bukak [bu.kaʔ] (Malay) *v* open
bukak kun [bu.kaʔ kun] (Malay), (Hokkien) *n* bride's assistant for kneeling and general help
bukan [bu.kan] (var. **kan**) (Malay) **1)** *interj* no **2)** Neg (noun)
bukit [bu.kit] (Malay) *n* hill
buku [bu.ku] (Malay) *n* book
bulan [bu.lan] (Malay) *n* **1)** moon **2)** month
bulat [bu.lat] (Malay) *adj* round
bulu [bu.lu] (Malay) *n* **1)** feather **2)** fine hair
bunbong [bun.boŋ] (Malay) *n* roof
bunchit [bun.tʃit] (Malay) *n* distended .stomach
bunga [bu.ŋa] (Malay) *n* flower
bungkus [buŋ.kus] (Malay) *n* bundle
bunoh [bu.noh] (Malay) *v* kill
buntot [bun.tot] (Malay) *n* **1)** tail **2)** backside
bunyi [bu.ɲi] (Malay) *n* sound
burok [bu.roʔ] (Malay) *adj* ugly
burong [bu.roŋ] (Malay) *n* bird
busok [bu.soʔ] (Malay) *adj* smelly comp. **ati busok**, comp. **mulot busok**
buta [bu.ta] (Malay) *adj* blind

C

chabot [tʃa.bot] (Malay) *v* pull out
chaiki [tʃaj.ki] (Hokkien) *n* banner
chaiteng [tʃaj.təŋ] (Hokkien) *n* nunnery that serves vegetarian food
chaiyen [tʃaj.jen] (Hokkien) *n* jelly
chakap [tʃaj.kap] (Malay) *v* speak
chakiak [tʃa.kjaʔ] (Hokkien) *n* clogs
cham 1 [tʃam] (Hokkien) *v* observe
cham 2 [tʃam] (Malay) (contr. of **macham**) *adv* like
champor [tʃam.por] (Malay) *v* mix

chanab [tʃa.nab] (Hokkien) *n* decorative altar stand
changkay [tʃaŋ.ke] (Malay) *n* cup
chanték [tʃan.teʔ] (Malay) *adj* beautiful
chap [tʃap] (Hokkien) *cardnum* ten id. **ati it gor it chap**
charék [tʃa.reʔ] (Malay) *v* find
chau [tʃaw] (Hokkien) *n* elder sister's husband
chaukah [tʃaw.kah] (Hokkien) *n* bad sport
chaukuan [tʃaw.kwan] (Hokkien) *n* bad type of person

chay [tʃe] (Hokkien) *n* beginning of lunar month
chay-em [tʃe.əm] (Hokkien) *n* mother-in-law (indirect address)
chék [tʃeʔ] (Hokkien) *n* father's younger brother
chék-gong [tʃeʔ-goŋ] (Hokkien) *n* grandfather's younger brother
chekék [tʃə.keʔ] (Malay) *v* strangle
chelop [tʃə.lop] (Malay) *v* dip in dye
chepat [tʃə.pat] (Malay) *adj* quick
chepuat [tʃə.pwat] (Hokkien) *n* family
cherdék [tʃər.deʔ] (Malay) *adj* streetwise
cherita [tʃə.ri.ta] (Malay) *n* story
cherkek [tʃər.keʔ] (Malay) *v* eat (vulgar)
cherki [tʃər.ki] (Hokkien) *n* Peranakan card game
chia [tʃja] (Hokkien) *n* car
chiam [tʃjam] (Hokkien) *n* divination stick
chichi [tʃi.tʃi] (Malay) *n* great-grandchild
chilaka [tʃi.la.ka] Javanese EXCLAM cursed one
chim [tʃim] (Hokkien) *n* father's younger brother's wife
chin [tʃin] (Hokkien) *adj* close to one another
China [tʃi.na] (Malay) *adj* Chinese
chinchai [tʃin.tʃaj] (Hokkien) *adj* not fussy

chinchang [tʃin.tʃaŋ] (Malay) *v* mince
chingkay [tʃiŋ.ke] (Hokkien) *n* **1)** parent-in-law **2)** father-in-law (indirect address)
chit [tʃit] (Hokkien) *cardnum* seven
chiwan [tʃi.wan] source unknown *n* toilet
cho [tʃo] (Hokkien) *n* **1)** great-grandparent **2)** great-grandmother **mak-cho**, comp. **gong-cho**
cho-cho [tʃo-tʃo] (Hokkien) *n* great-grandmother
cho-gong [tʃo-goŋ] (Hokkien) *n* great-grandfather
cho-po [tʃo-po] (Hokkien) *n* great-grandaunt
chobak [tʃo.baʔ] (Malay) *v* taste
chobék [tʃo.beʔ] (Malay) *adj* long-jawed
chonténg [tʃon.teŋ] (Malay) *v* draw
chu-lang [tʃu.laŋ] (Hokkien) *n* bridegroom's family's host
chuchi [tʃu.tʃi] (Malay) *v* wash
chuchu [tʃu.tʃu] (Malay) *n* grandchild
chuikuéh [tʃwi.kweh] (Hokkien) *n* rice cake
chukop [tʃu.kop] (Malay) *adv* enough
chupak [tʃu.paʔ] (Malay) *clf* cylindrincal measure of quarter gallon of rice
chutsi [tʃut.si] (Hokkien) *n* birth

D

dadair [da.dɛ] refined var. of **dadar**
dadar [da.dar] (var. **dadair**) (Malay) *n* omelette (coarse)
dagin [da.gin] (Malay) *n* meat
dahi [da.hi] (var. **dai**) (Malay) *n* forehead
dai [daj] var. of **dahi**
dalam [da.lam] (Malay) *prep* inside
daoun [da.own] (Malay) *n* leaves
dapat [da.pat] (Malay) *v* **1)** get **2)** receive
dapor [da.pɔ] (Malay) *n* kitchen
darah [da.rah] (Malay) *n* blood comp. **naik darah**
dari [da.ri] (Malay) *prep* from
datang [da.taŋ] (Malay) *v* come
degil [də.gil] (Malay) *adj* stubborn
dekat [də.kat] (var. **kat**) (Malay) **1)** *prep* at **2)** *prep* near **3)** *prep* Prep
dengair [də.ŋɛ] refined var. of **dengar** comp. **buat tak dengair** pretend to not hear
dengar [də.ŋar] (var. **dengair**) (Malay) *v* listen (coarse)

depan [də.pan] (Malay) *prep* front
di [di] (Malay) *prep* Prep comp. **diluar**
dia [dja] (Malay) **1)** *pro* 3.SG; **2)** *pro* 3.PL
diam [djam] (Hokkien) *adj* quiet
diam diam [djam djam] (Hokkien) *adv* quietly
dia-orang [dja-o.raŋ] (Malay) 3. PL *pro*
diluar [di.lwar] (var. **duluar**) (Malay) (comp. of **di**, **keluar**) *prep* outside
diri [di.ri] (Malay) *v* stand
dit [dit] var. of **duit**
dondang [don.daŋ] *n* melody
dua [dwa] (Malay) *cardnum* two
dudok [du.doʔ] (Malay) *v* **1)** sit **2)** stay
duit [dwit] (var. **dit**) (Dutch) *n* money
dulu [du.lu] (Malay) *adv* **1)** before **2)** long ago **3)** first
duluar [du.lwar] var. of **diluar**
dunya [du.ɲa] (Arabic) *n* world comp. **mulot dunya**

E

éh [eh] source unknown EXCLAM jibe
ékor [e.kor] (Malay) *clf* animal
éla [e.la] var. of **helay**
em [əm] (Malay) *n* **1)** father's elder brother's wife **2)** old aunty **sangkék-em**
embair-embair [əmbɛ-əmbɛ] (Malay) *adj* half-cooked (refined)
embar-embar [əmbar-əmbar] (Malay) *adj* half-cooked (coarse)
embok-embok [əm.boʔ-əm.boʔ] (Hokkien) *n* traditional Peranakan elder contr. **bok-bok**
empat [əm.pat] (Malay) *cardnum* four
enam [e.nam] (Malay) *cardnum* six
eng- [əŋ] (Hokkien) honorific prefix for familial relations

G

gaga [ga.ga] (Hokkien) *adj* daring
gambair [gam.bɛ] refined var. of **gambar gambar** [gam.bar] (var. **gambair**) (Malay) *n* picture (coarse)
ganjil [gan.jil] (Malay) *adj* odd-numbered
gantang [gan.taŋ] (Malay) *clf* cylindrical measure of one gallon of rice
gantong [gan.toŋ] (Malay) *v* hang
gaou [ga.ow] (Malay) *v* mix
garam [ga.ram] (Malay) *n* salt
garang [ga.raŋ] (Malay) *adj* fierce
gasak [ga.saʔ] (Malay) *v* guess
gatair [ga.tɛ] refined var. of **gatal** comp. **mulot gatair** uncontrollable mouth
gatal [ga.tal] (var. **gatair**) (Malay) *adj* itchy (coarse)
gau [gaw] (Hokkien) *cardnum* nine
gaya [ga.ja] (Malay) *v* splurge
gedebak-gedebuk [gə.də.baʔ-gə.də.buʔ] (Malay) onomatopoia thudding of the heart
gedebang-gedebong [gə.də.baŋ-gə.də.boŋ] (Malay) onomatopoeia loud noises
gelang [gə.laŋ] (Malay) *n* bracelet
gelap [gə.lap] (Malay) *adj* dark comp. **mata gelap**
geléték [gə.le.teʔ] (Malay) *v* tickle comp. **naik geléték**
gemoh [gə.moh] (Malay) *v* sun dry
gemok [gə.moʔ] (Malay) *adj* fat
geram [gə.ram] (Malay) *adj* furious comp. **naik geram**

gerang [gə.raŋ] (Malay) *n* enthusiasm
gerja [gər.dʒa] (var. **greja**) (Portuguese) *n* church
gerong [gə.roŋ] (Malay) *v* scratch
gertak [gər.taʔ] (var. **gretak**) (Malay) *v* threat
gigi [gi.gi] (Malay) *n* tooth
gigit [gi.git] (Malay) *v* bite
gila [gi.la] (Malay) *adj* mad comp. **naik gila**
gitu [gi.tu] var. of **begitu**
gonchang [gon.tʃaŋ] (Malay) *v* shake
gong [goŋ] (Hokkien) **1)** *n* grandparent **2)** grandfather comp. **gong-cho**
gong-cho [goŋ-tʃo] (Hokkien) (comp. of **gong, cho**) *n* ancestors
gonggong [goŋ-goŋ] (Malay) *v* bark
gor [gɔ] (Hokkien) *cardnum* five id. **ati it gor it chap**
gorblok [gɔ.bloʔ] Indonesian *adj* stupid
goréng [go.reŋ] (Malay) *v* fry
gostan [go.stan] (English) *v* reverse
goyang [go.jaŋ] (Malay) **1)** *vi* rock **2)** *vt* shake
greja [grə.dʒa] var. of **gerja**
gretak [grə.taʔ] var. of **gertak**
gua [gwa (coarse)] (Hokkien) *pro* 1.SG
guék [gweʔ] (Hokkien) *n* lunar month
gugol [gu.gol] (Malay) *n* dried fruit
gui [gwi] (Hokkien) *v* kneel
gula [gu.la] (Malay) *n* sugar
guna [gu.na] (Malay) **1)** *v* use **2)** *n* use
gunong [gu.noŋ] (Malay) *n* mountain

H

ha'us [ha.ʔus] (var. **a'us**) (Malay) *adj* **1)** thirsty **2)** worn out
habis [ha.bis] (var. **abis**; var. **abi**) (Malay) **1)** *v* finish 1.1) *adv* finish **2)** *conn* finish

hak [haʔ] (Hokkien) *adj* suitable
halo [ha.lo] (Malay) *v* chase away
hantok [han.toʔ] (Malay) *v* bang
harap [ha.rap] (var. **arap**) (Malay) *v* hope
harga [har.ga] (var. **arga**) (Sanskrit) *n* price
hari [ha.ri] (var. **ari**) (Malay) *n* day **tengah hari**
harimo [ha.ri.mo] (var. **arimo**) (Malay) *n* tiger
hati [ha.ti] (var. **ati**) (Malay) *n* **1)** heart **2)** liver
haulam [haw.lam] (Hokkien) *n* male mourner
hauli [haw.li] (Hokkien) *n* female mourner
helay [hə.le] (var. **lay**; var. **éla**) (Malay) *clf* sheet
héran [he.ran] (Malay) *v* wonder
hia [hja] (Hokkien) *n* elder brother
hidong [hi.doŋ] (var. **idong**) (Malay) *n* nose
hijo [hi.dʒo] (var. **ijo**) (Malay) *adj* green
hilang [hi.laŋ] (Malay) *v* lose

hitam [hi.tam] (var. **itam**) (Malay) *adj* black
ho [ho] (Hokkien) *adj* good
homia [ho.mja] (Hokkien) *interj* good life (comp. of **ho, mia**)
hormat [hor.mat] (var. **ormat**) (Malay) *v* respect
horpau [hor.paw] (var. **orpau**) (Hokkien) *n* purse
hu [hu] (Hokkien) *n* amulet
huahi [hwa.hi] (Hokkien) *adj* happy
huantiok [hwan.tjoʔ] (Hokkien) *v* meet ill spiritual forces
huat [hwat] (Hokkien) *v* **1)** expand **2)** prosper
huésio [hwe.sjo] (Hokkien) *n* monk
hujan [hu.dʒan] (var. **ujan**) (Malay) *n* rain
hutan [hu.tan] (var. **utan**) (Malay) *n* jungle
huyi [hu.ji] (Hokkien) *n* fishball

I

idong [i.doŋ] var. of **hidong**
ijo [i.dʒo] var. of **hijo**
ikan [i.kan] (Malay) *n* fish comp. **mata ikan**
ikat [i.kat] (Malay) *v* tie
ikot [i.kot] (Malay) *v* follow
ilang [i.laŋ] (Malay) *v* lose
ingat [i.ŋat] (Malay) *v* **1)** remember **2)** think
ini [i.ni] (Malay) *dem* this contr. **ni**

intan [in.tan] (Malay) *n* diamond chip
iris [i.ris] (Malay) *v* slice
isi [i.si] (Malay) *n* flesh
it [it] (Hokkien) *cardnum* one id. **ati it gor it chap**
itam [i.tam] var. of **hitam**
iték [i.teʔ] (Malay) *n* duck
itu [i.tu] (Malay) *dem* that contr. **tu**

J

ja.ou [dʒa.ow] (Malay) *adj* far
jadi [dʒa.di] (Malay) *v* **1)** happen **2)** become
jaga [dʒa.ga] (Malay) *v* **1)** guard **2)** take care of someone or something
jahat [dʒa.hat] (Malay) *adj* evil comp. **mulot jahat**
jait [dʒajt] (Malay) *v* sew
jalan [dʒa.lan] (Malay) *v* walk **tengah jalan**
jam [dʒam] (Malay) *n* **1)** time **2)** hour
jambu [dʒam.bu] (Malay) *n* Syzygium fruit (pink)
jangan [dʒa.ŋan] (Malay) *adv* do not
jantan [dʒan.tan] (Malay) *n* male
jantong [dʒan.toŋ] (Malay) *n* heart comp. **jantong ati**
jantong ati [dʒan.toŋ a.ti] (Malay) (comp. of **jantong, ati**) *n* beloved
jarang [dʒa.raŋ] (Malay) *adv* seldom

jari [dʒa.ri] (Malay) *n* finger
jati [dʒa.ti] (Malay) **1)** *n* teak **2)** *adj* pure
jatoh [dʒa.toh] (Malay) *v* **1)** fall **2)** drop
jawab [dʒa.wab] (Malay) *v* answer
ji [dʒi] (Hokkien) *cardnum* two
jin [dʒin] (Hokkien) *v* recognize
jinak [dʒi.naʔ] (Malay) *adj* tame
jodoh [dʒo.doh] (Malay) *n* match of love
jogét [dʒo.get] (Malay) *v* stylised dance
juair [dʒwɛ] refined var. of **jual**
jual [dʒwal] (var. **juair**) (Malay) *v* sell (coarse)
judi [dʒu.di] (Malay) *v* gamble
jugak [dʒu.gaʔ] (Malay) *adv* also
juling [dʒu.liŋ] (Malay) *adj* squinty comp. **mata juling**
jumoh [dʒu.moh] (Malay) *v* dry in the sun
jumpa [dʒum.pa] (Malay) *v* meet

K

ka [ka] (Hokkien) *conn* or
kabair [ka.bɛ] refined var. of **kabar**
kabar [ka.bar] (var. **kabair**) (Arabic) *n* news (coarse)
kacho [ka.tʃo] (Malay) *v* disturb
kachua [ka.tʃwa] (Hokkien) *n* cockroach
kain [kajn] (Malay) *n* cloth
kaki [ka.ki] (Malay) *n* **1)** leg **2)** friend
kala [ka.la] (Malay) *n* time **sinjakala**
kalah [ka.lah] (Malay) *v* lose (opposed to win)
kalang-kabot [ka.laŋ-ka.bot] (Malay) *v* fumble
kali [ka.li] (Malay) *n* time
kalo [ka.lo] var. of **kalu**
kalu [ka.lu] (var. **kalo**) (Malay) *conn* if
kambing [kam.biŋ] (Malay) *n* **1)** goat **2)** sheep
kampong [kam.poŋ] (Malay) *n* village
kamsiah [kam.sjah] (Hokkien) *interj* thank you
kamtiok [kam.tjoʔ] (Hokkien) *v* develop an illness
kamwan [kam.wan] (Hokkien) *adj* satisfied
kan [kan] var. of **bukan**
-kan [kan] (Malay) Tr
kanan [ka.nan] (Malay) *adv* right
kangkong [kaŋ.koŋ] (Malay) *n* water spinach
kapair [ka.pɛ] refined var. of **kapal**
kapal [ka.pal] (var. **kapair**) (Malay) *n* ship (coarse)
kasair [ka.sɛ] refined var. of **kasar**
kasar [ka.sar] (var. **kasair**) (Malay) *adj* coarse (coarse)
kasi [ka.si] Indonesian *v* **1)** give **2)** let **3)** cause **4)** Pass
kasot [ka.sot] (Malay) *n* shoe
kat [kat] var. of **dekat**
kata [ka.ta] (Malay) *v* say
katék [ka.teʔ] (Hokkien) *adj* short
kawan [ka.wan] (Malay) *n* friend
kawin [ka.win] (Hokkien) *v* marry
kaya 1 [ka.ja] (Malay) *adj* rich
kaya 2 [ka.ja] (Malay) *n* coconut jam
kayu [ka.ju] (Malay) *n* wood
kebaya [kə.ba.ja] (Malay) *n* traditional blouse
kebun [kə.bun] (Malay) *n* garden
kechik [kə.tʃiʔ] (Malay) *adj* small comp. **buang ayé kechik keday** [kə.de] (Malay) *n* shop
kejair [kə.dʒɛ] refined var. of **kejar**
kejar [kə.dʒar] (var. **kejair**) (Malay) *v* chase (coarse)
kejut [kə.dʒut] (Malay) *adj* shock
kék [keʔ] (English) *n* cake
kéksim [keʔ.sim] (Hokkien) *adj* unhappy

kelaka [kə.la.ka] (Malay) *v* joke
kelék.kelék [kəleʔ.kəleʔ] (Malay) *v* blink
keluak [kə.lwaʔ] (Malay) *n* Pangium.edule (black fruit with hard shell)
keluar [kə.lwar] (refined var. **kuluair**; var. **kuluar**) (Malay) *v* go out (coarse) comp. **diluar**
kemair [kə.mɛ] refined var. of **kemas**
kemantin [kə.man.tin] (Malay) *n* bride
kemas [kə.mas] (var. **kemair**) (Malay) *v* tidy (coarse)
kena [kə.na] (Malay) **1)** *v* Pass **2)** *v* subjected to
kenair [kə.nɛ] (Malay) *v* (refined var. **kenal**)
kenal [kə.nal] (Malay) *v* know a person (coarse)
kenang [kə.naŋ] (Malay) *v* reminisce
kenonay [kə.no.ne] source unclear *adj* proper
kenyang [kə.ɲaŋ] (Malay) *adj* full from eating
kepala [kə.pa.la] (Malay) *n* head
kepék [kə.peʔ] (Malay) *v* pinch
kepéng [kə.peŋ] (Malay) *clf* piece
kepok [kə.poʔ] (Malay) *n* box
kerair [kərɛ] refined var. of **keras**
keras [kəras] (var. **kerair**) (Malay) *adj* hard (coarse)
kerekot [kə.re.kot] (Malay) *adj* bent and curled up
keréta [kə.re.ta] (Malay) *n* car
kering [kə.riŋ] (Malay) **1)** *n* hay **2)** *adj* dry comp. **mulot kering**
kerja [kər.dʒa] (var. **kreja**) (Malay) **1)** *v* work **2)** *n* work
kerosi [kə.ro.si] (Malay) *n* chair
kertair [kər.tɛ] refined var. of **kertas**
kertas [kər.tas] (var. **kertair**) (Malay) *n* paper (coarse)
ketawa [kə.ta.wa] (Malay) *v* laugh
ketok [kə.toʔ] (Malay) *v* knock
kéwat [ke.wat] source unknown *adj* fussy
kiam [kjam] (Hokkien) *adj* stingy
kiamchai [kjam.tʃaj] (Hokkien) *n* preserved vegetables
kiamsiap [kjam.sjap] (Hokkien) *adj* miserly
kiasai [kjasaj] (Hokkien) *n* **1)** son-in-law **2)** groom
kim [kim] (Hokkien) *n* mother's brother's wife
kipas [ki.pas] (Malay) *n* fan
kita [ki.ta] (Malay) *pro* 1.PL
ko 1 [ko] (Hokkien) *n* father's sister **mak-ko**
ko 2 [ko] (Hokkien) *n* elder brother (non-familial)
kochék [ko.tʃeʔ] (Malay) *n* pocket
kodok [ko.doʔ] (Malay) *n* frog
koktok [kɔʔ.tɔʔ] (Hokkien) *v* ill-treat

kolomi [ko.lo.mi] (Hokkien) *n* type of noodles
konchi [kon.tʃi] (Malay) *n* key
kopék [ko.peʔ] (Hokkien) *v* peel
kopi [ko.pi] (Malay) *n* coffee
kopiah [ko.pjah] source unknown *n* hat
kopiau [ko.pjaw] (Hokkien) *n* paternal cousins
kotor [ko.tor] (Malay) *adj* dirty
koya [ko.ja] (Malay) *n* green bean cookies
koyak [ko.jaʔ] (Malay) *adj* torn
kreja [krə.dʒa] var. of **kerja**
ku 1 [ku] (Hokkien) *n* tortoise
ku 2 [ku] (Hokkien) *n* mother's brother comp. **ku-ku**
ku-ku [ku-ku] (Hokkien) (comp. of **ku** 2) *n* mother's eldest brother
kua 1 [kwa] (Malay) *n* gravy
kua 2 [kwa] (Hokkien) *n* father-in-law
kuat [kwat] (Hokkien) *adj* strong
kuatay [kwa.te] (Malay) *v* worry **kuching** [ku.tʃiŋ] (Malay) *n* cat comp. **kuching belanda**, comp. **mata kuching**
kuching belanda [ku.tʃiŋ bəlanda] (Malay) (comp. of **kuching, belanda**) *n* rabbit
kuda [ku.da] (Malay) *n* horse
kudut [ku.dut] (Malay) *adj* crumpled

kuéh [kweh] (Hokkien) *n* traditional cakes comp. **kuéh-yi**
kuéh-yi [kweh-ji] (Hokkien) (comp. of **kuéh, yi 1**) *n* glutinous rice balls
kuku [ku.ku] (Malay) *n* fingernail
kukus [ku.kus] (Malay) *v* steam
kulit [ku.lit] (Malay) *n* skin
kuluair [ku.lwɛ] refined var. of **keluar**
kuluar [ku.lwar] var. of **keluar**
kun 1 [kun] (Hokkien) *n* skirt
kun 2 [kun] var. of **pun**
kunang [ku.naŋ] source unclear *adj* under the influence of black magic
kuning [ku.niŋ] (Malay) *adj* yellow
kuntum [kun.tum] (Malay) *clf* bloom
kupas [ku.pas] (Malay) *v* peel
kuping [ku.piŋ] (Portuguese) *n* ear
kupu-kupu [ku.pu-ku.pu] (Malay) *n* butterfly
kura-kura [ku.ra-ku.ra] (Malay) *n* tortoise
kurang [ku.raŋ] (Malay) *adv* less
kuro [ku.ro] (Malay) *n* threadfin fish
kurus [ku.rus] (Malay) *adj* thin
kus semangat [kus sə.ma.ŋat] (Malay) Exclam cry to a dead spirit
kuya [ku.ja] (Hokkien) *n* groom's boy assistant

L

labi-labi [la.bi-la.bi] (Malay) *n* turtle
lagik [la.giʔ] (Malay) **1)** *adv* more **2)** *adv* still **3)** *adv* again
lagu [la.gu] (Malay) *n* song
lah [lah] (Hokkien) *prt* Emp
lain [lajn] (Malay) *adv* other
lak [laʔ] (Hokkien) *cardnum* six
laki [la.ki] (Malay) (contr. of **lelaki**) *n* husband
lalu [la.lu] (Malay) *v* pass
lama [la.ma] (Malay) *adj* long time
lambat [lam.bat] (Malay) *adj* late
lambong [lam.boŋ] (Malay) *v* toss
lampu [lam.pu] (Dutch) *n* lamp
lanchang [lan.tʃaŋ] (Malay) *adj* fluent
langgair [laŋ.gɛ] refined var. of **langgar**
langgar [laŋ.gar] (var. **langgair**) (Malay) *v* crash (coarse)
langit [la.ŋit] (Malay) *n* sky
langkék [laŋ.keʔ] (Hokkien) *n* guest
langsong [laŋ.soŋ] (Malay) *adv* straightaway
lantay [lan.te] (Malay) *n* floor

lapair [la.pɛ] refined var. of **lapar**
lapan [la.pan] (Malay) *cardnum* eight
lapar [la.par] (var. **lapair**) (Malay) *adj* hungry (coarse)
lapchai [lap.tʃaj] (Hokkien) *n* wedding gift exchange ceremony
lari [la.ri] (Malay) *v* run
lauk [lawʔ] (Malay) *n* cooked food
laut [lawt] (Malay) *n* **1)** sea **2)** pond
lawa [la.wa] (Malay) *adj* stylish **lawan** [la.wan] (Malay) *v* race
lay [le] var. of **helay**
lebat [lə.bat] (Malay) *adj* heavy
lebéh [lə.beh] (Malay) *adv* more
léihéi [lej.hej] (Malay) *n* neck
lekair [lə.kɛ] refined var. of **lekas**
lekas [lə.kas] (var. **lekair**) (Malay) *adj* quick (coarse)
lelaki [lə.la.ki] (Malay) *n* boy contr. **laki**
lemak [lə.maʔ] (Malay) *adj* cooked in coconut milk comp. **naik lemak**

lembéh [ləm.beh] (Malay) *adj* soft
lembu [ləm.bu] (Malay) *n* cow comp. **mata lembu**
lembut [ləm.but] (Malay) *adj* supple
lémo [le.mo] (Malay) *n* lemon
lentang [lən.taŋ] (Malay) *v* fall backwards
lepas [lə.pas] (Malay) *prep* after
letak [lə.taʔ] (Malay) *v* park
letay [lə.te] (Malay) *adj* exhausted
liar [ljar] (Malay) *n* wildness
lichin [li.tʃin] (Malay) *adj* smooth
lidah [li.dah] (Malay) *n* tongue
lihai [li.haj] (Hokkien) *adj* cunning
lima [li.ma] (Malay) *cardnum* five
lio [ljo] (Malay) *n* saliva
lipat [li.pat] (Malay) *v* fold

lobang [lo.baŋ] (Malay) *n* hole
lochéng [lo.tʃeŋ] (Hokkien) *n* bell
logong [lo.goŋ] (Malay) *v* carry baby
lompat [lom.pat] (Malay) *v* jump
longkang [loŋ.kaŋ] (Malay) *n* drain
lontong [lon.toŋ] (Malay) *n* rice cake served in spicy gravy
lor [lor] (Hokkien) Emp
loténg [lo.teŋ] (Hokkien) *adv* upstairs
lu [lu] (Hokkien) *pro* 2.Sg
luan [lwan] (Hokkien) *adj* messy
luka [luka] (Malay) **1)** *adj* wounded **2)** *n* wound
lun [lun] (Hokkien) *adj* intercalary
lun-guék [lun gweʔ] (Hokkien) *n* intercalary month
lupa [lu.pa] (Malay) *v* forget

M

mabok [ma.boʔ] (Malay) *adj* giddy
macham [ma.tʃam] (Malay) **1)** *adv* like **2)** *adv* seems **3)** *adv* like that **amcham**, comp. **apa cham**, comp. **apa macham**, contr. **cham 2**
magam [ma.gam] (Malay) *adj* overripe
mahal [ma.hal] (Malay) *adj* expensive comp. **buat mahal**
main [majn] (Malay) **1)** *v* play **2)** *v* perform
mair [mɛ] refined var. of **mas**
mak [maʔ] (Hokkien) *n* mother **mak bapak, mak-cho, mak-ko, mak-yi**
mak bapak [maʔ ba.paʔ] (Hokkien), (Malay) (**mak, bapak**) *n* parents
mak-cho [maʔ-tʃo] (Hokkien) (**mak, cho**) *n* great-grandmother
mak-ko [maʔ-ko] (Hokkien) (**mak, ko 1**) *n* father's eldest sister
mak-yi [maʔ-ji] (Hokkien) (**mak, yi 2**) *n* second mother
makan [ma.kan] (Malay) **1)** *v* eat **2)** *n* food
maki [ma.ki] (Malay) *v* scold
malair [ma.lɛ] refined var. of **malas**
malam [ma.lam] (Malay) *n* night **malas** [ma.las] (var. **malair**) (Malay) *adj* lazy (coarse)
malu [ma.lu] (Malay) *adj* embarrassed comp. **buat malu**
mamak [ma.maʔ] (Hokkien) *n* grandmother
mampus [mam.pus] (Malay) Exclam dead
mana [ma.na] (Malay) *interrog* **1)** where **2)** which

mandi [man.di] (Malay) *v* bathe
manék [ma.neʔ] (Malay) *n* bead
mangkok [maŋ.koʔ] (Malay) *n* bowl
mangun [ma.ŋun] (Malay) *v* wake
manis [ma.nis] (Malay) *adj* sweet comp. **mulot manis**
manyak [ma.ɲaʔ] (Malay) *adv* many
marah [ma.rah] (Malay) *adj* angry
mari [ma.ri] (Malay) *v* come let us
mas [mas] (var. **mair**) (Malay) *n* gold (coarse)
masak [ma.saʔ] (Malay) **1)** *v* cook **2)** *adj* ripe
masok [ma.soʔ] (Malay) **1)** *v* enter **2)** *v* put in
mata [ma.ta] (Malay) *n* eye **mata ayé, mata beliak**, comp. **bijik mata**, comp. **buang mata**, comp. **mata ari**, comp. **mata gelap**, comp. **mata ikan**, comp. **mata juling**, comp. **mata kuching**, comp. **mata lembu**, comp. **mata piso**, comp. **tanda mata**
mata ari [ma.ta a.ri] (Malay) (comp. of **mata, ari**) *n* sun
mata ayé [ma.ta a.je] (Malay) (**mata, ayé**) *n* sweetheart
mata beliak [ma.ta bə.ljaʔ] (Malay) (**mata, beliak**) *n* protruding eyes
mata gelap [ma.ta gə.lap] (Malay) (comp. of **mata, gelap**) *n* detective
mata ikan [ma.ta i.kan] (Malay) (comp. of **mata, ikan**) *n* wart
mata juling [ma.ta dʒu.liŋ] (Malay) (comp. of **mata, juling**) *n* cockeyed

mata kuching [ma.ta ku.tʃiŋ] (Malay) (comp. of **mata, kuching**) *n* longan fruit
mata lembu [ma.ta ləm.bu] (Malay) (comp. of **mata, lembu**) *n* fried egg with yolk intact
mata piso [ma.ta pi.so] (Malay) (comp. of **mata, piso**) *n* blade of knife
mati [ma.ti] (Malay) **1)** *v* die **2)** *adj* dead
mayang [ma.jaŋ] (Malay) *n* palm blossom
méh [meh] (Hokkien) *n* night (when referring to lunar dates)
méja [me.dʒa] (Portuguese) *n* table
melekat [mə.lə.kat] (Malay) *adj* sticky
mémang [me.maŋ] (Malay) *adv* indeed
memisék [mə.mi.seʔ] (Malay) *v* whisper
menang [mə.naŋ] (Malay) *v* win
menangis [mə.na.ŋis] (Malay) *v* cry
mengantok [mə.ŋan.toʔ] (Malay) **1)** *v* yawn **2)** *adj* sleepy
mengintar [mə.ŋin.tar] (Malay) *v* shiver
menidi [mə.ni.di] (Malay) *adj* boiling
menjéla [mən.dʒe.la] (Portuguese) *n* window
mentah [mən.tah] (Malay) *adj* raw
mentéga [mən.te.ga] (Portuguese) *n* butter
menyalap [mə.ɲa.lap] (Malay) *v* howl
menyanyi [mə.ɲa.ɲi] (var. **nyanyi**) (Malay) *v* sing
mérah [me.rah] (Malay) *adj* red
mesti [məs.ti] (Malay) *v* must
mia1 [mja] (Hokkien) *n* life
mia2 [mja] (Malay) (contr. of **punya**) **1)** *v* Poss **2)** Rel
mimpi [mim.pi] (Malay) *v* dream
mincharok [min.tʃa.roʔ] (Malay) *v* curse
minggu [miŋ.gu] (Malay) *n* week
minit [mi.nit] (English) *n* minute
mintak [min.taʔ] (Malay) *v* ask sincerely
minum [mi.num] (Malay) *v* drink
minyak [mi.ɲak] (Malay) *n* **1)** grease **2)** oil
miskin [mis.kin] (Malay) *adj* poor **mo** [mo] (Malay) *v* want
mudah [mu.dah] (Malay) *adj* young

muilang [mwi.laŋ] (Hokkien) *n* matchmaker
mula [mu.la] (Malay) *adj* original
mula mula [mu.la mu.la] (Malay) *adv* originally
mulot [mu.lot] (Malay) *n* mouth comp. **buang mulot**, comp. **mulot asin**, comp. **mulot béngok**, comp. **mulot berat**, comp. **mulot bocho**, comp. **mulot busok**, comp. **mulot dunya**, comp. **mulot gatair**, comp. **mulot jahat**, comp. **mulot kering**, comp. **mulot manis**, comp. **mulot pantat ayam**, comp. **mulot ringan**
mulot asin [mu.lot a.sin] (Malay) (comp. of **mulot, asin**) *n* ability to make accurate predictions
mulot béngok [mu.lot be.ɲoʔ] (Malay) (comp. of **mulot, béngok**) *n* twisted mouth
mulot berat [mu.lot bə.rat] (Malay) (comp. of **mulot, berat**) *n* inability to express oneself
mulot bocho [mu.lot bo.tʃo] (Malay) (comp. of **mulot, bocho**) *n* inability to keep a secret
mulot busok [mu.lot bu.soʔ] (Malay) (comp. of **mulot, busok**) *n* bad breath
mulot dunya [mu.lot du.ɲia] (Malay), (Arabic) (comp. of **mulot, dunya**) *n* public opinions
mulot gatair [mu.lot ga.tɛ] (Malay) (comp. of **mulot, gatair**) *n* uncontrollable mouth
mulot jahat [mu.lot dʒa.hat] (Malay) (comp. of **mulot, jahat**) *n* caustic mouth
mulot kering [mu.lot kə.riŋ] (Malay) (comp. of **mulot, kering**) *n* inability to say more
mulot manis [mu.lot ma.nis] (Malay) (comp. of **mulot, manis**) *n* ability to speak sweetly
mulot pantat ayam [mu.lot pan.tat a.jam] (Malay) (comp. of **mulot, pantat, ayam**) *n* deceitful mouth
mulot ringan [mu.lot ri.ŋan] (Malay) (comp. of **mulot, ringan**) *n* polite character
mungka [muŋ.ka] (Malay) *n* face comp. **buat mungka**
musim [mu.sim] (Arabic) *n* season

N

na [na] (Hokkien) *interj* here you go
naik [najʔ] (Malay) *v* **1)** climb **2)** rise **3)** ascend comp. **naik baik**, comp. **naik darah**, comp. **naik geléték**, comp. **naik geram**, comp. **naik gila**, comp. **naik lemak**, comp. **naik pangkat**, comp. **naik sedap**, comp. **naik seram**

naik baik [najʔ bajʔ] (Malay) (comp. of **naik, baik**) *v* change for good
naik darah [najʔ da.rah] (Malay) (comp. of **naik, darah**) *v* be angry
naik geléték [najʔ gə.le.teʔ] (Malay) (comp. of **naik, geléték**) *v* be up to mischief

naik geram [najʔ gə.ram] (Malay) (comp. of **naik, geram**) *v* be furious
naik gila [najʔ gi.la] (Malay) (comp. of **naik, gila**) *v* be mad
naik lemak [najʔ lə.maʔ] (Malay) (comp. of **naik, lemak**) *v* be up to mischief
naik pangkat [najʔ paŋ.kat] (Malay) (comp. of **naik, pangkat**) *v* be promoted
naik sedap [najʔ sə.dap] (Malay) (comp. of **naik, sedap**) *v* be satisfied
naik seram [najʔ sə.ram] (Malay) (comp. of **naik, seram**) *v* be frightened
nama [na.ma] (Malay) *n* name
nampak [nam.paʔ] (Malay) *v* see
nang [naŋ] var. of **yang**
nangis [na.ŋis] (Malay) *v* cry
nanti [nan.ti] (Malay) *adv* later
napas [na.pas] (Malay) *n* breath
napsu [nap.su] (Malay) **1)** *v* desire **2)** *n* desire
nasik [na.siʔ] (Malay) *n* cooked rice
nganga [ŋa.ŋa] (Malay) *adj* mouth agap
ngéngé [ŋe.ŋe] (Hokkien) *adj* obstinate
ni [ni] (Malay) (contr. of **ini**) *dem* this
nia [ɲa] (Malay) (**punya**) **1)** *v* Poss **2)** REL
nio [njo] (Hokkien) *n* mother-in-law
nua [nwa] (Hokkien) *adj* smashed up
numbor [num.bor] (English) *n* number
nya [ɲa] (Portuguese) (contr. of **Nyonya**) *n* **1)** mother **2)** daughter
nyanyi [ɲa.ɲi] var. of **menyanyi**
Nyonya [ɲo.ɲa] (Portuguese) *n* Peranakan female contr. **nya**

O

onéng.onéng [o.neŋ.o.neŋ] (Malay) *n* great-great grandchild
opan [o.pan] (Hokkien) *n* freckles
orang [o.raŋ] (Malay) *n* **1)** people **2)** person
ormat [or.mat] var. of **hormat**
orna [or.na] (Malay) *n* colour
orpau [or.paw] var. of **horpau**
otak [o.taʔ] (Malay) *n* brain

P

paderi [pa.də.ri] (Portuguese) *n* priest
pagi [pa.gi] (Malay) *n* morning
paiséh [paj.seh] (Hokkien) *adj* embarassed
pait [pajt] (Malay) *adj* bitter
pak [paʔ] (Malay) *n* male person
pak-chindék [paʔ-tʃin.deʔ] (Malay) *n* groom's ceremonial assistant
pakay [pa.ke] (Malay) *v* **1)** wear **2)** use
paksa [paʔ.sa] (Malay) *v* force
paku [pa.ku] (Malay) *n* nail
panair [pa.nɛ] refined var. of **panas**
panas [pa.nas] (var. **panair**) (Malay) *adj* hot (coarse)
panday [pan.de] (Malay) *adj* clever
panggang [paŋ.gaŋ] (Malay) *v* roast
panggay [paŋ.ge] (Malay) *v* call
panggong [paŋ.goŋ] (Malay) *n* stage
pangkat [paŋ.kat] (Malay) *n* rank **pangkat adek beradek**, comp. **naik pangkat**
pangkat adek beradek [paŋ.kat a.deʔ bə.ra.deʔ] (Malay) (**pangkat, adék beradék**) *n* cousins
panjang [pan.dʒaŋ] (Malay) *adj* long
panjat [pan.dʒat] (Malay) *v* climb
pantang [pan.taŋ] (Malay) *adj* superstitious
pantat [pan.tat] (Malay) *n* buttocks comp. **mulot pantat ayam**
parang [pa.raŋ] (Malay) *n* chopper
pasair 1 [pa.sɛ] refined var. of **pasar**
pasair 2 [pa.sɛ] refined var. of **pasal** contr. **sair 1** matter reason
pasal [pa.sal] (var. **pasair 2**) (Malay) *n* **1)** matter (coarse) **2)** reason comp. **apa pasal**
pasang 1 [pa.saŋ] (Malay) *v* use
pasang 2 [pa.saŋ] (Malay) *clf* pair
pasar [pa.sar] (var. **pasair 1**) (Malay) *n* market (coarse)
paser [pa.ser] (Malay) *n* sand
patah [pa.tah] (Malay) *v* snap
pati [pa.ti] (Malay) *n* first cream of coconut
paya [pa.ja] (English) *n* papaya
payong [pa.joŋ] (Malay) *n* umbrella
pé'él [peʔe] (Arabic) *n* good character
pechah [pə.tʃah] (Malay) *v* break
pégang [pe.gaŋ] (Malay) *v* hold
pegi [pə.gi] (Malay) *v* go contr. **pi**
pék [peʔ] (Hokkien) *n* father's elder brother

pék-pék [peʔ-peʔ] (Hokkien) *n* father's eldest brother
pekak [pə.kaʔ] (Malay) *adj* deaf
pekara [pə.ka.ra] (Malay) *n* matter
pekat [pə.kat] (Malay) *adj* thick (describing liquid)
pekék [pə.keʔ] (Malay) *v* shout
pékji [peʔ.dʒi] (Hokkien) (**puay**) *n* eight characters of Chinese horoscope
pelan [pə.lan] (Malay) *adj* slow comp. **pelan pelan**
pelan pelan [pə.lan pə.lan] (Malay) (comp. of **pelan**) *adv* slowly
peléchok [pə.le.tʃoʔ] (Malay) *v* to twist one's foot
penat [pə.nat] (Malay) *adj* tired
péndék [pen.deʔ] (Malay) *adj* short
pengapék [pəŋ.ga.peʔ] (Malay) *n* bride's girl assistant
pengat [pə.ŋat] (Malay) *n* sweet dessert of thick coconut milk with banana chunks
péngsan [peŋ.san] (Malay) *v* faint
penoh [pə.noh] (Malay) *adj* full
perah [pə.rah] (Malay) *v* wring
perama [pə.ra.ma] (Malay) *adj* polite
Peranakan [pə.ra.na.kan] (Malay) *n* Straits-born Chinese
peranjat [pə.ran.dʒat] (Malay) *adj* surprised comp. **terperanjat**
perchaya [pər.tʃa.ja] (Malay) *v* trust
periok [pə.rjoʔ] (Malay) *n* cooking pot
pernah [pər.nah] (Malay) *adv* ever
perompuan [pə.rom.pwan] (Malay) *n* female
perot [pə.rot] (Malay) *n* **1)** belly **2)** stomach
pertama [pər.ta..a] (Malay) *adj* first
pésan [pe.san] (Malay) *v* instruct

petang [pə.taŋ] (Malay) *n* evening
petay [pə.te] (Malay) *n* flat bean
peték [pə.teʔ] (Malay) *v* pluck
pi [pi] (Malay) (contr. of **pegi**) *v* go
piara [pja.ra] (Malay) *v* raise children
pikay [pi.ke] (Arabic) *v* think
piléh [pi.leh] (Malay) *v* choose
pilu [pi.lu] (Malay) *n* sorrow
pinggan [piŋ.gan] Persian *n* plate
pinggang [piŋ.gaŋ] (Malay) *n* waist
pinjak [pin.dʒaʔ] (Malay) *v* step on
pinjam [pin.dʒam] (Malay) *v* lend
pintu [pin.tu] (Malay) *n* door
pisang [pi.saŋ] (Malay) *n* banana
piso [pi.so] (Malay) *n* knife comp. **mata piso**
po [po] (Hokkien) *n* grand-aunt
pokok [po.koʔ] (Malay) *n* tree
popiah [po.pjah] (Hokkien) *n* spring roll with turnip
potong [po.toŋ] (Malay) *v* cut
puay [pwe] (Hokkien) *cardnum* eight **pékji**
pukol [pu.kol] (Malay) *v* **1)** hit **2)** strike
pulak [pu.laʔ] (Malay) *adv* instead
pulang [pu.laŋ] (Malay) *v* return
puloh [pu.loh] (Malay) *cardnum* ten
pulot [pu.lot] (Malay) *n* glutinous rice
pun [pun] (var. **kun 2**) (Malay) *adv* also
punggot [puŋ.got] (Malay) *v* pick up
punya [pu.ɲa] (Malay) **1)** *v* POSS **2)** REL **nia**, contr. **mia 2**
purot [pu.rot] (Malay) *n* stomach
pusing [pu.siŋ] (Malay) *v* **1)** whirl **2)** turn
putéh [pu.teh] (Malay) *adj* white

R

raba [ra.ba] (Malay) *v* touch
radat [ra.dat] (Malay) *adj* greed (vulgar)
raja [ra.dʒa] (Sanskrit) *n* king
rambat [ram.bat] (Malay) *n* hallway
rambot [ram.bot] (Malay) *n* **1)** hair **2)** coarse hair
ranjang [ran.dʒaŋ] (Malay) *n* bed
rasa [ra.sa] (Sanskrit) **1)** *v* feel **2)** *v* think
ratus [ra.tus] (Malay) *cardnum* hundred
rebus [rə.bus] (Malay) *v* boil
rendah [rən.dah] (Malay) *adj* low
renjis [rən.dʒis] (Malay) *v* to water plants
reti [rə.ti] (Malay) *v* understand
ribu [ri.bu] (Malay) *cardnum* thousand

rindu [rin.du] (Malay) *v* miss
ringan [ri.ŋan] (Malay) *adj* slim comp. **mulot ringan**
riyang [ri.jaŋ] (Malay) *adj* lively
ronggéng [roŋ.geŋ] (Malay) *n* faster version of jogét
rosak [ro.saʔ] (Malay) *adj* spoilt
roti [ro.ti] (Sanskrit) *n* bread
ruboh [ru.boh] (Malay) *v* collapse
rumah [ru.mah] (Malay) *n* house
rumpot [rum.pot] (Malay) *n* grass
rupa [ru.pa] (Sanskrit) *n* appearance
rusak [ru.saʔ] (Malay) *adv* day after tomorrow

S

sa [sa] (Hokkien) *cardnum* three
sahja [sa.dʒa] (Malay) *adv* only
sair 1 [sɛ] (Malay) (contr. of **pasair 2**) **1)** *n* matter **2)** *n* reason contr. **apa sair**
sair 2 [sɛ] (Malay) *prt* Confirmative
sakit [sa.kit] (Malay) *adj* sick
salah [sa.lah] (Malay) **1)** *n* mistake **2)** *adj* wrong
salat [sa.lat] (Malay) *n* custard rice
salin [sa.lin] (Malay) *v* transfer
sama [sa.ma] (Sanskrit) **1)** *adj* same **2)** *conn* and **3)** *prep* with
sambal [sam.bal] (Malay) *n* chilli paste made with shrimps or anchovies
sampay [sam.pe] (Malay) **1)** *prep* until **2)** *v* reach
samplang [sam.plaŋ] source uncertain *adj* promiscuous **samséng** [sam.seŋ] (Hokkien) *n* offering of three meats
sana [sa.na] (Malay) *adv* there
sandah [san.dah] (Malay) *v* lean
sangat [sa.ŋat] (Malay) *adv* very
sangka [saŋ.ka] (Malay) *v* expect
sangkék-em [saŋ.keʔ-əm] (Hokkien) (**em**) *n* bride's ceremonial assistant
sapu [sa.pu] (Malay) *v* sweep
satu [sa.tu] (Malay) *cardnum* one contr. **se**
saya (Sanskrit) *pers* 1.Sg (refined)
sayang [sa.jaŋ] (Malay) **1)** *v* care **2)** *n* care **3)** *interj* pity
sayor [sa.jor] (Malay) *n* vegetables
sayup [sa.jup] (Malay) *adj* faint
se [sə] (Malay) (contr. of **satu**) *cardnum* one
sebelair [sə.bə.lɛ] refined var. of **sebelas**
sebelas [sə.bə.las] (var. **sebelair**) (Malay) *cardnum* eleven (coarse)
seberang [sə.bə.raŋ] (Malay) *v* cross
sébok [se.boʔ] (Malay) *adj* busy
sedang [sə.daŋ] (Malay) *adj* medium
sedap [sə.dap] (Malay) *adj* delicious comp. **naik sedap**
sedéh [sə.deh] (Malay) *adj* sad
segan [sə.gan] (Malay) *adj* shy comp. **buang segan**
séhjit [seh.dʒit] (Hokkien) *n* birthday
séisema [sej.sə.ma] (Malay) *n* cold
sejok [sə.dʒoʔ] (Malay) *adj* cold
sekair [sə.kɛ] (Malay) *adv* indeed (refined) (unsystematic variant of sekali)
sekali [sə.ka.li] (Malay) *adv* **1)** very **2)** indeed
sekarang [sə.ka.raŋ] (Malay) *adv* now
sekejab [sə.kə.dʒab] (Malay) *adv* awhile
sekolah [sə.ko.lah] (Dutch) *n* school
selalu [sə.la.lu] (Malay) *adv* always
selamat [sə.la.mat] (Arabic) *adj* safe
seluar [sə.lwar] (var. **suluar**) (Malay) *n* pants (coarse)
semayang [sə.ma.jaŋ] (Malay) *v* pray
semilan [sə.mi.lan] (Malay) *cardnum* nine
semonyet [sə.mo.ɲet] (Malay) *v* hide
sempang [səm.paŋ] (Malay) *n* traffic junction
senang [sə.naŋ] (Malay) **1)** *adj* easy **2)** *adj* free
sendiri [sən.di.ri] (Malay) *n* self
séndok [sen.doʔ] (Malay) *n* spoon
sengbuay [səŋ.bwe] (Hokkien) *n* sour plums
séngét [se.ŋeʔ] (Malay) *adj* crooked
séngkang [seŋ.kaŋ] (Malay) *v* block
senyap [səɲap] (Malay) *adj* silent
senyum [sə.ɲum] (Malay) **1)** *v* smile **2)** *n* smile
sepekah [sə.pə.kah] (Malay) *adj* acceptable
seram [sə.ram] (Malay) *adj* frightening comp. **naik seram**
seronoh [sə.ro.noh] (Malay) *adj* proper
setuju [sə.tu.dʒu] (Malay) *v* agree
shiok [ʃjoʔ] (Punjabi) **1)** *adj* satisified feeling **2)** Exclam satisfaction
si 1 [si] Indonesian *dem* Person
si 2 [si] (Hokkien) *cardnum* four
siang [sjaŋ] (Malay) **1)** *adj* early **2)** *n* day
siap [sjap] (Malay) *v* prepared
siap-siap [sjap-sjap] (Malay) *adv* perpetually
siapa [sja.pa] (Malay) *interrog* who
sién [sjen] (Hokkien) *n* Chinese.immortal
sihat [si.hat] (Malay) *adj* healthy
siki [si.ki] (Hokkien) *n* death anniversary
sikit [si.kit] (Malay) *adv* little
simpan [sim.pan] (Malay) *v* keep something safe
sini [si.ni] (Malay) *adv* here
sinjakala [sin.dʒa.ka.la] (Malay) (**kala**) *n* dusk
sinkék [sin.keʔ] (Hokkien) *n* newcomer from China
siram [si.ram] (Malay) *v* flush with water
siséh [si.seh] Indonesian *n* comb **sisék** [si.seʔ] (Hokkien) *n* four colours cardgame
siut [sjut] (Hokkien) *v* singe
so 1 [so] (Hokkien) *v* burn **so.hio**
so 2 [so] (Hokkien) *n* elder brother's wife

so.hio [sohjo] (Hokkien) (**so 1**) *v* burn incense
sua [swa] (Malay) (contr. of **sudah**) *adv* already
suap [swap] source unclear *v* feed
suay [swe] (Hokkien) *adj* unlucky comp. **buat suay**
sudah [su.dah] (Malay) *adv* already contr. **sua**
suka [su.ka] (Malay) *v* like
suluair [su.lwɛ] refined var. of **suluar**
suluar [su.lwar (coarse)] (var. **suluair**) var. of **seluar**
sumua [su.mwa] (Arabic) *adv* all
sunggay [suŋ.ge] (Malay) *n* river
sunggu [suŋ.gu] (Malay) *adv* really
sup [sup] (English) *n* soup
surat [su.rat] (Malay) *n* letters
susah [su.sah] (Malay) *adj* difficult
susu [su.su] (Malay) *n* milk

T

tachi [ta.tʃi] (Hokkien) *n* elder sister
tadi [ta.di] (Malay) *adv* just
tahan [ta.han] (Malay) *v* withstand
tait [tajt] (Malay) *n* excrement
tak [taʔ] (Malay) *adv* Neg verb comp. **buat tak dengair**
takot [ta.kot] (Malay) *v* afraid
taman [ta.man] (Malay) *n* garden
tambah [tam.bah] (Malay) *v* add on
tampair [tam.pɛ] refined var. of **tampal**
tampal [tam.pal] (var. **tampair**) (Malay) *v* mend (coarse)
tanah [ta.nah] (Malay) *n* **1)** soil **2)** ground **3)** earth
tanam [ta.nam] (Malay) *v* plant
tanda [tan.da] (Malay) *n* sign comp. **tanda mata**
tanda mata [tan.da ma.ta] (Malay) (comp. of **tanda, mata**) *n* heirloom
tandok [tan.doʔ] (Malay) *n* horn
tangan [ta.ŋan] (Malay) *n* hand
tangchék [taŋ.tʃeʔ] (Hokkien) *n* Winter Solstice
tangga [taŋ.ga] (Malay) *n* **1)** ladder **2)** stairs
tangkap [taŋ.kap] (Malay) *v* capture
tanya [tan.ja] (Malay) *v* ask
taoun [ta.own] (Malay) *n* year
tapay [ta.pe] (Malay) *n* fermented rice dessert
tapi [ta.pi] (Sanskrit) *conn* but
tapis [ta.pis] (Malay) *v* filter
tarék [ta.reʔ] (Malay) *v* pull
tarok [ta.roʔ] (Malay) *v* put
tau [taw] (Malay) *v* know
taukay [taw.ke] (Hokkien) *n* boss
tauyu [taw.ju] (Malay) *n* dark soya sauce
tawair [ta.wɛ] refined var. of **tawar**
tawar [ta.war] (var. **tawair**) (Malay) *adj* tasteless (coarse)
téh [teh] (Hokkien) *n* tea
teloh [tə.loh] (Malay) *n* egg
téloh [te.loh] (Malay) *n* accent
témbok [tem.boʔ] (Malay) *n* wall
tempat [təm.pat] (Malay) *n* place
tendang [tən.daŋ] (Malay) *v* kick
tengah [tə.ŋah] (Malay) *adj* middle **tengah hari, tengah jalan tengah hari** [tə.ŋah ha.ri] (Malay) (**tengah, hari**) *n* midday
tengah jalan [tə.ŋah dʒa.lan] (Malay) (**tengah, jalan**) *n* road
tenggelam [təŋ.gə.lam] (Malay) *v* sink
téngok [te.ŋoʔ] (Malay) *v* **1)** look **2)** see
tentu [tən.tu] (Malay) *adj* definite
tepi [tə.pi] (Malay) **1)** *n* side **2)** *adv* side
tepok [tə.poʔ] (Malay) *v* clap
ter- [tər] (Malay) **1)** accidental **2)** uncontrolled movement comp. **terperanjat**
terang [tə.raŋ] (Malay) *adj* **1)** bright **2)** clear
terbang [tər.baŋ] (var. **trebang**) (Malay) *v* fly
terbantot [tər.ban.tot] (Malay) *adj* unripe
terbiat [tər.bjat] (Malay) *n* attitude comp. **buang tebiét**
teriak [tə.rjaʔ] (Malay) *v* call out
terima [tə.ri.ma] (Malay) *v* accept
terlalu [tə.la.lu] (Malay) *adv* too
terok [tə.roʔ] (Malay) *adj* terrible
terompak [tə.rom.paʔ] (Malay) *n* slippers
terperanjat [tər.pə.ran.dʒat] (Malay) (comp. of **ter-, peranjat**) *adj* be shocked
terus [tə.rus] (Malay) *adj* straight
téték [te.teʔ] (Malay) *n* breast
ti-gong [ti-goŋ] (Hokkien) *n* sky-deity (Jade Emperor)
tiap [tjap] (Malay) *adv* every
tiarap [tja.rap] (Malay) *v* fall on one's front
tidor [ti.dor] (Malay) *v* sleep
tiga [ti.ga] (Malay) *cardnum* three

tikam [ti.kam] (Malay) *v* **1)** stab **2)** bet
tim [tim] (Hokkien) *v* double-boil
timbang [tim.baŋ] (Malay) *v* weigh
timbol [tim.bol] (Malay) *v* float
timun [ti.mun] (Malay) *n* cucumber
tinggair [tiŋ.gɛ] refined var. of **tinggal**
tinggal [tiŋ.gal] (var. **tinggair**) (Malay) *v* **1)** live (coarse) **2)** stay (coarse)
tinggi [tiŋ.gi] (Malay) *adj* tall
tio [tjo] (Hokkien) *n* parent's sister's husband
tio-tio [tjo-tjo] (Hokkien) *n* **1)** parents' eldest sister's husband **2)** second father
tiop [tjop] (Malay) *v* blow
tipu [ti.pu] (Malay) *v* cheat
titék [ti.teʔ] source unclear *n* spice paste (for papaya soup)
tok [toʔ] (Hokkien) *n* table
toksa [toʔ.sa] (Malay) *v* do not need
tolak [to.laʔ] (Malay) *v* push
tolong [to.loŋ] (Malay) *v* help
tompang [tom.paŋ] (Malay) *v* hitch (a ride)
tongchit [toŋ.tʃit] (Cantonese) *v* eat all (mahjong term)
tongkat [toŋ.kat] (Malay) *n* walking stick

tork [tɔʔ] (Hokkien) *adj* **1)** poisonous **2)** evil (used in particular for describing stepmothers)
trebang [trə.baŋ] var. of **terbang**
tu [tu] (Malay) (contr. of *itu*) *dem* that
tua [twa] (Hokkien) *adj* **1)** old **2)** big
tuaban [twa.ban] (Hokkien) *adj* handsome
tuakang [twa.kaŋ] (Hokkien) *adj* generous
tuan [twan] (Malay) *n* boss
tuang [twaŋ] (Malay) *v* pour and serve
tujoh [tu.dʒoh] (Malay) *cardnum* seven
tukair [tu.kɛ] refined var. of **tukar**
tukang [tu.kaŋ] (Malay) *n* laborer
tukar [tu.kar] (var. **tukair**) (Malay) *v* change (coarse)
tulang [tu.laŋ] (Malay) *n* bone
tulis [tu.lis] (Malay) *v* write
tumbok [tum.boʔ] (Malay) *v* pound
tumis [tu.mis] (Malay) *v* saute spices
tumpus [tum.pus] (Malay) *adj* blunt **tunggang** [tuŋ.gaŋ] (Malay) *v* ride
tunggu [tuŋ.gu] (Malay) *v* wait
tunjok [tun.dʒoʔ] (Malay) *v* show
turun [tu.run] (Malay) *v* descend
tutop [tu.top] (Malay) *v* close

U

udang [u.daŋ] (Malay) *n* prawn
ujan [u.dʒan] var. of **hujan**
ulam [u.lam] (Malay) *n* mixed herbs rice with shredded anchovies
ular [u.lar] (var. **uluair**) (Malay) *n* snake (coarse)

uluair [u.lɛ] refined var. of **ular**
umor [u.mor] (Arabic) *n* age
untok [un.toʔ] (Malay) *adv* for
utan [u.tan] var. of **hutan**

W

wak [waʔ] (Malay) *n* elderly Malay person
wangi [wa.ŋi] (Malay) *adj* fragrant
wayang [wa.jaŋ] (Malay) *n* play

wilo [wi.lo] (Hokkien) *n* hot pot for lunar new year reunion dinner

Y

ya [ja] (Malay) *interj* yes
yang [jaŋ] (var. **nang**) (Malay) REL
yauguai [jaw.gwaj] (Hokkien) *n* demon
yaukin [jau.kin] (Hokkien) *adj* important
yénchi [jen.tʃi] (Hokkien) *n* rouge
yi 1 [ji] (Hokkien) *n* food in the shape of a ball comp. **kuéh-yi**

yi 2 [ji] (Hokkien) *n* mother's sister **mak-yi**
yi-yi [ji-ji] (Hokkien) *n* mother's eldest sister
yok.hun [joʔ.hun] (Hokkien) *n* Chinese medicinal powder

7.3.2 English- Baba Malay reversal index

1
1.PL kita [ki.ta] *pro*
1.SG (coarse) gua [gwa] *pro*

1.SG (refined) saya [saja] *pro*

2
2.SG lu [lu] *pro*

3
3.SG dia [dja] *pro*

3.PL dia [dja] *pro*; dia-orang [dja-o.raŋ] *pro*

A

ability to make accurate predictions mulot asin [mu.lot a.sin] (comp. of mulot, asin) *n*
ability to speak sweetly mulot manis [mu.lot ma.nis] (comp. of mulot, manis) *n*
accent téloh [te.loh] *n*
accept terima [tə.ri.ma] *v*
acceptable sepekah [sə.pə.kah] *adj*
accidental ter- 1 [tər] (comp. terperanjat)
add on tambah [tam.bah] *v*
afraid takot [ta.kot] *v*
after lepas [lə.pas] *prep*
again balék 4 [ba.leʔ] *adv*; lagik 3 [la.giʔ] *adv*
age umor [u.mor] *n*
agree setuju [sə.tu.dʒu] *v*
alcohol arat [a.rat] *n*
all sumua [su.mwa] *adv*
already sua [swa] (contr. of sudah) *adv*; sudah [su.dah] *adv*
also jugak [dʒu.gaʔ] *adv*; kun 2 [kun] (var. of pun) *adv*; pun [pun] *adv*
always selalu [sə.la.lu] *adv*
amulet hu [hu] *n*
ancestors gong-cho [goŋ-tʃo] (comp. of gong, cho) *n*

anchovy bilis [bi.lis] *n*
and sama 2 [sa.ma] *conn*;
angry marah [ma.rah] *adj*
animal ékor [e.kor] *clf*
anonymous ano [a.no] *adj*
answer jawab [dʒa.wab] *v*
appearance rupa [ru.pa] *n*
argue (coarse) bertengkar [bər.təŋ.kar] *v*
argue (refined) bertengkair [bər.təŋ.kɛ] *v*
ascend naik 3 [najʔ] *v* (comp. naik baik comp. naik darah comp. naik geléték comp. naik geram comp. naik gila comp. naik lemak comp. naik pangkat comp. naik sedap comp. naik seram)
ash abu [a.bu] *n*
aside from buang sebelah [bwaŋ sə.bə.lah] (comp. of buang, sebelah) *adv*
ask tanya [tan.ja] *v*
ask sincerely mintak [min.taʔ] *v*
at dekat 1 [də.kat] (var. kat) *prep*
attitude terbiat [tər.bjat] *n* (comp. buang tebiét)
awhile sekejab [sə.kə.dʒab] *adv*

B

back balék 3 [ba.leʔ] *adv*
backside buntot 2 [bun.tot] *n*
bad breath mulot busok [mu.lot bu.soʔ] (comp. of mulot, busok) *n*
bad sport chaukah [tʃaw.kah] *n*

bad type of person chaukuan [tʃaw.kwan] *n*
bag bég [beʔ] *n*
bald botak [bo.taʔ] *adj*
banana pisang [pi.saŋ] *n*
bang hantok [han.toʔ] *v*

banner chaiki [tʃaj.ki] *n*
bark gonggong [goŋ-goŋ] *v*
basket bakol [ba.kol] *n*
bathe mandi [man.di] *v*
be angry naik darah [najʔ da.rah] (comp. of naik, darah) *v*
be frightened naik seram [najʔ sə.ram] (comp. of naik, seram) *v*
be furious naik geram [najʔ gə.ram] (comp. of naik, geram) *v*
be mad naik gila [najʔ gi.la] (comp. of naik, gila) *v*
be promoted naik pangkat [najʔ paŋ.kat] (comp. of naik, pangkat) *v*
be satisfied naik sedap [najʔ sə.dap] (comp. of naik, sedap) *v*
be shocked terperanjat [tər.pə.ran.dʒat] (comp. of ter-, peranjat) *adj*
be sour-faced buat mungka [bwat muŋ.ka] (comp. of buat, mungka) *v*
be up to mischief naik geléték [najʔ gə.le.teʔ] (comp. of naik, geléték) *v*; naik lemak [najʔ lə.maʔ] (comp. of naik, lemak) *v*
bead manék [ma.neʔ] *n*
bear beruang [bə.rwaŋ] *n*
beautiful chanték [tʃan.teʔ] *adj*
become jadi 2 [dʒa.di] *v*
bed ranjang [ran.dʒaŋ] *n*
before belom 2 [bə.lom] *adv*; dulu 1 [du.lu] *adv*
beginning of lunar month chay [tʃe] *n*
behind belakang [bə.la.kaŋ] *prep*
bell lochéng [lo.tʃeŋ] *n*
belly perot 1 [pə.rot] *n*
beloved jantong ati [dʒan.toŋ a.ti] (comp. of jantong, ati) *n*
bent and curled up kerekot [kə.re.kot] *adj*
bet tikam 2 [ti.kam] *v*
big besar [bə.sar] (var. besair) *adj*; tua 2 [twa] *adj*
big (refined) besair [bə.sɛ] (var. of besar) *adj* (comp. buang ayé besair)
bird burong [bu.roŋ] *n*
birth chutsi [tʃut.si] *n*
birthday séhjit [seh.dʒit] *n*
bite gigit [gi.git] *v*
bitter pait [pajt] *adj*
black hitam [hi.tam] (var. itam) *adj*; itam [i.tam] *adj*

blade of knife mata piso [ma.ta pi.so] (comp. of mata, piso) *n*
blessing of the marital bed ancheng [an.tʃəŋ] *n*
blind buta [bu.ta] *adj*
blink kelék.kelék [kəleʔ.kəleʔ] *v*
block séngkang [seŋ.kaŋ] *v*
blood darah [da.rah] *n* (comp. naik darah)
bloom kuntum [kun.tum] *clf*
blow tiop [tjop] *v*
blunt tumpus [tum.pus] *adj*
body badan [ba.dan] *n*
boil rebus [rə.bus] *v*
boiling menidi [mə.ni.di] *adj*
bone tulang [tu.laŋ] *n*
book buku [bu.ku] *n*
boss taukay [taw.ke] *n*; tuan [twan] *n*
bottle botol [bo.tol] *n*
bowl mangkok [maŋ.koʔ] *n*
box kepok [kə.poʔ] *n*
boy lelaki [lə.la.ki] *n* (contr. laki)
bracelet gelang [gə.laŋ] *n*
brain otak [o.taʔ] *n*
bread roti [ro.ti] *n*
break pechah [pə.tʃah] *v*
breast téték [te.teʔ] *n*
breath napas [na.pas] *n*
bride kemantin [kə.man.tin] *n*
bridegroom's family's host chu-lang [tʃu.laŋ] *n*
bride's assistant for kneeling and general help bukak kun [bu.kaʔ kun] *n* (comp. of kun 2)
bride's ceremonial assistant sangkék-em [saŋ.keʔ-əm] *n* (comp of em)
bride's girl assistant pengapék [pəŋ.ga.peʔ] *n*
bright terang 1 [tə.raŋ] *adj*
bring bawak [ba.waʔ] *v*
brush berus [bə.rus] *v*
bundle bungkus [buŋ.kus] *n*
burn so 1 [so] *v* (comp. sohio)
burn (coarse) bakar [ba.kar] *v*
burn (refined) bakair [ba.kɛ] *v*
burn incense sohio [sohjo] (comp of so 1)
busy sébok [se.boʔ] *adj*
but tapi [ta.pi] *conn*
butter mentéga [mən.te.ga] *n*
butterfly kupu-kupu [ku.pu-ku.pu] *n*
buttocks pantat [pan.tat] *n* (comp. mulot pantat ayam)
buy beli [bə.li] *v*

C

cake kék [keʔ] *n*
call panggay [paŋ.ge] *v*
call out teriak [tə.rjaʔ] *v*
can boléh [bo.leh] *v*
capture tangkap [taŋ.kap] *v*
car chia [tʃja] *n*; keréta [kə.re.ta] *n*
care sayang 1 [sa.jaŋ] *v*; sayang 2 [sa.jaŋ] *n*
carry angkat 4 [aŋ.kat] *v*
carry baby logong [lo.goŋ] *v*
cat kuching [ku.tʃiŋ] *n* (comp. kuching belanda comp. mata kuching)
cause kasi 3 [ka.si]
cause embarrassment buat malu [bwat ma.lu] (comp. of buat, malu) *v*
cause misfortune buat suay [bwat swe] (comp. of buat, suay) *v* **caustic mouth** mulot jahat [mu.lot dʒa.hat] (comp. of mulot, jahat) *n*
cave batu 3 [ba.tu] *n*
chair kerosi [kə.ro.si] *n*
change (coarse) tukar [tu.kar] *v*
change (refined) tukair [tu.kɛ] *v*
change for good naik baik [najʔ bajʔ] (comp. of naik, baik) *v*
character budi [bu.di] *n*
chase (coarse) kejar [kə.dʒar] *v*
chase (refined) kejair [kə.dʒɛ] *v*
chase away halo [ha.lo] *v*
cheat tipu [ti.pu] *v*
chicken ayam [a.jam] *n* (comp. mulot pantat ayam)
child anak [a.naʔ] *n*; budak [bu.daʔ] *n*
chilli paste made with shrimps or anchovies sambal [sam.bal] *n*
Chinese China [tʃi.na] *adj*
Chinese medicinal powder yok.hun [joʔ.hun] *n*
Chinese.immortal sién [sjen] *n*
choose piléh [pi.leh] *v*
chopper parang [pa.raŋ] *n*
church gerja [gər.dʒa] (var. greja) *n*; greja [grə.dʒa] *n*
clap tepok [tə.poʔ] *v*
clean bersi [bər.si] (var. bresi) *v*; bersi [bər.si] *n*
clear terang 2 [tə.raŋ] *adj*
clever panday [pan.de] *adj* ever
climb naik 1 [najʔ] *v* (comp. naik baik comp. naik darah comp. naik geléték comp. naik geram comp. naik gila comp. naik lemak comp. naik pangkat comp. naik sedap comp. naik seram); panjat [pan.dʒat] *v*

clogs chakiak [tʃa.kjaʔ] *n*
close tutop [tu.top] *v*
close to one another chin [tʃin] *adj*
cloth kain [kajn] *n*
clothes baju [ba.dʒu] *n*
cloud awan [a.wan] *n*
coarse (coarse) kasar [ka.sar] *adj*
coarse (refined) kasair [ka.sɛ] *adj*
coarse hair rambot 2 [ram.bot] *n*
cockeyed mata juling [ma.ta dʒu.liŋ] (comp. of mata, juling) *n*
cockroach kachua [ka.tʃwa] *n*
coconut cookie bangkit [baŋ.kit] *n*
coconut jam kaya 2 [ka.ja] *n*
coffee kopi [ko.pi] *n*
cold séisema [sej.sə.ma] *n*; sejok [sə.dʒoʔ] *adj*
collapse ruboh [ru.boh] *v*
colour orna [or.na] *n*
comb siséh [si.seh] *n*
come datang [da.taŋ] *v*
come let us mari [ma.ri] *v*
Confirmative sair 2 [sɛ] *prt*
convey by speaking (as opposed to writing) buang mulot [bwaŋ mu.lot] (comp. of buang, mulot) *v*
cook masak 1 [ma.saʔ] *v*
cooked food lauk [lawʔ] *n*
cooked in coconut milk lemak [lə.maʔ] *adj*
cooked rice nasik [na.siʔ]
cooking pot periok [pə.rjoʔ] *n*
Cop ada 5 [a.da] (var. a) *v*
correct betol 1 [bə.tol] *adj*
cousins pangkat adek beradek [paŋ.kat a.deʔ bə.ra.deʔ] (comp. of pangkat, adék beradék) *n*
cow lembu [ləm.bu] *n* (comp. mata lembu)
crash (coarse) langgar [laŋ.gar] *v*
crash (refined) langgair [laŋ.gɛ] *v*
crawl belangkat [bə.laŋ.kat] *v*
crooked séngét [se.ŋeʔ] *adj*
cross seberang [sə.bə.raŋ] *v*
crowded beramay [bə.ra.me] *adj*
cruel ati busok [a.ti bu.soʔ] (comp. of ati, busok) *adj*
crumpled kudut [ku.dut] *adj*
cry menangis [mə.na.ŋis] *v*; nangis [na.ŋis] *v*
cucumber timun [ti.mun] *n*
cunning lihai [li.haj] *adj*

cup changkay [tʃaŋ.ke] *n*
curse mincharok [min.tʃa.roʔ] *v*
custard rice salat [sa.lat] *n*
cut potong [po.toŋ] *v*

cylindrical measure of one gallon of rice gantang [gan.taŋ] *clf*
cylindrincal measure of quarter gallon of rice chupak [tʃu.paʔ] *clf*

D

daring gaga [ga.ga] *adj*
dark gelap [gə.lap] *adj* (comp. mata gelap)
dark soya sauce tauyu [taw.ju] *n*
daughter nya 2 [ɲa] (contr. of Nyonya) *n*
day ari [a.ri] (var. of hari) *n* (comp. mata ari); hari [ha.ri] (var. ari) *n* (comp. tengah hari); siang 2 [sjaŋ] *n*
day after tomorrow rusak [ru.saʔ] *adv*
dead mati 2 [ma.ti] *adj*
deaf pekak [pə.kaʔ] *adj*
death anniverary siki [si.ki] *n*
deceitful mouth mulot pantat ayam [mu.lot pan.tat a.jam] (comp. of mulot, pantat, ayam) *n*
decorative altar stand chanab [tʃa.nab] *n*
defecate bérak [be.raʔ] *v*; buang ayé besair [bwaŋ a.je bə.sɛ] (comp. of buang, ayé, besair) *v*
definite tentu [tən.tu] *adj*
delicious sedap [sə.dap] *adj* (comp. naik sedap)
demon yauguai [jaw.gwaj] *n*
descend turun [tu.run] *v*
desire napsu 1 [nap.su] *v*; napsu 2 [nap.su] *n*
detective mata gelap [ma.ta gə.lap] (comp. of mata, gelap) *n*
develop an illness kamtiok [kam.tjoʔ] *v*
diamond belién [bə.ljen] *n*
diamond chip intan [in.tan] *n*
die mati 1 [ma.ti] *v*
difficult susah [su.sah] *adj*

dip in dye chelop [tʃə.lop] *v*
dirty kotor [ko.tor] *adj*
distended stomach bunchit [bun.tʃit] *n*
disturb kacho [ka.tʃo] *v*
divination stick chiam [tʃjam] *n*
do bikin 2 [bi.kin] *v*; buat 1 [bwat] *v* (comp. buat bodoh comp. buat mahal comp. buat malu comp. buat mungka comp. buat suay comp. buat tak dengair)
do not jangan [dʒa.ŋan] *adv*
do not need toksa [toʔ.sa] *v*
dog anjing [an.dʒiŋ] *n*
door pintu [pin.tu] *n*
double-boil tim [tim] *v*
drain longkang [loŋ.kaŋ] *n*
draw chonténg [tʃon.teŋ] *v*
dream mimpi [mim.pi] *v*
dried fruit gugol [gu.gol] *n*
drink minum [mi.num] *v*
drip berléiléi [bər.lej.lej] *v*
drop jatoh 2 [dʒa.toh] *v*
dry kering 2 [kə.riŋ] *adj* (comp. mulot kering)
dry in the sun jumoh [dʒu.moh] *v*
duck iték [i.teʔ] *n*
durian flesh uluair 2 [u.lɛ] (var. of ular) *clf*
dusk sinjakala [sin.dʒa.ka.la] (comp. of kala) *n*
Dutch belanda [bə.lan.da] (comp. kuching belanda)

E

ear kuping [ku.piŋ] *n*
early siang 1 [sjaŋ] *adj*
earrings anting-anting [an.tiŋ-an.tiŋ] *n*
earth tanah 3 [ta.nah] *n*
easy senang 1 [sə.naŋ] *adj*
eat makan 1 [ma.kan] *v*
eat (vulgar) cherkek [tʃər.keʔ] *v*
eat all (mahjong term) tongchit [toŋ.tʃit] *v*
egg teloh [tə.loh] *n*
eight lapan [la.pan] *cardnum*; puay [pwe] *cardnum* (comp. pékji)

eight characters of Chinese horoscope pékji [peʔ.dʒi] (comp. of puay) *n*
elder brother hia [hja] *n*
elder brother (non-familial) ko 2 [ko] *n*
elder brother's wife so 2 [so] *n*
elder sister tachi [ta.tʃi] *n*
elder sister's husband chau [tʃaw] *n*
elderly Malay person wak [waʔ] *n*
eleven (coarse) sebelas [sə.bə.las] *cardnum*
eleven (refined) sebelair [sə.bə.lɛ] *cardnum*

embarassed malu [ma.lu] *adj* (comp. buat malu); paiséh [paj.seh] *adj*
EMP lah [lah] *prt*; lor [lor] *prt*
enough chukop [tʃu.kop] *adv*
enter masok 1 [ma.soʔ] *v*
enthusiasm gerang [gə.raŋ] *n*
estimate agak [a.gaʔ] *v* (comp. agak agak)
evening petang [pə.taŋ] *n*
ever pernah [pər.nah] *adv*
every tiap [tjap] *adv*
evil jahat [dʒa.hat] *adj* (comp. mulot jahat)
evil (used in particular for describing stepmothers) tork 2 [tɔʔ] *adj*
EXCLAM annoyance aiya [aj.ja]
EXCLAM cry to a dead spirit kus semangat [kus sə.ma.ŋat]
EXCLAM cursed one chilaka [tʃi.la.ka]
EXCLAM dead mampus [mam.pus]
EXCLAM dismay alamak [a.la.maʔ]
EXCLAM irritation aiyo [aj.jo]
EXCLAM jibe éh [eh]
EXCLAM regret ala [a.la]
EXCLAM satisfaction shiok 2 [ʃjoʔ]
EXCLAM surprise amboi [am.boj]; ayi [a.ji]
excrement tait [tajt] *n*
exhausted letay [lə.te] *adj*
EXIST ada 3 [a.da] (var. a) *v*
exorcise buang buang [bwaŋ bwaŋ] (comp. of buang) *v*
expand huat 1 [hwat] *v*
expect sangka [saŋ.ka] *v*
expensive mahal [ma.hal] *adj* (comp. buat mahal)
eye mata [ma.ta] *n* (comp. bijik mata comp. buang mata comp. mata ari mata ayé mata beliak comp. mata gelap comp. mata ikan comp. mata juling comp. mata kuching comp. mata lembu comp. mata piso comp. tanda mata)

F

face mungka [muŋ.ka] *n* (comp. buat mungka)
faint péngsan [peŋ.san] *v*; sayup [sa.jup] *adj*
fall jatoh 1 [dʒa.toh] *v*
fall backwards lentang [lən.taŋ] *v*
fall on one's front tiarap [tja.rap] *v*
family chepuat [tʃə.pwat] *n*
fan kipas [ki.pas] *n*
far ja.ou [dʒa.ow] *adj*
faster version of jogét ronggéng [roŋ.geŋ] *n*
fat gemok [gə.moʔ] *adj*
father baba [ba.ba] (var. of bapak) *n*; bapak [ba.paʔ] *n* (comp. mak bapak)
father-in-law kua 2 [kwa] *n*
father-in-law (indirect address) chingkay 2 [tʃiŋ.ke] *n*
father's elder brother pék [peʔ] *n*
father's elder brother's wife em 1 [əm] *n* (comp. sangkék-em)
eldest brother pék-pék [peʔ-peʔ]
father's eldest sister mak-ko [maʔ-ko] (comp. of mak, ko 1) *n*
father's sister ko 1 [ko] *n* (comp. mak-ko)
father's younger brother chék [tʃeʔ] *n*
father's younger brother's wife chim [tʃim] *n*
favourite child bijik mata [bi.dʒiʔ ma.ta] (comp. of bijik, mata) *n*
feather bulu 1 [bu.lu] *n*

feed suap [swap] *v*
feel rasa 1 [ra.sa] *v*
feign ignorance buat bodoh [bwat bo.doh] (comp. of buat, bodoh) *v*
female perompuan [pə.rom.pwan] *n*
female mourner hauli [haw.li] *n*
fermented rice dessert tapay [ta.pe] *n*
fierce bengis 1 [bə.nis] *adj*; garang [ga.raŋ] *adj*
filter tapis [ta.pis] *v*
find charék [tʃa.reʔ] *v*
fine hair bulu 2 [bu.lu] *n*
finger jari [dʒa.ri] *n*
fingernail kuku [ku.ku] *n*
finish abi [a.bi] (var. of habis) *conn*; abis [a.bis] (var. of habis) *v*; habis [ha.bis] 1 *v*; habis 2 [ha.bis] *adv*
fire api [a.pi] *n*
first dulu 3 [du.lu] *adv*; pertama [pər.ta.ma] *adj*
first cream of coconut pati [pa.ti] *n*
fish ikan [i.kan] *n* comp. mata ikan
fishball huyi [hu.ji] *n*
five gor [gɔ] *cardnum* id. ati it gor it chap; lima [li.ma] *cardnum*
flat bean petay [pə.te] *n*
flesh isi [i.si] *n*
float timbol [tim.bol] *v*
floor lantay [lan.te] *n*

flower bunga [bu.ŋa] *n*
fluent lanchang [lan.tʃaŋ] *adj*
flush with water siram [si.ram] *v*
fly terbang [tər.baŋ] (var. trebang) *v*; trebang [trə.baŋ] *v*
fold lipat [li.pat] *v*
follow ikot [i.kot] *v*
food makan 2 [ma.kan] *n*
food in the shape of a ball yi 1 [ji] *n* (comp. kuéh-yi)
force paksa [paʔ.sa] *v*
for untok [un.toʔ] *adv*
forehead dahi [da.hi] (var. dai) *n*; dai [daj] *n*
forget lupa [lu.pa] *v*
forgive ampun 1 [am.pun] *v*
forgiveness ampun 2 [am.pun] *n*
four empat [əm.pat] *cardnum*; si 2 [si] *cardnum*
four colours cardgame sisék [si.seʔ] *n*

fragrant wangi [wa.ŋi] *adj*
freckles opan [o.pan] *n*
free senang 2 [sə.naŋ] *adj*
fried egg with yolk intact mata lembu [ma.ta ləm.bu] (comp. of mata, lembu) *n*
friend kaki 2 [ka.ki] *n*; kawan [ka.wan] *n*
frightening seram [sə.ram]
frog kodok [ko.doʔ] *n*
from dari [da.ri] *prep*
front depan [də.pan] *prep*
fruit buah [bwah] *n*
fry goréng [go.reŋ] *v*
full penoh [pə.noh] *adj*
full from eating kenyang [kə.ɲaŋ] *adj*
fumble kalang-kabot [ka.laŋ-ka.bot] *v*
furious geram [gə.ram] *adj* (comp. naik geram)
fussy kéwat [ke.wat] *adj*

G

gamble judi [dʒu.di] *v*
garden kebun [kə.bun] *n*; taman [ta.man] *n*
generous tuakang [twa.kaŋ] *adj*
get dapat 1 [da.pat] *v*
giddy mabok [ma.boʔ] *adj*
give kasi 1 [ka.si] *v*
glare beliak [bə.ljaʔ] *v* (comp. mata beliak)
glutinous rice pulot [pu.lot] *n*
glutinous rice balls kuéh-yi [kweh-ji] (comp. of kuéh, yi 1) *n*
go pegi [pə.gi] *v* contr. pi; pi [pi] *v*
go out (coarse) keluar [kə.lwar] (var. kuluar) (comp. diluar); kuluar [ku.lwar] *v*
go out (refined) kuluair [ku.lwɛ] *v*
goat kambing 1 [kam.biŋ] *n*
gold (coarse) mas [mas] *n*
gold (refined) mair [mɛ] *n*
good bagus [ba.gus] *interj*; baik [bajʔ] *adj* (comp. ati baik, comp. naik baik); ho [ho] *adj* (comp. homia)
good character pé'él [peʔe] *n*
good life homia [ho.mja] *interj* (comp. of ho, mia)
grand-aunt po [po] *n*
grandchild chuchu [tʃu.tʃu] *n*
grandfather gong 2 [goŋ] (comp. gong-cho)
grandfather's younger brother chék-gong [tʃeʔ-goŋ] *n*

grandmother mamak [ma.maʔ] *n*
grandparent gong 1 [goŋ] *n* comp. gong-cho
grass rumpot [rum.pot] *n*
gravy kua 1 [kwa] *n*
grease minyak 1 [mi.ɲak] *n*
great-grandaunt cho-po [tʃo-po] *n*
great-grandchild chichi [tʃi.tʃi] *n*
great-grandfather cho-gong [tʃo-goŋ] *n*
great-grandmother cho 2 [tʃo] *n* (comp. gong-cho, mak-cho); cho-cho [tʃo-tʃo] *n*; mak-cho [maʔ-tʃo] (comp. of mak, cho) *n*
great-grandparent cho 1 [tʃo] *n* (comp. gong-cho mak-cho)
great-great grandchild onéng.onéng [o.neŋ.o.neŋ] *n*
greed (vulgar) radat [ra.dat] *adj*
green hijo [hi.dʒo] (var. ijo) *adj*; ijo [i.dʒo] *adj*
green bean cookies koya [ko.ja] *n*
groom kiasai 2 [kjasaj] *n*
groom's ceremonial assistant pak-chindék [paʔ-tʃin.deʔ] *n*
groom's boy assistant kuya [ku.ja] *n*
ground tanah 2 [ta.nah] *n*
guard jaga 1 [dʒa.ga] *v*
guess gasak [ga.saʔ] *v*
guest langkék [laŋ.keʔ] *n*

H

HAB ada 6 [a.da] (var. a) *v*
hair rambot 1 [ram.bot] *n*
half-cooked (coarse) embar-embar [əmbar-əmbar] *adj*
half-cooked (refined) embair-embair [əmbɛ-əmbɛ] *adj*
hallway rambat [ram.bat] *n*
hand tangan [ta.ŋan] *n*
handkerchief binpo [bin.po] *n*
handsome tuaban [twa.ban] *adj*
hang gantong [gan.toŋ] *v*
happen jadi 1 [dʒa.di] *v*
happy huahi [hwa.hi] *adj*
hard (coarse) keras [kəras] *adj*
hard (refined) kerair [kərɛ] *adj*
hat kopiah [ko.pjah] *n*
have a [a] (var. of ada) *v*; ada 1 [a.da] (var. a) *v*
hay kering 1 [kə.riŋ] *n* comp. mulot kering
head kepala [kə.pa.la] *n*
healthy sihat [si.hat] *adj*
heart ati 1 [a.ti] (var. of hati) *n* (comp. ati baik, comp. ati busok, comp. jantong ati (id. ati it gor it chap); hati 1 [ha.ti] *n*; jantong [dʒan.toŋ] *n* (comp. jantong ati)
heavy berat [bə.rat] *adj* (comp. mulot berat); lebat [lə.bat] *adj*
heirloom tanda mata [tan.da ma.ta] (comp. of tanda, mata) *n*
help tolong [to.loŋ] *v*

here sini [si.ni] *adv*
here you go na [na] *interj*
hide semonyet [sə.mo.ɲet] *v*
hill bukit [bu.kit] *n*
hit pukol 1 [pu.kol] *v*
hitch (a ride) tompang [tom.paŋ] *v*
hold angkat 2 [aŋ.kat] *v*; pégang [pe.gaŋ] *v*
hole lobang [lo.baŋ] *n*
honorific prefix for familial relations eng- [əŋ]
hope arap [a.rap] (var. of harap); harap [ha.rap] *v*
horn tandok [tan.doʔ] *n*
horse kuda [ku.da] *n*
hot (coarse) panas [pa.nas] *adj*
hot (refined) panair [pa.nɛ] *adj* hot
hot pot for lunar new year reunion dinner wilo [wi.lo] *n*
hour jam 2 [dʒam] *n*
house rumah [ru.mah] *n*
how (coarse) amcham [am.tʃam] (var. of apa cham [a.pa.tʃam]; apa macham [a.pa ma.tʃam], comp. of apa, macham) *interrog*
how (refined) apa pasair [a.pa pa.sɛ] *interrog*
how many berapa 1 [bə.ra.pa] *interrog*
howl menyalap [mə.ɲa.lap] *v*
hundred ratus [ra.tus] *cardnum*
hungry (coarse) lapar [la.par] *adj*
hungry (refined) lapair [la.pɛ] *adj*
husband laki [la.ki] (contr. of lelaki) *n*

I

if kalo [ka.lo] (var. of kalu) *conn*; kalu [ka.lu] *conn*
ill-treat koktok [kɔʔ.tɔʔ] *v*
important yaukin [jau.kin] *adj*
inability to express oneself mulot berat [mu.lot bə.rat] (comp. of mulot, berat) *n*
inability to keep a secret mulot bocho [mu.lot bo.tʃo] (comp. of mulot, bocho) *n*
inability to say more mulot kering [mu.lot kə.riŋ] (comp. of mulot, kering) *n*
indeed mémang [me.maŋ] *adv*; sekali 2 [sə.ka.li] *adv*

indeed (refined) (unsystematic variant of sekali) sekair [sə.kɛ] *adv*
inside dalam [da.lam] *prep*
instead pulak [pu.laʔ] *adv* instead instead
instruct pésan [pe.san] *v* instruct instruct
intercalary lun [lun] *adj* intercalary intercalary
intercalary month lun-guék [lun gweʔ] *n* (comp. of lun, guék)
iron besi [bə.si] *n* iron iron
itchy (coarse) gatal [ga.tal] *adj* itchy
itchy (refined) gatair [ga.tɛ] *adj* (comp. mulot gatair)

J

jelly chaiyen [tʃaj.jen] *n*
joke kelaka [kə.la.ka] *v*
jump lompat [lom.pat] *v*

jungle hutan [hu.tan] (var. utan) *n*; utan [u.tan] *n*
just baru 2 [ba.ru] *adv*; tadi [ta.di] *adv*

K

keep an eye on someone or something buang mata [bwaŋ ma.ta] (comp. of buang, mata) *v*
keep something safe simpan [sim.pan] *v*
key konchi [kon.tʃi] *n*
kick tendang [tən.daŋ] *v*
kill bunoh [bu.noh] *v*
kind ati baik [a.ti bajʔ] (comp. of ati, baik) *adj*

king raja [ra.dʒa] *n*
kitchen dapor [da.pɔ] *n*
kneel gui [gwi] *v*
knife piso [pi.so] *n* (comp. mata piso)
knock ketok [kə.toʔ] *v*
know tau [taw] *v*
know a person (coarse) kenal [kə.nal] *v*
know a person (refined) kenair [kə.nɛ] *v*

L

laborer tukang [tu.kaŋ] *n*
ladder tangga 1 [taŋ.ga] *n*
lamp lampu [lam.pu] *n*
language bahasa [ba.ha.sa] *n*
late lambat [lam.bat] *adj*
later nanti [nan.ti] *adv*
laugh ketawa [kə.ta.wa] *v*
lazy (coarse) malas [ma.las] *adj*
lazy (refined) malair [ma.lɛ] *adj*
leaky bocho [bo.tʃo] *adj* (comp. mulot bocho)
lean sandah [san.dah] *v*
learn (coarse) belajar [bə.la.dʒar] *v*
learn (refined) belajair [bə.la.dʒɛ] *v*
leaves daoun [da.own] *n*
leg kaki 1 [ka.ki] *n*
lemon lémo [le.mo] *n*
lend pinjam [pin.dʒam] *v*
less kurang [ku.raŋ] *adv*
let kasi 2 [ka.si] *v*
letters surat [su.rat] *n*
lie bohong [bo.hoŋ] *n*
lie down baring [ba.riŋ] *v*
life mia 1 [mja] *n*
lift angkat 1 [aŋ.kat] *v*
like suka [su.ka] *v*
like cham 2 [tʃam] (contr. of macham) *adv*; macham 1 [ma.tʃam] *adv* (comp. apa cham, comp. apa macham)

like that macham 3 [ma.tʃam] *adv* (comp. apa cham comp. apa macham)
like that begi [bə.gi] (contr. of begitu), gitu [gi.tu] (contr. of begitu) *adv*; begitu [bə.gi.tu] *adv*,
listen (coarse) dengar [də.ŋar] *v*
listen (refined) dengair [dəŋ.ɛ] *v* (comp. buat tak dengair)
little sikit [si.kit] *adv*
live (coarse) tinggal 1 [tiŋ.gal] *v*
live (refined) tinggair 1 [tiŋ.gɛ] *v*
lively riyang [ri.jaŋ] *adj*
liver ati 2 [a.ti] (var. of hati) *n* (comp. ati baik, comp. ati busok, id. ati it gor it chap, comp. jantong ati); hati 2 [ha.ti] *n*
long panjang [pan.dʒaŋ] *adj*
long ago dulu 2 [du.lu] *adv*
long and thin batang [ba.taŋ] *clf*
long time lama [la.ma] *adj*
longan fruit mata kuching [ma.ta ku.tʃiŋ] (comp. of mata, kuching) *n*
long-jawed chobék [tʃo.beʔ] *adj*
lose hilang [hi.laŋ]; ilang [i.laŋ] *v*
lose (opposed to win) kalah [ka.lah] *v*
low rendah [rən.dah] *adj*
lunar month guék [gweʔ] *n*

M

mad gila [gi.la] *adj* (comp. naik gila)
make bikin 1 [bi.kin] *v*; buat 2 [bwat] *v* (comp. buat bodoh, comp. buat mahal, comp. buat malu, comp. buat mungka, comp. buat suay, comp. buat tak dengair)
male jantan [dʒan.tan] *n*
male mourner haulam [haw.lam] *n*
male person pak [paʔ] *n*
many manyak [ma.ɲaʔ] *adv*
market (coarse) pasar [pa.sar] *n*
market (refined) pasair 1 [pa.sɛ] *n*
marry kawin [ka.win] *v*
match of love jodoh [dʒo.doh] *n*
matchmaker muilang [mwi.laŋ] *n*
matter pekara [pə.ka.ra] *n*; sair 1 [sɛ] (contr. of pasair 2) *n* (comp. apa sair)
matter (coarse) pasal 1 [pa.sal] *n* (comp. apa pasal)
matter (refined) pasair 2 [pa.sɛ] *n* (contr. sair 1)
meat dagin [da.gin] *n*
medium sedang [sə.daŋ] *adj*
meet jumpa [dʒum.pa] *v*
meet ill spiritual forces huantiok [hwan.tjoʔ] *v*
melody dondang [don.daŋ] *n*
mend (coarse) tampal [tam.pal] *v*
middle tengah [tə.ŋah] *adv* (comp tengah jalan)
milk susu [su.su] *n*
mince chinchang [tʃin.tʃaŋ] *v*
minute minit [mi.nit] *n*
miserly kiamsiap [kjam.sjap] *adj*
miss rindu [rin.du] *v*
mistake salah 1 [sa.lah] *n*

mix champor [tʃam.por] *v*; gaou [ga.ow] *v*
mixed herbs rice with shredded anchovies ulam [u.lam] *n*
money dit [dit] (var. of duit) *n*; duit [dwit] *n*
monk huésio [hwe.sjo] *n*
month bulan 2 [bu.lan] *n*
moon bulan 1 [bu.lan] *n*
more lagik 1 [la.giʔ] *adv*; lebéh [lə.beh] *adv*
morning pagi [pa.gi] *n*
mother mak [maʔ] *n* (comp. mak bapak, mak-cho, mak-ko, mak-yi); nya 1 [ɲa] (contr. of Nyonya) *n*
mother-in-law nio [njo] *n*
mother-in-law (indirect address) chay-em [tʃe.əm] *n*
mother's brother ku 2 [ku] *n* (comp. ku-ku)
mother's brother's wife kim [kim] *n*
mother's eldest brother ku-ku [ku-ku] (comp. of ku 2) *n*
mother's eldest sister yi-yi [ji-ji] *n*
mother's sister yi 2 [ji] *n* (comp. mak-yi)
mountain gunong [gu.noŋ] *n*
mouth mulot [mu.lot] *n* (comp. buang mulot, comp. mulot asin, comp. mulot béngok, comp. mulot berat, comp. mulot bocho, comp. mulot busok, comp. mulot dunya, comp. mulot gatair, comp. mulot jahat, comp. mulot kering, comp. mulot manis, comp. mulot pantat ayam, comp. mulot ringan)
mouth agape nganga [ŋa.ŋa] *adj*
move bergerak [bər.gə.raʔ] *v*
movement (that is uncontrolled) ter- 2 [tər] (comp. terperanjat)
must mesti [məs.ti] *v*

N

nail paku [pa.ku] *n*
name nama [na.ma] *n*
near dekat 2 [də.kat] (var. kat) *prep*
neck léihéi [lej.hej] *n*
Neg kan [kan] (contr of bukan 1) *interj*; tak [taʔ] *adv* (comp. buat tak dengair)
Neg (noun) bukan 2 [bu.kan]
nervous ati it gor it chap [a.ti it gɔ it tʃap] (id. of ati, it, gor, chap) *adj*
new baru 1 [ba.ru] *adj*
newcomer from China sinkék [sin.keʔ] *n*

news (coarse) kabar [ka.bar] *n*
news (refined) kabair [ka.bɛ] *n*
night malam [ma.lam] *n*
night (when referring to lunar dates) méh [meh] *n*
nine gau [gaw] *cardnum*; semilan [sə.mi.lan] *cardnum*
no bukan 1 [bu.kan] (var. kan) *interj*
noisy bising [bi.siŋ] *adj*
Nom -an [-an]
nose hidong [hi.doŋ] (var. idong) *n*; idong [i.doŋ] *n*

not fussy chinchai [tʃin.tʃaj] *adj*
not yet belom 1 [bə.lom] *adv*
now sekarang [sə.ka.raŋ] *adv*

O

observe cham 1 [tʃam] *v*
obstinate ngéngé [ŋe.ŋe] *adj*
odd-numbered ganjil [gan.jil] *adj*
offering of three meats samséng [sam.seŋ] *n*
oil minyak 2 [mi.ɲak] *n*
old tua 1 [twa] *adj*
old aunty em 2 [əm] *n* (comp. sangkék-em)
older Peranakan woman bibik [bi.biʔ] *n*
omelette (coarse) dadar [da.dar] *n*
omelette (refined) dadair [da.dɛ] *n*
one it [it] *cardnum* (id. ati it gor it chap); satu [sa.tu] *cardnum* (contr. se [sə])
onion bawang [ba.waŋ] *n*
only sahja [sa.dʒa] *adv*

number numbor [num.bor] *n*
nunnery that serves vegetarian food chaiteng [tʃaj.təŋ] *n*

onomatopoeia loud noises gedebang-gedebong [gə.də.baŋ-gə.də.boŋ]
onomatopoia thudding of the heart gedebak-gedebuk [gə.də.baʔ-gə.də.buʔ]
open bukak [bu.kaʔ] *v*
or ka [ka] *conn*
original mula [mu.la] *adj*
originally mula mula [mu.la mu.la] *adv*
other lain [lajn] *adv*
outside diluar [di.lwar] (var. duluar) (comp. of di, keluar) *prep*; duluar [du.lwar] (var. of diluar) *prep*
overripe magam [ma.gam] *adj*

P

pail baldi [bal.di] *n*
pair pasang 2 [pa.saŋ] *clf*
palm blossom mayang [ma.jaŋ] *n*
Pangium.edule (black fruit with hard shell) keluak [kə.lwaʔ] *n*
pants (coarse) suluar [su.lwar] (var. seluair) *n*
pants (coarse) seluar [sə.lwar] *n*
pants (refined) suluair [su.lwɛ] *n*
papaya paya [pa.ja] *n*
paper (coarse) kertas [kər.tas] *n*
paper (refined) kertair [kər.tɛ] *n*
parent-in-law chingkay 1 [tʃiŋ.ke] *n*
parents mak bapak [maʔ ba.paʔ] (comp. of mak, bapak) *n*
parents' eldest sister's husband tio-tio 1 [tjo-tjo] *n*
parent's sister's husband tio [tjo] *n*
park letak [lə.taʔ] *v*
pass lalu [la.lu] *v*
PASS kena 1 [kə.na] *v*; kasi 4 [ka.si] *v*
paternal cousins kopiau [ko.pjaw] *n*
pay (coarse) bayar [ba.jar] *v*
pay (refined) bayair [ba.jɛ] *v*;
peel kopék [ko.peʔ] *v*; kupas [ku.pas] *v*
people orang 1 [o.raŋ] *n*
Peranakan female Nyonya [ɲo.ɲa] *n* (contr. nya)
Peranakan male Baba 1 [ba.ba] *n* (contr. ba)

Peranakan card game cherki [tʃər.ki] *n*
perform main 2 [majn] *v*
perpetually siap-siap [sjap-sjap] *adv*
person orang 2 [o.raŋ] *n*
PERSON si 1[si] *dem*
PFV ada 4 [a.da] (var. a) *v*
pick up angkat 3 [aŋ.kat] *v*; punggot [puŋ.got] *v*
picture (coarse) gambar [gam.bar] *n*
picture (refined) gambair [gam.bɛ] *n*
piece kepéng [kə.peŋ] *clf*
piece of fabric or paper lay [le] (var. of helay) *clf*
pig babi [ba.bi] *n*
pinch kepék [kə.peʔ] *v*
pity sayang 3 [sa.jaŋ] *interj*
place tempat [təm.pat] *n*
plant tanam [ta.nam] *v*
plate pinggan [piŋ.gan] *n*
play main 1 [majn] *v*; wayang [wa.jaŋ] *n*
play hard to get buat mahal [bwat ma.hal] (comp. of buat, mahal) *v*
pluck peték [pə.teʔ] *v*
pocket kochék [ko.tʃeʔ] *n*
poisonous tork 1 [tɔʔ] *adj*
polite perama [pə.ra.ma] *adj*
polite character mulot ringan [mu.lot ri.ŋan] (comp. of mulot, ringan) *n*

pond laut 2 [lawt] *n*
poor miskin [mis.kin] *adj*
porridge bubor [bu.bɔ] *n*
Poss mia 2 [mja] (contr. of punya) *v*; nia 1 [ɲa] *v*; punya 1 [pu.ɲa] *v*
pound tumbok [tum.boʔ] *v*
pour and serve tuang [twaŋ] *v*
prawn udang [u.daŋ] *n*
pray semayang [sə.ma.jaŋ] *v*
Prep dekat 3 [də.kat] (var. kat) *prep*; di [di] *prep* (comp. diluar); kat [kat] *prep*
prepared siap [sjap] *v*
preserved vegetables kiamchai [kjam.chaj] *n*
pretend to not hear buat tak dengair [bwat taʔ dəŋ.ɛ] (comp. of buat, tak, dengair) *v*
price arga [ar.ga] (var. of harga) *n*; harga [har.ga] *n*
priest paderi [pa.də.ri] *n*

Prog ada 2 [a.da] (var. a) *v*
promiscuous samplang [sam.plaŋ] *adj*
proper kenonay [kə.no.ne] *adj*; seronoh [sə.ro.noh] *adj*
prosper huat 2 [hwat] *v*
protruding eyes mata beliak [ma.ta bə.ljaʔ] (mata, beliak) *n*
public opinions mulot dunya [mu.lot du.ɲia] (comp. of mulot, dunya) *n*
pull tarék [ta.reʔ] *v*
pull out chabot [tʃa.bot] *v*
pummel bedék [bə.deʔ] *v*
pure jati 2 [dʒa.ti] *adj*
purse horpau [hor.paw] (var. orpau) *n*; orpau [or.paw] *n*
push tolak [to.laʔ] *v*
put tarok [ta.roʔ] *v*
put in masok 2 [ma.soʔ] *v*

Q
quarrel berkelay [bər.kə.le] *v*
quick chepat [tʃə.pat] *adj*
quick (coarse) lekas [lə.kas] *adj*

quick (refined) lekair [lə.kɛ] *adj*
quiet diam [djam] *adj*
quietly diam diam [djam djam] *adv*

R
rabbit kuching belanda [ku.tʃiŋ bəlanda] (comp. of kuching, belanda) *n*
race lawan [la.wan] *v*
rain hujan [hu.dʒan] (var. ujan) *n*; ujan [u.dʒan] *n*
raise children piara [pja.ra] *v*
rank pangkat [paŋ.kat] *n* (comp. naik pangkat, pangkat adek beradek)
rational (coarse) benal [bə.nal] *adj*
rational (refined) benair [bə.nɛ] *adj*
raw mentah [mən.tah] *adj*
reach sampay 2 [sam.pe] *v*
read bacha [ba.tʃa] *v*
really betol 3 [bə.tol] *adv*; sunggu [suŋ.gu] *adv*
reason (refined) pasair 2 [pa.sɛ] *n* (contr. sair 1); sair 1 [sɛ] (contr. of pasair) *n* (comp. apa sair)
reason (coarse) pasal 2 [pa.sal] *n* (comp. apa pasal)
receive dapat 2 [da.pat] *v*
recognize jin [dʒin] *v*
red mérah [me.rah] *adj*

red packet of monetary gift angpau [aŋ.paw] *n*
Rel mia 2 [mja] (contr. of punya), nia 2 [ɲa] (contr. of punya) *rel*, punya 2 [pu.ɲa] *rel*; nang [naŋ] (var. of yang) *rel*; yang [jaŋ] *rel*
remember ingat 1 [i.ŋat] *v*
reminisce kenang [kə.naŋ] *v*
repent beruba [bə.ru.ba] *v*
respect hormat [hor.mat] (var. ormat) *v*; ormat [or.mat] *v*
resting platform balay-balay [ba.le-ba.le] *n*
return balék 1 [ba.leʔ] *v*; pulang [pu.laŋ] *v*
reverse gostan [go.stan] *v*
rice cake chuikuéh [tʃwi.kweh] *n*
rice cake served in spicy gravy lontong [lon.toŋ] *n*
rich kaya 1 [ka.ja] *adj*
ride tunggang [tuŋ.gaŋ] *v*
right kanan [ka.nan] *adv*
ripe masak 2 [ma.saʔ] *adj*
rise naik 2 [najʔ] *v* (comp. naik baik, comp. naik darah, comp. naik geléték, comp. naik geram, comp. naik gila, comp. naik lemak,

comp. naik pangkat, comp. naik sedap, comp. naik seram)
river sunggay [suŋ.ge] *n*
road tengah jalan [tə.ŋah dʒa.lan] (comp. of tengah, jalan) *n*
roast panggang [paŋ.gaŋ] *v*
rock batu 1 [ba.tu] *n*
rock goyang 1 [go.jaŋ] *v*

roof bunbong [bun.boŋ] *n*
room bilék [bi.leʔ] *n*
root (coarse) akar [a.kar] *n*
root (refined) akair [a.kɛ] *n*
rouge yénchi [jen.tʃi] *n*
roughly agak agak [a.gaʔ a.gaʔ] (agak) *adv*
round bulat [bu.lat] *adj*
run lari [la.ri] *v*

S

sad sedéh [sə.deh] *adj*
safe selamat [sə.la.mat] *adj*
saliva lio [ljo] *n*
salt garam [ga.ram] *n*
salty asin [a.sin] *adj* der. asién asin comp. mulot asin
same sama 1 [sa.ma] *adj*
sand paser [pa.ser] *n*
satisfied kamwan [kam.wan] *adj*
satisified feeling shiok 1 [ʃjoʔ] *adj*
saute spices tumis [tu.mis] *v*
say kata [ka.ta] *v*
school sekolah [sə.ko.lah] *n*
scold maki [ma.ki] *v*
scratch gerong [gə.roŋ] *v*
sea laut 1 [lawt] *n*
season musim [mu.sim] *n*
second father tio-tio 2 [tjo-tjo] *n*
second mother mak-yi [maʔ-ji] (comp. of mak, yi 2) *n*
see nampak [nam.paʔ] *v*; téngok [te.ŋoʔ] *v*
seed bijik 2 [bi.dʒiʔ] *n* (comp. bijik mata)
seems macham 2 [ma.tʃam] *adv*; amcham (comp. of apa cham), (comp. apa macham, contr. cham 2)
seldom jarang [dʒa.raŋ] *adv*
self sendiri [sən.di.ri] *n*
selfish auban [aw.ban] *adj*
sell (coarse) jual [dʒwal] *v*
sell (refined) juair [dʒwɛ] *v*
serious bengis 2 [bə.ŋis] *adj*
seven chit [tʃit] *cardnum*; tujoh [tu.dʒoh] *cardnum*
sew jait [dʒajt] *v*
shadow bayang [ba.jaŋ] *n*
shake gonchang [gon.tʃaŋ] *v*; goyang 2 [go.jaŋ] *v*
sheep kambing 2 [kam.biŋ] *n*

sheet éla [e.la] (var. of helay) *clf*; lay [le] (var. of helay); helay [hə.le] *clf*
ship (coarse) kapal [ka.pal] *n*
ship (refined) kapair [ka.pɛ] *n* ship
shiver mengintar [mə.ŋin.tar] *v*
shock kejut [kə.dʒut] *adj*
shoe kasot [ka.sot] *n*
shop keday [kə.de] *n*
short katék [ka.teʔ] *adj*; péndék [pen.deʔ] *adj*
shoulder bahu [ba.hu] (var. bau) *n* shoulder shoulder; bau [baw] *n*
shout pekék [pə.keʔ] *v*
show tunjok [tun.dʒoʔ] *v*
shy segan [sə.gan] *adj* comp. buang segan
sibling adék 1 [a.deʔ] *n* (der. adék beradék)
siblings adék beradék 1 [a.deʔ bə.ra.deʔ] (der. of adék) *n* (comp. pangkat adek beradek)
sick sakit [sa.kit] *adj*
side belah [bə.lah] *prep*; tepi 1 [tə.pi] *n*; tepi 2 [tə.pi] *adv*
sign tanda [tan.da] *n* (comp. tanda mata)
silent senyap [sə.ɲap] *adj*
similar to bagi [ba.gi] *adv*
sing menyanyi [mə.ɲa.ɲi] (var. nyanyi) *v*; nyanyi [ɲa.ɲi] *v*
singe siut [sjut] *v*
sink tenggelam [təŋ.gə.lam] *v*
sit dudok 1 [du.doʔ] *v*
six enam [e.nam] *cardnum* six six; lak [laʔ] *cardnum*
skin kulit [ku.lit] *n*
skirt kun 1 [kun] *n*
sky langit [la.ŋit] *n*
sky-deity (Jade Emperor) ti-gong [ti-goŋ] *n*
sleep tidor [ti.dor] *v*
sleepy mengantok 2 [me.ŋan.toʔ] *v*
slice iris [i.ris] *v*
slim ringan [ri.ŋan] *adj* (comp. mulot ringan)

slippers terompak [tə.rom.paʔ] *n*
slow pelan [pə.lan] *adj* (comp. pelan pelan)
slowly pelan pelan [pə.lan pə.lan] (der. of pelan) *adv*
small kechik [kə.tʃiʔ] *adj* (comp. buang ayé kechik)
small and round bijik 1 [bi.dʒiʔ] *clf* (comp. bijik mata)
small clock aloji 1 [a.lo.dʒi] *n*
smashed up nua [nwa] *adj*
smell ba'u [ba.ʔu] *n*
smelly busok [bu.soʔ] *adj* (comp. ati busok, comp. mulot busok)
smile senyum 1 [sə.ɲum] *v*; senyum 2 [sə.ɲum] *n*
smoke asap [a.sap] *n*
smooth lichin [li.tʃin] *adj*
snake (coarse) ular [u.lar] *n* snake
snake (refined) uluair 1 [u.lɛ] *n*
snap patah [pa.tah] *v*
socks boik [bojk] *n*
soft lembéh [ləm.beh] *adj*
soil tanah 1 [ta.nah] *n*
some berapa 2 [bə.ra.pa] *adv*
somewhat salty asién asin [a.sjen asin] (der. of asin) *adj*
son ba [ba] (contr. of Baba) *n*; Baba 2 [ba.ba] *n*
song lagu [la.gu] *n*
son-in-law kiasai 1 [kjasaj] *n*
sorrow pilu [pi.lu] *n*
sound bunyi [bu.ɲi] *n*
soup sup [sup] *n*
sour asam 2 [a.sam] *adj*
sour plums sengbuay [səŋ.bwe] *n*
speak chakap [tʃaj.kap] *v*
spend belanja 1 [bə.lan.dʒa] *v*
spice paste (for papaya soup) titék [ti.teʔ] *n*
splurge gaya [ga.ja] *v*
spoilt rosak [ro.saʔ] *adj*
spoon séndok [sen.doʔ] *n*
spring roll with turnip popiah [po.pjah] *n*
squinty juling [dʒu.liŋ] *adj* (comp. mata juling)
stab tikam 1 [ti.kam] *v*
stage panggong [paŋ.goŋ] *n*
stairs tangga 2 [taŋ.ga] *n*
stale basi [ba.si] *adj*
stand diri [di.ri] *v*

standard baku [ba.ku] *adj*
star bintang [bin.taŋ] *n*
stay dudok 2 [du.doʔ] *v*
stay (coarse) tinggal 2 [tiŋ.gal] *v* stay
stay (refined) tinggair 2 [tiŋ.gɛ] *v*
steam kukus [ku.kus] *v*
step on pinjak [pin.dʒaʔ] *v*
sticky melekat [mə.lə.kat] *adj*
still lagik 2 [la.giʔ] *adv*
stingy kiam [kjam] *adj*
stomach perot 2 [pə.rot] *n*; purot [pu.rot] *n*
stone batu 2 [ba.tu] *n*
story cherita [tʃə.ri.ta] *n*
straight terus [tə.rus] *adj*
straightaway langsong [laŋ.soŋ] *adv*
Straits-born Chinese Peranakan [pə.ra.na.kan] *n*
strangle chekék [tʃə.keʔ] *v*
streetwise cherdék [tʃər.deʔ] *adj*
stretch upon waking up buang segan [bwaŋ sə.gan] (comp. of buang, segan) *v*
strike pukol 2 [pu.kol] *v*
strong kuat [kwat] *adj*
stubborn degil [də.gil] *adj*
stupid bodoh [bo.doh] *adj* (comp. buat bodoh); gorblok [gɔ.bloʔ] *adj*
stylised dance jogét [dʒo.get] *v*
stylish lawa [la.wa] *adj*
subjected to kena 2 [kə.na] *v*
sugar gula [gu.la] *n*
suitable hak [haʔ] *adj*
sun mata ari [ma.ta a.ri] (comp. of mata, ari) *n*
sun dry gemoh [gə.moh] *v*
superstitious pantang [pan.taŋ] *adj*
supple lembut [ləm.but] *adj*
surprised peranjat [pə.ran.dʒat] *adj* (comp. terperanjat)
sweep sapu [sa.pu] *v*
sweet manis [ma.nis] *adj* (comp. mulot manis)
sweet dessert of thick coconut milk with banana chunks pengat [pə.ŋat] *n*
sweetheart mata ayé [ma.ta a.je] (comp. of mata, ayé) *n*
swim berenang [bə.rə.naŋ] *v*
Syzygium fruit (pink) jambu [dʒam.bu] *n*

T

table méja [me.dʒa] *n*; tok [toʔ] *n*
tail buntot 1 [bun.tot] *n*
take amék [a.meʔ] *v*
take care of someone or something jaga 2 [dʒa.ga] *v*
tall tinggi [tiŋ.gi] *adj*
tamarind asam 1 [a.sam] *n*
tame jinak [dʒi.naʔ] *adj*
tapioca ambun [am.bun] *n*
taste chobak [tʃo.baʔ] *v*
tasteless (coarse) tawar [ta.war] *adj*
tasteless (refined) tawair [ta.wɛ] *adj*
tea téh [teh] *n*
teach (coarse) ajar [a.dʒar] *v*
teach (refined) ajair [a.dʒɛ] *v*
teak jati 1 [dʒa.ti] *n*
tell bilang [bi.laŋ] *v*
tell a lie bédék [be.deʔ] *v*
ten chap [tʃap] *cardnum* (id. ati it gor it chap); puloh [pu.loh] *cardnum*
ten (coarse) belas [bə.las] *cardnum*
ten (refined) belair [bə.lɛ] *cardnum*
terrible terok [tə.roʔ] *adj*
thank you kamsiah [kam.sjah] *interj*
that itu [i.tu] *dem* (contr. tu)
there [sa.na] *adv*
thick (describing liquid) [pə.kat] *adj*
thin kurus [ku.rus] *adj*
thing barang [ba.raŋ] *n*
think ingat 2 [i.ŋat] *v*; pikay [pi.ke] *v*; rasa 2 [ra.sa] *v*
thirsty a'us 1 [a.ʔus] (var. of ha'us) *adj*; ha'us 1 [ha.ʔus] *adj*
this ini [i.ni] *dem* (contr. ni)
thousand ribu [ri.bu] *cardnum*
threadfin fish kuro [ku.ro] *n*
threat gertak [gər.taʔ] (var. gretak) *v*; gretak [grə.taʔ] *v*
three sa [sa] *cardnum*; tiga [ti.ga]
throw buang [bwaŋ] *v* (comp. buang ayé, comp. buang ayé besair, comp. buang ayé kechik, comp. buang buang, comp. buang mata, comp. buang mulot, comp. buang sebelah, comp. buang segan, comp. buang tebiét)
throw tantrum buang tebiét [bwaŋ tə.bjet] (comp. of buang, terbiat) *v*

tickle geléték [gə.le.teʔ] *v* (comp. naik geléték)
tidy (coarse) kemas [kə.mas] *v* tidy
tidy (refined) kemair [kə.mɛ] *v*
tie ikat [i.kat] *v*
tiger arimo [a.ri.mo] (var. of harimo) *n*; harimo [ha.ri.mo] *n*
time jam 1 [dʒam] *n*; kala [ka.la] *n* (comp. sinjakala); kali [ka.li] *n*
tired penat [pə.nat] *adj* **to twist one's foot** peléchok [pə.le.tʃoʔ] *v*
to water plants renjis [rən.dʒis] *v*
toilet chiwan [tʃi.wan] *n*
tomorrow bésok [be.soʔ] *adv*
tongue lidah [li.dah] *n*
too terlalu [tə.la.lu] *adv*
tooth gigi [gi.gi] *n*
top atas [a.tas] *prep*
torn koyak [ko.jaʔ] *adj*
tortoise ku 1 [ku] *n*; kura-kura [ku.ra-ku.ra] *n*
toss lambong [lam.boŋ] *v*
touch raba [ra.ba] *v*
Tʀ -kan [kan]
traditional blouse kebaya [kə.ba.ja] *n*
traditional cakes kuéh [kweh] *n*. (comp. kuéh-yi)
traditional Peranakan elder bok-bok [boʔ-boʔ] (contr. of **embok-embok**) *n*; embok-embok [əm.boʔ-əm.boʔ] *n*
traffic junction sempang [səm.paŋ] *n*
transfer salin [sa.lin] *v*
treat belanja 2 [bə.lan.dʒa] *v*
tree pokok [po.koʔ] *n*
tremble (coarse) bergetar [bər.gə.tar] *v*
tremble (refined) bergetair [bər.gə.tɛ] *v*
true betol 2 [bə.tol] *adj*
trust perchaya [pər.tʃa.ja] *v*
turn bélok [be.loʔ] *v*; **pusing** 2 [pu.siŋ] *v*
turn over balék 2 [ba.leʔ] *v*
turnip bangkuang [baŋ.kwaŋ] *n*
turtle labi-labi [la.bi-la.bi] *n*
twisted béngok [be.ŋoʔ] *adj* (comp. mulot béngok)
twisted mouth mulot béngok [mu.lot be.ŋoʔ] (comp. of mulot, béngok) *n*
two dua [dwa] *cardnum*; ji [dʒi] *cardnum*
type of noodles kolomi [ko.lo.mi] *n*

U

ugly burok [bu.roʔ] *adj*
umbrella payong [pa.joŋ] *n*
unbleached cotton outfit used for mourning
  belachu [bə.la.tʃu] *n*
uncontrollable mouth mulot gatair [mu.lot ga.tɛ]
  (comp. of mulot, gatair) *n*
under bawah [ba.wah] *prep*
under the influence of black magic kunang
  [ku.naŋ] *adj*
understand reti [rə.ti] *v*
unhappy kéksim [keʔ.sim] *adj*

unlucky suay [swe] *adj* (comp. buat suay)
unripe terbantot [tər.ban.tot] *adj*
until sampay 1 [sam.pe] *prep*
upstairs loténg [lo.teŋ] *adv*
urinate buang ayé kechik [bwaŋ a.je kə.chiʔ]
  (comp. of buang, ayé, kechik) *v*; buang ayé
  [bwaŋ a.je] (comp. of buang, ayé) *v*
use guna 1 [gu.na] *v*; guna 2 [gu.na] *n*; pakay 2
  [pa.ke] *v*; pasang 1 [pa.saŋ] *v*
used to it biasa [bja.sa] *adj*

V

vegetables sayor [sa.jor] *n*
very sangat [sa.ŋat] *adv* v; sekali 1 [sə.ka.li] *adv*

village kampong [kam.poŋ] *n*

W

waist pinggang [piŋ.gaŋ] *n*
wait tunggu [tuŋ.gu] *v*
wake mangun [ma.ŋun] *v*
walk jalan [dʒa.lan] *v* (comp. tengah jalan)
walking stick tongkat [toŋ.kat] *n*
wall témbok [tem.boʔ] *n*
want mo [mo] *v*
wart mata ikan [ma.ta i.kan] (comp. of mata,
  ikan) *n*
wash chuchi [tʃu.tʃi] *v*
water ayé [a.je] *n* (comp. buang ayé, comp.
  buang ayé besair, comp. buang ayé kechik,
  mata ayé)
water spinach kangkong [kaŋ.koŋ] *n*
wear pakay 1 [pa.ke] *v*
wedding gift exchange ceremony lapchai
  [lap.tʃaj] *n*
week minggu [miŋ.gu] *n*
weigh timbang [tim.baŋ] *v*
what apa [a.pa] *interrog* (comp amcham, comp.
  apa cham, comp. apa macham, comp. apa
  pasal, contr. apa sair)
when bila [bi.la] *adv*
where mana 1 [ma.na] *interrog*
which mana 2 [ma.na] *interrog*
whirl pusing 1 [pu.siŋ] *v*
whisper memisék [mə.mi.seʔ] *v*
white putéh [pu.teh] *adj*

who siapa [sja.pa] *interrog*
why (coarse) apa pasal [a.pa pa.sal] (comp. of
  apa, pasal) *interrog*
why (refined) apa sair [a.pa sɛ] (contr. of apa,
  sair 1) *interrog* why
wife bini [bi.ni] *n*
wildness liar [ljar] *n*
win menang [mə.naŋ] *v*
wind angin [a.ŋin] *n*
window menjéla [mən.dʒe.la] *n*
Winter Solstice tangchék [taŋ.tʃeʔ] *n*
with sama 3 [sa.ma] *prep*
withstand tahan [ta.han] *v*
wonder héran [he.ran] *v*
wood kayu [ka.ju] *n*
work kerja 1 [kər.dʒa] (var. kreja) *v*; kerja 2 [kər.
  dʒa] (var. kreja) *n*; kreja 1 [krə.dʒa] *v*; kreja
  2 [krə.dʒa] *n*
world dunya [du.ɲa] *n* (comp. mulot dunya)
worn out ha'us 2 [ha.ʔus] (var. a'us) *adj*; a'us 2
  [a.ʔus] *adj*
worry kuatay [kwa.te] *v*
wound luka 2 [luka] *n*
wounded luka 1 [luka] *adj*
wring perah [pə.rah] *v*
wrist watch aloji 2 [a.lo.dʒi] *n*
write tulis [tu.lis] *v*
wrong salah 2 [sa.lah] *adj*

Y

yawn mengantok 1 [mə.ŋan.toʔ] *v*
year taoun [ta.own] *n*
yellow kuning [ku.niŋ] *adj*
yes ya [ja] *interj*
young mudah [mu.dah] *adj*

younger sibling adék 2 [a.deʔ] *n* (der. adék beradék)
younger siblings adék beradék 2 [a.deʔ bə.ra.deʔ] (der. of adék) *n*
youngest (only for familial relations) bongsu [boŋ.su] *adj*

List of Tables

Table 1	The vowel inventory of Baba Malay	4
Table 2	The consonant inventory of Baba Malay	4
Table 3	Population of Malacca and Singapore in 1836 (Newbold 1839: 136, 283)	26
Table 4	Ethnic composition of Malacca and Singapore (Malaysia 2016; Singapore 2015)	27
Table 5	Consonant chart of Baba Malay	34
Table 6	Bilabial consonants by position	37
Table 7	Alveolar consonants by position	39
Table 8	Post-alveolar consonants by position	43
Table 9	Velar consonants by position	45
Table 10	Glottal consonants by position	47
Table 11	Glides by position	49
Table 12	Vowel chart of Baba Malay	50
Table 13	Vowels and formant values for a proficient speaker of Baba Malay in Singapore	53
Table 14	Distinctive features of vowels and glides in Baba Malay spoken in Singapore	64
Table 15	Distinctive features of consonants in Baba Malay	64
Table 16	Examples illustrating syllable-final velar plosive to glottal stop rule	65
Table 17	Examples illustrating optional word-initial *h* deletion rule	66
Table 18	Examples illustrating optional *ə* and *r* metathesis rule	66
Table 19	Examples illustrating optional V to *u* before *lw* assimilation rule	67
Table 20	Examples illustrating vowel raising to *ɛ* rule	68
Table 21	Examples illustrating final *l, r, s* deletion post- *ɛ* vowel raising	68
Table 22	Ordering of vowel raising to *ɛ*, then final *l, r, s* deletion	69
Table 23	Ordering of vowel raising to *ɛ* and final *l, r, s* deletion, then *u* assimilation	69
Table 24	Writing system of Baba Malay used by this grammar	72
Table 25	Some nominal compounds in Baba Malay using *ati* 'heart', *mata* 'eye' and *mulot* 'mouth'	95
Table 26	Noun classifiers in Baba Malay	96
Table 27	Mass classifiers in Baba Malay	97
Table 28	Personal pronouns in Baba Malay	99
Table 29	Interrogative pronouns in Baba Malay	104
Table 30	List of some verbal compounds in Baba Malay	114
Table 31	Interrogative adverbs in Baba Malay	119
Table 32	Baba Malay numerals derived from Malay	123
Table 33	Baba Malay numerals derived from Hokkien	124
Table 34	List of prepositions in Baba Malay	127
Table 35	List of conjunctions in Baba Malay	135
Table 36	List of common interjections in Baba Malay	138
Table 37	List of commonly used functional adverbs that modify verb phrases and their distributions	180
Table 38	List of phrases, their word orders and general tendency	194
Table 39	List of interrogative pronouns and adverbs in Baba Malay	216
Table 40	Vowel chart of Malacca Baba Malay	232
Table 41	Consonant chart of Malacca Baba Malay	232
Table 42	Swadesh 100-word list in Baba Malay	248

Table 43	Kinship terms in Baba Malay —— 251
Table 44	Days of the week in Baba Malay —— 254
Table 45	Months in Baba Malay —— 255
Table 46	Important dates on the lunar calendar in Baba Malay —— 255
Table 47	General diurnal expressions in Baba Malay —— 256
Table 48	Specific time in Baba Malay —— 256
Table 49	Transcription conventions for texts —— 257
Table 50	A list of ten *pantun* by Albert Ku —— 338

List of Figures

Figure 1	Pages in *Hua yi tong yu* provide Sinicized pronunciations for various numerals and silver currencies in Malay (Collection of National Library, Singapore) —— 17
Figure 2	A 1920s photograph of a Peranakan couple in Singapore —— 19
Figure 3	Map of key locales in the development of Baba Malay —— 23
Figure 4	Waveform and spectrogram of [p] in [panas] 'hot' —— 38
Figure 5	Waveform and spectrogram of [b] in [bakol] 'basket' —— 38
Figure 6	Wave form and spectrogram of [m] in [sama] 'same, and, with' —— 39
Figure 7	Waveform and spectrogram of [t] in [tareʔ] 'pull' —— 40
Figure 8	Waveform and spectrogram of [d] in [dataŋ] 'come' —— 40
Figure 9	Waveform and spectrogram of [s] in [sama] 'same, and, with' —— 41
Figure 10	Waveform and spectrogram of [n] in [mana] 'where, which' —— 41
Figure 11	Waveform and spectrogram of [l] in [labilabi] 'tortoise' —— 42
Figure 12	Waveform and spectrogram of [l] in [bakol] —— 42
Figure 13	Waveform and spectrogram of [r] in [garaŋ] 'fierce' —— 43
Figure 14	Waveform and spectrogram of [tʃ] in [tʃərita] 'story' —— 44
Figure 15	Waveform and spectrogram of [dʒ] in [dʒaga] 'take care of someone or something, guard' —— 44
Figure 16	Waveform and spectrogram of [ɲ] in [maɲaʔ] 'many' —— 45
Figure 17	Waveform and spectrogram of [k] in [kaki] 'leg' —— 46
Figure 18	Waveform and spectrogram of [g] in [garaŋ] 'fierce' —— 46
Figure 19	Waveform and spectrogram of [ŋ] in [garaŋ] 'fierce' —— 47
Figure 20	Waveform and spectrogram of [h] in [habis] 'finish' —— 48
Figure 21	Waveform and spectrogram of [ʔ] in [budaʔ] 'child' —— 48
Figure 22	Waveform and spectrogram of [w] in [wajaŋ] 'play (performance)' —— 49
Figure 23	Waveform and spectrogram of [j] in [wajaŋ] 'play (performance)' —— 50
Figure 24	Waveform and spectrogram of [i] in [abi] 'then' —— 53
Figure 25	Vowel space of a Baba Malay speaker in Singapore —— 56
Figure 26	Vowel space of a more proficient Baba Malay speaker in Singapore —— 87
Figure 27	Vowel space of a less proficient Baba Malay speaker in Singapore —— 87
Figure 28	Normalized vowel plots of six Baba Malay speakers in Singapore —— 88
Figure 29	Tense and aspect system of Baba Malay —— 171
Figure 30	Vowel space of a Malacca Baba Malay speaker —— 231
Figure 31	Vowel space of a Singapore Baba Malay speaker —— 231

References

Abdul, Aziz Mohd. Sharif (1981): *The Baba language*. University of York (= Master of Arts thesis).
Aikhenvald, Alexandra Y. (2005): Serial verb constructions in typological perspective. In Alexandra Y. Aikhenvald & R.M.W Dixon (eds.), *Serial verb constructions: a cross-linguistic typology*, 1–68. Oxford: Oxford University Press.
Andaya, Barbara Watson & Leonard Y. Andaya (2001): *A history of Malaysia, 2nd edition*. London: Macmillan Education.
Ansaldo, Umberto (2009): *Contact languages: Ecology and evolution in Asia*. Cambridge: Cambridge University Press.
Ansaldo, Umberto, Lisa Lim & Salikoko S. Mufwene (2007): The sociolinguistic history of the Peranakans: What it tells us about "creolization". In Umberto Ansaldo, Stephen Matthews & Lisa Lim (eds.), *Deconstructing Creole. Typological Studies in Language. 73.*, 203–226. Amsterdam: John Benjamins.
Ansaldo, Umberto & Stephen Matthews (1999): The Minnan substrate and creolization in Baba Malay. *Journal of Chinese Linguistics* 27(1). 38–68.
Babel, Molly (2009): The phonetic and phonological obsolescence in Northern Paiute. In James N. Stanford & Dennis R. Preston (eds.), *Variation in indigenous minority languages*, 23–46. Amsterdam: John Benjamins.
Berez, Andrea (2011): *Directional reference, discourse and landscape in Ahtna*. University of California Santa Barbara (= PhD dissertation).
Blust, Robert (1998): In Defense of Dempwolff: Austronesian Dipthongs Once Again. *Oceanic Linguistics* 37(2). 354–62.
Bodman, Nicholas C. (1955): *Spoken Amoy Hokkien, Volume 1*. Kuala Lumpur: The Government of the Federation of Malaya.
Bodman, Nicholas C. (1958): *Spoken Amoy Hokkien, Volume 2*. Kuala Lumpur: The Government of the Federation of Malaya.
Boersma, Paul & David Weenink (2013): *Praat: doing phonetics by computer [Computer program]*. Version 5.3.59, retrieved 20 November 2013 from http://www.praat.org/.
Bossong, Georg (2021): DOM and linguistic typology. A personal view. In Johannes Kabatek (ed.), *Differential Object Marking in Romance: The third wave*. Walter De Gruyter.
Brunelle, Marc (2009): Diglossia and monosyllabization in Eastern Cham: A sociolinguistic study. In James N. Stanford & Dennis R. Preston (eds.), *Variation in indigenous minority languages*, 47–76. Amsterdam: John Benjamins.
Campbell, Lyle & Martha C. Muntzel (1989): The structural consequences of language death. In Nancy Dorian (ed.), *Investigating obsolescence: Studies in language contraction and death*, 181–196. Cambridge: Cambridge University Press.
Chan, Kenneth (2018): *Mari Chakap Baba: A comprehensive guide to the Baba Nyonya language*. Singapore: Gunong Sayang Association.
Chan, Philip (2007): *Speak Baba Malay: The easy way*. Singapore: Baba Nyonya Sayang.
Chao, Yuen-Ren (1930): A system of tone-letters. *Le Maître Phonétique* 45. 24–27.
Chia, Felix (1980): *The Babas*. Singapore: Times Books International.
Chia, Felix (1983a): *Ala Sayang!* Singapore: Eastern Universities Press.
Chia, Felix (1983b): Peeping through the nonya window curtain and seeing the decline of the Baba culture. A talk held at the Central Library, National University of Singapore on 19th August. Singapore.
Chia, Felix (1994): *The Babas revisited*. Singapore: Heinemann Asia.
Clammer, John R. (1980): *Straits Chinese Society*. Singapore: Singapore University Press.
Clynes, Adrian & David Deterding (2011): Illustrations of the IPA: Standard Malay (Brunei). *Journal of the International Phonetic Association* 41(2). 259–268.

Comrie, Bernard (1976): *Aspect: An Introduction to the Study of Verbal Aspect and Related Problems*. Cambridge: Cambridge University Press.

Comrie, Bernard (1989): *Language Universals and Linguistic Typology*. Chicago: University of Chicago Press.

De Witt, Dennis (2008): *History of the Dutch in Malaysia*. Kuala Lumpur: Nutmeg Publishing.

Dempwolff, Otto (1934): Vergleichende Lautlehre des austronesischen Wortschatzes. *Zeitschrift für Eingeborenen-Sprachen. I. Induktiver Aufbau einer indonesischen Ursprache, Supplement 15 (1934); 2. Deduktive Anwendung des Urindonesischen auf austronesische Einzelsprachen, Supplement 17 (1937); 3. Austronesisches Wörterverzeichnis, Supplement 19 (1938)*. Berlin: Reimer.

Department of Statistics Singapore (2015): *General Household Survey*. Singapore: Department of Statistics, Ministry of Trade & Industry, Republic of Singapore.

Department of Statistics Singapore (2017): *Statistics on Population Trends 2017*. Singapore: Department of Statistics, Ministry of Trade & Industry, Republic of Singapore.

Dhoraisingam, Samuel S. (2006): *Peranakan Indians of Singapore and Melaka: Indian Babas and Nonyas- Chitty Melaka*. Singapore: Institute of Southeast Asian Studies.

Du Bois, John, Susanna Cumming, Stephan Schuetze-Coburn & Danae Paolino (eds.) (1992): *Discourse Transcription*. California: University of California Santa Barbara.

Evers, Vincent, Henning Reetz & Aditi Lahiri (1998): Crosslinguistic acoustic categorization of sibilants independent of phonological status. *Journal of Phonetics* 26. 345–370.

Fei, Hsin (1436): *Hsing-ch'a sheng-lan: the overall survey of the Star Raft. (Republished in South China and Maritime Asia. 4. Translated by John Vivian Gottlieb Mills. Edited and annotated by Roderich Ptak)*. Wiedsbaden: Harrassowitz Verlag.

Freedman, Maurice (1979): *The study of Chinese societies: essays*. Stanford: Stanford University Press.

Greenberg, Joseph (1963): *Universals of language*. Cambridge, Massachusetts: MIT Press.

Groeneveldt, W.P. (1880): *Notes on the Malay Archipelago and Malacca: Compiled from Chinese Sources. Verhandelingen van het Bataviaasch Genootschap van Kunsten en Wetenschappen*. 39: i-x. 1–144.

Gunong Sayang Association (2018): Wayang Peranakan. *Gunong Sayang Association* https://www.gsa.org.sg/wayang-peranakan (letzter Zugriff 26.08.2018).

Gwee, William Thian Hock (1993): *Mas sepuloh: Baba conversational gems*. Singapore: Armour Publishing.

Gwee, William Thian Hock (2006): *A Baba Malay Dictionary: The First Comprehensive Compendium of Straits Chinese Terms and Expressions*. Singapore: Tuttle Publishing.

Hardwick, Patricia Ann (2008): „Neither fish nor fowl": constructing Peranakan identity in colonial and post-colonial Singapore. *Folklore of East Asia* 31(1). 36–55.

Hayes, Marriott (1921): The peoples of Singapore: inhabitants and population. In Walter Makepeace, Gilbert E. Brooke & Roland St. J. Braddell (eds.), *One hundred years of Singapore. Volume I*. London: John Murray (Republished by Oxford University Press in 1991. Introduction by C. M. Turnbull.).

Hong, Jose (2017): Keeping the Peranakan language alive. Text *The Straits Times* http://www.straitstimes.com/singapore/keeping-the-peranakan-language-alive (letzter Zugriff 03.03.2018).

Hung, Feng-Sheng (1996): *Prosody and the acquisition of grammatical morphemes in Chinese languages*. University of Hawai'i (= PhD dissertation).

Johnson, Keith (2012): *Acoustic and Auditory Phonetics. Third edition*. Oxford: Wiley-Blackwell.

Johnson, Keith, Peter Ladefoged & Mona Lindau (1993): Individual differences in vowel production. *Journal of the Acoustical Society of America* 94. 701–14.

Khoo, Joo Ee (1996): *The Straits Chinese: A Cultural History*. Kuala Lumpur: Pepin Press.
Khoo, Kay Kim (1998): Malaysia: Immigration and the growth of a plural society. *Journal of the Malaysian Branch of the Royal Asiatic Society* 71(1). 1–25.
Ladefoged, Peter (2003): *Phonetic Data Analysis: An Introduction to Fieldwork and Instrumental Techniques*. Oxford: Blackwell Publishing.
Ladefoged, Peter, Joseph DeClerk, Mona Lindau & George Papcun (1972): An auditory-motor theory of speech production. *UCLA Working Papers in Phonetics* 22(48–75).
Ladefoged, Peter & Keith Johnson (2011): *A Course in Phonetics, Sixth Edition. International Edition*. Canada: Wadsworth Cengage Learning.
Lee, Gwyneth A. Mae-En (1999): *A descriptive grammar of spoken Peranakan*. National University of Singapore (= Honour's thesis).
Lee, Meiyu (2016): A dictionary that bridged two races. *BiblioAsia* 11(4). Web version: http://www.nlb.gov.sg/biblioasia/2016/01/26/a-dictionary-that-bridged-two-races/.
Lee, Nala H. (2014): *A grammar of Baba Malay with sociophonetic considerations*. University of Hawai'i (= PhD dissertation).
Lee, Nala H. (2018): Baba Malay: Diverging trends in two ecologies. *Journal of Pidgin and Creole Languages* 33(1). 136–173.
Lee, Nala H. (2019): Peranakans in Singapore: Responses to language endangerment and documentation. (Ed.) Mário Pinharanda-Nunes & Cardoso, Hugo C. *Language Documentation & Conservation. Special issue on Documentation and conservation of contact languages in Southeast Asia and East Asia: Current issues and ongoing initiatives* 19. 123–140.
Lee, Nala H. (2020): Utilizing the Matched-guise as a Method of Examining Perceptual Change in an Endangered Creole. *Applied Linguistics* 42. 207–229.
Lee, Nala H. (in prep): The early Baba Malay continuum.
Lee, Nala H. & John Van Way (2016): Assessing levels of endangerment in the Catalogue of Endangered Languages (ELCat) using the Language Endangerment Index (LEI). *Language in Society* 45(2). 271–292.
Lee, Nala H. (2009): *One substrate, two lexifiers and the lexifier effect*. National University of Singapore (= MA thesis).
Lee, Nala H. (2012): Relativization and the lexifier effect. Paper presented at the Society of Pidgin and Creole Linguistics. 5 January. Portland, USA.
Lee, Nala H. (2013): Review of Shure WH30XLR cardioid headset microphone and Countryman E6 omnidirectional earset microphone. *Language Documentation & Conservation* 7. 177–184.
Lee, Yong Hock (1960): *A history of the Straits Chinese British Association, 1900–1959*. University of Singapore (= PhD dissertation).
Lewis, M Paul & Gary F. Simons (2010): Assessing endangerment: expanding Fishman's GIDS. *Revue Roumaine de Linguistique* 55(2). 103–120.
Lewis, M. Paul, Gary F. Simons & Charles D. Fennig (eds.) (2015): *Ethnologue: Languages of the World, Eighteenth edition*. Dallas, Texas: SIL International. Online version: http://www.ethnologue.com.
Lim, Catherine G.S. (2003): *Gateway to Peranakan culture*. Singapore: Asiapac.
Lim, Joo-Hock (1967): Chinese female immigration into the Straits Settlements 1860–1901. *Journal of the South Seas Society* 22. 58–110.
Lim, Lisa (2016a): Multilingual mediators: the role of the Peranakans in the contact dynamics of Singapore. In Li (ed.), *Multilingualism in the Chinese diaspora world-wide*, 216–236. New York: Routledge.
Lim, Lisa (2016b): The art of losing: Beyond java, patois and postvernacular vitality – Repositioning the periphery in global Asian ecologies. In Luna Filipović & Martin Pütz (eds.), *Endangered languages and lanugages in danger: Issues of documentation, policy, and language rights*, 283–312. Amsterdam: John Benjamins.

Lim, Sonny (1981): *Baba Malay: the language of the „Straits-born" Chinese*. Monash University (= MA thesis).
Lim, Sonny (1988): Baba Malay: The language of the „Straits-born" Chinese. *Papers in Western Austronesian Linguistics* 3. 1–61.
Lin, Heng-nan (1883): *Hua Yi Tong Yu: Chinese migrants' vernacular*. Singapore: S.n.
Lobanov, Boris M. (1971): Classification of Russian vowels spoken by different listeners. *Journal of the Acoustical Society of America* 49. 606–08.
Malaysia, Department of Statistics (2016): Laporan kiraan permulaan: preliminary count report. Online version: https://www.statistics.gov.my.
Marsden, William (1812): *A grammar of the Malayan language*. London: Cox and Baylis.
McWhorter, John H. (2001): The world's simplest grammars are creole grammars. *Linguistic Typology* 5. 125–126.
Michael, Franz H. (1971): *The Taiping Rebellion: history and documents*. Washington: University of Washington.
Mintz, Malcom W. (1994): *A student grammar of Malay and Indonesian*. Singapore: EPB Publishers.
Nathan, J (1922): *The Census of British Malaysia*. London: Waterloo & Sons.
Newbold, Thomas John (1839): Political and statistical account of the British settlements in the Straits of Malacca. Vol 1. London: J. Murray. [Re-issued in 1971 by Oxford University Press, Kuala Lumpur].
Omar, Asmah Haji (1989): The Malay Spelling Reform. *Journal of the Simplified Spelling Society* 2. 9–13.
Omar, Asmah Haji (1993): The First Congress for Malay. In Joshua Fishman (ed.), *The Earliest Stage of Language Planning: The „First Congress" Phenomenon*, 181–198. Berlin: Mouton de Gruyter.
Onn, Farid M. (1980): *Aspects of Malay Phonology and Morphology: A Generative Approach*. Kuala Lumpur: Penerbit University Malaya.
Paauw, Scott Horan (2009): *The Malay Contact Varieties of Eastern Indonesia: A Typological Comparison*. State University of New York at Buffalo (= PhD dissertation).
Pakir, Anne (1986): *A linguistic investigation of Baba Malay*. University of Hawai'i (= PhD dissertation).
Pakir, Anne (1994): Educational linguistics: looking to the East. In James Alatis (ed.), *Georgetown University Round Table on Languages and Linguistics*, 370–383. Washington DC: Georgetown University Press.
Pan, Lynn (ed.) (2006): *The Encyclopedia of the Chinese Overseas*. Singapore: Chinese Heritage Centre.
Peranakan Museum (2018): *Amek Gambar. Exhibition at the Peranakan Museum*. Singapore: National Heritage Board.
Purcell, Victor (1967): *The Chinese in Malaya*. Oxford: Oxford University Press (originally published in 1948).
Purcell, Victor (1980): *The Chinese in Southeast Asia*. Issued under the auspices of the Royal Institute of International Affairs [by] Oxford University Press.
Rappa, Antonio L. & Lionel Wee (2006): *Language Policy and Modernity in Southeast Asia: Malaysia, the Philippines, Singapore, and Thailand*. New York: Springer.
Reinecke, John E., Stanley M. Tsuzaki, David de Camp, Ian F. Hancock & R. Wood (1975): *A Bibliography of Pidgin and Creole Languages*. Honolulu: The University of Hawai'i Press.
Ryan, Neil Joseph (1976): *A History of Malaysia and Singapore*. Oxford: Oxford University Press.
Salleh, Hood (2006): *Peoples and traditions. Encyclopedia of Malaysia 12*. Kuala Lumpur: Archipelago Press.
Sebba, Mark (1987): *The syntax of serial verbs*. Amsterdam: John Benjamins.

Shellabear, William G. (1913): Baba Malay: an introduction to the language of the Straits-born Chinese. Attached as appendix in J.R. Clammer (1980). *Straits Chinese Society*, 153–165. Singapore: Singapore University Press.

Shih, Meng-Yi (2009): *The Hokkien substrate in Baba Malay*. National Tsing-Hua University (= MA thesis).

Simons, Gary F. & Charles D. Fennig (2017): *Ethnologue: Languages of the World, 20th edition*. Dallas, Texas: SIL International. Online version: http://www.ethnologue.com.

Singapore, Department of Statistics (2015): Popuation trends 2015. Online version: http://www.singstat.gov.sg/docs/default-source/default-document-library/publications/publications_and_papers/population_and_population_structure/population2015.pdf.

Skinner, G William (1996): Creolized Chinese Societies in Southeast Asia. In Anthony Reid & Kristine Aililunas-Rodgers (eds.), *Sojourners and settlers: Histories of Southeast Asia and the Chinese*, 51–93. Hawai'i: University of Hawai'i Press.

Smith, Carlota S. (1991): *The parameter of aspect*. Dordrecht: Kluwer.

Song, Ong-Siang (1967): *One hundred years' history of the Chinese in Singapore*. First published in 1923. Singapore: University of Malaya Press.

Swadesh, Morris (1955): Towards greater accuracy in lexicostatistic dating. *International Journal of American Linguistics* 21(121–137).

Tan, Bonny (2007): *A Baba Malay Bibliography: A select annotated listing of sources on the Peranakan Chinese in Singapore and Malaysia*. Singapore: National Library Board.

Tan, Chee Beng (1979): *Baba and Nyonya: a study of the ethnic identity of the Chinese Peranakan in Malacca*. Cornell University.

Tan, Ling Ling, Azlina Musa & Maggie Seaton (2007): *Easy Learning Malay Dictionary*. Glasglow: Colins Publishers.

Teoh, Boon Seong (1994): *The Sound System of Malay Revisited*. Kuala Lumpur: Ministry of Education Malaysia.

Teoh, Boon Seong, Beng Soon Lim & Liang Hye Lee (2017): A study of Penang Peranakan Hokkien. *Journal of Modern Languages* 15(1). 169–181.

Thomas, Erik R. & Tyler Kendall (2014): *The Vowel Normalization and Plotting Suite NORM [Computer program]*. Version 1.1, retrieved 12 February 2014 from http://ncslaap.lib.ncsu.edu/tools/norm/.

Thomason, Sarah G. (2003): Social factors and linguistic processes in the emergence of stable mixed languages. In Yaron Matras & Peter Bakker (eds.), *The Mixed Language Debate: Theoretical and Empirical Advances*, 21–40. Berlin: Mouton de Gruyter.

Thurgood, Elzbieta (1998): *A description of nineteenth century Baba Malay: a Malay variety influenced by language shift*. University of Hawai'i.

Traugott, Elizabeth Closs, Alice ter Meulen, Judy Snitzer Reilly & Charles A. Ferguson (eds.) (1986): *On Conditionals*. Cambridge: Cambridge University Press.

Tsao, Feng-fu (2004): Semantics and Syntax of Verbal and Adjectival Reduplication in Mandarin and Taiwanese. In Hilary Chappell (ed.), *Sinitic grammar: Synchronic and diachronic perspectives*, 285–308. New York: Oxford University Press.

Tsunoda, Tasaku (2005): *Language endangerment and language revitalization: an introduction*. Berlin: Mouton de Gruyter.

Vaughan, J. D. (1879): *Manners and customs of the Chinese in the Straits Settlements*. Singapore: The Mission Press.

Wade, Geoffrey Philip (1994): *The Ming-Shi-lu (veritable records of the Ming dynasty)*. University of Hong Kong (= PhD dissertation).

Wan, Aslynn (2012): *Instrumental phonetic study of the rhythm of Malay*. Newcastle University (= PhD thesis).

Wang, Gungwu (1964): The opening of relations between China and Malacca, 1403–5. In John Bastin & R Roolvink (eds.), *Malayan and Indonesian Studies: essays presented to Sir Richard Windstedt on his 85th birthday*, 87–104. Oxford: Clarendon Press.

Wee, Kim Soon Gabriel (2000): *Intonation of the Babas: an auditory and instrumental study*. National University of Singapore (= Honours thesis).

Wee, Lionel (2003): Linguistic Instrumentalism in Singapore. *Journal of Multilingual and Multicultural Development* 24(3). 211–224. doi:10.1080/01434630308666499.

Wee, Peter (2013): Memories relived. Talk presented at the Asian Civilizations Museum, Singapore. 19 April.

Widodo, Johannes (2002): A celebration of diversity: Zheng He and the origins of the pre-colonial coastal urban pattern in Southeast Asia. *Journal of Southeast Asian Architecture* 6. 11–22.

Windstedt, Richard O. (1948): The Malay founder of medieval Malacca. *Bulletin of the School of Oriental and African Studies. Presented to Lionel David Barnett by his colleagues, past and present.* 12(3/4). 726–729.

Wright, Martha Susan (1983): *A metrical approach to tone sandhi in Chinese dialects*. University of Massachusetts (= PhD dissertation).

Yeo, Zoe (2017): Straits Chinese British Association. *Singapore Infopedia* http://eresources.nlb.gov.sg/infopedia/articles/SIP_496_2004-12-20.html (letzter Zugriff 30.07.2018).

Yoong, S.K. & A.N. Zainab (2002): Chinese literary works translated into Baba Malay: A bibliometric study. *Malaysian Journal of Library & Information Science* 7(2). 1–23.

Index

acoustic 36
active 4, 9
active voice 112
adjectival phrase 160, 183, 190, 191, 209, 214, 242
adjective 62, 91, 108, 115, 116, 117, 118, 120, 126, 142, 154, 155, 172, 186, 187, 189, 193, 196, 201, 234
adjunct 204
adverb 62, 108, 117, 118, 170, 171, 172, 175, 176, 178, 180, 183, 186, 187, 190, 191, 193, 206, 222
adverbial clause 119, 204, 205, 206, 207, 211, 212, 214, 215, 219, 222
adverbial compound 119
adverbial phrase 127, 191, 192, 193, 194, 214, 242, 243, 246
adversative passive 9, 165, 166
affix 1, 4, 5, 21, 60, 91, 93, 94, 106, 107, 110, 117, 119, 234, 236, 237, 238
affricate 43, 44, 58, 59
alignment 8
alveolar 39, 40, 41, 42, 43
anaphora 102
approximant 49, 50
articulator 37, 38
aspect 2, 105, 160, 170, 171, 173, 174, 175, 183, 205, 240, 241, 381
aspiration 37, 38, 40, 46
assimilation 20, 67, 69, 218
Austronesian 1, 57
auxiliary 157, 160, 164, 170, 171, 174, 183, 240
auxiliary verb 165

Bazaar Malay 1, 135
benefactive 2, 166, 169
beneficiary 166, 168
bilabial 38
bilabials 37
bilingual 10, 27, 30, 86

calquing 100, 163
causative 2, 164, 166, 169
change 57, 89, 90
circumfix 234, 238
classifier 1, 92, 95, 96, 97, 98, 144, 147, 150, 152, 157, 218

clause 195, 197, 211, 224
coarse 1, 39, 58, 60, 67, 68, 89, 94, 99, 137, 332
coda 58, 59, 60
Colloquial Singapore English 139
common noun 146
comparative 134, 183, 185, 186, 187, 188, 191, 242, 243, 246
comparative of equality 186, 191
comparative of similarity 187, 191
complement 115, 127, 157, 159, 160, 185, 194
complement clause 201
compound words 37, 71
conditional 136, 208
conjunction 133, 135, 193, 209, 210, 212, 243, 244, 245
consonant 33, 58, 232
consonant cluster 58, 59
consonants 33
contact language 1, 2, 17, 32, 33, 90, 139, 247
content question 82, 83, 85, 216, 228
contracted form 24, 70, 101, 115, 119, 127, 140, 152, 157, 171, 181, 187, 210, 224, 241
contracted forms 145
coordinating conjunction 209, 245, 246
copula 159, 160, 171, 186, 196, 215, 240
copula verb 91
counterfactual 208
creole 1, 2, 22, 135, 380

declarative 82, 85, 222, 226
definite 147
deixis 121, 122, 147, 149
deletion 65, 68, 69, 71
demonstrative 92, 121, 142, 147, 148, 149, 157, 238, 246
demonstrative determiner 122
demonstrative pronoun 121
deontic modality 160, 161, 162, 163
derivational affix 107, 237
derivational morphology 237
derivational prefix 108
derivational suffix 108
determiner 120, 147, 238, 239, 240
dialect 1, 25, 230

differential object marking 135
diphthong 33, 57, 63
direct object 166, 168, 169, 201
direct speech 203
discourse 13, 137, 139, 140, 222, 257
distal 147
distinctive features 63
disyllabic 62, 71, 75, 78, 80
ditransitive 164, 166, 167, 168
duration 74
Dutch 2, 33, 71
dynamic modality 161
dynamic verb 178

ecology 26, 27, 230, 246, 247
endangerment 1, 14, 28, 29, 31, 32, 85
English 2, 20, 27, 29, 30, 33, 240
epistemic modality 160, 161, 162, 163
etymology 342
excessive degree 188, 191
existential 157, 171, 240
experiential perfect 2, 170, 173
expressions for day 254
expressions for diurnal cycle 256
expressions for month 255
expressions for time 256

fast speech 58, 60, 70
first person 99, 203
first person plural exclusive 100
first person plural inclusive 100
first person singular 67, 99
flap 20, 39, 43
formal 67
formant 36, 37, 52, 53, 74, 86, 230
fricative 39, 41, 47, 48, 70, 72
future 170, 175, 205, 206

gap-type relativization 201
genitive 142, 144, 146
glide 49, 58, 59
glottal 47, 48, 58, 59, 65
grammaticalization 128, 132, 212, 221
grammatical relations 91, 197

habitual 2, 170, 171, 174
head 96, 142, 144, 145, 149, 150, 152, 153, 154, 155, 157, 159, 183, 188, 189, 190, 191, 194, 195, 199, 201

Hokkien 1, 2, 3, 17, 21, 22, 25, 28, 33, 37, 47, 57, 58, 59, 62, 63, 66, 67, 73, 78, 79, 80, 81, 89, 96, 99, 100, 123, 124, 135, 139, 163, 165, 166, 167, 169, 170, 175, 199, 214, 222, 230, 244, 245, 246, 247, 250, 254, 255, 379, 383
home language 3, 18, 31, 247

imperative 106, 112, 182, 228
imperfective 171, 173, 174
indirect object 166, 168, 169, 201
indirect speech 203
inflectional affix 107
inflectional morphology 37
informal 67
intensity 74
interjection 137, 138
intermarriage 1, 18, 21, 22, 24, 30, 31
interrogative 83, 85, 104, 154, 159, 212, 220, 222, 228, 229
interrogative adverb 104, 119, 120, 216, 219, 222
interrogative pronoun 104, 119, 216, 217, 219, 222
intonation 14, 73, 82, 83, 85, 228, 257, 258
intonation unit 14, 257
intransitive 5, 6, 9, 102, 105, 107, 134, 198
isolating 37, 91, 142

Javanese 17, 22, 25, 26

kinship terms 2, 15, 21, 22, 26, 62, 94, 121, 123, 124, 248, 250

labiovelar 49
language documentation 10, 11, 12, 31, 36, 52
language policy 27, 30
lateral 39, 42, 66, 67
lexical stress 73, 74, 75, 77
lexicon 2, 15, 18, 33, 112, 342
lexifier 1, 33, 73, 90, 96, 100, 167, 230, 247, 381
liquid 58, 59, 66, 70
location 192, 204, 206, 220
logical subject 9, 164, 166, 197
long vowel 33

Malay 1, 2, 3, 4, 11, 12, 17, 18, 22, 27, 33, 57, 60, 61, 63, 66, 71, 73, 86, 89, 94, 96, 99, 100, 101, 110, 112, 121, 123, 128, 165, 188, 199,

230, 232, 234, 236, 237, 238, 240, 241,
    243, 245, 246, 250, 256
Mandarin 27, 30
manner 193, 204
metathesis 58, 59, 60, 66, 70
middle voice 110, 236
minimal pairs 33, 50
modality 160, 164
Modern Baba Malay 2, 3
modifier 96, 114, 142, 152, 153, 154, 157, 158,
    178, 188, 189, 191, 192, 193, 194, 195, 199,
    204, 207
monolingual 10, 27, 28
monomorphemic 37
monophthong 52, 63
monophthongization 63, 232
monosyllabic 62, 78
mood 170
moribund 28, 31
morphology 2, 3, 4, 15, 20, 91, 93, 94, 106, 107,
    110, 116, 117, 230, 234, 237, 246
multilingualism 27, 247

nasal 37, 38, 39, 41, 42, 43, 45, 47
nasal murmur 42
near-minimal pairs 33
negation 156, 157, 180, 182, 183, 222, 224,
    226, 228
negative imperative 228
nominal compound 95, 96
nominalizer 20, 60, 65, 94, 117, 235, 236,
    238, 246
nominative-accusative 8, 198
noun 62, 92, 93, 96, 97, 115, 120, 122, 126,
    147, 148, 149, 154, 218, 234, 238, 239,
    240, 246
noun phrase 91, 92, 95, 99, 104, 119, 127, 134,
    142, 145, 149, 150, 154, 156, 157, 185, 186,
    187, 188, 191, 192, 196, 198, 201, 206, 209,
    214, 215, 216, 217, 218, 224, 238
nucleus 57, 58
null-subject 197, 203
numeral 17, 62, 79, 92, 97, 123, 124, 142, 144,
    147, 150, 157, 250

object 8, 92, 101, 164, 166, 197, 214
object complement 91
object control 202
object noun phrase 103

oblique 165, 166, 185
Old Baba Malay 2, 3
onomatopoeia 61
onset 58, 59, 60

palatal 49, 50
palatalization 70
palatoalveolar 41
particle 137, 139, 140
partitive 96, 97, 152, 157
part of speech 91, 107
parts of speech 15, 91
passive 2, 9, 10, 160, 164, 165, 166,
    169, 197
past 205, 206
patient 166
perfective 2, 170, 171, 174, 175, 240,
    241, 246
personal pronoun 99, 100, 120
person marker 92, 120, 121, 142, 144, 147,
    150, 157
phoneme 3, 4, 33, 50, 85
phoneme inventory 33
phonetic 71
phonetics 3, 33, 230, 246
phonological rules 62, 63, 65, 68, 69
phonology 33, 230, 234, 246
phonotactics 58, 59
pitch 74, 76, 78, 79, 80, 81, 139, 140
pitch contour 82, 257
plosive 37, 39, 40, 45, 46, 47, 48, 65, 101
plural marker 60, 62
Portuguese 2, 20, 21, 33, 59, 135
possessive 2, 146, 217
possessor 7, 144, 146, 200, 201, 218
post-alveolar 43, 44, 45
postnominal relativization 2, 7, 8, 199, 201
potential mood 161, 162
predicate 214
prefix 4, 5, 20, 77, 94, 101, 107, 110, 112, 114,
    123, 165, 189, 236, 237, 238
prenominal relativization 2, 7, 8, 199, 201
preposition 127, 128, 130, 132, 133
prepositional phrase 160, 191, 192, 193
present 205
primary stress 75, 76, 77
progressive 2, 170, 171, 173, 174, 240, 246
pronoun 7, 8, 67, 99, 100, 142, 146,
    203, 217

proper noun 92, 146
proximal 147

quantifier 126, 142, 147, 153, 154, 157

r-coloring 43
recent perfect 2, 170, 172
reciprocal 103
reduplication 2, 60, 61, 62, 93, 94, 106, 116, 118, 170, 175
refined 1, 67, 68, 69, 71, 89, 99
reflexive 101, 102
register 1, 67, 99
relative 7
relative clause 1, 2, 7, 8, 115, 142, 145, 149, 152, 155, 157, 183, 188, 191, 198, 199, 200, 201
relexification 170
resyllabification 60
reversal index 342
revitalization 32, 383
rhoticity 43
rule feeding 69
rule ordering 69

secondary stress 76, 77
second person 99, 203
second person plural 100
second person singular 100
semivowel 63
serial verb construction 105, 157, 177
sibilant 41
Sinitic 1, 17, 175
spectrogram 53, 74
spectrograms 36
stative verb 178
subject 6, 8, 9, 12, 30, 91, 92, 101, 102, 159, 160, 164, 165, 166, 186, 187, 197, 198, 199, 201, 202, 214, 215
subject control 202
subordinate clause 136, 149, 155, 199, 201, 202, 203, 211, 212, 213
subordinate clauses 208
subordinating conjunction 136, 208, 212, 213
substrate 1, 2, 3, 73, 96, 100, 135, 139, 167, 170, 175, 199, 214, 230, 247, 379, 381, 383
suffix 5, 20, 60, 94, 107, 108, 112
superlative 183, 188, 191

Swadesh 100-word list 248
syllable 20, 21, 36, 37, 57, 58, 59, 60, 65, 70, 72, 74, 75, 76, 77, 80, 112
syllable-timed 36, 73, 75
syntactic distribution 91, 105, 147
syntax 142, 230, 246

tag 159
tag question 82, 85, 216, 222, 224, 225, 227, 228, 258
Tamil 33
temporal 192, 204, 205, 206, 220
tense 170, 173, 175, 183, 205
tentative 2, 62, 106, 116, 170, 175
text 12
texts 257, 338
theme 166, 168, 169
third person 203
third person plural 100
tone 21, 22, 73, 78, 79, 80, 81, 82, 379, 384
topicalization 10, 197, 214, 215
transcription 11, 13, 14, 79
transitive 5, 6, 9, 60, 91, 105, 107, 108, 134, 167, 198, 224, 236, 238
transitive suffix 60, 107, 110
transitive verb 108
trisyllabic 62, 75, 76, 78

variation 56, 57, 63, 85, 103, 212, 342
velar 45, 46, 47, 65, 72
velar pinch 46, 47
verb 91, 92, 105, 106, 115, 117, 134, 157, 159, 160, 168, 187, 189, 194, 195, 197, 201, 234, 240
verbal compound 114, 177
verb phrase 9, 92, 115, 157, 161, 164, 166, 169, 175, 178, 180, 182, 183, 192, 193, 194, 197, 207, 210, 214, 215, 224, 228, 240
vocoid 57
voice bar 37, 40, 44
voiced 37, 38, 39, 40, 43, 44, 45, 46, 101
voiceless 37, 39, 40, 43, 44, 45, 46, 47, 48
voice onset time 38
volition 165
volitional 163
vowel 33, 50, 52, 56, 58, 230
vowel inventory 3, 4
vowel merger 56, 89
vowel normalization 86

vowel raising 68, 69, 71
vowel reduction 70
vowel sequence 57
vowel space 57, 85, 230, 232

waveform 74
waveforms 36

word order 3, 6, 7, 8, 91, 96, 142, 145, 146, 147, 149, 156, 157, 160, 180, 183, 190, 191, 194, 195, 197, 198, 208, 212, 213, 228, 238, 239, 240, 246
writing system 71

zero strategy 203

www.ingramcontent.com/pod-product-compliance
Lightning Source LLC
Chambersburg PA
CBHW080406230426
43662CB00016B/2332